AF411606

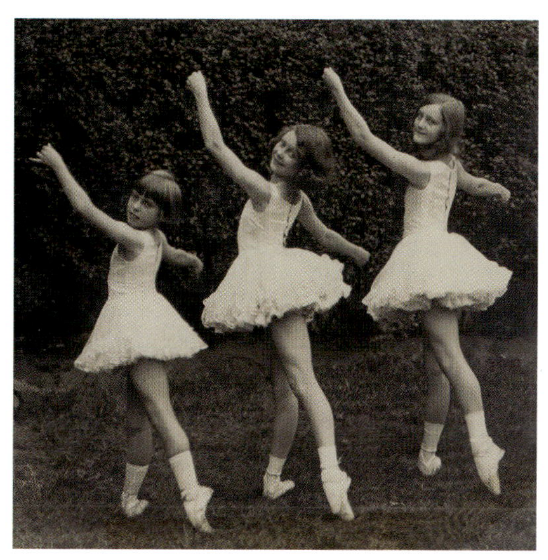

Royal Academy of Dance

Celebrating 100 years

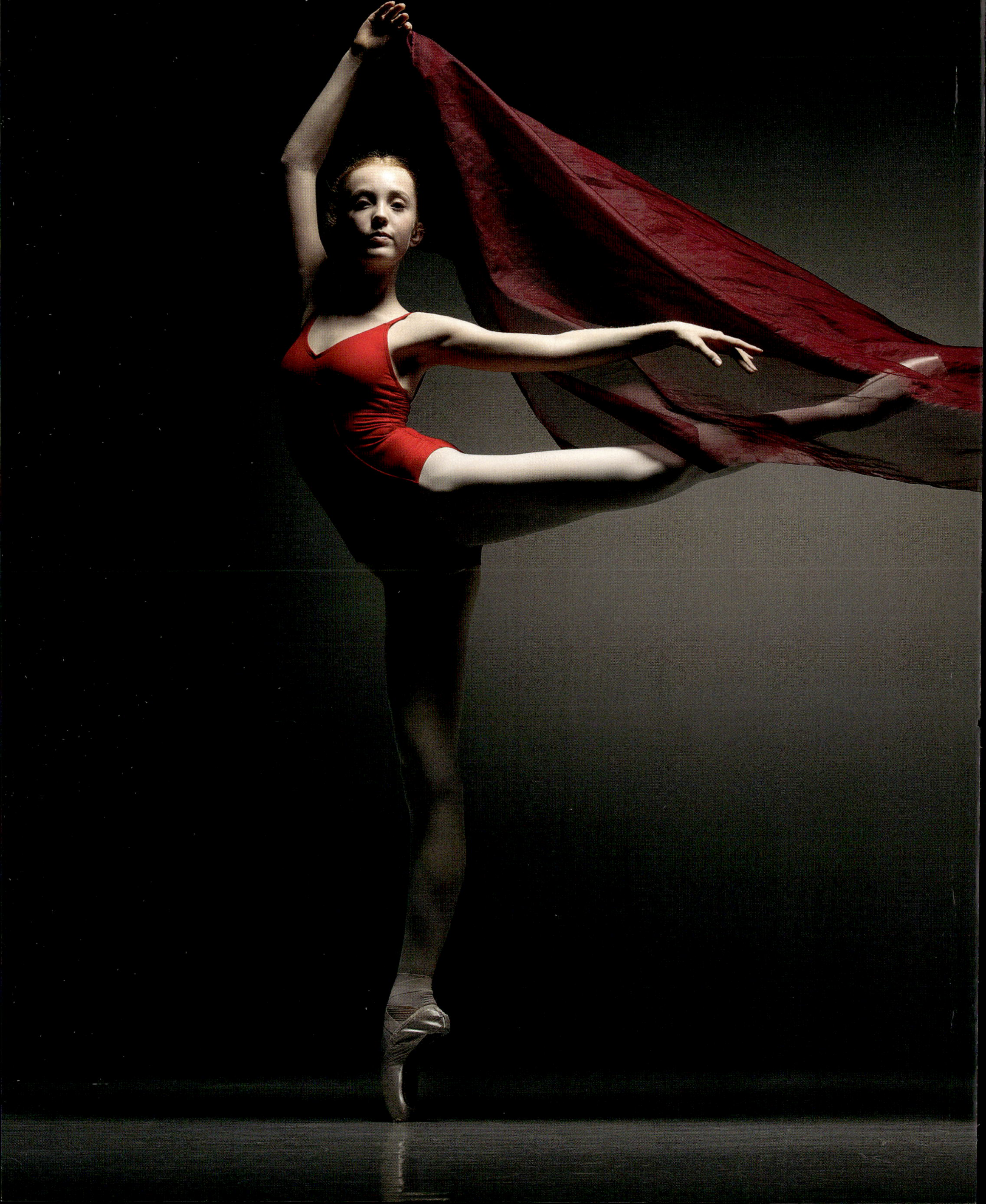

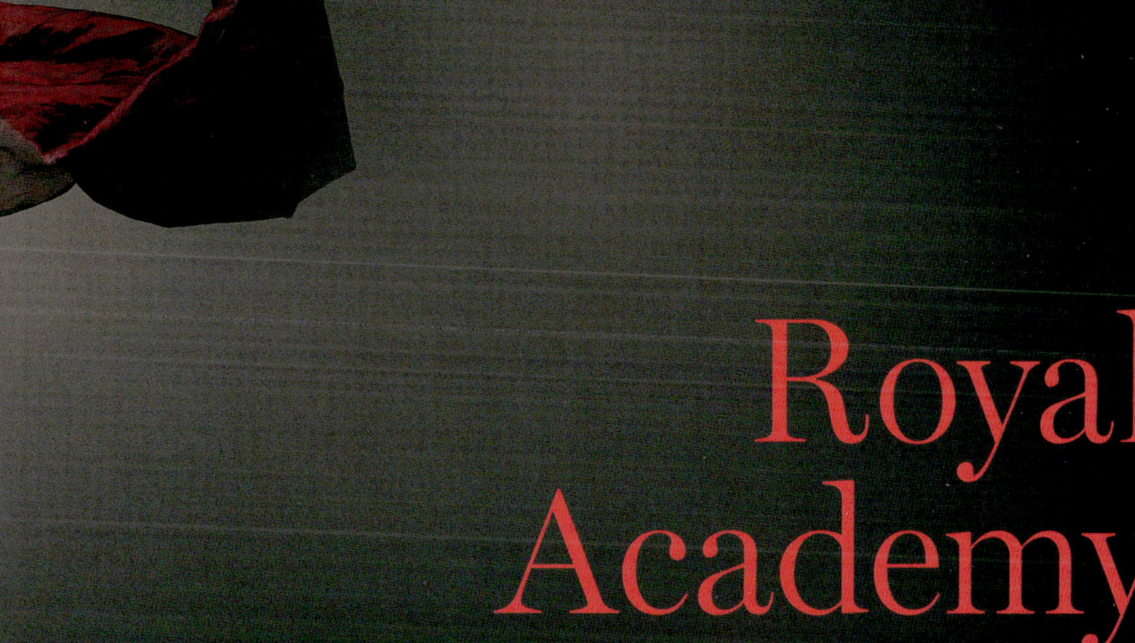

Royal Academy of Dance

Celebrating 100 years

SCALA

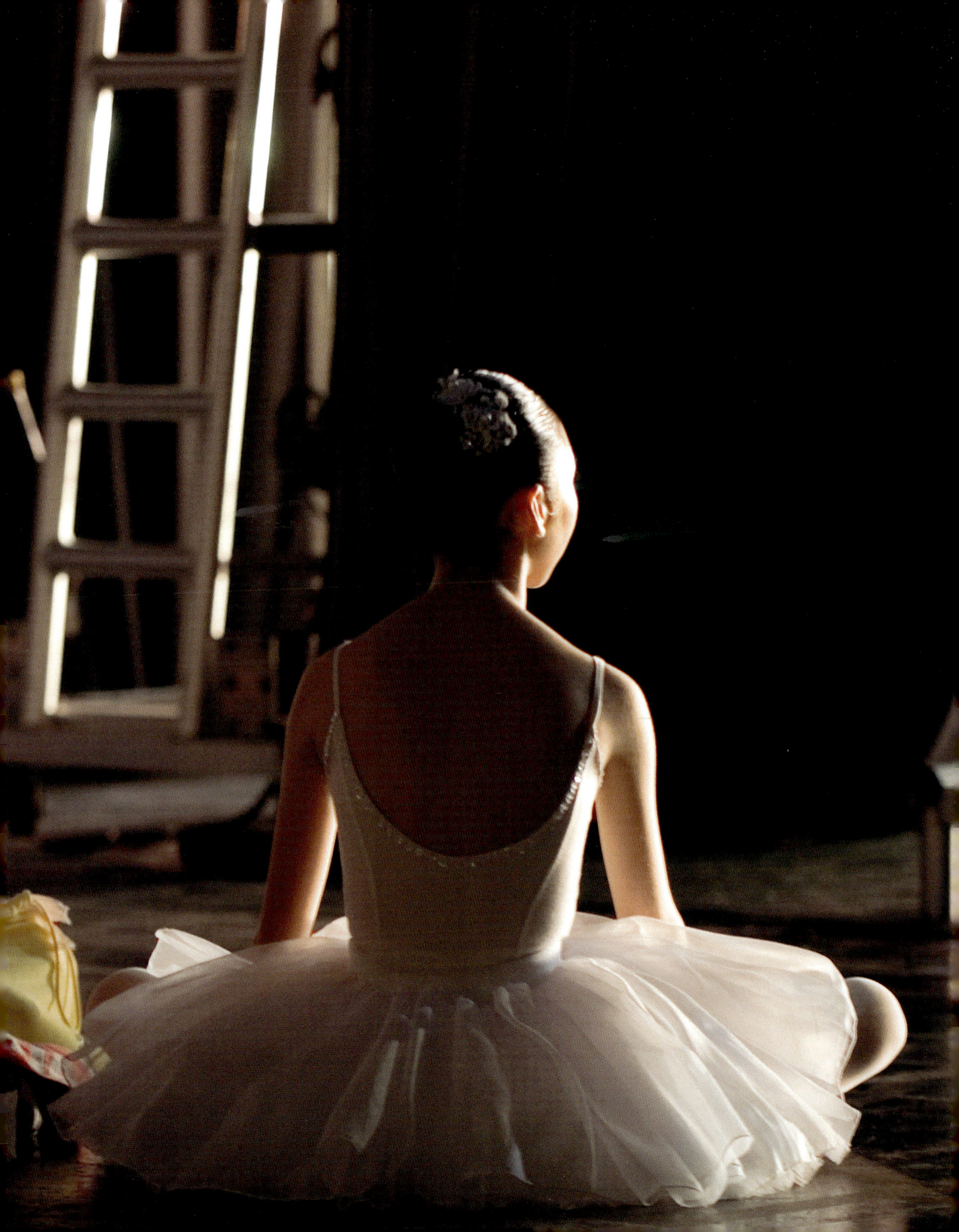

CONTENTS

PRESIDENT'S FOREWORD

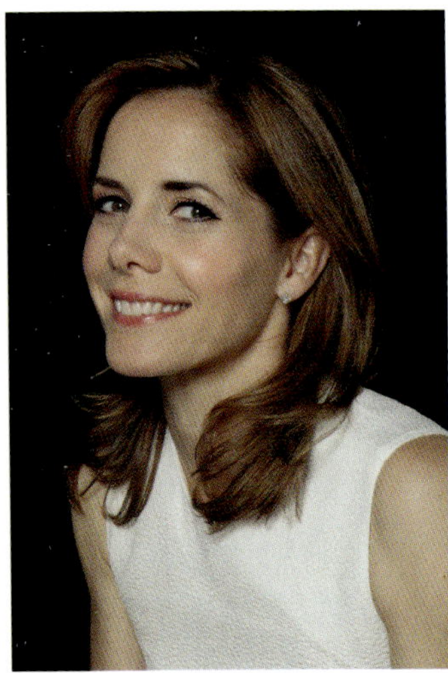

As the Royal Academy of Dance reaches its centenary, this wonderful book celebrates the RAD's history, beginning from the dream of a small group of determined and ambitious individuals at its foundation, right through to the prestigious worldwide organisation that it is today.

You will meet some of the key figures responsible for building the RAD and making it so respected and admired. You will find the stories of some of the most renowned dancers of their day; names like Genée, de Valois and Fonteyn alongside the stories of the teachers, examiners, students and dance lovers, who were, and continue to be, the very heartbeat of the RAD.

The book explores the evolution of the syllabus and examinations, the music, dance shoes, choreography and the costumes, and describes how the story of the RAD is also one of royal patronage, the Genée International Ballet Competition (which will be renamed the Margot Fonteyn International Ballet Competition from 2020 onwards) and legendary gala performances.

The RAD's important outreach work in the community is also highlighted, from RADiate, where our teachers work with children with learning disabilities, to Project B, which encourages more boys into dance. Our alumni make an appearance in the 'Where are they now' section, and there's a feature on past Presidents of the RAD who have all contributed to making the RAD such a success.

Lastly, we look to the future of the RAD. Our brand new, purpose-built headquarters is set to be the home of dance for our local and global dance communities.

The RAD has brought so much beautiful ballet into the lives of so many. I am privileged and extremely proud to be its President as we celebrate our centenary and I look forward to the future with real optimism.

I know that you will enjoy this stunning overview of the RAD's history and work.

DAME DARCEY BUSSELL
President of the Royal Academy of Dance

VICE PRESIDENT'S FOREWORD

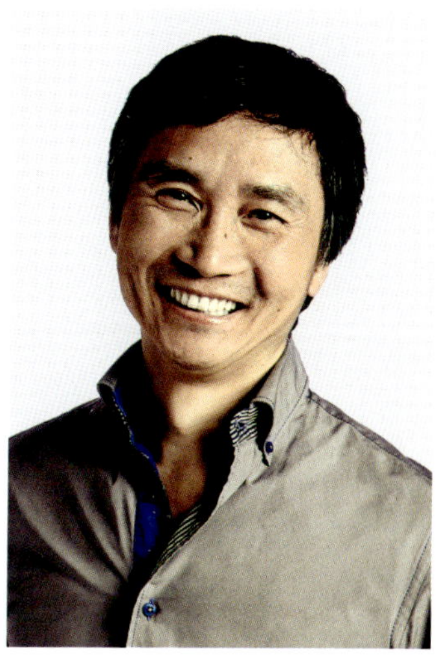

Over one hundred years the Royal Academy of Dance has grown to become an institution admired and respected around the world for the rigour of its ballet syllabi and examinations, as well as the quality of its teacher training.

The inspirational teachers that the RAD produces offer the chance for dancers of all ages, abilities and ambitions to enjoy the beautiful art form, to express themselves and develop their passion. They may dream of dancing with a professional company (perhaps Queensland Ballet!) or they may just want to dance with friends for the joy it brings.

My own passion for ballet was kindled by an incredible teacher – someone who changed my outlook on life, who inspired my hunger for excellence. This inspiration kept me going through years of hard work and being away from my family. The importance and value of good teachers cannot be understated, and RAD's contribution in this area is a valuable part of its history and legacy.

After an association of many years, I was pleased and honoured to be made a Vice President of the RAD in 2014. Looking over these pages has given me an opportunity to reflect on the important role the RAD plays in the lives of so many, and I am truly struck by the breadth, ambition and value of its work.

I look forward with great anticipation and pride to seeing what the next century will bring for this organisation, which has already transformed the lives and careers of so many.

LI CUNXIN
Vice President of the Royal Academy of Dance
Artistic Director of Queensland Ballet

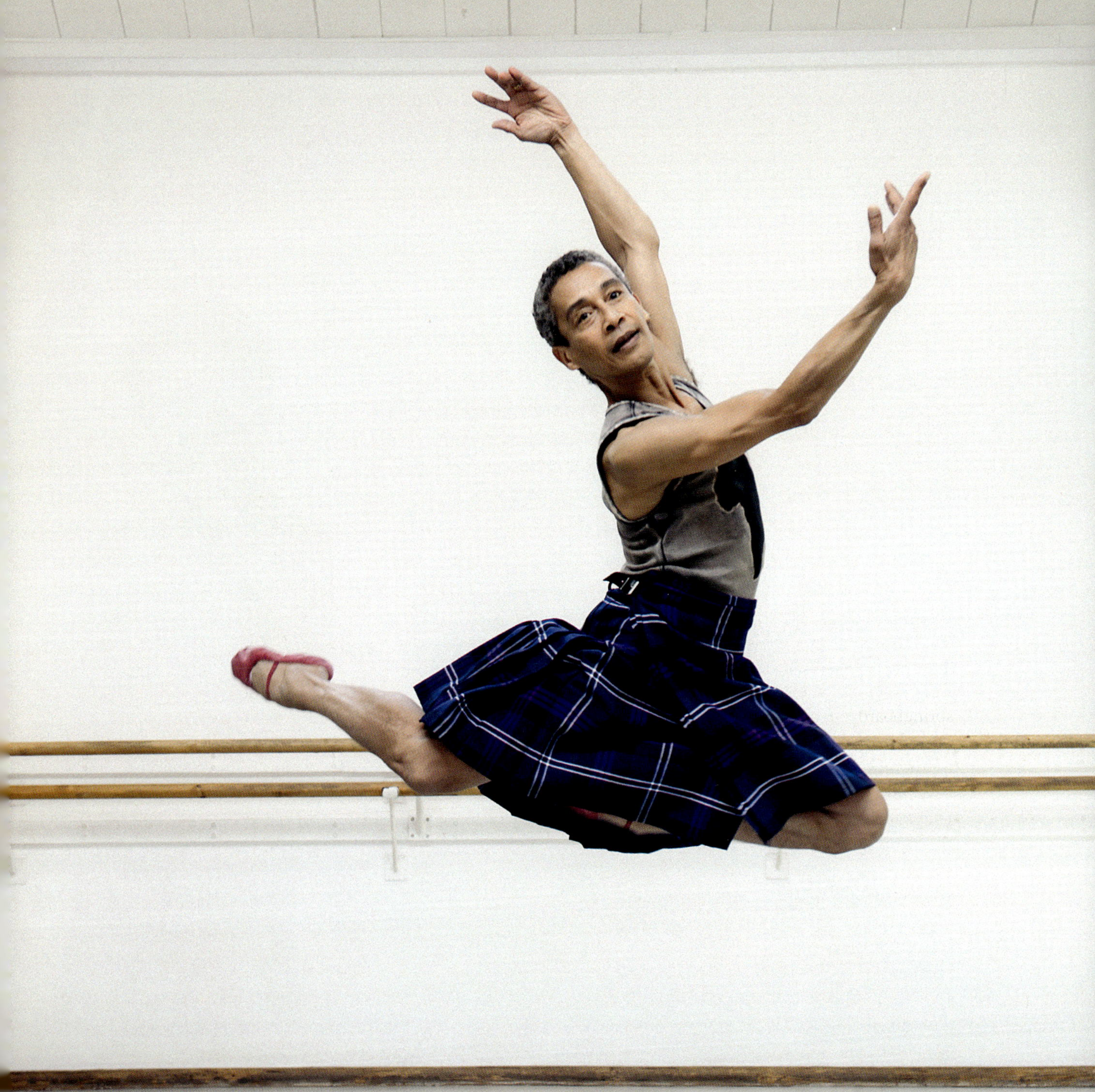

VINCENT HANTAM, 2017
Professional Dancers' Teaching Diploma
(PDTD) programme.

MANY THINGS TO MANY PEOPLE

Gerald Dowler

ONE hundred years on from its founding, what actually is the Royal Academy of Dance? It is perhaps a question easier to ask than to answer. Is it an organisation set up to teach the teachers of dance? Certainly – that was its avowed intention in 1920 when interested parties, horrified at the generally appalling nature of dance teaching in the United Kingdom at the time, established the Association of Teachers of Operatic Dancing (as ballet was commonly referred to at the time), but it was and is not only that. Is it then an organisation to teach ballet to young people? It is that too. Is it the awarding body for graded examinations in a dance syllabus of its own devising not only in the UK but now across the world? Undoubtedly. Is it 'home' to the 'once-a-week' dancer for whom dance will never be their chosen career path or is it the springboard and a showcase for young dancers who have chosen to make their career in dancing, some of whom ascend to the very highest ranks in some of the world's finest classical companies? It is both. Difficult to categorise, impossible to pigeon-hole, the Royal Academy of Dance derives its undoubted strength from its inherent polyvalent nature – it has always been many things to many different people.

That the RAD is all the above and more should, perhaps, come as little surprise because it has always been an organisation of many functions, established as it was to address a perceived need and not out of the whim of an individual or a state bureaucracy. It is this essential element to its existence that has shaped and continues to shape the Academy and its members and students for whom it represents much more than an examination board. Inherent to the RAD now, as it was then, is the dissemination of its work beyond the shores of the United Kingdom, firstly to the Empire/Commonwealth and, increasingly, to the world as a whole. This internationalism is one of the RAD's enduring strengths, as is the feeling of commonality that the Academy's global network provides – it is reassuring for teachers and learners alike to have the knowledge of belonging to a wider organisation, one that sees examiners criss-crossing the globe and which can bring the whole family together for such an important event as the Genée International Ballet Competition. But then, the international nature of the Academy cannot come as much of a surprise given that its founders one hundred years ago were Danish, Russian, Italian and British – it is simply part of its DNA.

The RAD syllabus taught and followed around the world was, from the outset, the product of a group of professionals to ensure that the fundamentals of classical dancing are logically and safely put in place for each and every learner; the Academy is, in many ways, an organisation born of an art form simply to serve that art form. The RAD syllabus is, in a sense, living history, conceived initially by representatives of the great classical ballet traditions: Adeline Genée (Danish), Tamara Karsavina (Russian), Lucia Cormani (Italian), Edouard Espinosa (French) and Phyllis Bedells (British). In this it differs from many of the main schools of ballet that emerged and developed to feed a single company, often in the service of a monarch. The Royal Danish Ballet, the pre-revolution Russian Imperial Ballet and what is now the Paris Opéra Ballet all began as court ensembles, their schools and programmes of teaching and learning focused on feeding them. Even in later, non-royal contexts, the relationship continued, so that the Vaganova Academy in Leningrad/St Petersburg, the Royal Ballet Schools and the School of American Ballet are all primarily designed to produce performers for identifiable, often state-sponsored ensembles.

But in the UK another context existed, that of pure entertainment, offered not to a rarefied

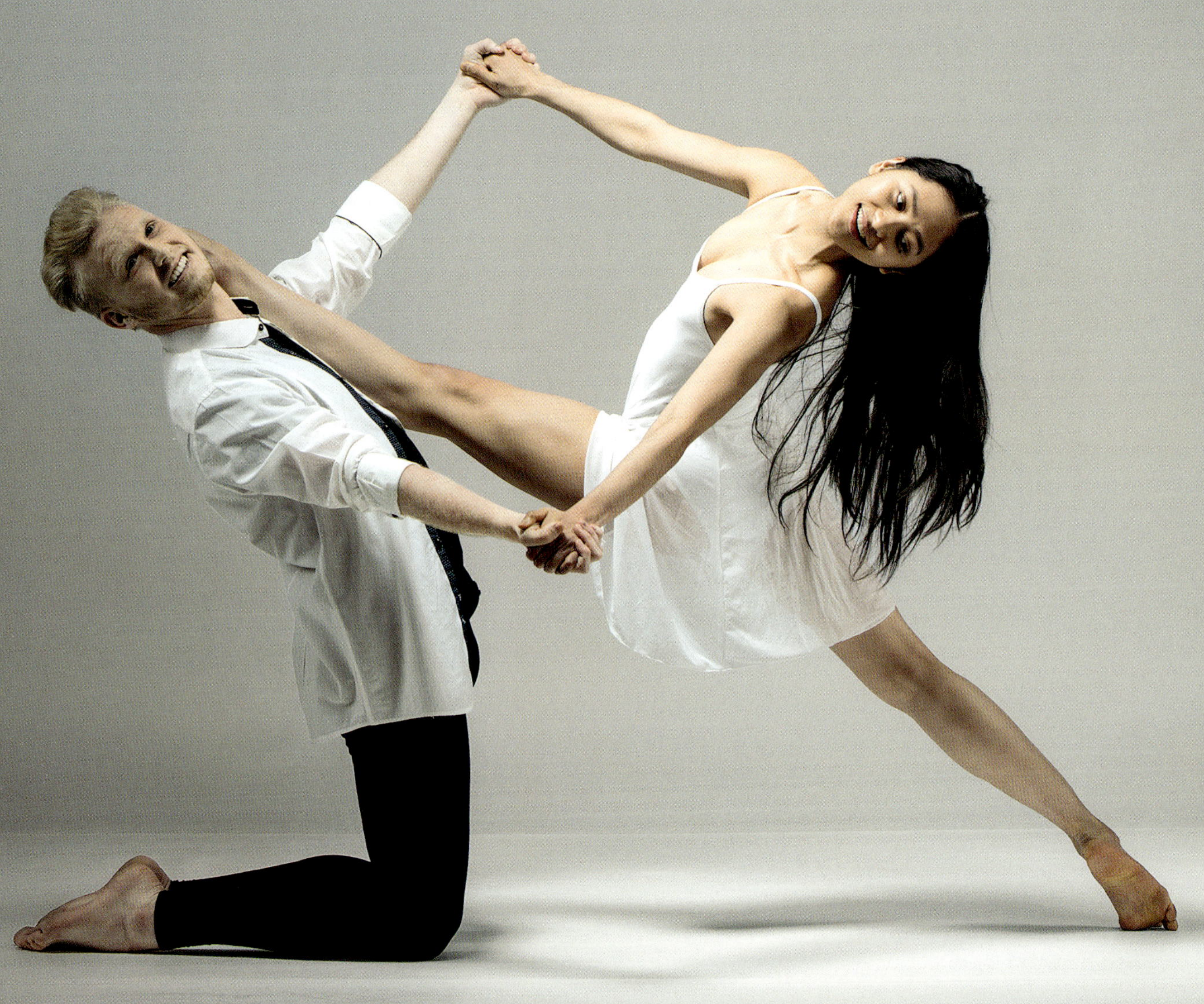

JAMES GROOM AND FELICIA SUNIASTARI, 2018
BA (Hons) Ballet Education (BABE) programme.

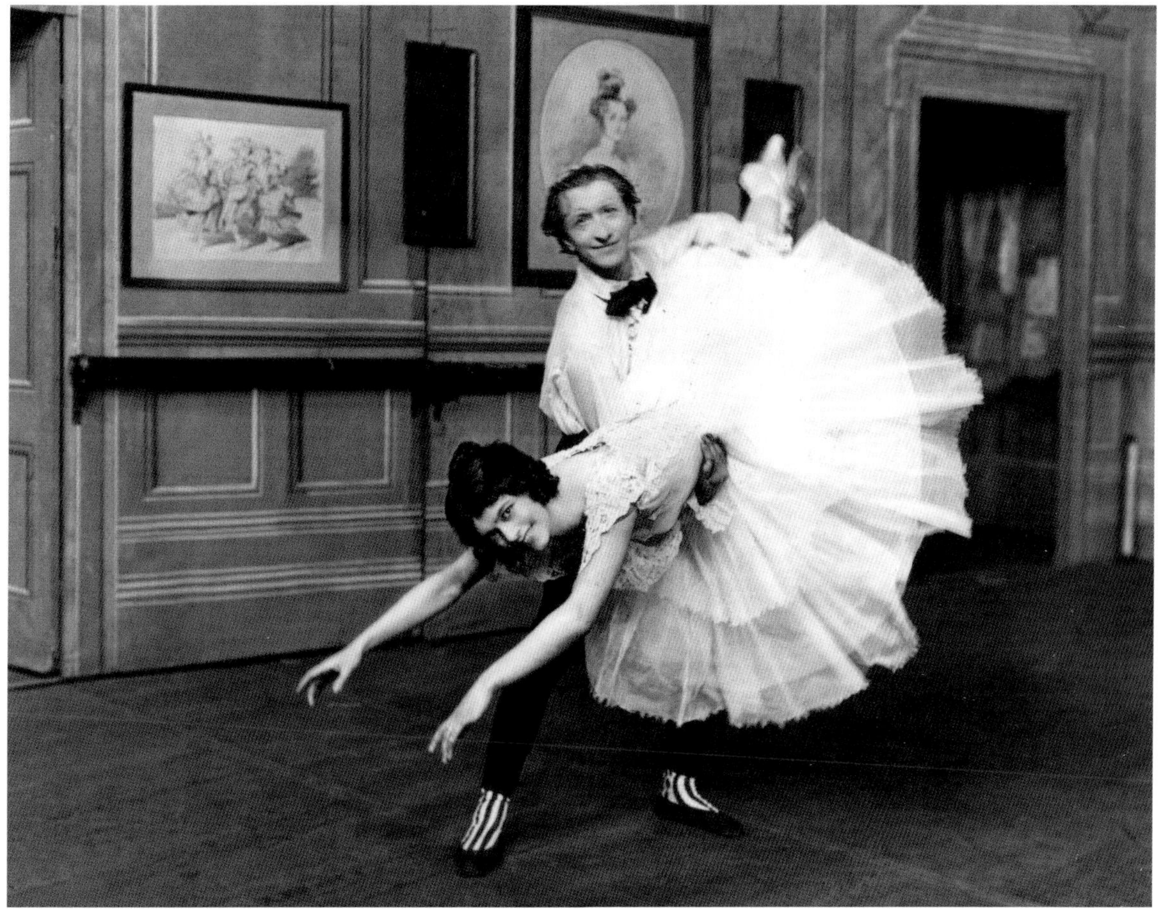

PHYLLIS BEDELLS AND EDOUARD ESPINOSA, 1913
Bedells and Espinosa in *The Dancing Master* at the
Empire Theatre, London. The ballet was revived for
the Association's first annual matinée in 1923 with
both Bedells and Espinosa in their original roles.

court audience but to a paying public – a ballet
performance at the great London music halls of
the early twentieth century, the Alhambra and the
Empire theatres, would have been seen mostly by
the middle and upper working classes. It was in
this context that the RAD's founding president,
Adeline Genée, regularly performed – she was
prima ballerina of the Empire from 1897 to 1907,
a position another RAD founder, Phyllis Bedells,
occupied from 1914 onwards, while Tamara
Karsavina, the great Russian ballerina (yet another
founding committee member), appeared at the

London Coliseum. The arrival of the Russian
ensembles, most notably Anna Pavlova's company
in 1910 and Sergei Diaghilev's Ballets Russes the
year after, brought something else to the British
dance world, but these exotic visitors were not
the RAD founding committee's motivation to
offer ratification for dance teachers – it was a
basic concern to ensure that learners were safe
in their hands.

It is no coincidence that Marie Rambert
established her own dance school in 1920, followed
by Ninette de Valois in 1926 – the founding

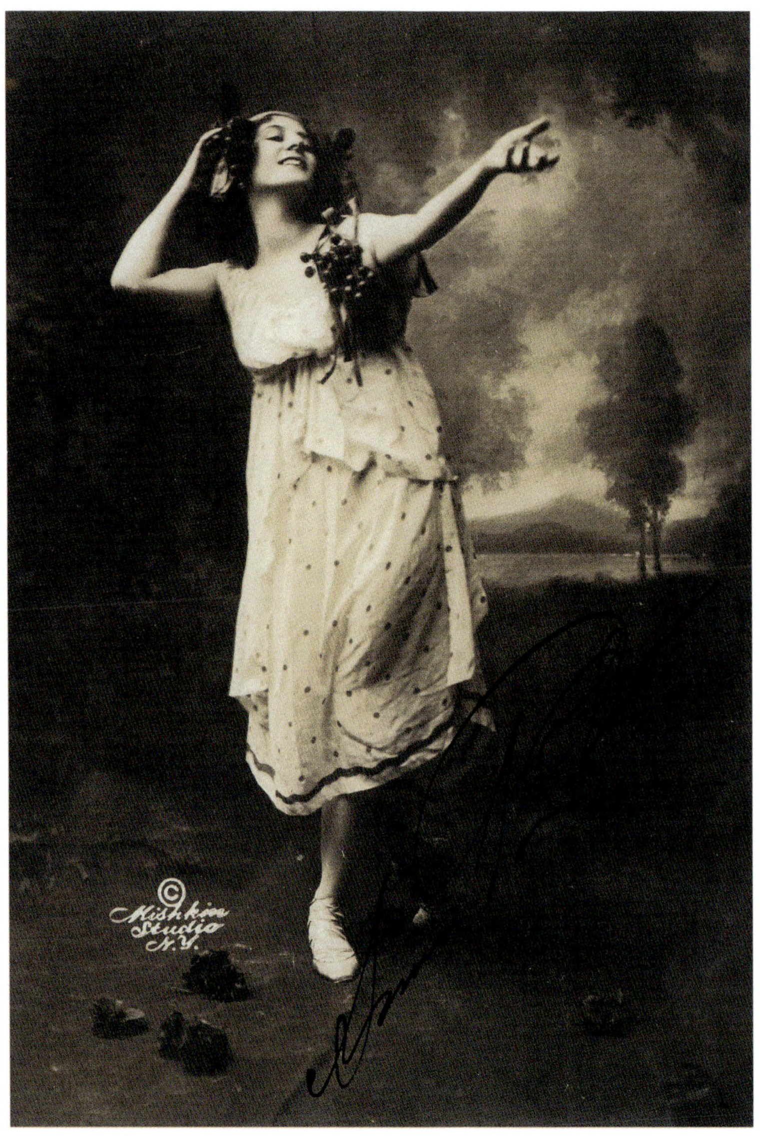

ANNA PAVLOVA, 1910
Pavlova in *Bacchanale*, arranged by
Mikhail Mordkin. The ballet was part
of the first London Season at the
Palace Theatre in 1910.

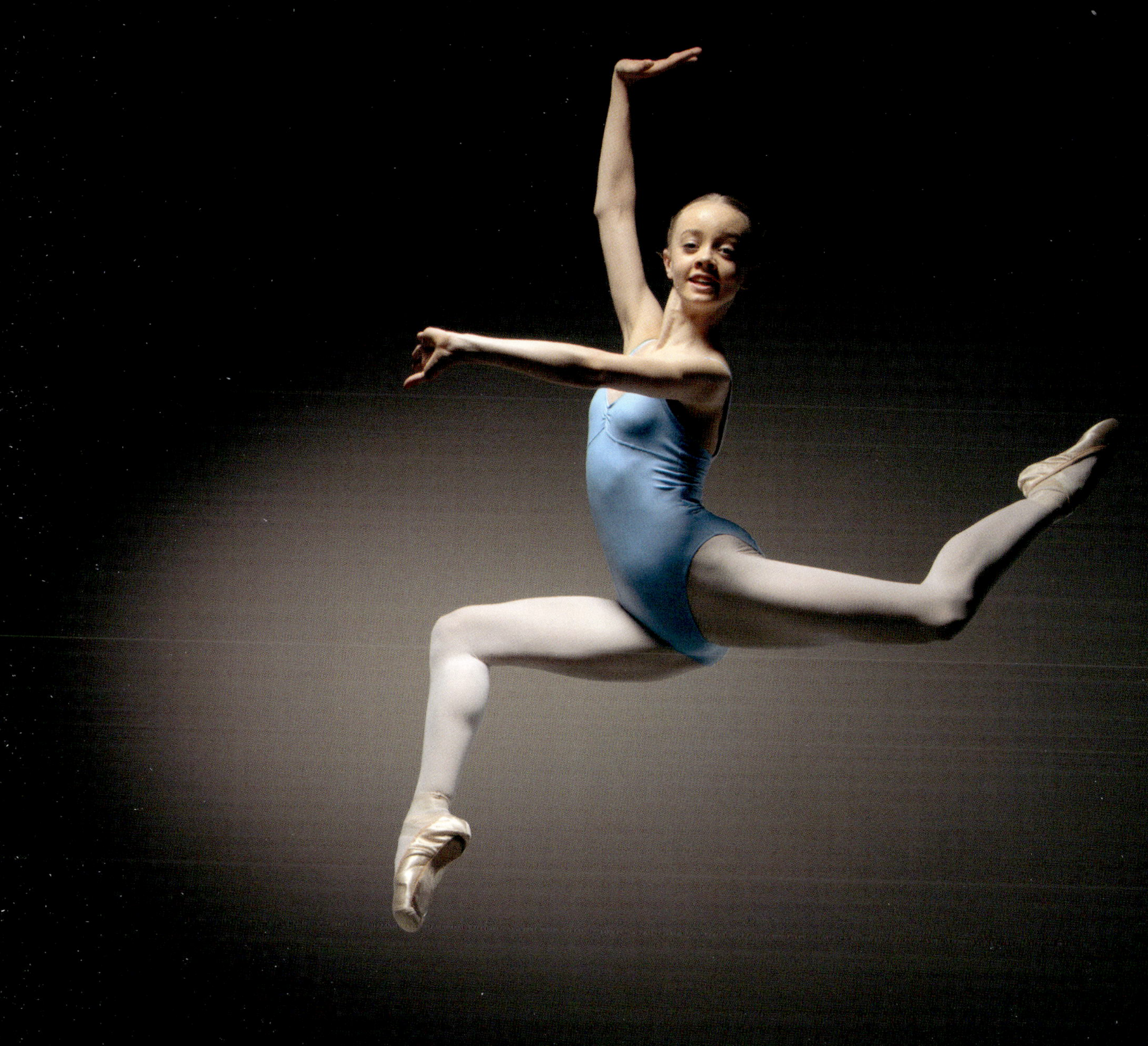
JESSICA TEMPLETON, 2018

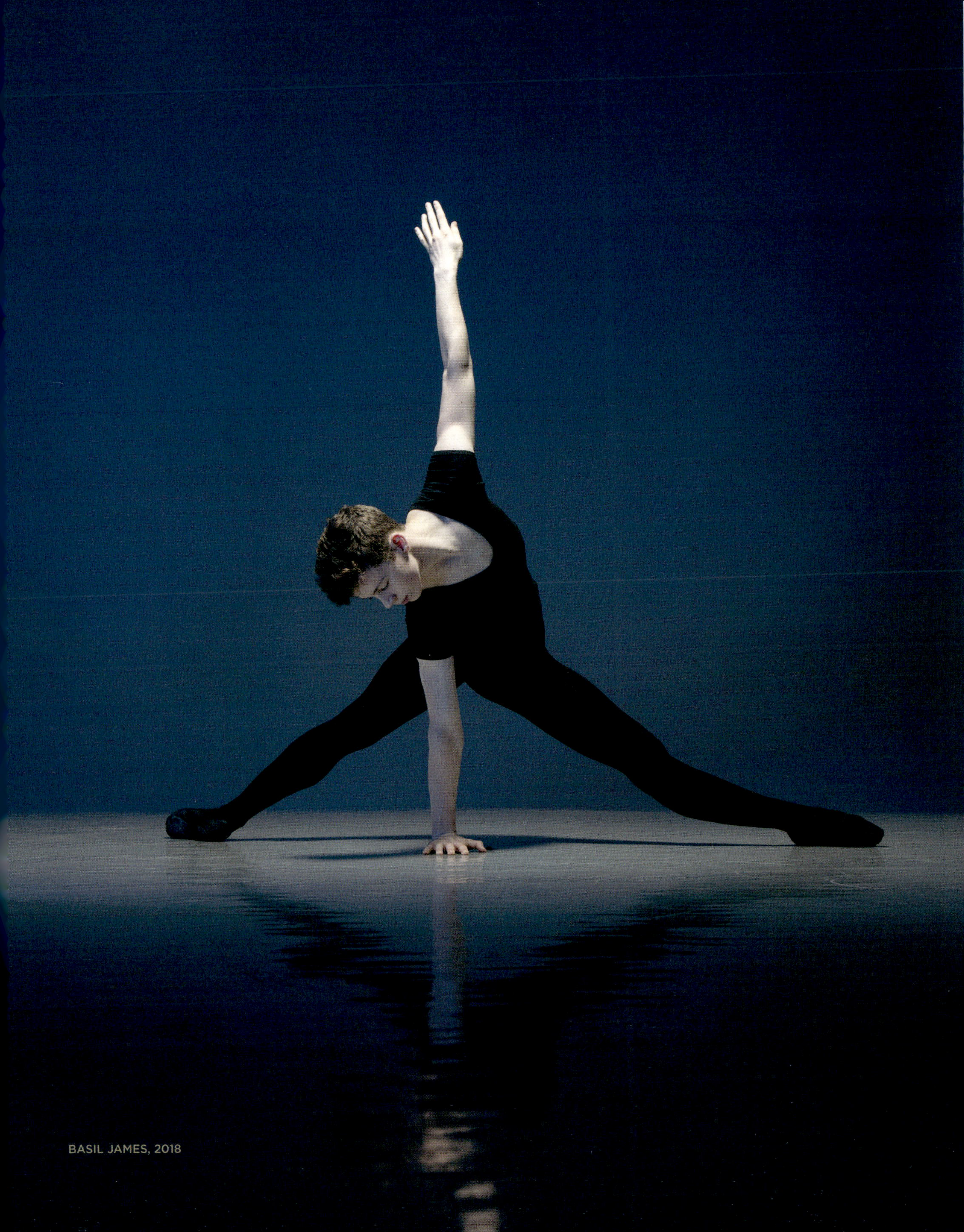
BASIL JAMES, 2018

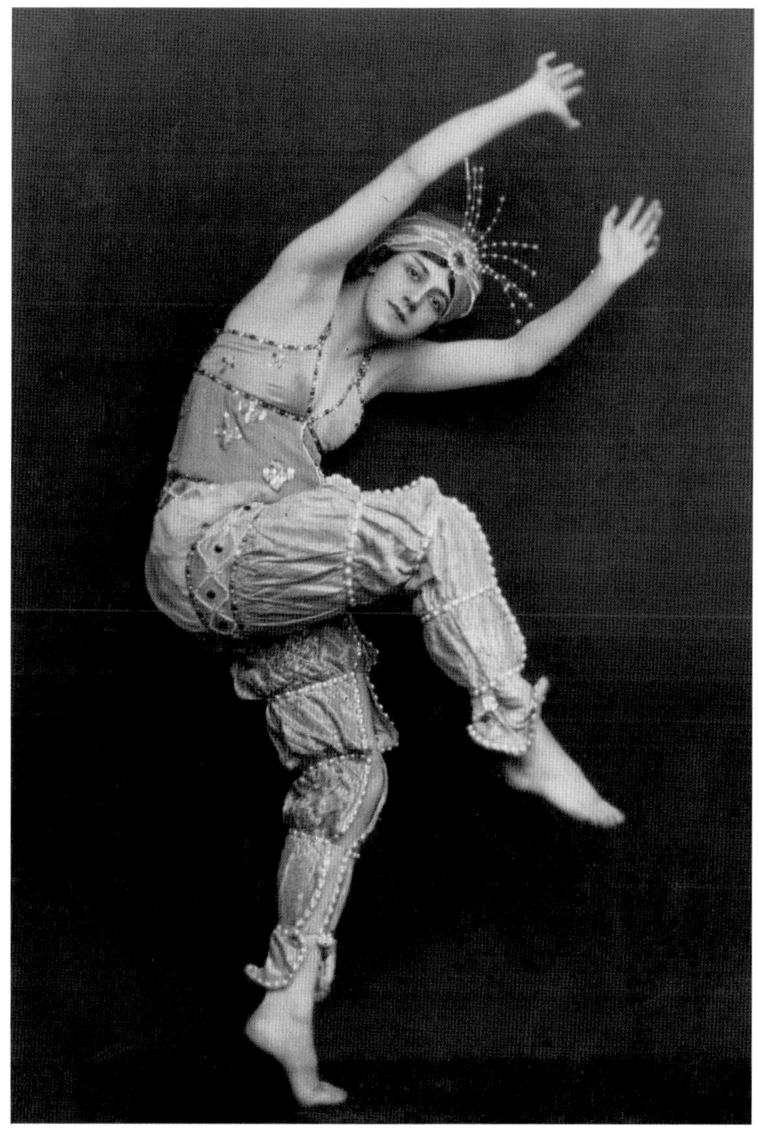

TAMARA KARSAVINA, 1914
Tamara Karsavina as Zobeide in Fokine's
Scheherazade, when she was part of Diaghilev's
Ballets Russes. Karsavina went on to be one of
the Founders of the RAD.

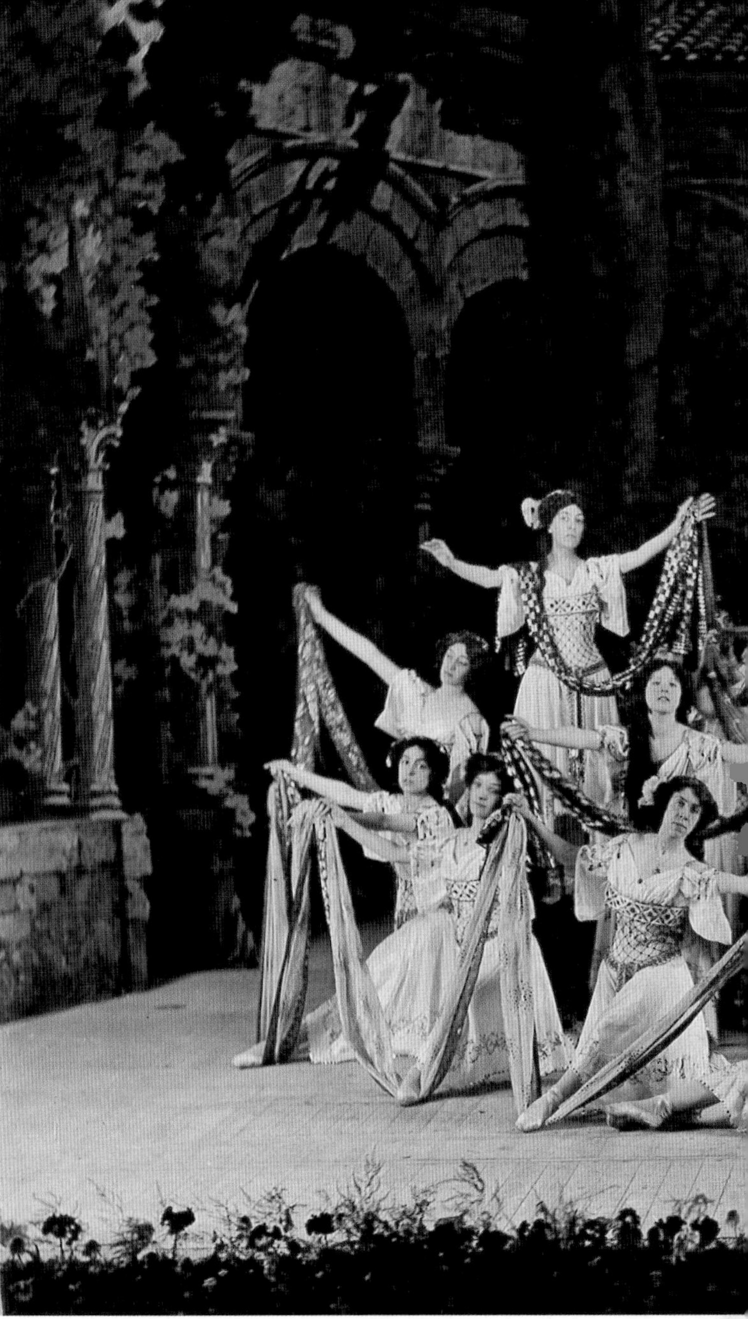

committee's desire to codify and assess dance teaching must be seen as part of a wider trend, not only in dance but across the arts, and was part of a process of catching up with other performance forms such as music and theatre, which had established syllabi and certification before the First World War. In addition, the war had engendered a social upheaval that, after peace finally came, led to a partial emancipation of women and confirmed the rise of the middle classes, who enjoyed greater disposable income and time from work to seek other pursuits – the dance education of their daughters was part and parcel of parents' social aspirations. If social optimism was indeed a factor, it is interesting to consider the founding of the Association of Teachers of Operatic Dancing in 1920 as part of that phenomenon of positivity – it might well not have happened after the financial disaster of the 1928 Wall Street Crash and the ensuing Depression.

The Danish Adeline Genée understood British society and its psyche quite well enough to strive for the cachet of a Royal Charter a mere ten years after the Association's inception – having the prefix 'Royal' would attract both teachers, who would proudly display their crested certificate, and parents who would value the weight given by it to their child's achievements. In a way, the royal cachet was and is something of an add-on, given the continuing unpretentious aims of the Academy. Genée and the Association were lucky to have the support of Queen Mary, who consented to become patron in 1928 and who, after the failed application for a Royal Charter in 1930, is said to have supported a successful second request five years later. But then it must be remembered that, as a young Princess Mary of Teck, she had been taught social dancing by none other than the great Romantic ballerina Marie Taglioni.

What then of the RAD's future? It is perhaps ironic that an organisation that is hard to pin down is likely to be an anchor in future decades for teachers and learners to come. Performed dance, perhaps in a reflection of modern society, is becoming more fractured, more disparate in nature, so it will undoubtedly be increasingly important for successive generations to be able to refer, if not to immutable dance truths, then at least to a code and structure that will allow those teaching and learning the idiom to do so in safety and in the knowledge that

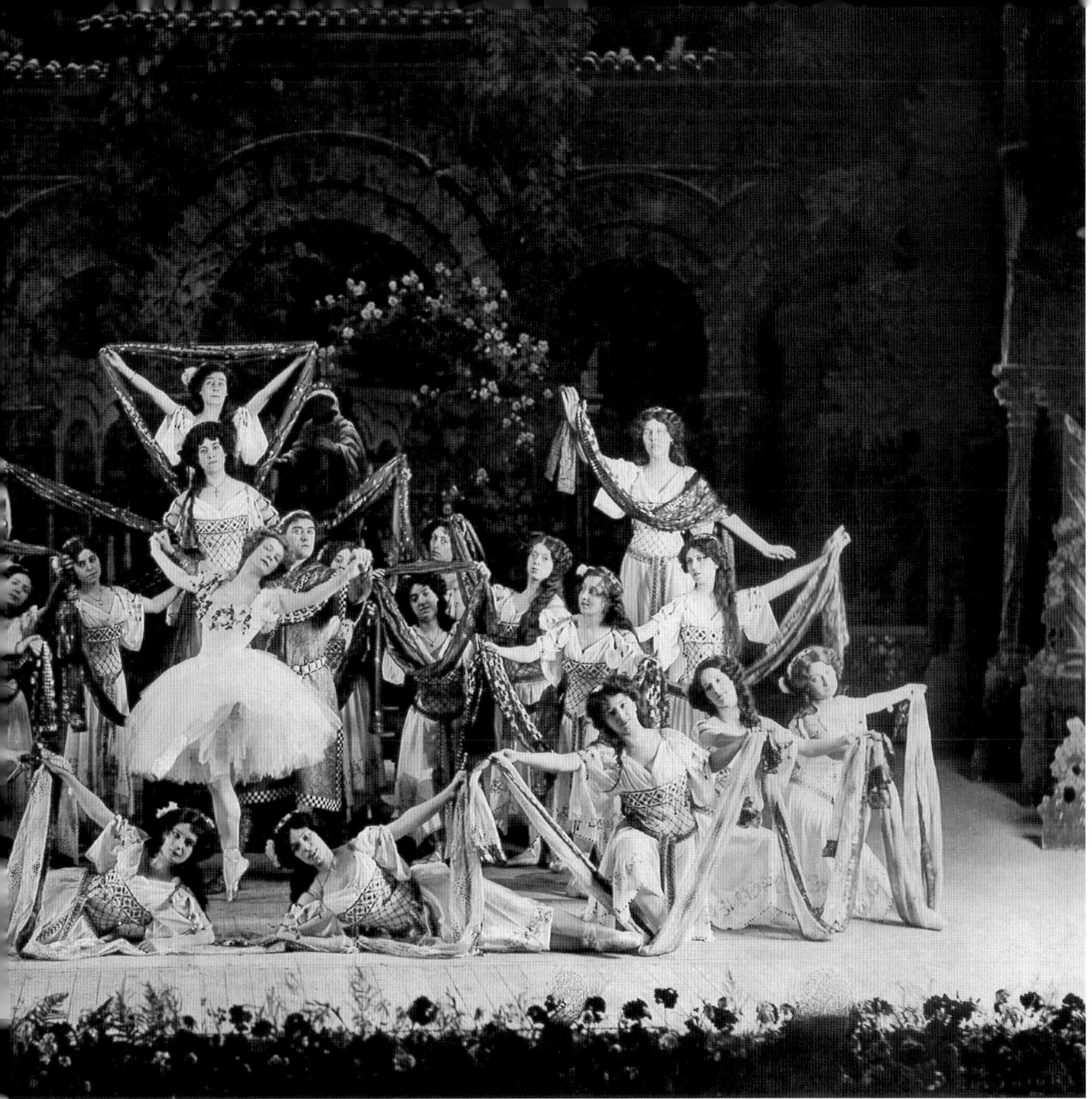

what they are doing has come from experience and understanding. The process is already under way, with a focus on dancing specifically for boys and an expansion into the market for adult classes. The Academy's somewhat amorphous nature will, it is likely, allow it to shift and adapt when and where it has to, something it has done successfully for a hundred years, and ensuring that it will remain many things to many different people.

Gerald Dowler reviews and writes on dance for several publications, which include The Financial Times, Dancing Times, Ballet 2000 *and* Ballet Review (New York). *He lives and works in London.*

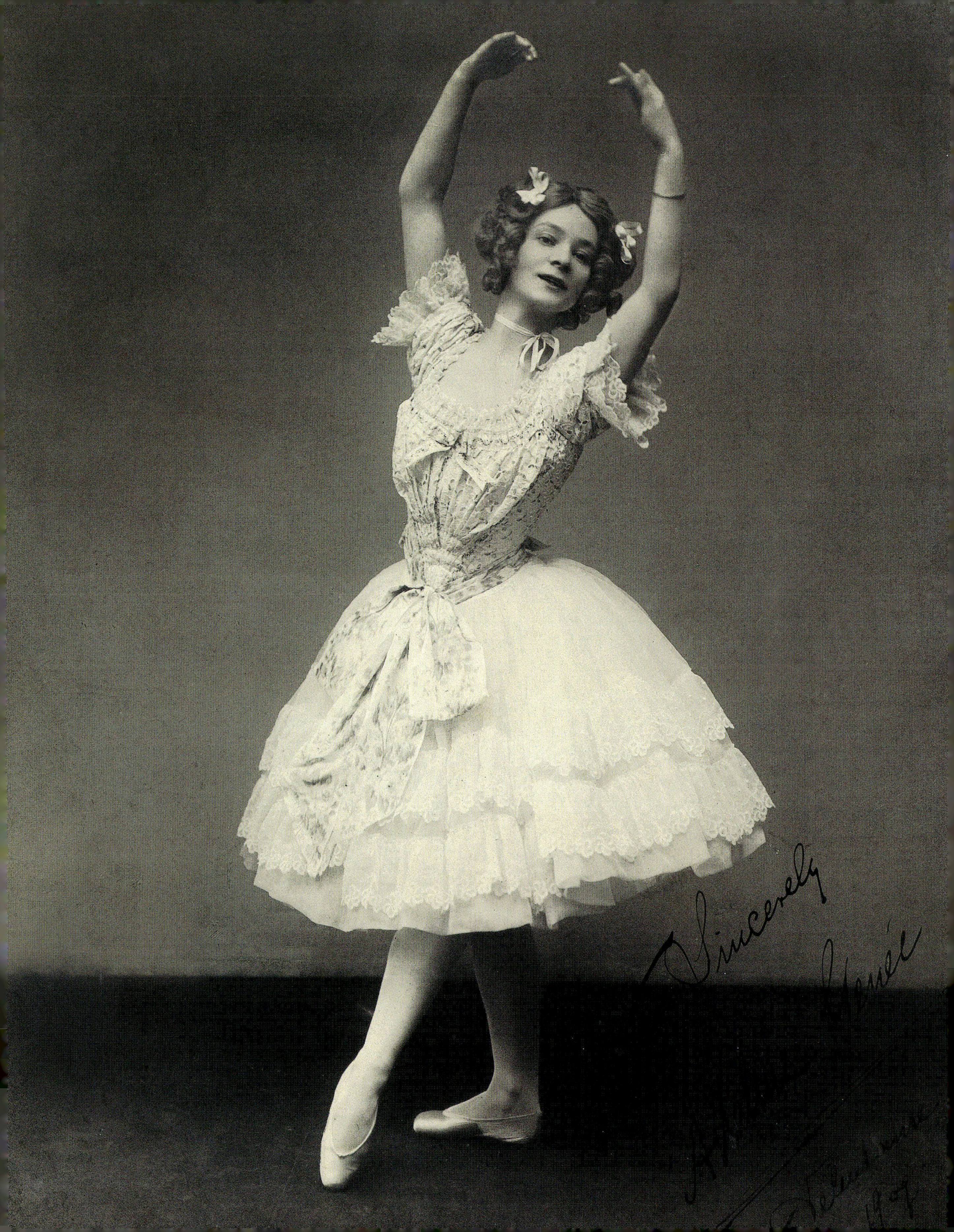

Sincerely
1909

1

HOW IT ALL BEGAN

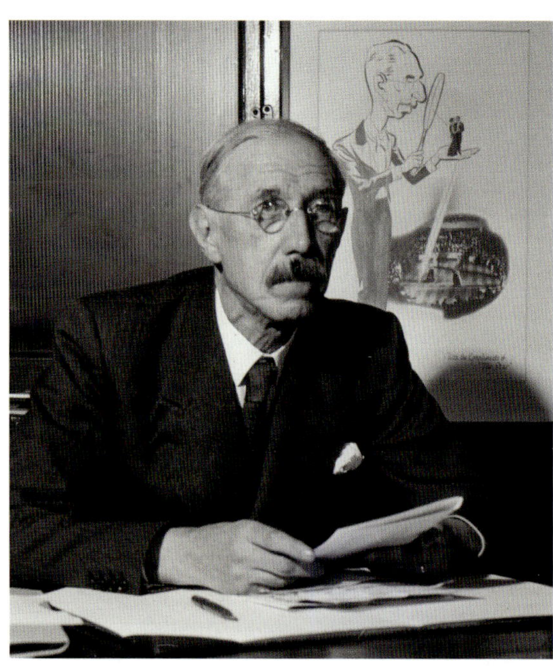

Genée as Delphine
Duvet in *The Débutante*.
Although the photo is
signed and dated 1907,
the ballet was first
produced at the Empire
Theatre in 1906.

PHILIP RICHARDSON

A key figure in the foundation of
the Association of Teachers of
Operatic Dancing of Great Britain
(later the RAD), Richardson was
editor of *The Dancing Times*
and a judge of ballroom dancing
competitions. The caricature on
the wall behind him shows him
'examining' a dancing couple.

THERE are many places where a history
of the Royal Academy of Dance might start. A meeting between Edouard Espinosa and the editor of
The Dancing Times, Philip Richardson, in 1912 is
one possibility. In 1913 Richardson published the
first edition of Espinosa's *Technical Dictionary
of Dancing*, which codified the classical ballet
vocabulary. In 1916 the drive to do something about
poor standards in dance teaching continued with
Espinosa's article 'What Every Teacher of Operatic
Dancing Ought to Know and Be Able to Teach', also
published in *The Dancing Times* and accompanied
by the suggestion of a professional 'tribunal' that
could issue certificates to those properly qualified
to teach.[1] Such developments were, however, overshadowed by the grim reality of the First World War
and progress was stalled until after the Armistice
in 1918.

The story can be picked up again in July 1920,
when some thirty people sat down to dinner in
the Oak Room at London's Trocadero Restaurant.
At 12s 6d (about £27 at today's value) a head,
the dinner was promoted as an opportunity for

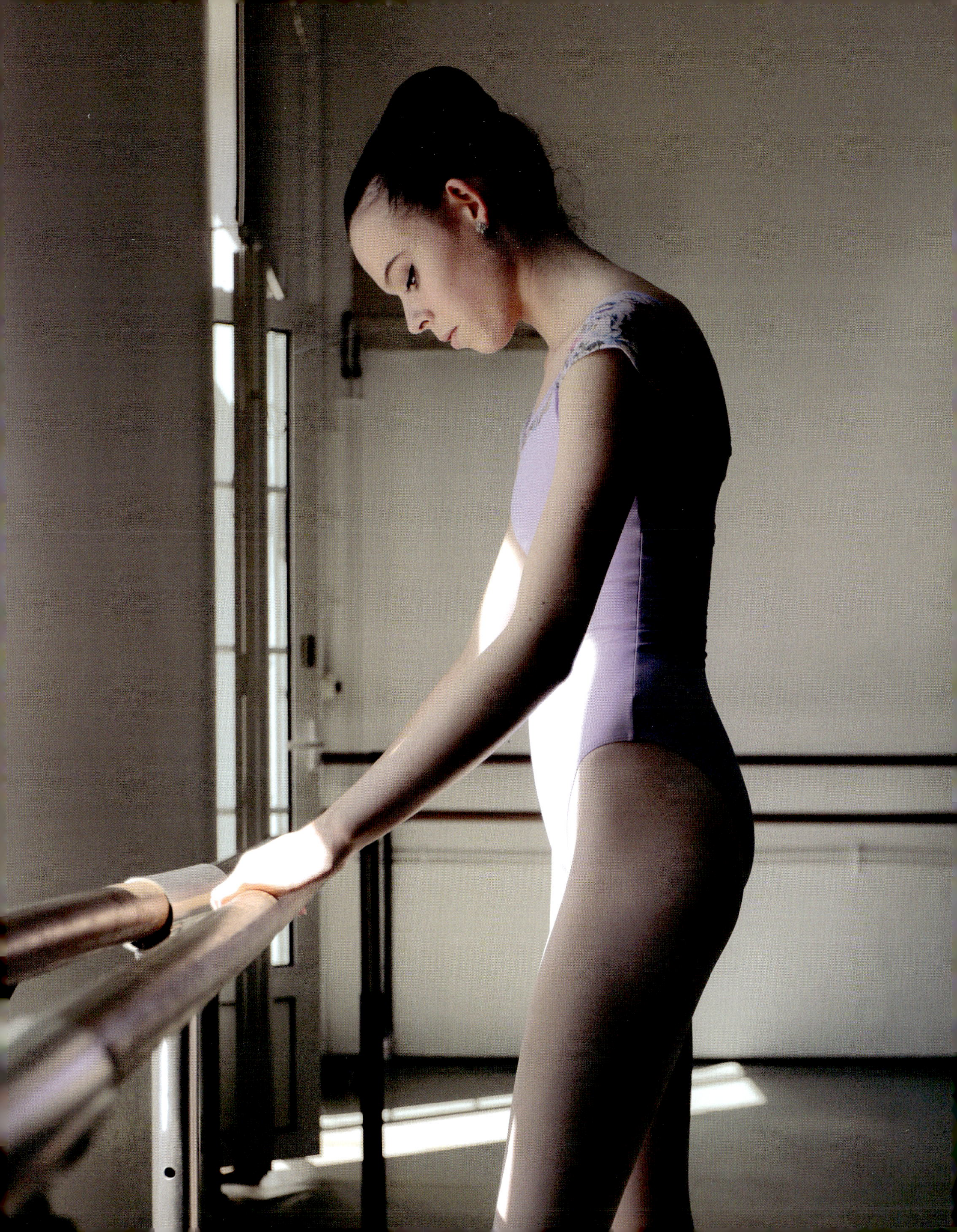

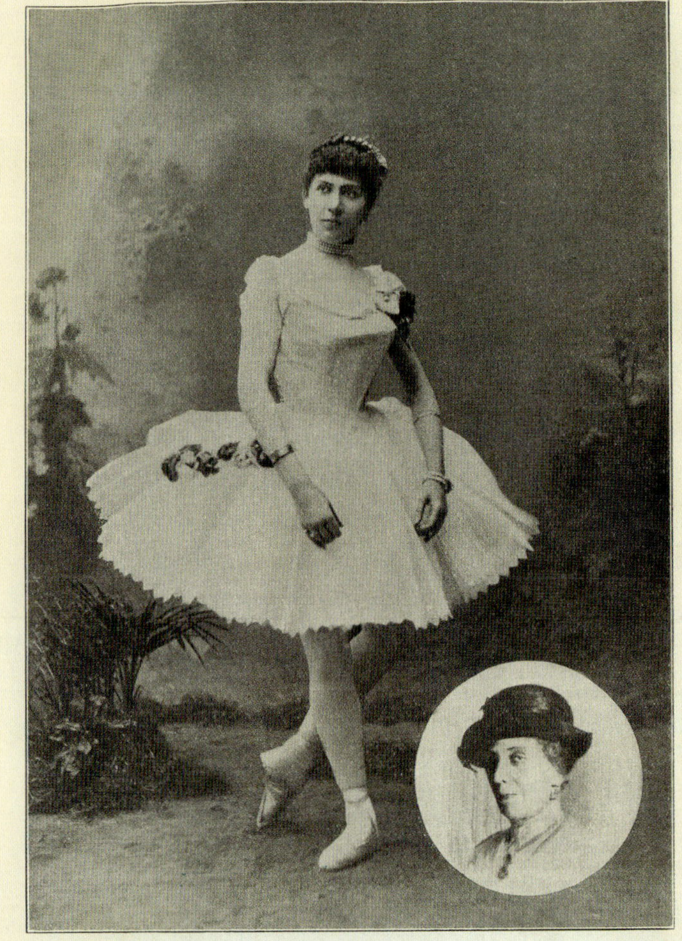

dancers and dance teachers in England to get to know each other and to consider the idea of an association that would preserve the traditions of ballet and raise the standard of teaching by providing a guide to correct technique.

Dance professionals swapped stories about some of the dance schools they had seen. Marie Rambert, who came to London during the First World War, was appalled to see 'little girls of three or four put into hard, real ballet shoes and running about on their points with contorted legs'.[2] Espinosa was equally dismayed: 'It is little short of criminal', he said, 'that people should be permitted to pose as teachers of dancing and take money from others when they do not know the very rudiments of the art which they profess to teach.'[3] Bad training was ruining the physique of young dancers, it was claimed, and adding to the perception that the English could not dance. Something needed to be done.

The dinner at the Trocadero was the first step in doing that something. The five guests of honour were among the most celebrated dancers and most respected teachers in the country at the time: Adeline Genée, Tamara Karsavina, Lucia Cormani, Edouard Espinosa and Phyllis Bedells. Each represented a different school of teaching 'operatic

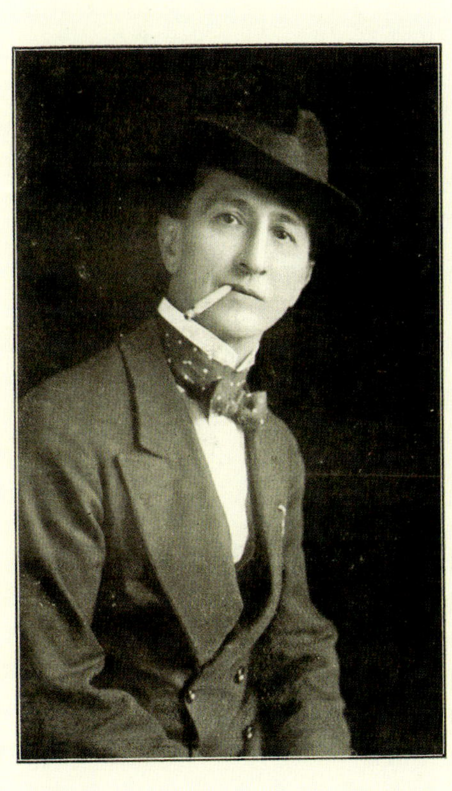

Technical Dictionary of Dancing

By ESPINOSA

" What the teacher must know."
" What the dancer should know."

PRICE SIX SHILLINGS.

Published at the Offices of
"THE DANCING TIMES,"
25, WELLINGTON STREET, STRAND, W.C.

dancing' (as ballet was then known), and were to some extent rivals, but all were concerned about the state of dance teaching in the UK at the time. The need for an association to raise the standards of dance teaching was discussed in more detail at a meeting held three months later, when the five guests of honour agreed to form a committee with Richardson as Honorary Secretary.

Their first task was to agree a syllabus. Phyllis Bedells, the only English dancer on the committee, remembered later that they started with Espinosa's original proposal: 'We took it to pieces and thrashed the pros and cons of the systems we each thought most suitable.'[4] There was clearly a lot of spirited discussion but after 'a good deal of give and take' an elementary syllabus was agreed. On 31 December 1920 it was presented to a meeting of more than a hundred dance teachers at the Grafton Galleries in Regent Street, at which the Association of Teachers of Operatic Dancing of Great Britain was officially established.

NOTES

1   Espinosa 1916, p. 327.
2   Rambert 1972, p. 124.
3   Richardson 1916, p. 326.
4   Bedells 1971, p. 5.

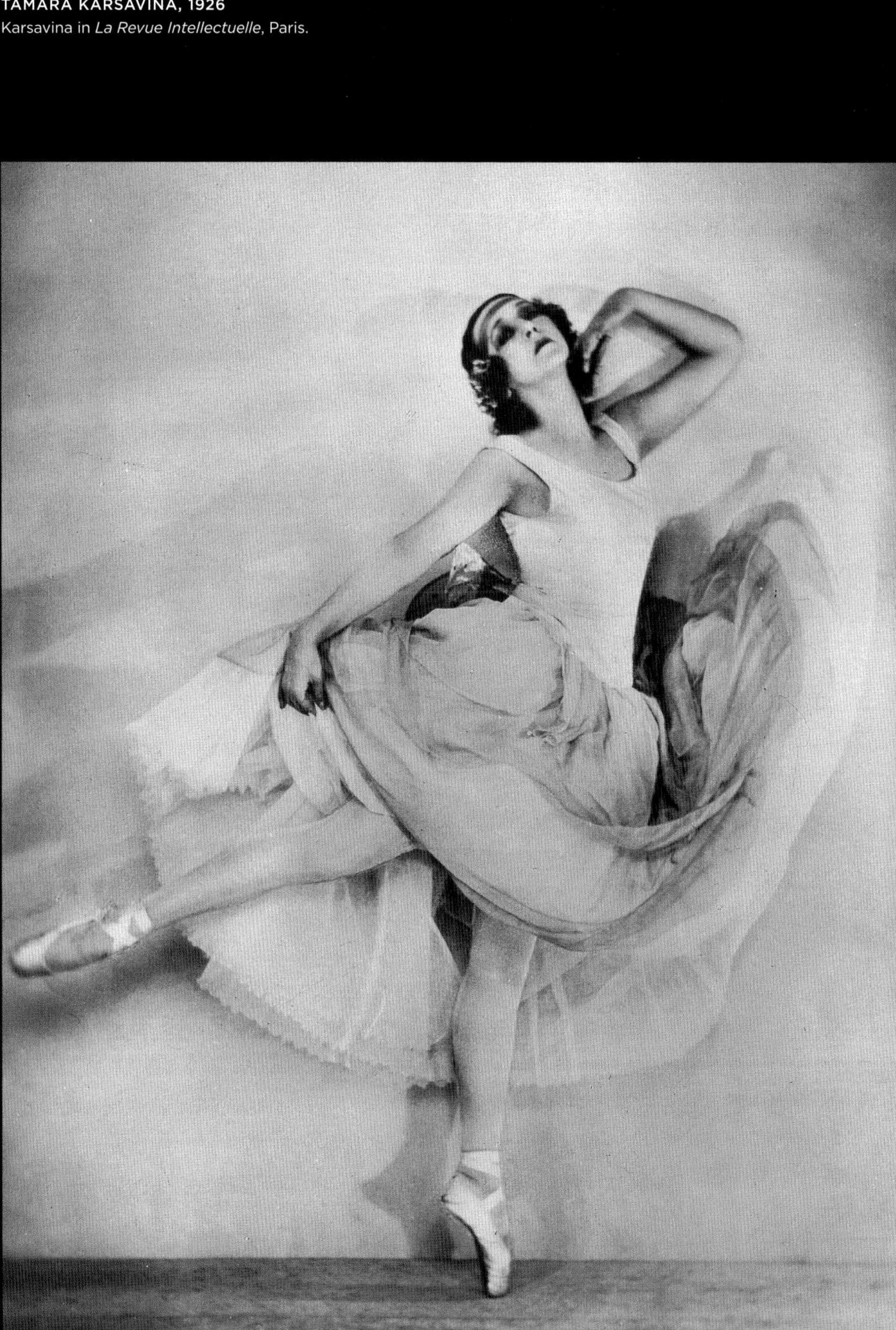
TAMARA KARSAVINA, 1926
Karsavina in *La Revue Intellectuelle*, Paris.

The ballet, with dances arranged by Espinosa,
was presented at the Empire Theatre in
London in the tense summer of 1914.

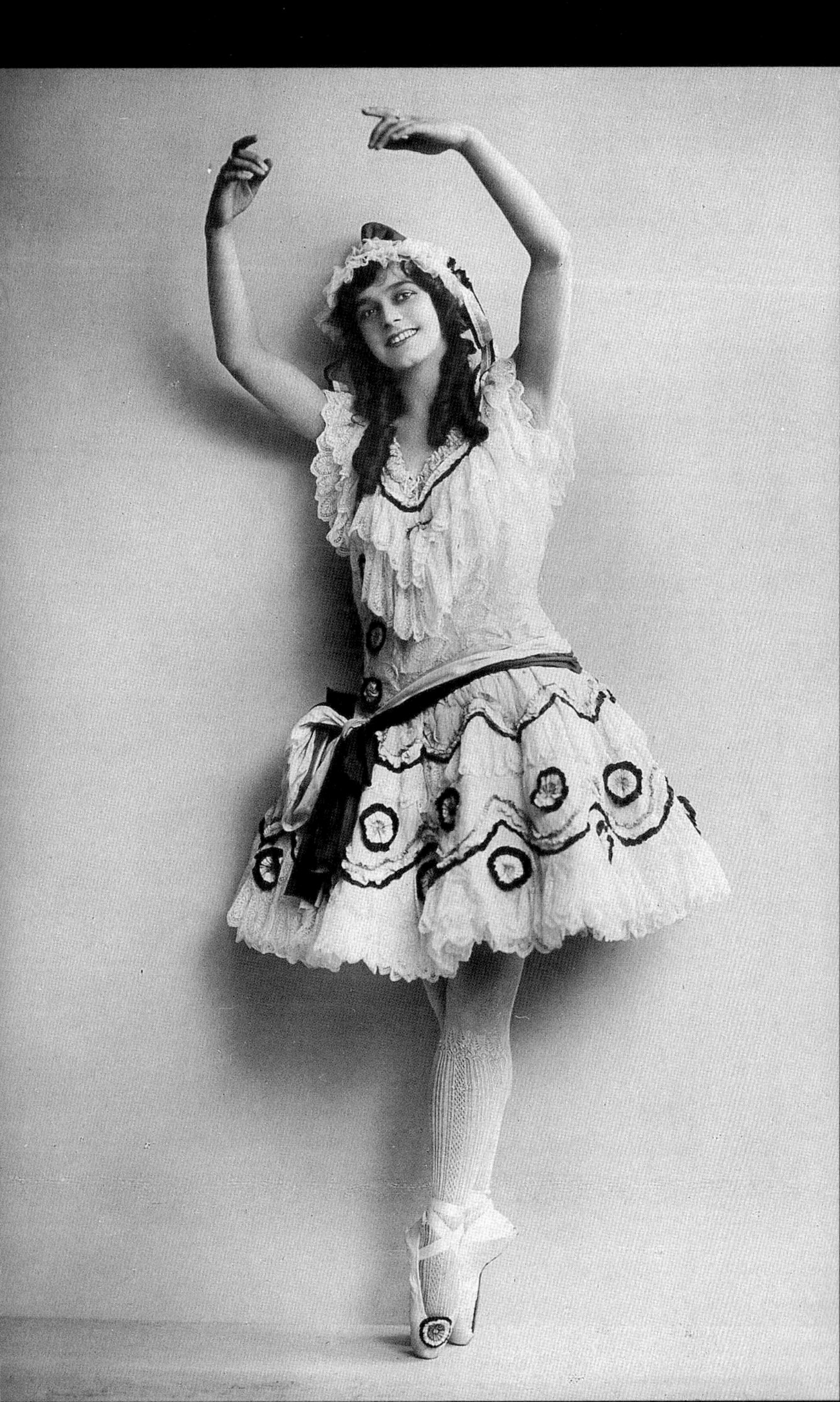

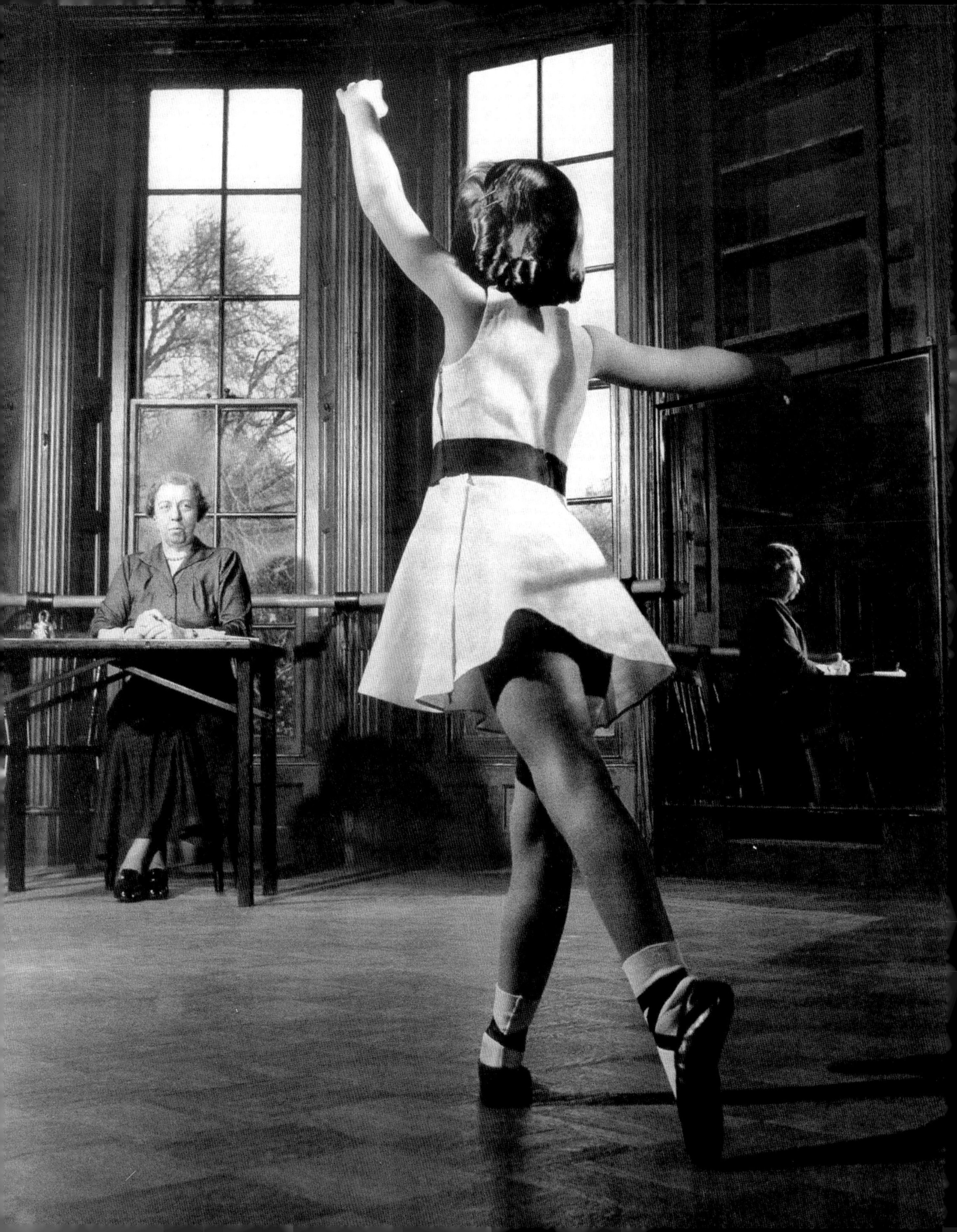

2

THE ACADEMY RISES

1920–1954

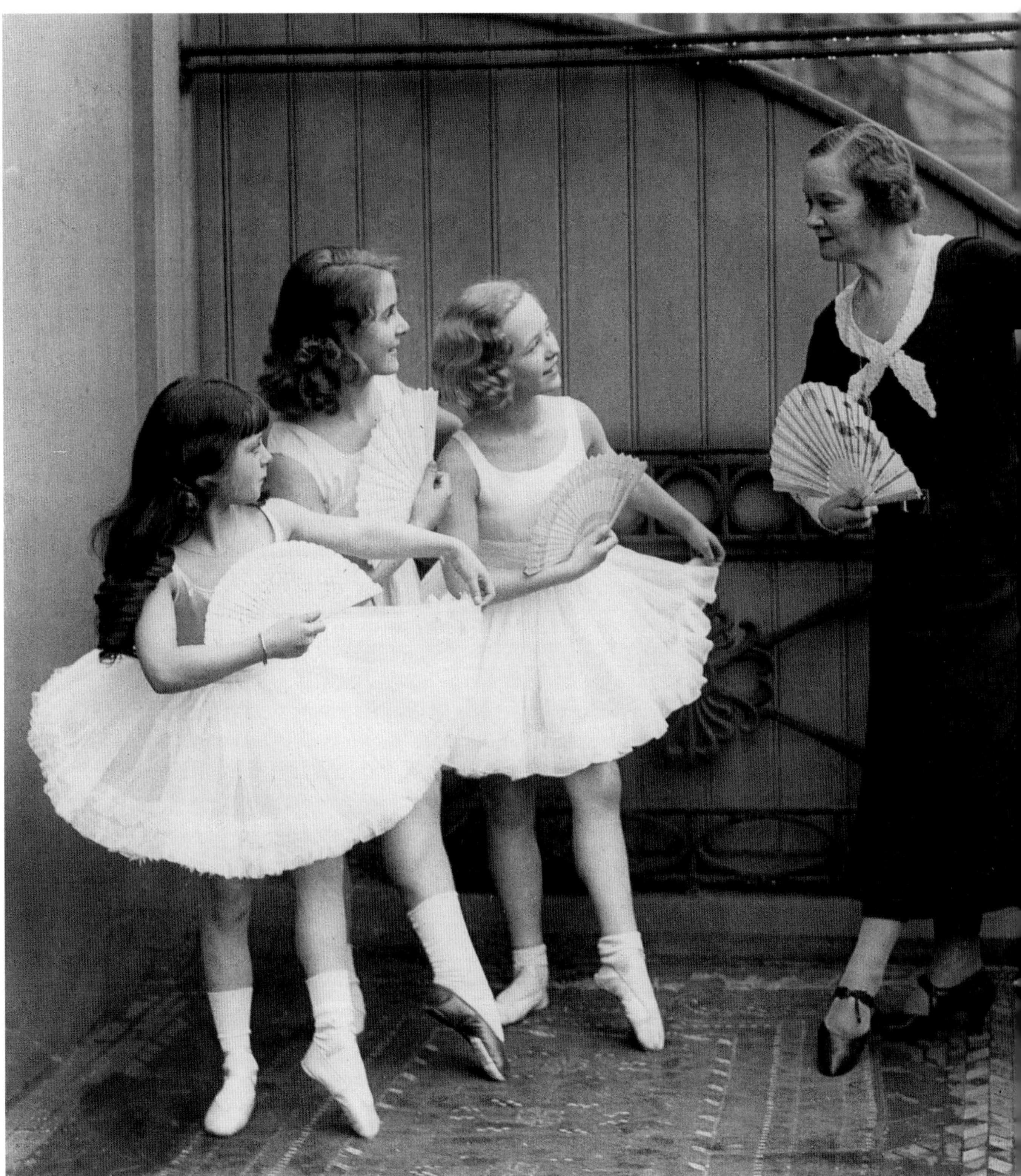

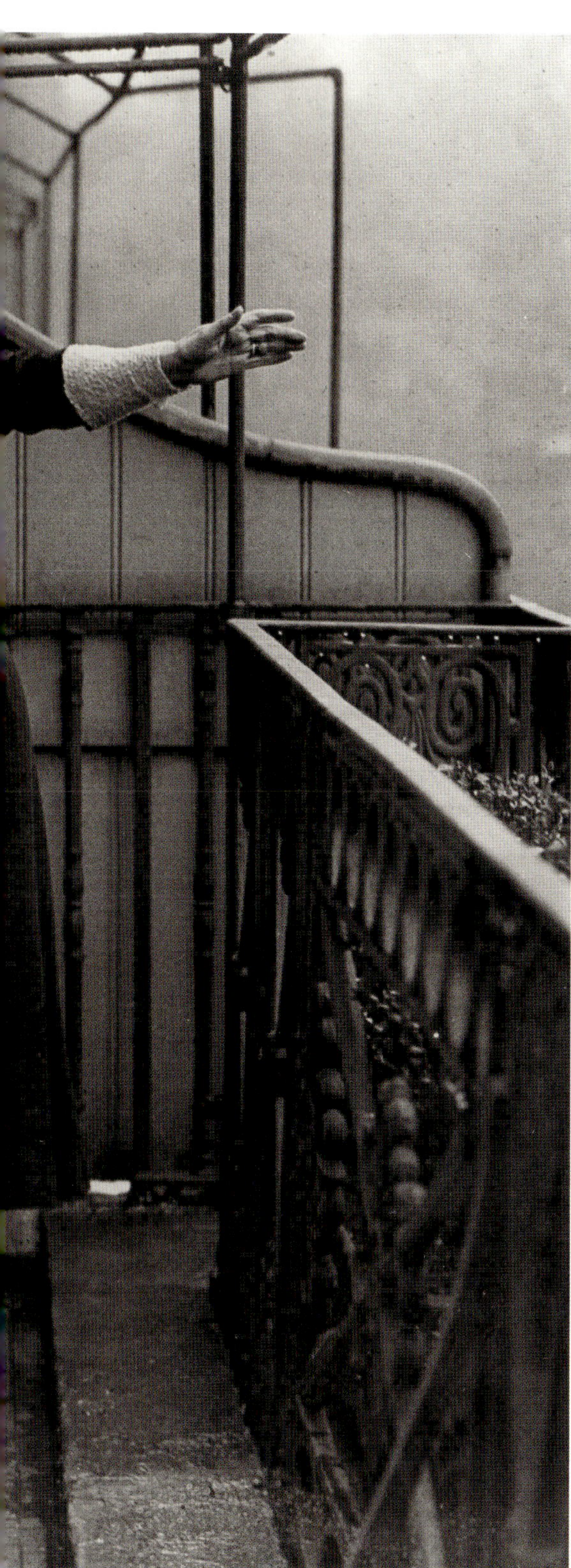

AS the first President of the Academy, Adeline Genée served in this role for nearly *35* years and many of its core activities today have their origins in her tenure. The establishment of syllabi for both the 'one-lesson-a-week' child and the vocational student, the development of teacher training, the Genée International Ballet Competition and the Queen Elizabeth II Coronation Award all date from this period. In addition, Genée launched the Building Fund, which enabled the organisation to find a home, and instigated various projects to aid the war effort during the Second World War.

In the early years, Genée's priority was to establish a safe and informed structure for the

PEGGY WHITELEY, 1921

One of the first probationers to be accepted as a Member of the Association, Whiteley was awarded her certificate – signed by all of the original members of the Association's founding committee – after successfully passing the Elementary examination session in May 1921. She ran her own ballet school during the 1930s but remained closely involved with the Academy in later years.

teaching of ballet. In this she was aided by a Technical Committee, which was able to provide a wealth of knowledge and experience. In combining the best of the French, Danish, Italian, Russian and English 'schools', the Association of Operatic Dancing, as it became known, set new standards in the teaching of ballet. Aspiring teachers were required to pass executant examinations to ensure knowledge of the ballet vocabulary and the ability to demonstrate steps and positions with accuracy. Indeed, it is worth noting that the Association began with 'Major' (now Vocational Graded) examinations for future performers and teachers. The first Elementary examinations were held in 1921, the Intermediate in 1922 and the Advanced in 1923. The prestigious Solo Seal examination, for holders of the Advanced Certificate, was introduced in 1928. Within a decade Genée and her committee had created an entire vocational training structure for ballet.

Children's examinations were introduced in 1924 and were designed to eliminate some of the poor practice that was prevalent at the time. As recorded by Phyllis Bedells, there were 523 candidates from across the UK. The syllabus was specifically designed for the 'one-lesson-a-week child' who was dancing for enjoyment rather than aiming for a dance career. The benefits of ballet classes were promoted by the Association from the first, Philip Richardson claiming that 'when properly given, classes form the finest form of physical culture, the best corrective of the minor bodily ailments, and one of the pleasantest steps in the direction of mental culture which a child can have'.[1] In 1925 the Association launched a scholarship scheme to support talented students in the UK, thus beginning a long-term commitment to widening access to dance that remains to this day.

From the outset, Genée sought both national and international expansion and recognition of the Association's work. Gaining the support of Queen

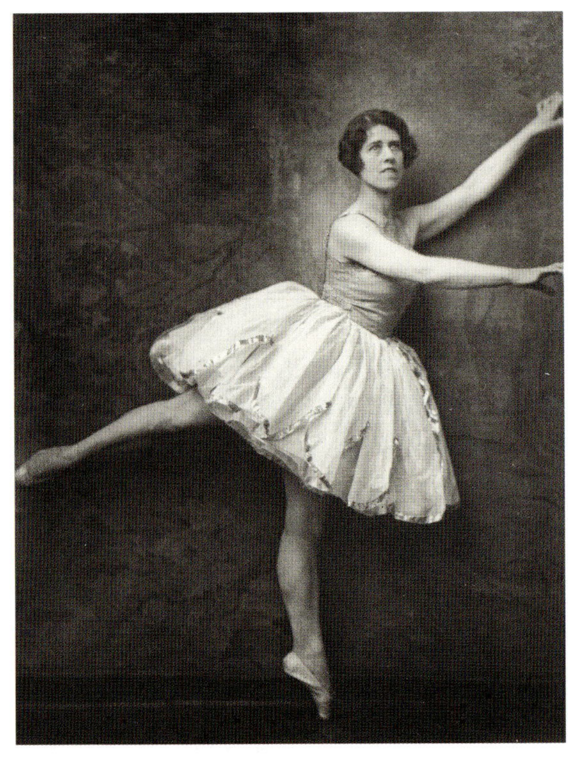

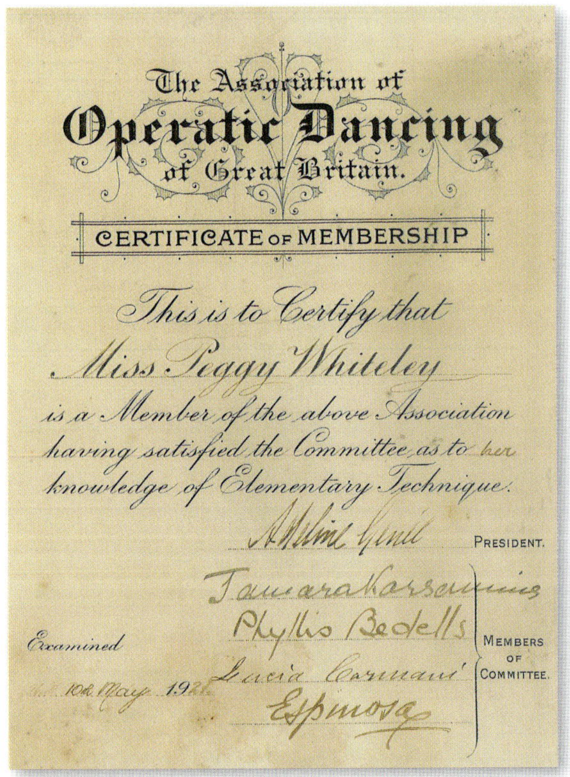

The Association of
Operatic Dancing
of Great Britain.

CERTIFICATE of MEMBERSHIP

This is to Certify that
Miss Peggy Whiteley
is a Member of the above Association having satisfied the Committee as to her knowledge of Elementary Technique.

Adeline Genée — PRESIDENT.

Tamara Karsavina
Phyllis Bedells
Lucia Cormani
Espinosa — MEMBERS OF COMMITTEE.

Examined
10th May 1921

PROGRAMME

1. OVERTURE - - "The Shoe" - - - - *Ansell*
Conducted by THE COMPOSER.

2. MENUET - - - - - - - - *Boccherini*
Danced by 'Scholars' of the Association.
BERYL LAVERICK   BARBARA ELLIS   BETTY ENGLAND   DENISE HUNT
PEGGY BANDY   MARGERY DUNHILL   KATHLEEN PEARCE   GWYNETH MATHEWS
Arranged by Madame GENEE.

3. "HOMMAGE AUX BELLES VIENNOISES" *Schubert*
(a) Pas de Trois - EILEEN BAKER, SHEILA McCARTHY, WALTER GORE
(b) Pas de Quatre - MABEL RODGER, EILEEN STEWART, MARY BUTTERWORTH, JEAN HORNE
(c) Pas de Huit - DOROTHY WHITAKER, JESSIE WILSON, JANET ROGERS, ANNE STEVENS, BETTY WEDGWOOD, MOYA KENNEDY, NESSIE BROOKING, GWYNETH MATHEWS
(d) Pas de Deux - NINETTE DE VALOIS, STANLEY JUDSON
Choregraphy by NINETTE DE VALOIS

4. DOT RICKINSON
"The Broken Rendezvous" - - *Cyril Scott*
Arranged by Miss GRACIE CONE

5. THE TRUE STORY OF KING ALFRED
(An anachron'stic ballet by MOLLIE SUFFIELD, set to the music of *Haydn*)
King Alfred - KATHLEEN ORMROD   *The Scullion* - PAT GREY
Queen Alfreda - EMILY HINDLE   *The Royal Cook* - RUTH BURTON
The King's Fool - PAULINE CRANKSHAW   *The Varlets and Ladies of the Court*

6. 'EN FAMILLE—A daily occurrence'
'One Touch of Humour makes the family grin'
Ballet Music by T. E. ATKINSON   Conducted by T. E. ATKINSON
Eddie - E. KELLAND ESPINOSA   *Babs* - YVETTE ESPINOSA   *Dad* - ESPINOSA
Records from THE COLUMBIA GRAMOPHONE Co.   Choregraphy by ESPINOSA

7. LUCIENNE LAMBALLE
(Première Danseuse Etoile from the Opera, Paris)
(a) Pizzicato - - - - - *Glazounow*
(b) Polichinelle - - - - - - *Rachmaninoff*
Choregraphy by Madame EGOROVA   Mlle. LAMBALLE appears by permission of M. ROUCHÉ

8. BRITISH DANCES
arranged by Mr. D. G. MacLENNAN
IRISH—(a) Four Hand Reel and Solo Reel Steps
DOROTHY CHAPLIN, EILEEN BAKER, MOLLY BERLANDINA, DOROTHY REED, DOROTHY GREENHILL,
(b) Irish Hornpipe
SHEILA GEERE, PHYLLIS WALLERS, MAVIS BITHEL
ENGLISH—Sailors' Hornpipe
ELSIE MAGDIN, OLIVE KILLINGBACK
SCOTTISH—Two old Highland Dances now revived for the first time by Mr. MacLENNAN
(a) Highland Laddie - - NANCY MUNRO
(b) Blue Bonnets - - ELSIE MAGDIN
First Performance of a New Eightsome Reel arranged by Mr. MacLENNAN
NANCY MUNRO   MOLLY BERLANDINA   DOROTHY CHAPLIN
NESSIE BROOKING   ELSIE MAGDIN   DOROTHY GREENHILL
EILEEN BAKER   DOROTHY REED
followed by a Modern Step Dance - - E. KELLAND ESPINOSA
evolved from the steps of the above National Dances
FINALE   ENSEMBLE   THE CHICKEN REEL

A SHORT INTERVAL

9. SELECTION - - - - "Coppelia" - - - - *Delibes*

10. An excerpt from the Ballet
"COPPELIA"
Produced by Mr. ALEXANDER GENEE
Swanilda - PHYLLIS BEDELLS   *Franz* - FELIX DEMERY   *The Doll* - NANCY MUNRO
Friends of Swanilla - NOREEN BUSH, EILEEN BAKER, DOROTHY CHAPLIN, JOAN COWLEY, EILEEN REED, IRENE STEWAT, SISSIE SMITH WILMA van DUSEN
Conducted by Mr. JOHN ANSELL
Mr. ANSELL appears by permission of the B.B.C.

11. VERA SAVINA
DANSÉ RUSSE - - - - - - - - *Tchaikowsky*
Arranged by M. MASSINE

12. ANTON DOLIN
"ESPAGNOL" - - - - - - - - - *Albeniz*

13. THAMAR KARSAVINA
VIENNESE WALTZ - - - - - - - *Lanner*
Madame KARSAVINA appears by permission of M. DIAGHILEFF

14. ANTON DOLIN AND VERA SAVINA
PAS DE DEUX - - - - - - - - - *Reval*
Arranged by Mr. DOLIN
Costumes by Miss PHYLLIS DOLTON
Mr. DOLIN appears by permission of M. DIAGHILEFF

15. DIVERTISSEMENT CLASSIQUE
Arranged by ESPINOSA. Music by T. E. ATKINSON. Introducing
LUCIENNE LAMBALLE
Supported by
BETTY ROYLANCE, D. REED, D. GREENHILL, M. DUNHILL, H. FISHER, P. NOBLE, M. DEACON, G. SIDES, M. DEACON, M. IRWIN, E. COLLIS B. MORGAN, P. FOSTER, E. REED, I. STEWART, M. BERLANDINA, G. HEAVEN, J. BARTLETT, B. SETH, C. AMBROSE, C. Y. AMBROSE, J. WATKINS, P. FROST, D. HOUSELY, D. HOLMAN, M. BARTON, Q. SMITH, K. O'DRISCOLL, J. LARRINGTON, P. HOOD, E. DUCKINFIELD, B. CLELLAND, M. TURNER, E. THELWELL, P. BROOKS, RUTH BERNEY.
THE BABIES:
BETTY ENGLAND, KATHLEEN PEARCE, JOAN McCARTHY, with NOREEN BUSH
Mlle. LAMBALLE'S 'Caprice' de Tcherepnin arranged by Madame EGOROVA
The Divertissement conducted by the Composer

Grand Piano kindly lent by CHAPPELL & Co.

GOD SAVE THE KING

Mary, who became the organisation's first Royal Patron in 1928, was a considerable coup. The Association's profile was raised further through a series of charity matinées held in well-known London theatres, which drew wide audiences. The second of these, at the Gaiety Theatre in July 1929, featured the first act of *Coppélia* with Phyllis Bedells as Swanilda (coached by Genée herself) and Felix Demery as Franz. Other performers included Ninette de Valois, Anton Dolin, Edouard Espinosa, Tamara Karsavina and Vera Savina. Such an illustrious cast sealed the link between the Association and the wider British ballet profession, a partnership that later Presidents, Margot Fonteyn, Antoinette Sibley and Darcey Bussell, continued to pursue.

In addition to UK developments, the 1920s saw the start of what would become a truly global organisation. As early as 1922, members of the Association were teaching in South Africa and the first examinations were held there in 1927.

A SPECIAL MATINÉE, 1929
Programme details for the 'Special Matinée' presented at the Gaiety Theatre on 4 July 1929.

ESPINOSA TEACHING, 1920s
Edouard Espinosa with his pupil Ruth Berney. Liverpool teachers Miss Butterworth and Shelagh Elliott-Clarke and theatre manager Maud Carpenter look on.

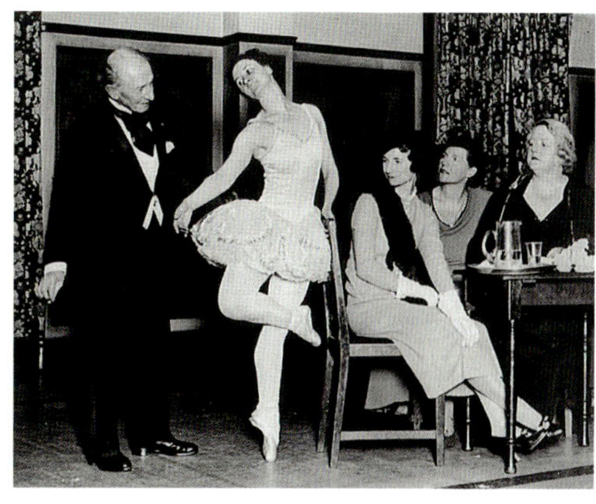

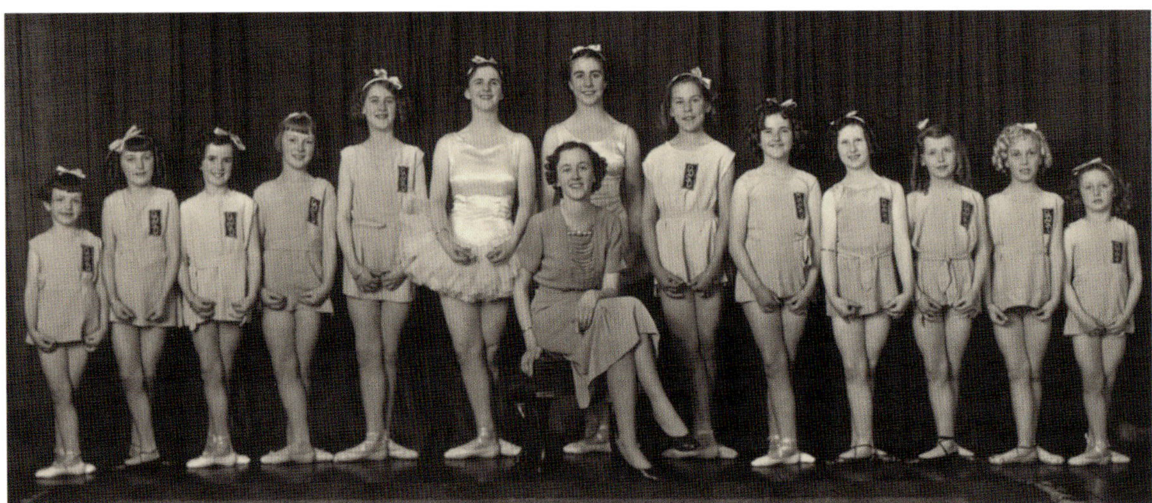

Espinosa was sent out to examine in 1927 and Donald MacLennan in 1929. The Association spread into Australia, New Zealand and Canada in the following decade, sending examiners out on long and somewhat arduous tours in the days before air travel. The first examinations in Australia and New Zealand took place in 1935 and the first examinations in Canada in 1941.

The Association's first decade closed with the resignation of Espinosa (who went on to form the British Ballet Organisation) and the appointment of his sister, Judith Espinosa, who was to serve as a loyal committee member for several years. In November 1930 the first issue of *The Operatic Association Gazette*, later renamed *Dance Gazette*, provided a much-needed line of communication with the increasing membership and remains a vital source of news and information for members today. In the same year a number of the Association's students were invited to perform at the Royal Opera House, Covent Garden. All in all there was much to celebrate on the organisation's tenth anniversary.

1930s

Throughout the 1930s the Association continued to show remarkable vision and unrelenting drive. The decade saw a number of important achievements, beginning in 1931 with the introduction of the first Teaching Certificate, the inauguration of the Adeline Genée Gold Medal (later the Genée International Ballet Competition) and the Pavlova Casket (awarded to the winners of a group competition). Performance opportunities were in abundance, with a trip to Copenhagen (in 1932) by the English Ballet Company, an ensemble formed of Association members and established British dancers, such as Anton Dolin, Alicia Markova, Ninette de Valois, Harold Turner and Phyllis Bedells. The company performed at the Royal Theatre before the King and Queen of Denmark and the Prince of Wales (later King Edward VIII). On the fourth and final performance Genée danced the closing number with Anton Dolin, receiving 'tumultous [*sic*] applause and curtain after curtain with the stage a bower of flowers looped and tied with the Danish and English colours'.[2]

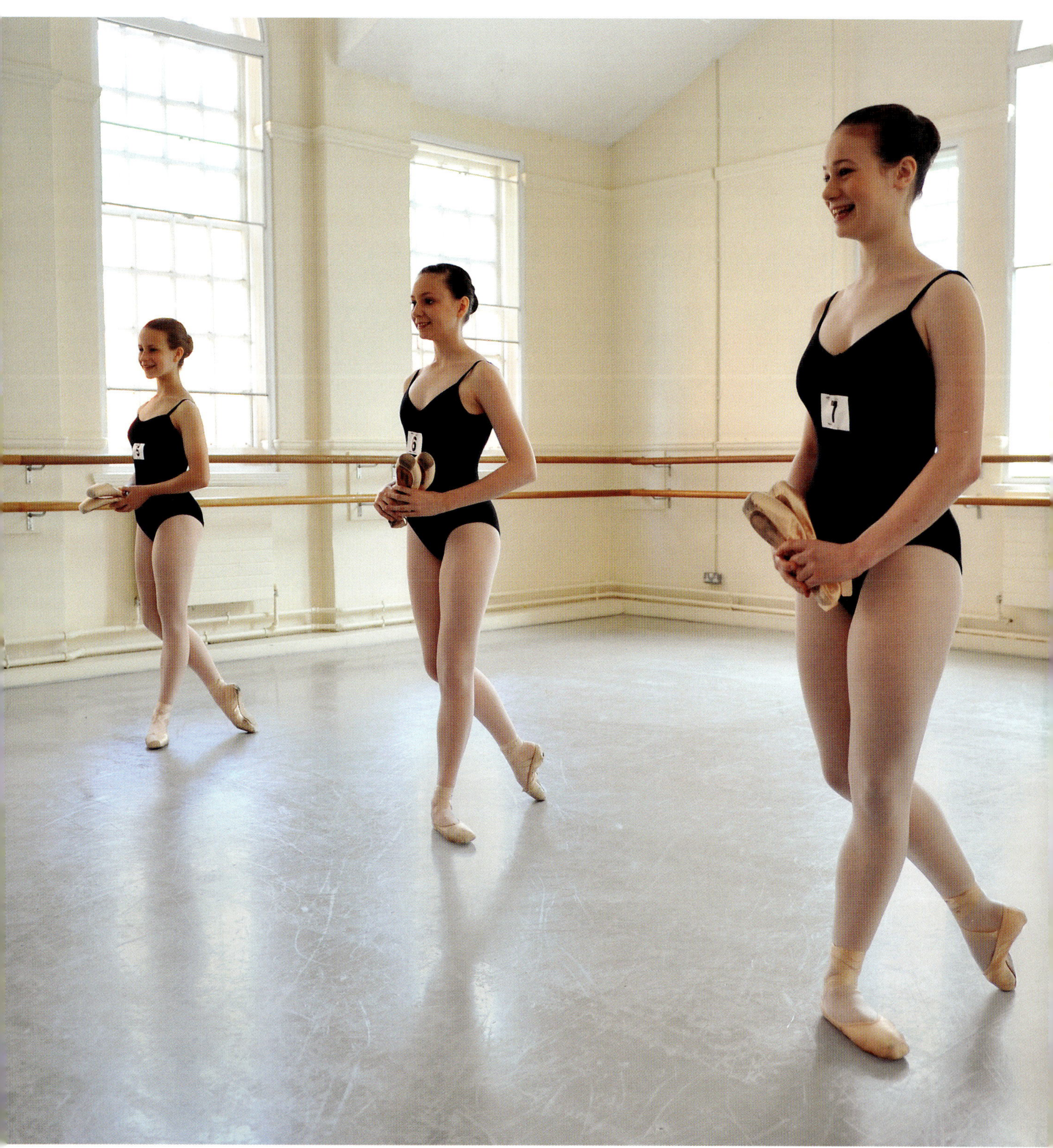

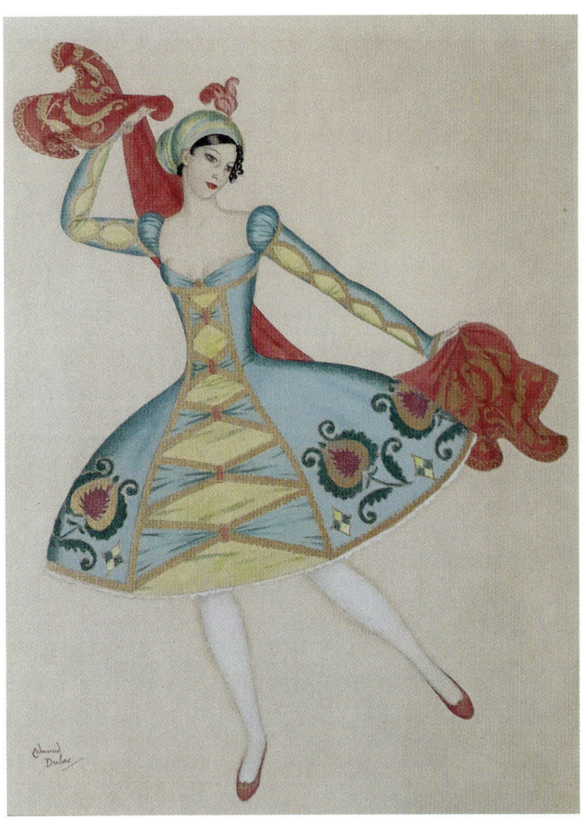

GALA, 1932

Adeline Genée performed at this Gala Matinée at Drury Lane in 1932 (programme design by Edmund Dulac) in a rare public appearance after her retirement in 1914. She repeated the performance later that year in Denmark.

COAT OF ARMS, 1937

Granted a Royal Charter in 1935, the Association's name was officially changed to the Royal Academy of Dancing and it acquired a coat of arms in 1937.

DENMARK, 1932

Sissie Smith, an Advanced Member of the Association of Operatic Dancing, travelled to Denmark to perform as part of the English Ballet Company. The autographed programme cover is for the Company's performances at the Royal Theatre in Copenhagen in 1932.

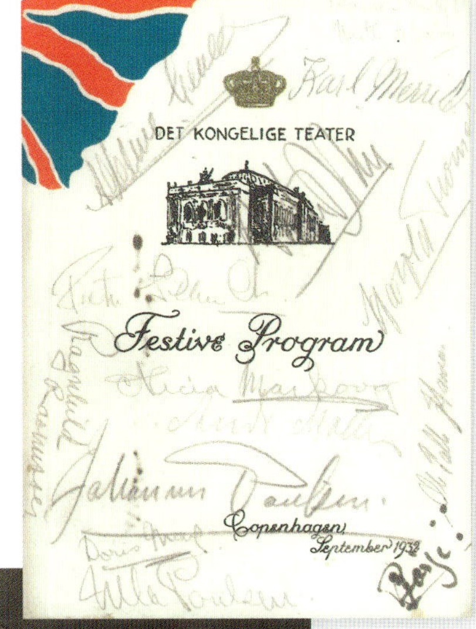

The following year, members of the Association appeared alongside Bedells and Harold Turner in *The Débutante* (at the Coliseum). Following the 1937 Annual General Meeting, members were accomplished enough to perform with the stars of Colonel de Basil's Ballets Russes. These and other opportunities showcased the standards being set under Genée and raised the organisation's profile within the dance profession.

Artistic goals were only one facet of Genée's vision: politics was another. Her ultimate aim of gaining national recognition was strengthened by the creation of a Grand Council and Executive Committee (in 1934) to support an application for a Royal Charter. In August 1935 King George V commanded that the Association should be known as The Royal Academy of Dancing. A few months later, on 20 December 1935, the application for the Royal Charter was approved. A coat of arms was designed in 1937, a year that ended well for the new Academy but brought unprecedented turmoil for the British monarchy following the abdication crisis of 1936.

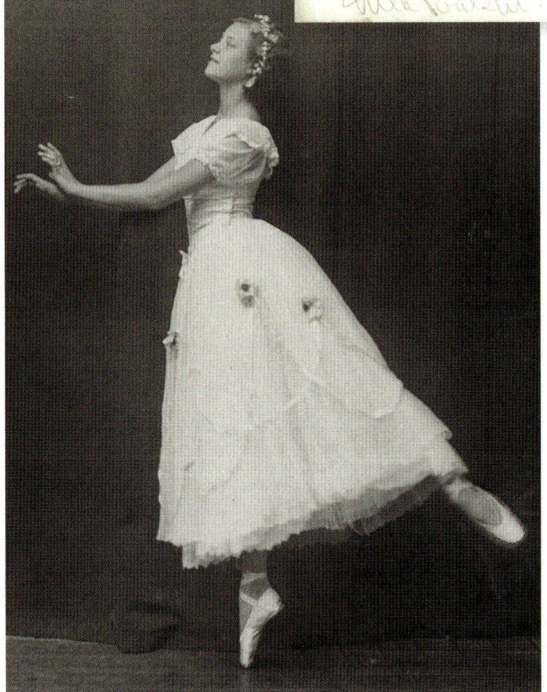

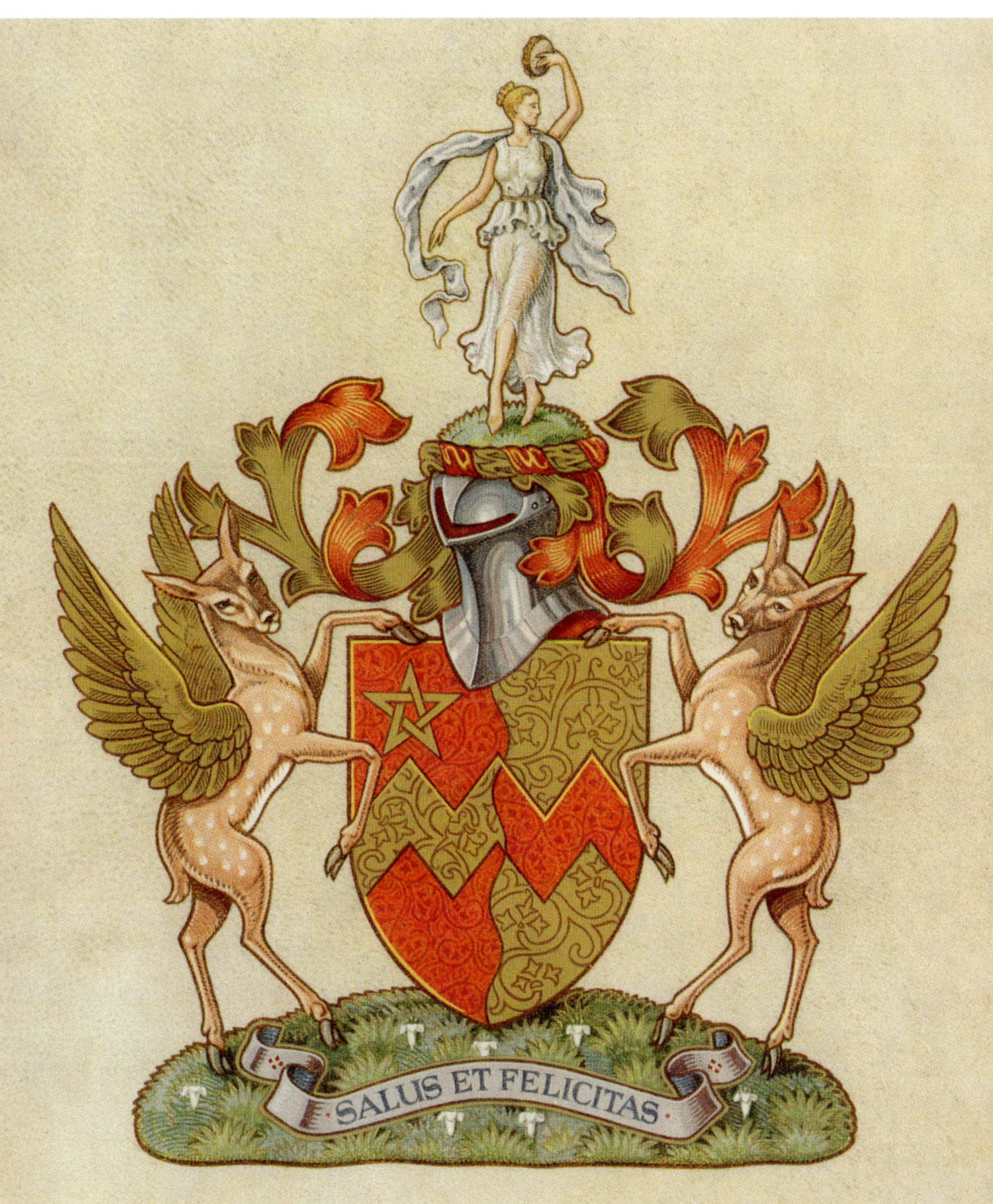

THE ARMORIAL BEARINGS OF

THE ROYAL ACADEMY
:: OF DANCING ::

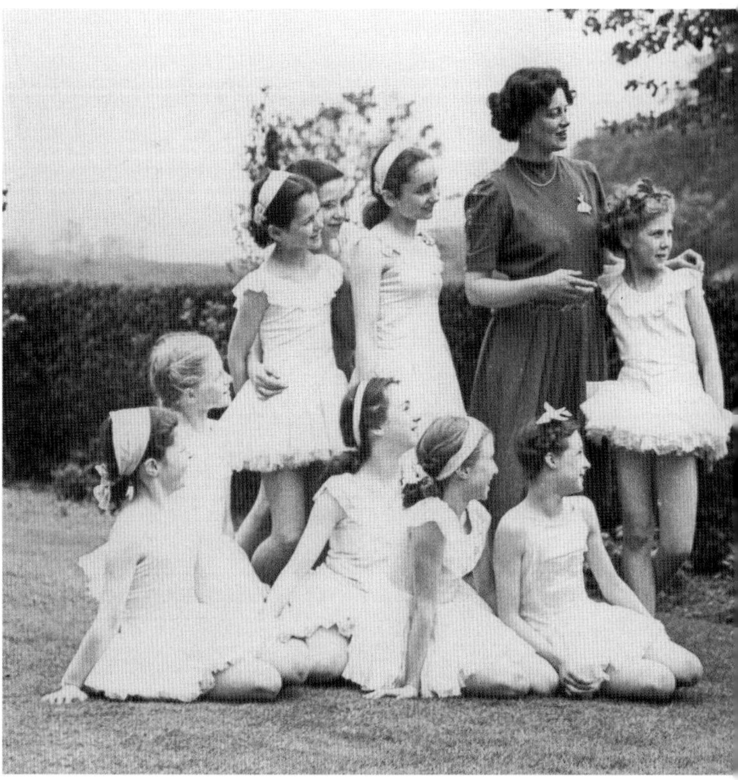

Having gained 'Royal Academy' status, attention was turned to more practical matters: the organisation needed a suitable home. The final year of the decade saw the launch of the Building Fund, a project that was to dominate the next few decades. In the November 1937 *Gazette*, Genée had pronounced: 'Unless we ourselves show the world that we are anxious to possess a building worthy of the patronage of Her Most Gracious Majesty Queen Mary, of the Royal Charter, and of the Art of Dancing, we cannot expect the outside support of which we so clearly stand in need.'[3]

Of equal significance, 1939 saw the publication of a lecture given by education expert Miss E.R. Gwatkin MA on a 'Suggested Training Course for Teachers of Dancing'. Here, for the first time, was a shift in perspective from 'what' to 'how' to teach and a proposal for dance teacher training that was comparable to other arts and academies.

THE WAR YEARS

The dynamic optimism of the 1930s was shattered by the outbreak of the Second World War in 1939, which brought inevitable disruption as schools were evacuated, theatres closed and many dancers and teachers over 18 joined the Armed Forces or served in other capacities. With the introduction of rationing it was difficult to buy or make uniforms, and skirts and tights were either swapped or hired. In spite of these practical difficulties, no fewer than 12,390 children took examinations during the six years of the Second World War.

Dance Gazette continued to be published throughout the war, albeit in shorter form. The newly launched Building Fund still managed to attract contributions and Genée instigated a 'knitting party' to provide much-needed garments for sailors on a minesweeper off the East Coast.

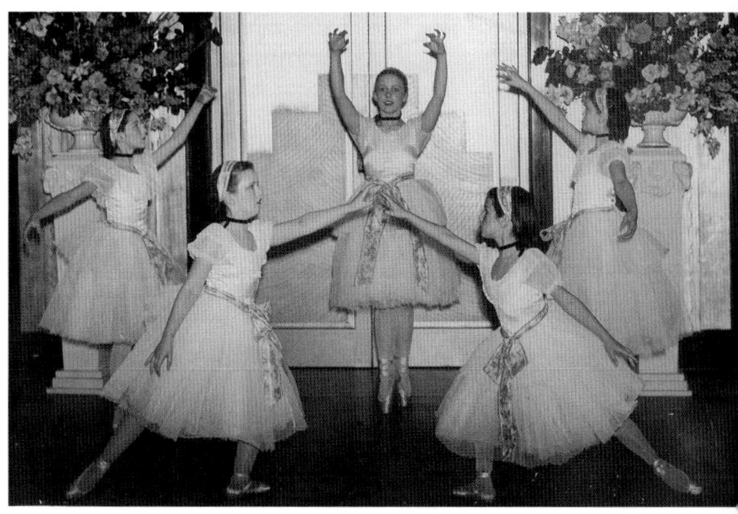

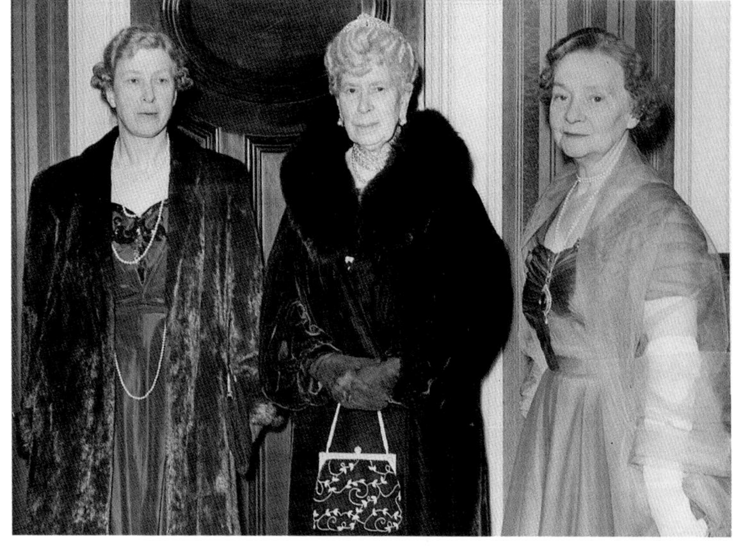

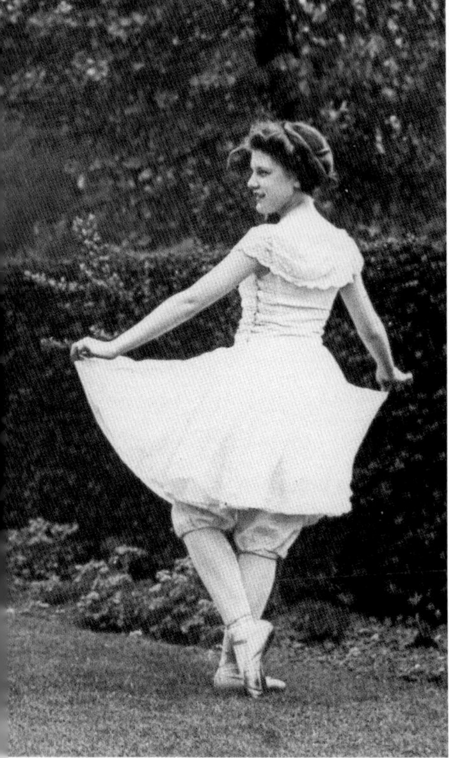

ROYAL PATRONAGE, 1950
Queen Mary became the Association's first Patron in 1928. Here, she attends a performance by the newly formed Festival Ballet in honour of Adeline Genée and the RAD in 1950. With Genée (right) and the Princess Royal (left).

OPPOSITE, BELOW
SILVER JUBILEE CELEBRATIONS, 1946
RAD scholars performing at the twenty-fifth anniversary celebrations at Claridge's Hotel on 15 January 1946.

DIPLOMA DAY, 1957
Students graduating from the Teachers' Training Course with course directors Lilian Charlesworth and Arnold Haskell at Fairfield Lodge.

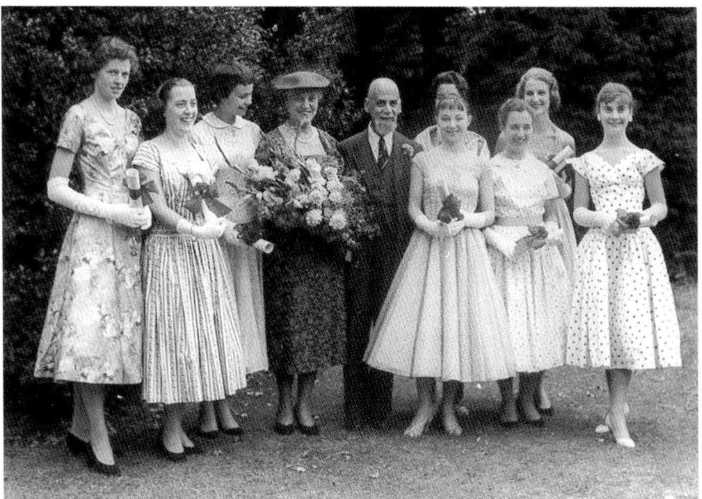

POST-WAR

The year 1945 marked both the end of the war and the Academy's Silver Jubilee. With peace came the chance to develop the three-year Teachers' Training Course that had been planned since the lecture by E.R. Gwatkin in 1939. Launched in October 1945, the programme aimed to give the dancing teacher a knowledge of the physical reasons behind ballet technique, a wide view of dance as an art, and of ballet as composite of the arts of dance, music, painting and drama. Students were required to live as boarders at Fairfield Lodge in the Holland Park area of London. In the summer of 1948, after a challenging course, successful graduates were rewarded with a Licentiate Award, followed by a grand party in the gardens of the Lodge on Diploma Day.

The years after the war were golden ones for British ballet. The success of Sadler's Wells Ballet, Festival Ballet and Ballet Rambert brought a new attention to the art form, while Margot Fonteyn, Dame Ninette de Valois and Frederick Ashton became household names. It was during the 1950s, too, that the Royal Academy of Dancing expanded further overseas, with examinations held in Mexico and the Caribbean, the USA, Belgium, the Netherlands, Norway, Germany, Italy, Malaysia, Singapore, India, Ceylon (now Sri Lanka), Rhodesia (now Zimbabwe) and Hong Kong.

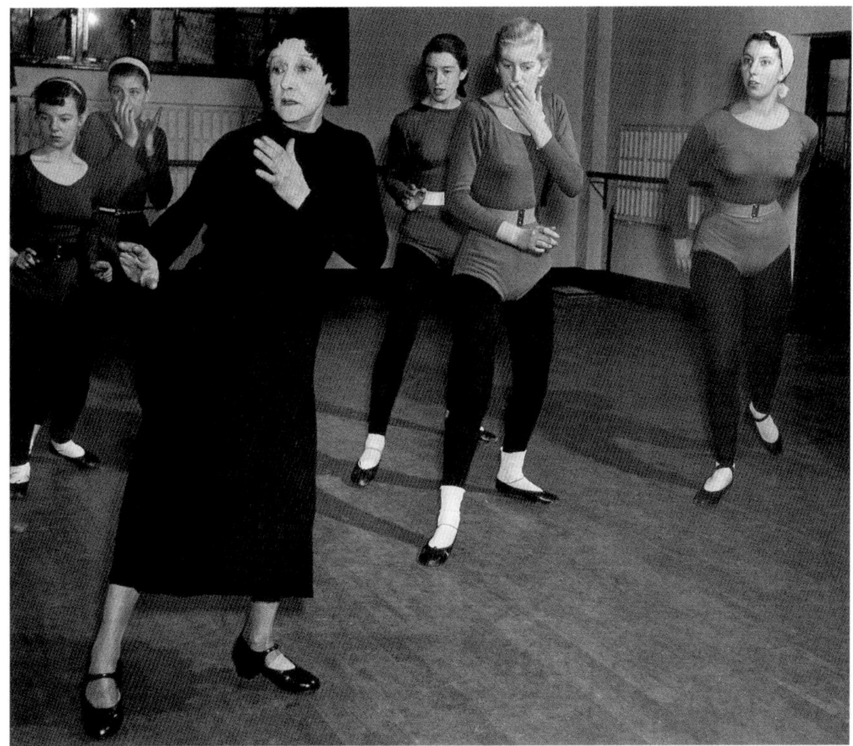

TEACHING MIME, 1952
Tamara Karsavina teaching
mime to students on the
Teachers' Training Course.
Karsavina is expressing
'surprise mingled with fear
at seeing an unexpected
ugly insect emerge from
a beautiful flower'.

PHYLLIS BEDELLS,
*c.*1956
Bedells teaching pupils at
her school in Quex Road,
North London.

OPPOSITE

**TEACHERS' TRAINING
COURSE STUDENTS,
1949**
In the studio at Fairfield
Lodge.

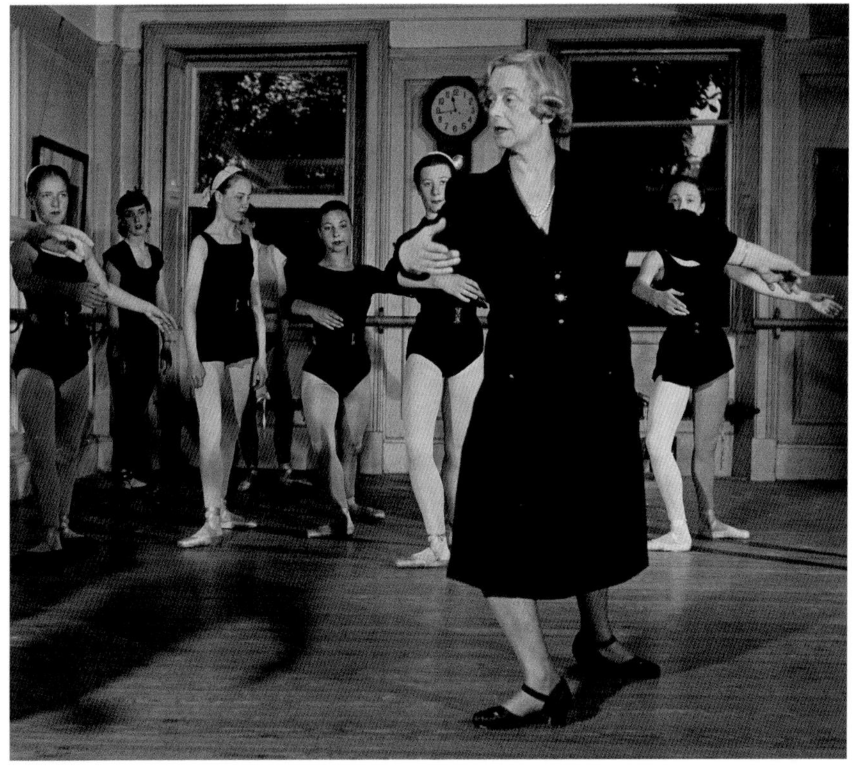

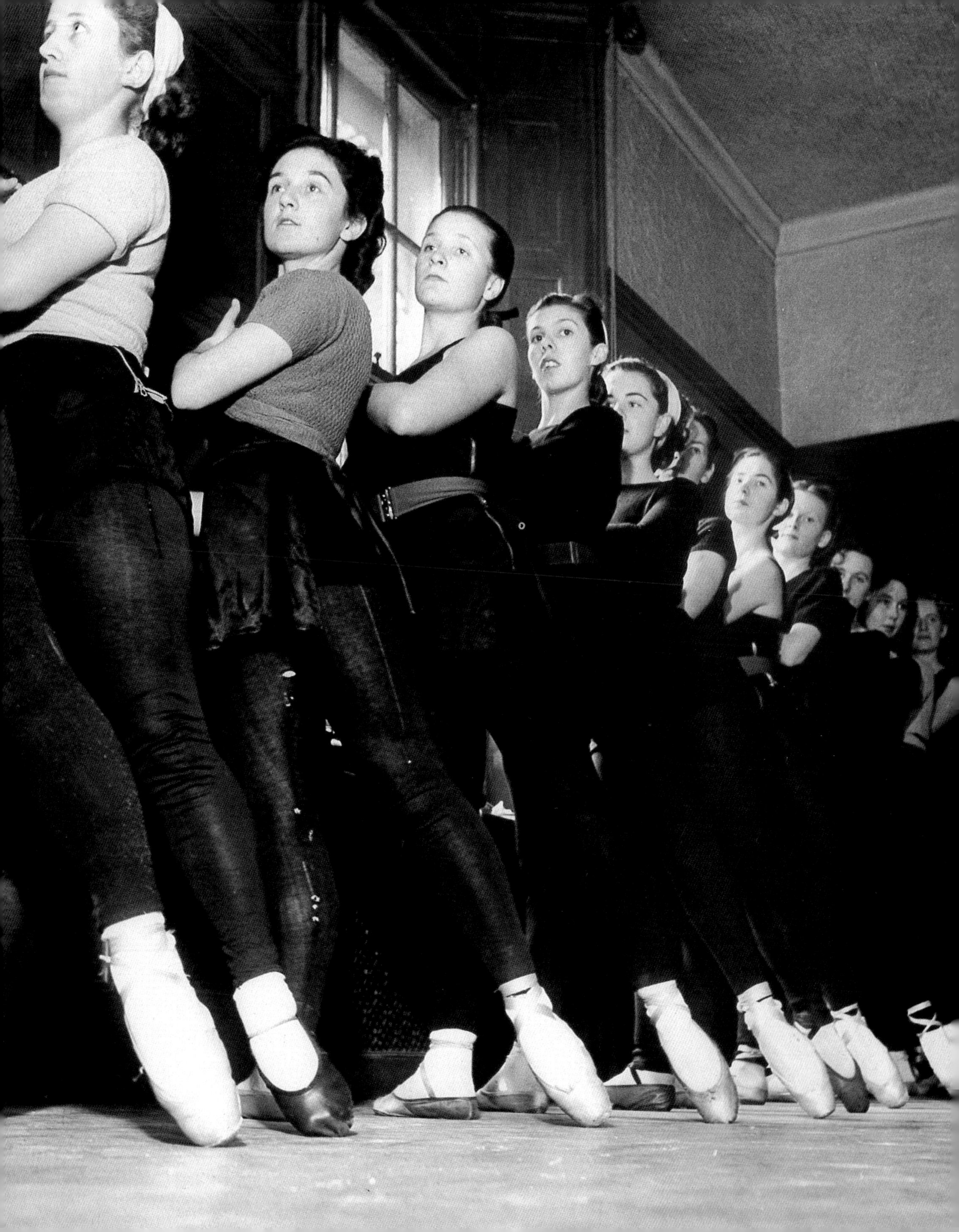

Phyllis Bedells[+]

MAJOR EXAMINATIONS, 1952
Candidates demonstrate an *arabesque en l'air sur pointe* for the examiners, Phyllis Bedells (left) and Dame Adeline Genée.

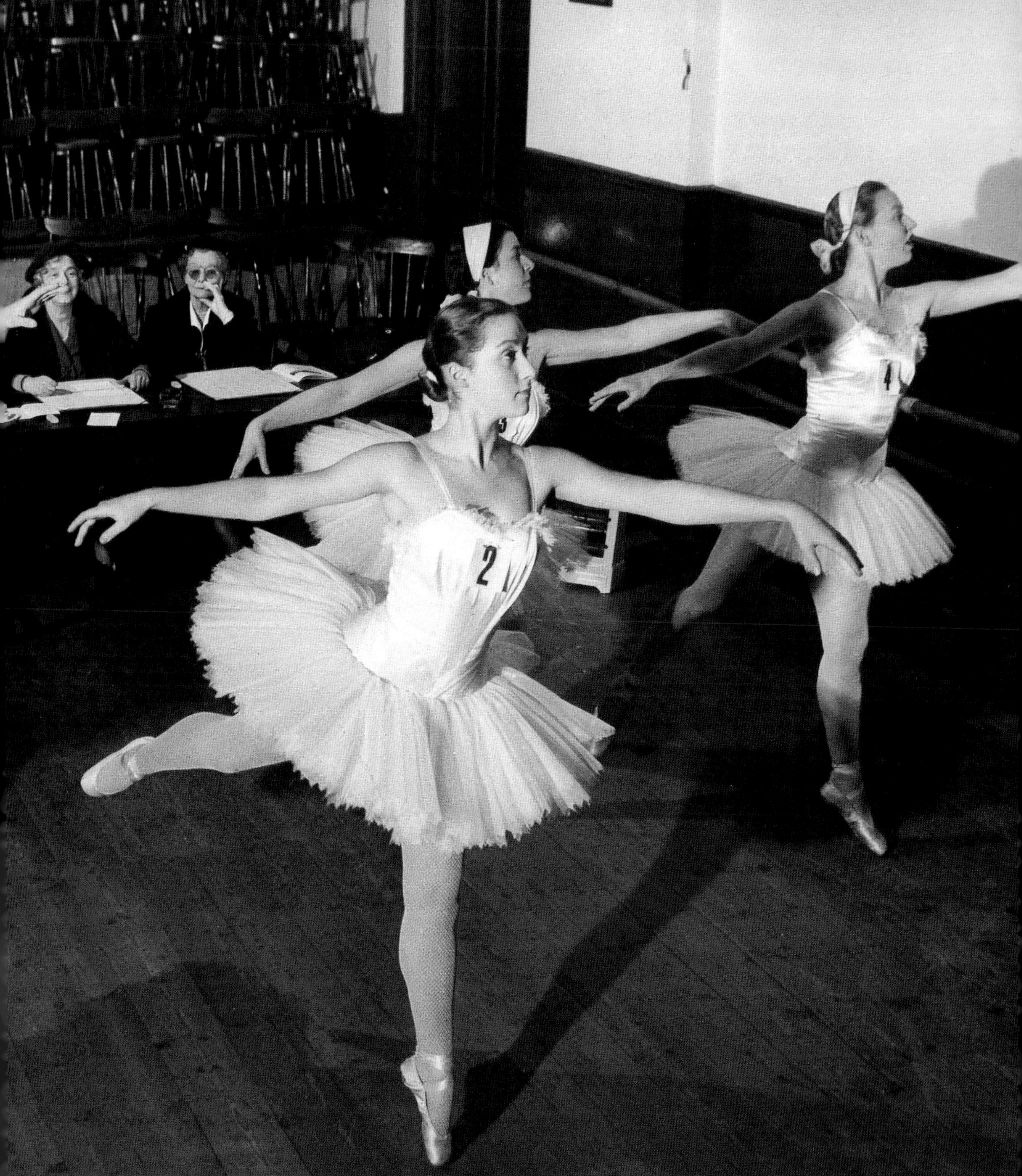

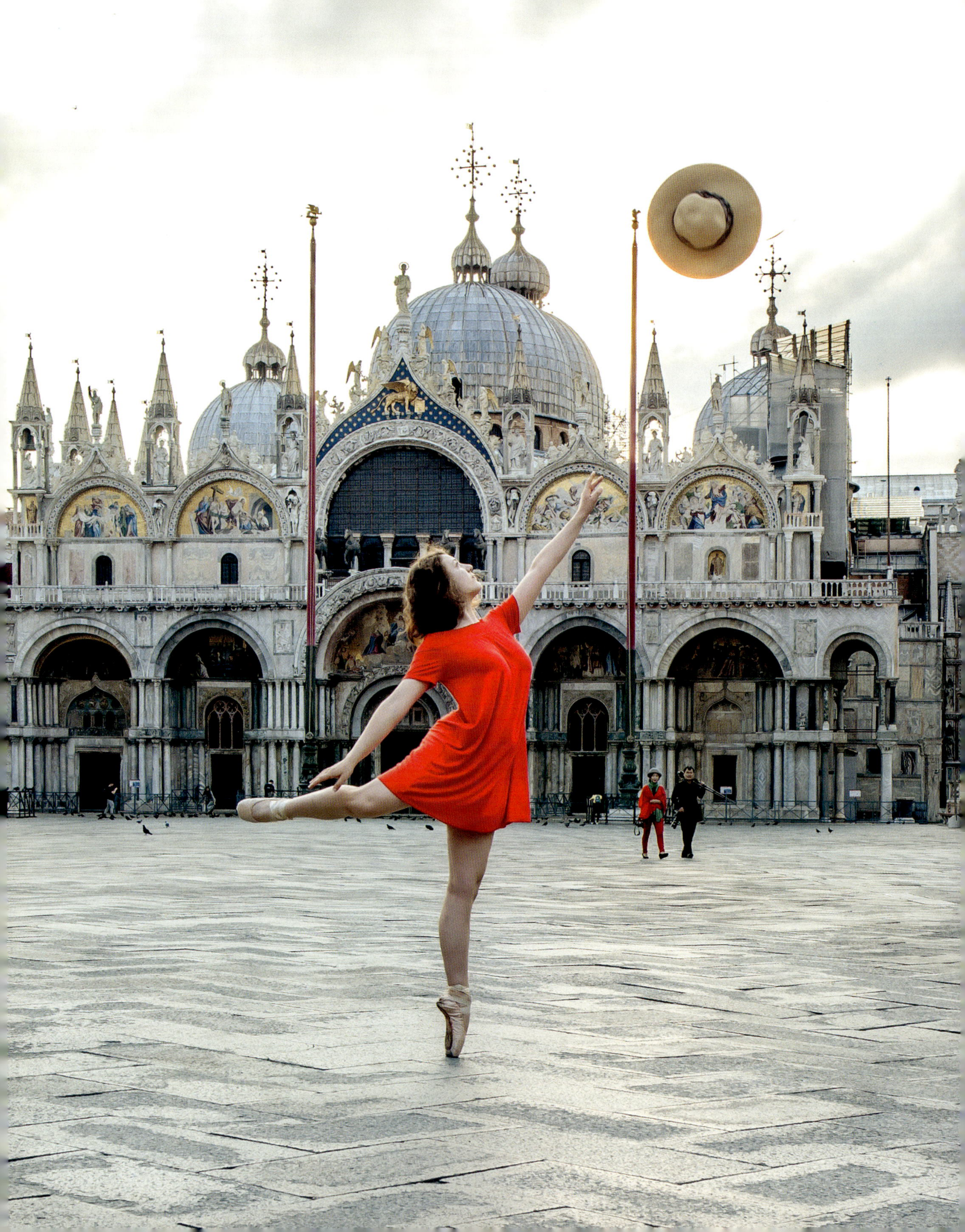

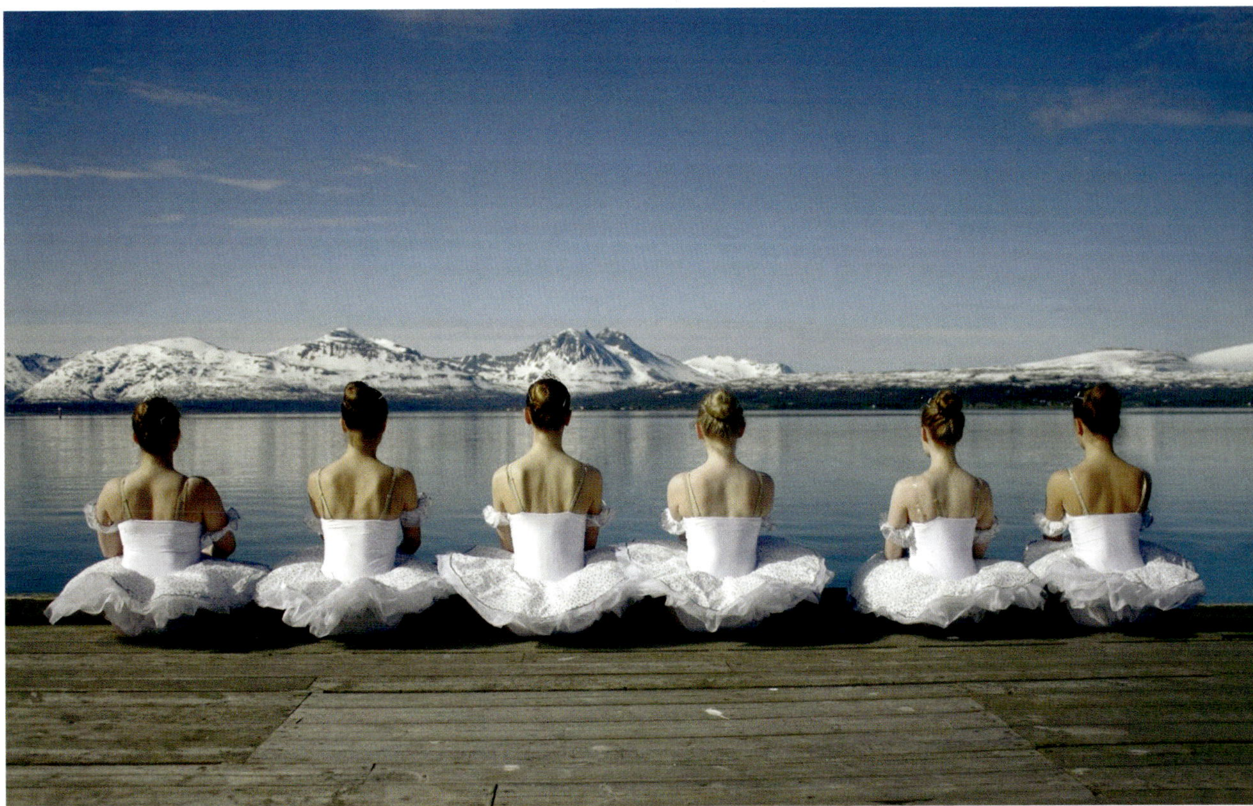

In 1953 Queen Mary died and the new Queen Elizabeth II agreed to become the second Royal Patron of the RAD, a post she has retained ever since. After 35 years, Genée marked her retirement by presenting the RAD with a silver plaque to be known as the Queen Elizabeth II Coronation Award, recognising individuals who have given outstanding services to the art of ballet. In her final address, as she passed the presidency of the RAD on to Margot Fonteyn, Genée acknowledged her faith in placing the role 'in the hands of one so greatly admired and beloved', adding that the appointment of Fonteyn as her successor 'makes the step so much easier for me'.[5]

NOTES

1   Richardson 1923, p. 900.
2   Bedells 1971, p. 7.
3   Genée 1937, p. 1.
4   Bedells 1971, p. 7
5   Genée 1954, p. 1.

QUEEN ELIZABETH II CORONATION AWARD

THE Queen Elizabeth II Coronation Award, gifted to the Academy by Adeline Genée, remains the RAD's highest honour. Created in 1953 to mark the coronation of the RAD's Royal Patron, the award is presented in recognition of outstanding services to the art of ballet. The first recipient was Dame Ninette de Valois, founder of The Royal Ballet, and the award has subsequently been given to many of the most famous names in ballet, including Sir Frederick Ashton, Rudolf Nureyev, Dame Gillian Lynne, Sir Matthew Bourne and Carlos Acosta. In 2014 the award was given to The Royal Ballet, the first time it had been presented to a company rather than to an individual.

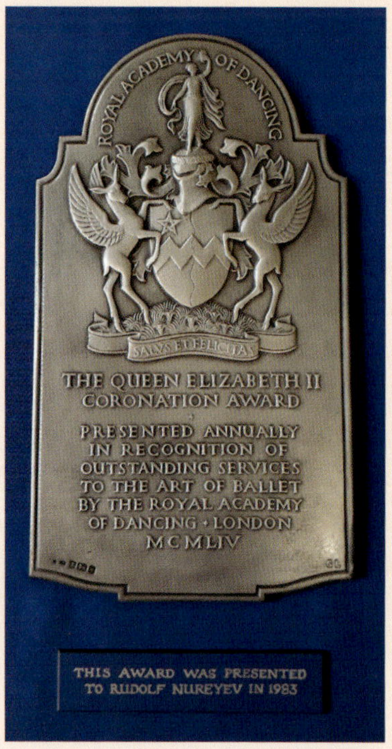

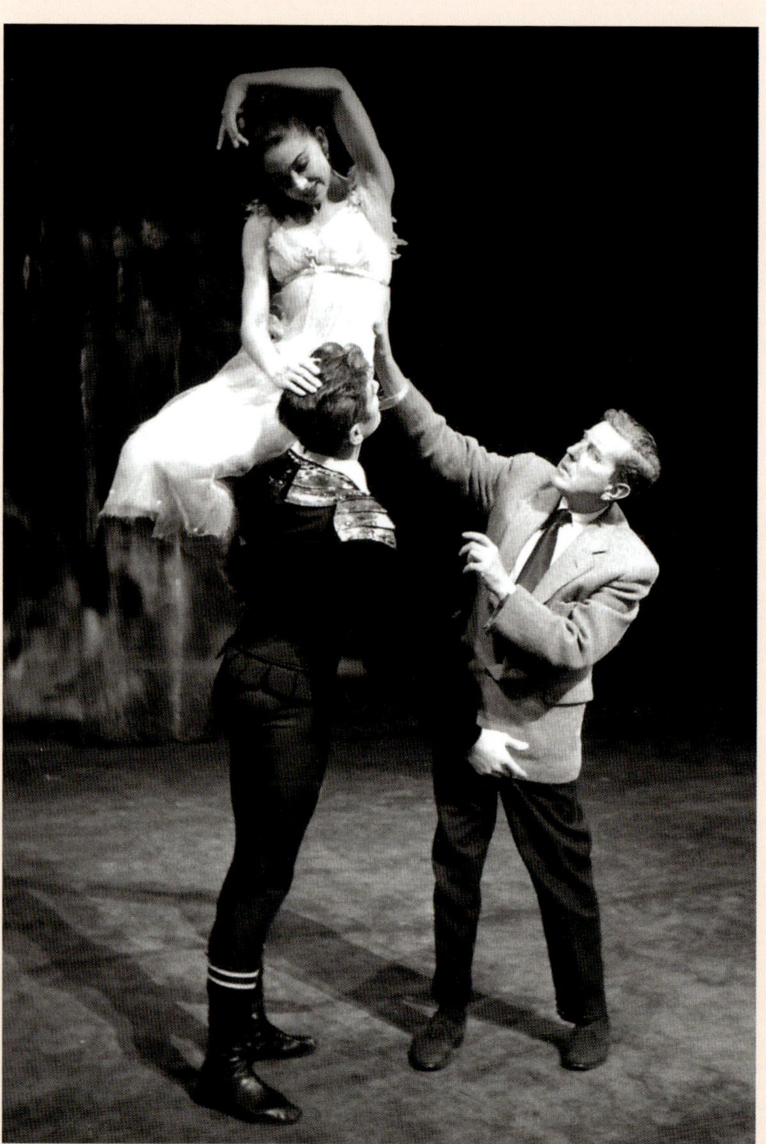

ORIGINAL PLAQUE, 1954
The original Queen Elizabeth II Coronation Award designed by Gilbert Ledward, RA.

SIR FREDERICK ASHTON, 1958
Ashton rehearsing Margot Fonteyn and Michael Somes in *Ondine*. He was awarded the Queen Elizabeth II Coronation Award the following year.

CARLOS ACOSTA, 2018
Darcey Bussell, President of the RAD, presents Carlos Acosta with the Queen Elizabeth II Coronation Award.

RECIPIENTS

1954	Dame Ninette de Valois OM, CH, DBE, FRAD
1955	Tamara Karsavina
1956	Dame Marie Rambert DBE
1957	Sir Anton Dolin
1958	Phyllis Bedells FRAD
1959	Sir Frederick Ashton OM, CH, CBE
1960	Sir Robert Helpmann
1961	Ursula Moreton
1962	Cyril Beaumont OBE
1963	Philip J.S. Richardson OBE (posthumously) and Dame Alicia Markova DBE
1964	Kathleen Gordon CBE, FRAD
1965	Dame Peggy van Praagh DBE
1966	Serge Grigorieff and Lubov Tchernicheva
1967	Lydia Sokolova
1968	Stanislas Idzikowski
1969	John Hart CBE
1970	John Gilpin
1971	Louise Browne OBE, FRAD
1972	Ruth French FRAD
1973	Norman Morrice
1974	Brian Shaw
1975	Robin Howard CBE
1976	Pamela May FRAD
1977	Winifred Edwards
1978	Sir Kenneth MacMillan
1979	Arnold Haskell CBE
1980	Glen Tetley
1981	Michael Somes CBE
1982	Dame Merle Park DBE
1983	Rudolf Nureyev
1984	Leslie Edwards OBE
1985	Antony Tudor
1986	Rudolf and Joan Benesh
1987	Peter Darrell
1988	John Lanchbery OBE
1989	Mary Clarke
1990	Sir Peter Wright CBE
1991	Ivor Guest MA, FRAD
1992	Clement Crisp
1993	Julia Farron FRAD
1994	Sir Anthony Dowell CBE
1995	Dame Beryl Grey
1996	Irina Baronova
1998	Lady Sainsbury (Anya Linden)
1999	Maina Gielgud
2000	Dame Gillian Lynne
2003	HRH Princess Margaret
2005	Sir John Tooley
2007	Alexander Grant
2009	Victor and Lilian Hochhauser
2010	Rachel Cameron
2011	Dame Monica Mason
2012	Dame Antoinette Sibley
2014	The Royal Ballet
2016	Sir Matthew Bourne OBE
2018	Carlos Acosta
2019	Karen Kain

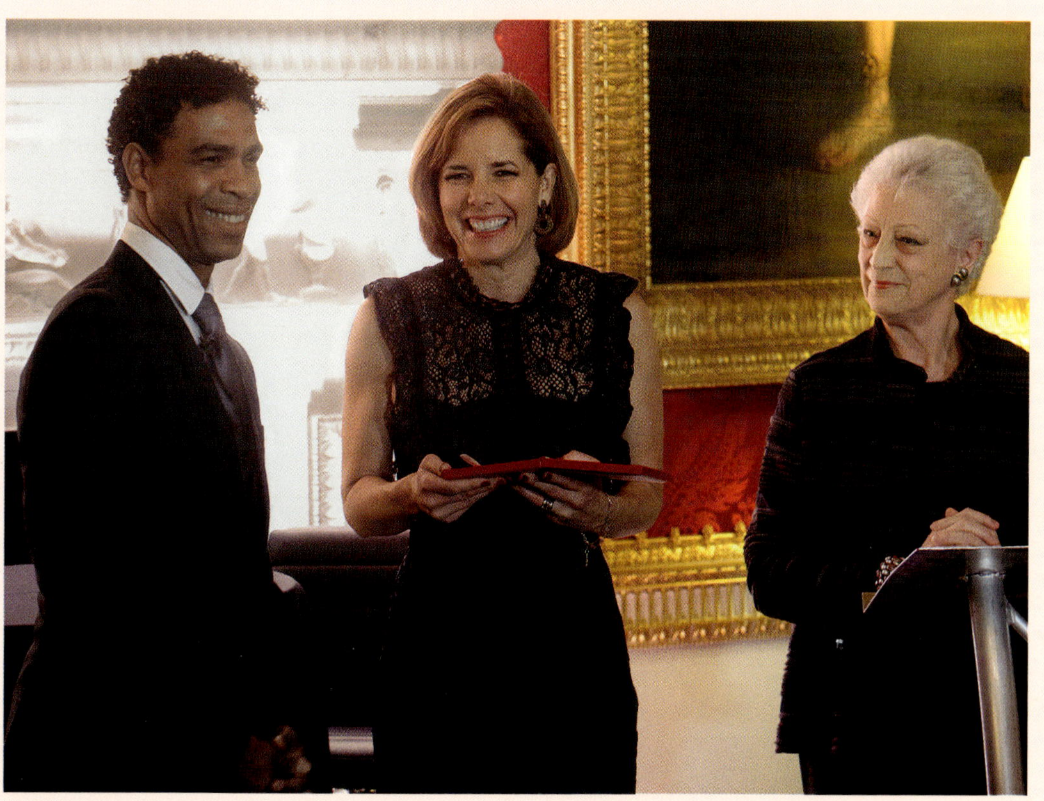

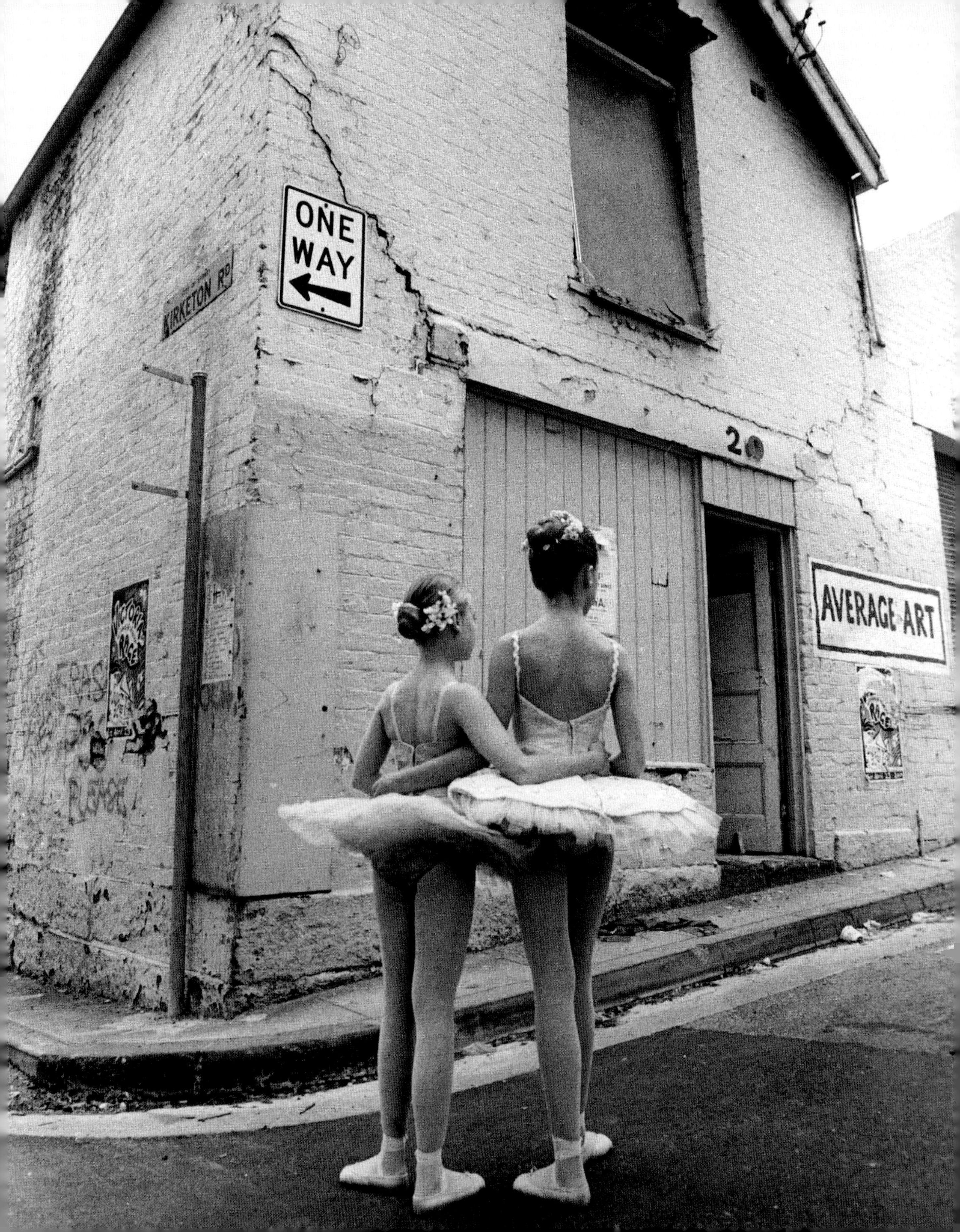

KIRKETON RD
ONE WAY
2
AVERAGE·ART

3

———

A HOME FOR DANCE

1954–1991

MARGOT Fonteyn was to
prove a popular and hard-working President who
led the RAD for nearly 37 years. Her presidency,
which crossed four decades, was to see a transformation in post-war society and culture, not just in
Britain but across the world. By 1954 Fonteyn was
an internationally famous ballerina who drew
intense media attention and huge audiences. During
the following decades she was able to combine two
equally demanding roles as a performer and RAD
President, bringing the Academy and the ballet
profession closer together than ever before. The
Gala Matinées that she organised for the RAD in
the 1950s and 1960s were glamorous, glittering
occasions, attended by royalty, which did much to
raise the profile of ballet in Britain.

1950s

The late 1950s saw a period of international
expansion, with examinations taking place in new
regions for the RAD, such as Pakistan and Trinidad.
In 1956 Adeline Genée was made a Dame of the
British Empire and the Academy launched the first
examinations of the Revised Major Syllabus. Two
years later Fonteyn proposed that Alicia Markova
be elected Vice President and, in honour of her
services to ballet and the RAD, Phyllis Bedells
received the Queen Elizabeth II Coronation Award.

The 1950s also saw two remarkable Gala
Matinées (both in aid of the Building Fund), which
demonstrated the Academy's status and the international ballet network that Fonteyn was able to call

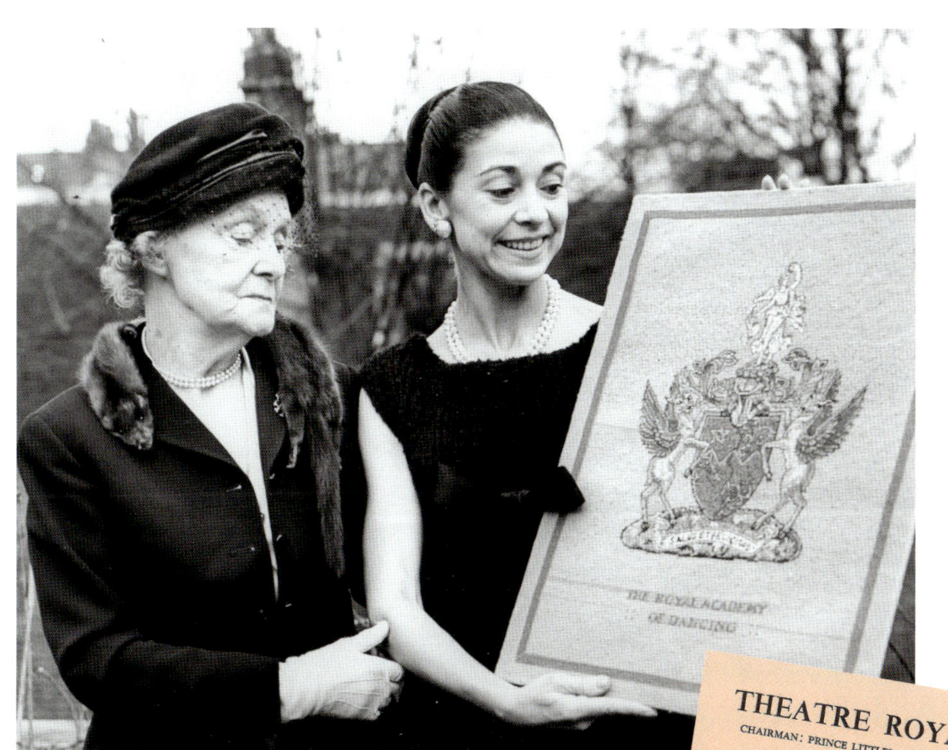

CHRISTMAS GIFT, 1960

Dame Margot Fonteyn receives an embroidered crest of the RAD as a Christmas gift from Dame Adeline Genée.

RAD GALA MATINÉE, 1958

HM Queen Elizabeth the Queen Mother meets ballet dancers Michael Somes and John Gilpin, following the RAD Gala Matinée at the London Coliseum. Margot Fonteyn has her back to the camera. The gala the following year was held at the Theatre Royal, Drury Lane.

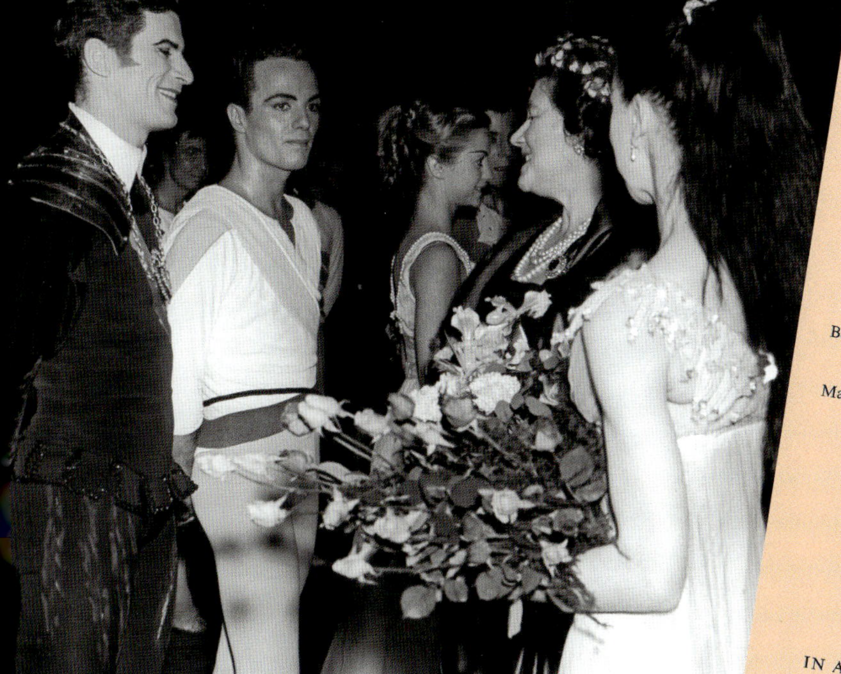

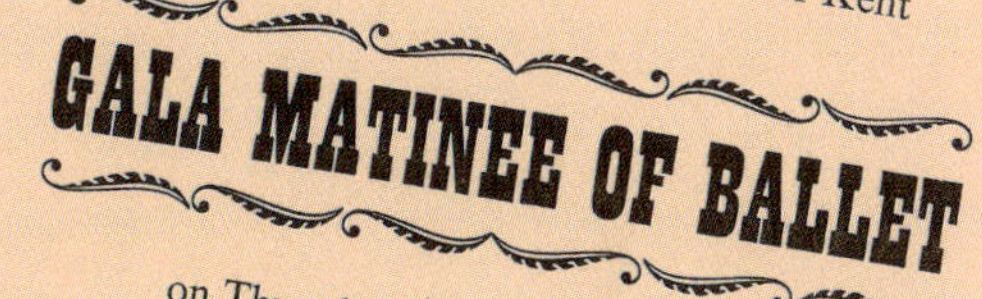

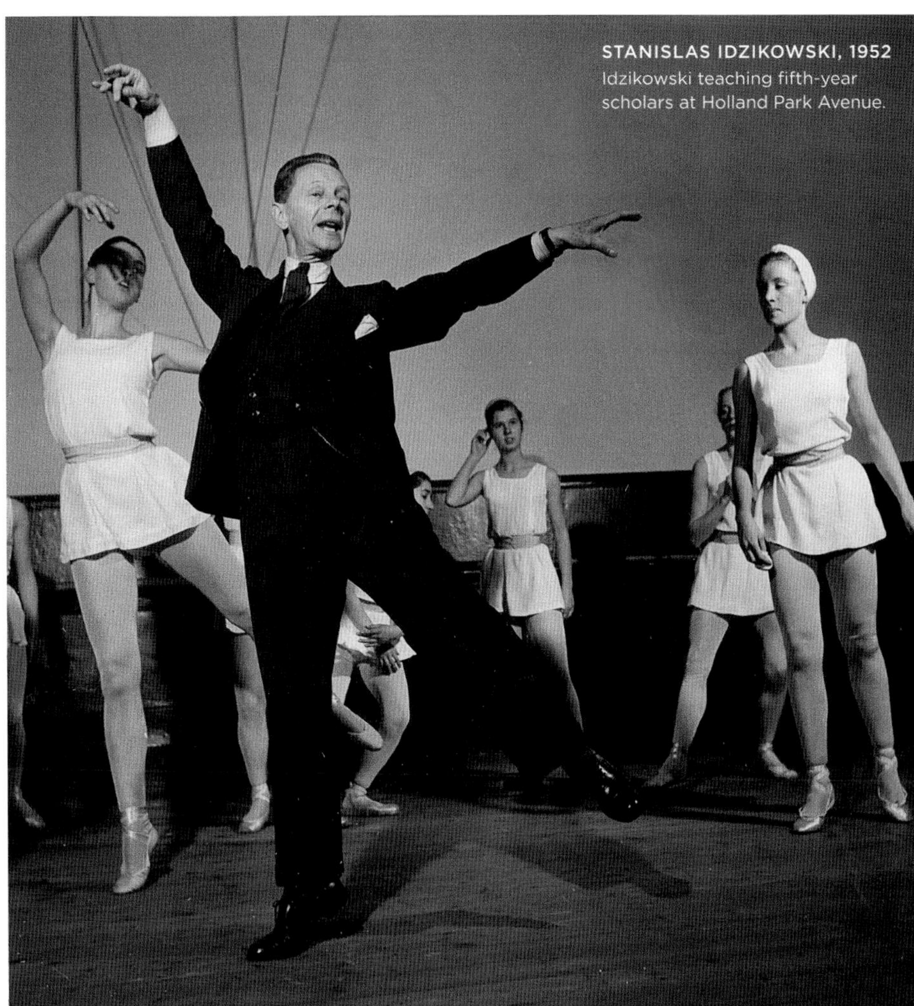

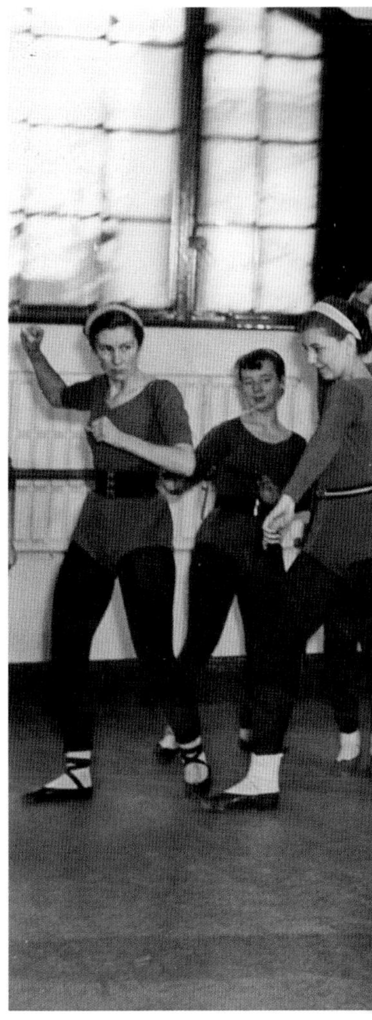

upon. The first gala took place in November 1958 and was attended by HM Queen Elizabeth The Queen Mother, HRH Princess Margaret and a very young Princess Anne. The programme (organised by de Valois and Anton Dolin) included extracts from the perennial favourite, *Coppélia*, and the pas de deux from Act 1 of Frederick Ashton's *Ondine*, performed by Fonteyn and Michael Somes. A second gala in 1959 reflected an increasingly international profile, with performances by the Polish Ballet, Ballets de Jean Babilée, Festival Ballet, Ballet Rambert and Roland Petit's company. Fonteyn again appeared with Somes, this time dancing Ashton's newly created pas de deux from *Raymonda*.

1960s

In 1960 the Academy introduced its Fellowship award, which was given to Tamara Karsavina and Stanislas Idzikowski, both of whom had made remarkable contributions to the RAD. However, the 1960s were dominated by financial concerns and the desperate need for a suitable new 'home' for the Academy. The organisation was granted charitable status in 1963 and by 1966 the Building Fund had reached £85,000; but suitable premises in central London were hard to find and expensive. The RAD embarked on a cycle of 'boom and bust' that was to leave it on the verge of bankruptcy three times before 1988. In 1967 a disastrous decision was

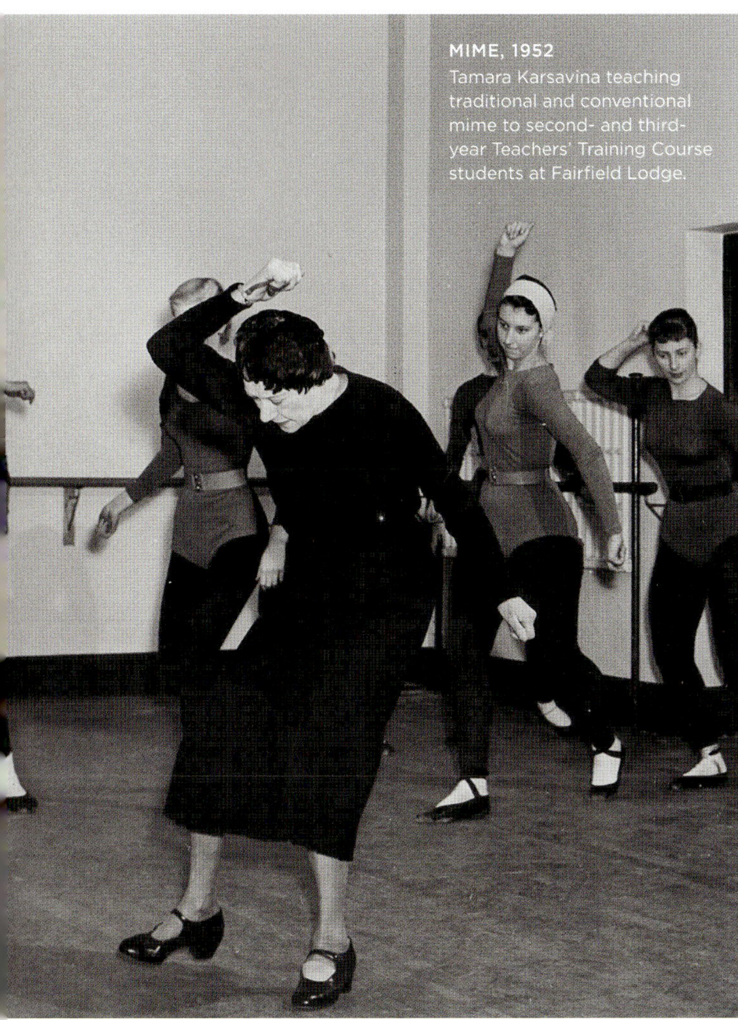

MIME, 1952
Tamara Karsavina teaching traditional and conventional mime to second- and third-year Teachers' Training Course students at Fairfield Lodge.

BOTTOM
FAREWELL PARTY, 1968
Kathleen Gordon (left) became the General Secretary in 1937 and in 1947 took on Directorial responsibilities, with Muriel Lehmann (centre) becoming General Secretary. Gordon resigned in 1968 after 44 years with the RAD.

BELOW
APPEAL BROCHURE, 1968
Appeal brochure for funding to buy South Lodge, Knightsbridge, as a new home for the Academy.

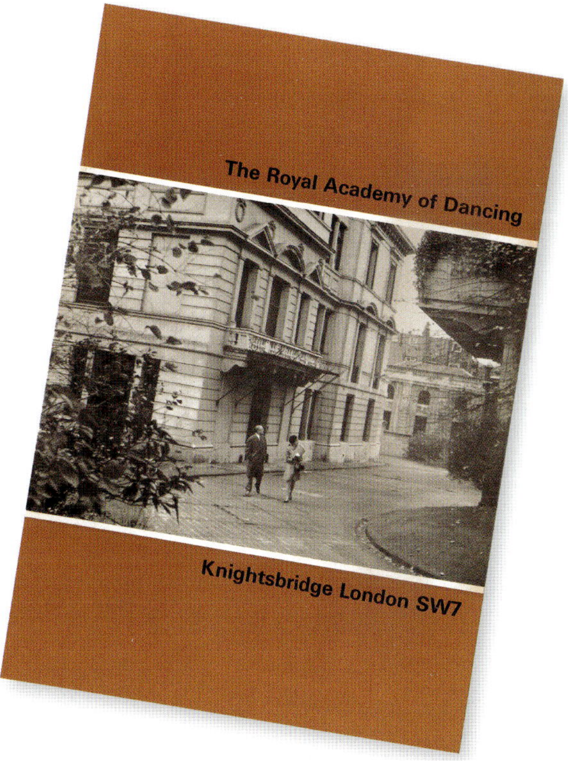

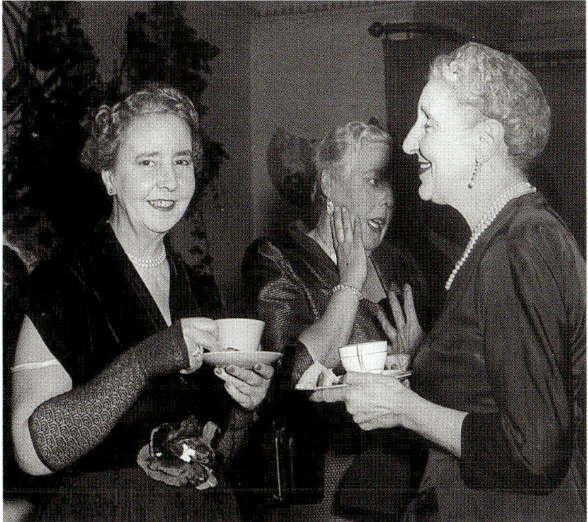

made to buy South Lodge, a substantial mansion in Knightsbridge. A bank loan was required to convert the building to offices, studios and a theatre: appeals for financial aid from members met with little enthusiasm. Bedells recalls that she was 'frightened at the immense financial risk we were taking' but that her concerns were outvoted.[1] A Members Appeal was launched in addition to the Building Fund (renamed the Development Fund) and various other money-making schemes were undertaken. However, by 1969 the looming prospect of bankruptcy led to several resignations and prompted the decision to separate the artistic and financial aspects of the organisation. South Lodge was sold, which left the RAD homeless until Fonteyn persuaded the

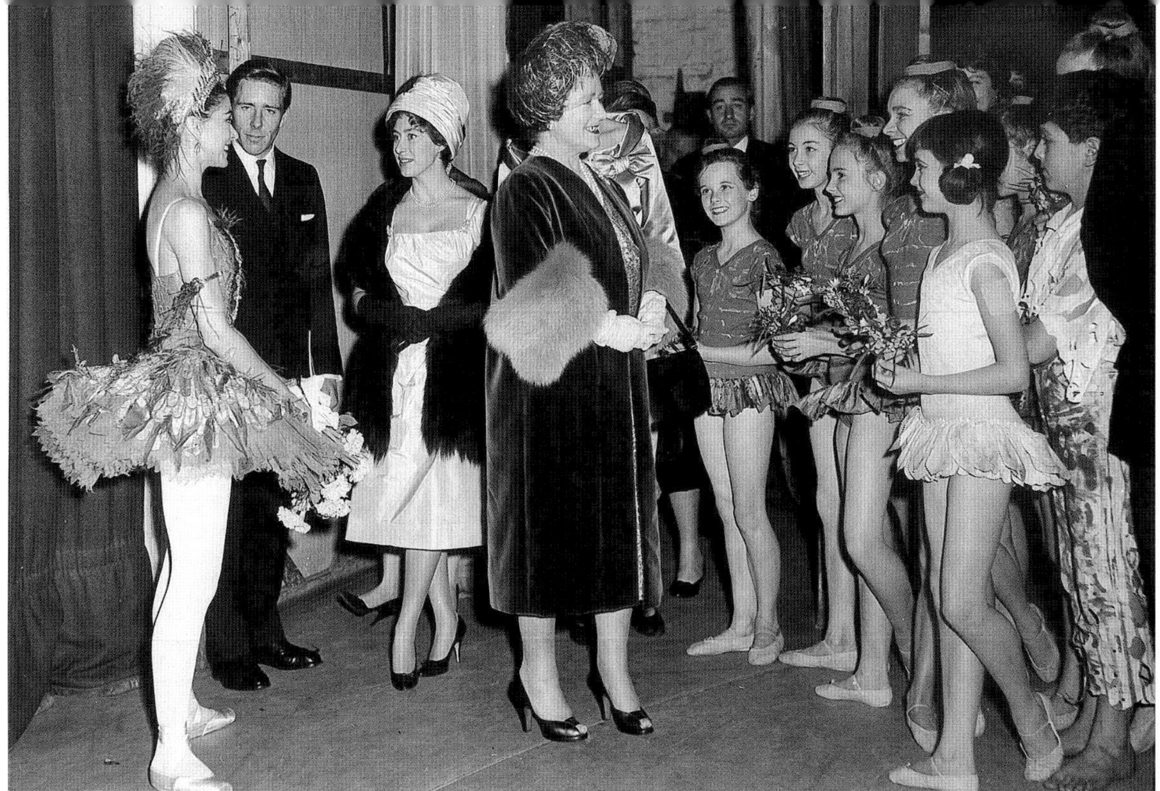

buyers to allow the Academy to remain in the building for a nominal rent for two and a half years. Financial problems aside, the decade saw positive developments in the growth of international membership. In August 1965 the first RAD summer school was held at Fairfield Lodge, bringing together members (students and teachers) from the USA, Canada, New Zealand and the UK. The faculty included Anton Dolin, John Gilpin, Maria Fay, Ruth French and Keith Lester, and members were offered a full programme of practical classes and workshops as well as lectures and demonstrations. Louise Browne directed both the UK summer schools and the early international ones. The event became an annual fixture in the RAD calendar, providing a showcase for new or revised syllabi and a rare opportunity to meet international members. By the end of the decade the event reflected the phenomenal work being done by the RAD outside the UK, with member representation from Canada, USA, Hong Kong, Austria, Rhodesia (now Zimbabwe), Italy, Greece, France, Malaysia, Norway, Holland, Mexico, Switzerland and Turkey.

Perhaps the greatest achievement of the 1960s was the series of fundraising galas made possible

GALA MATINÉE, 1960

Queen Elizabeth the Queen Mother and Princess Margaret, accompanied by Antony Armstrong-Jones, meet Margot Fonteyn and young performers backstage following the Gala Matinée of Ballet at the Theatre Royal, Drury Lane. Princess Margaret was a keen supporter of ballet; in 2003 she was the recipient of the Queen Elizabeth II Coronation Award.

REHEARSING, 1960

Erik Bruhn and Maria Tallchief rehearsing the Black Swan pas de deux for the RAD Gala Matinée at Drury Lane in December.

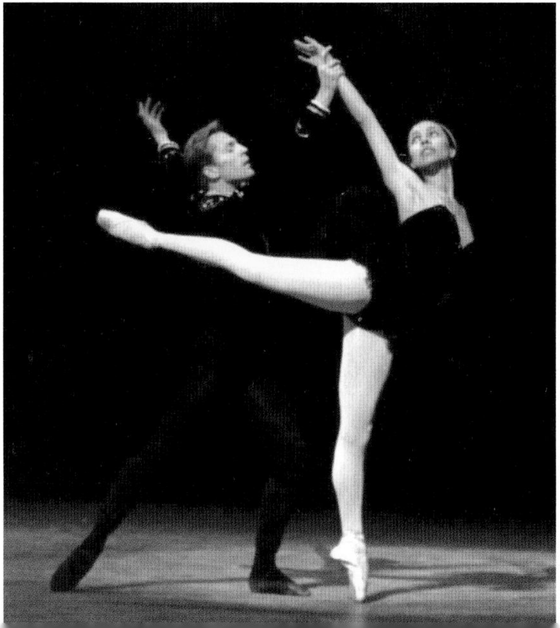

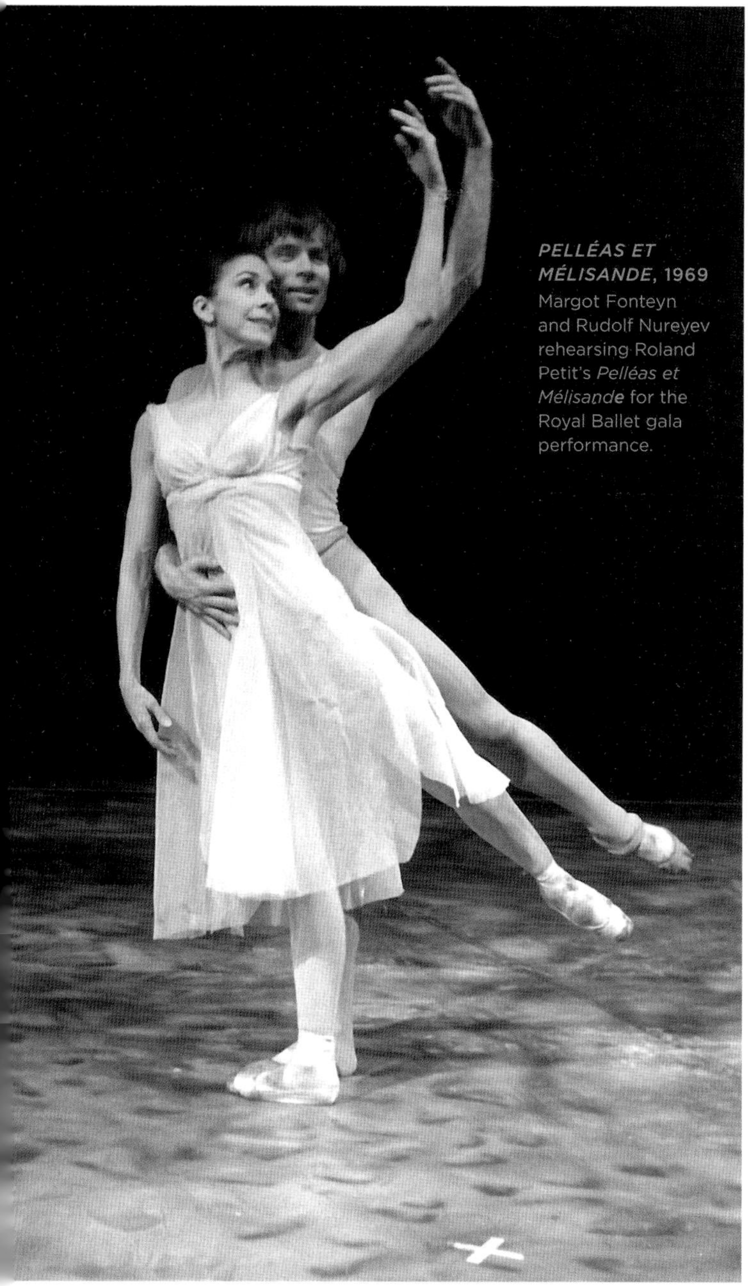

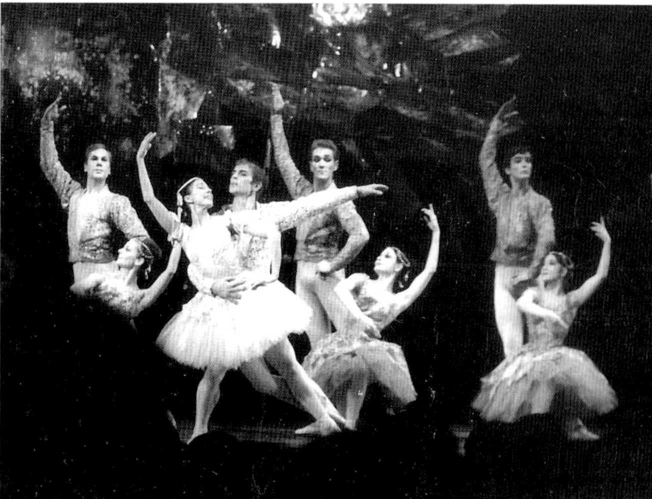

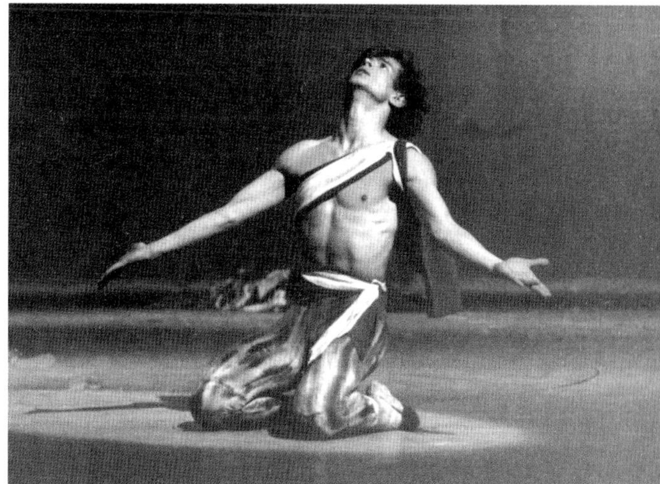

PELLÉAS ET MÉLISANDE, 1969
Margot Fonteyn and Rudolf Nureyev rehearsing Roland Petit's *Pelléas et Mélisande* for the Royal Ballet gala performance.

by Fonteyn's status and popularity within the international ballet world. As noted by Derek Parker, the RAD galas were 'treasured by every ballet lover … and almost every notable dancer in the world performed at some time or other'.[2] In December 1960 the audience at Drury Lane Theatre was treated to an array of star performers including Erik Bruhn, Maria Tallchief, George Skibine, Ballet Rambert, Margot Fonteyn and Michael Somes, John Gilpin and Alicia Markova. The following year the RAD Gala Matinée introduced a young Rudolf Nureyev to London audiences for the first time, a momentous occasion that would inspire a generation of male dancers.

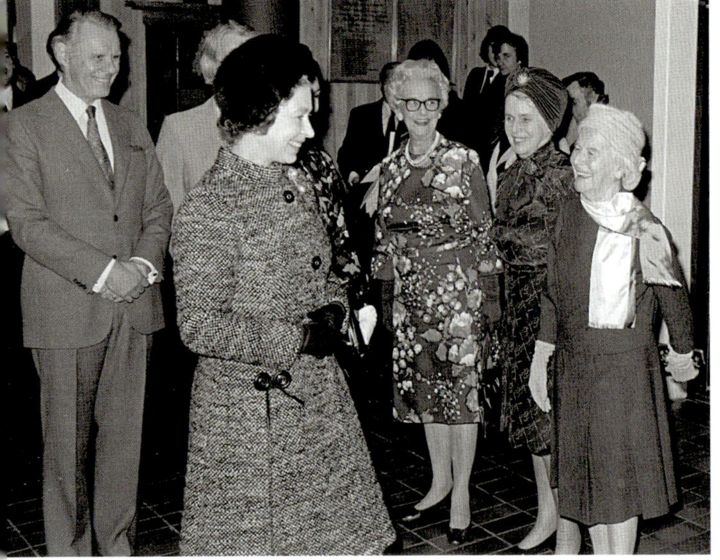

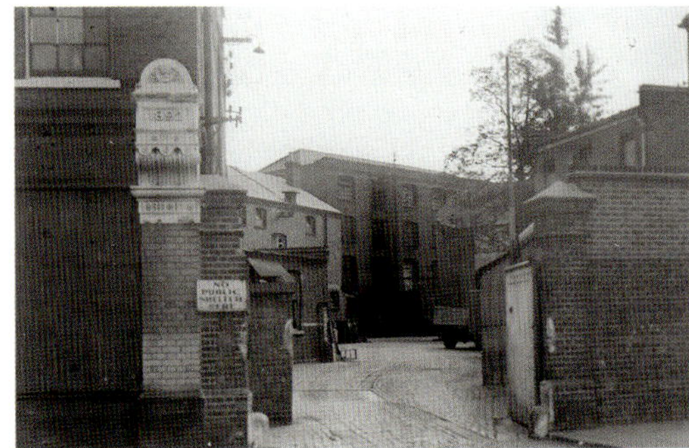

In 1962 injury prevented Nureyev from appearing in the gala as planned, but he returned in 1963 to dance the pas de deux from *Les Sylphides* with Fonteyn. Further gala performances by the iconic partnership of Fonteyn and Nureyev included an excerpt from *Paquita* (1964) and a full-length evening performance with the Australian Ballet in *Raymonda* (1965).

A special gala performance took place at Covent Garden in March 1969, celebrating 35 years since Fonteyn's first appearance with The Royal Ballet. Attended by HM The Queen, the programme included Merle Park in an extract from Ashton's *Enigma Variations*, Marcia Haydée and Richard Cragun in Cranko's *Romeo and Juliet* and Carla Fracci and Erik Bruhn in part of Act II from *La Sylphide*. The evening ended with Fonteyn and Nureyev in *Pelléas et Mélisande*, a new ballet created for them by the French choreographer Roland Petit. In May of the same year, Fonteyn appeared in another high-profile gala to benefit the RAD, this time in New York (see p. 61).

As a coda to a difficult decade, the new Children's syllabus was launched in 1968. The work, which was to become known as the 'Fonteyn syllabus', was immensely popular with teachers and students alike and was to serve the RAD well for the next two decades.

1970s

Following its fiftieth anniversary, the Academy's financial situation gradually improved and, in 1971, new permanent quarters were found in a former warehouse in Battersea. The building was converted into a set of studios and offices. The administrative staff arrived in July 1972, and in September the Teachers' Training Course took up residence on the top floor. Over the years, additions were made to the main building and in 1990 the Fonteyn Centre was added, providing additional studios and changing facilities.

During the 1970s the Academy reorganised its management structure with the introduction of the role of Artistic Director, whose task would be to guide artistic strategy and development. At the same time, administrative and financial management was to be strengthened by the appointment of a General Administrator. The Chairman of the Executive Committee, Ivor Guest, was also pivotal in steering the RAD through the 1970s and 1980s, dealing once again with financial crisis and threatened bankruptcy. John Field was elected the Academy's first Artistic Director in 1975. A year later, the full-time Teachers' Training Course became the College of the RAD. The Professional Dancers' Teaching Course, designed to retrain professional dancers as teachers, was also introduced.

**VALENCIA SUMMER
SCHOOL, 1984**
Phyllis Bedells' daughter
Jean teaching at the first
'mini' summer school in
Valencia, Spain.

BRAZIL CANDIDATES, 1986
Candidates for the Margot Fonteyn
Bursary in Brazil, with RAD examiner
Tina Stuart and Stephen Rimmer,
assistant director of the São Paulo
regional British Council. That year's
Bursary was won by Daniela Steck (no. 4).

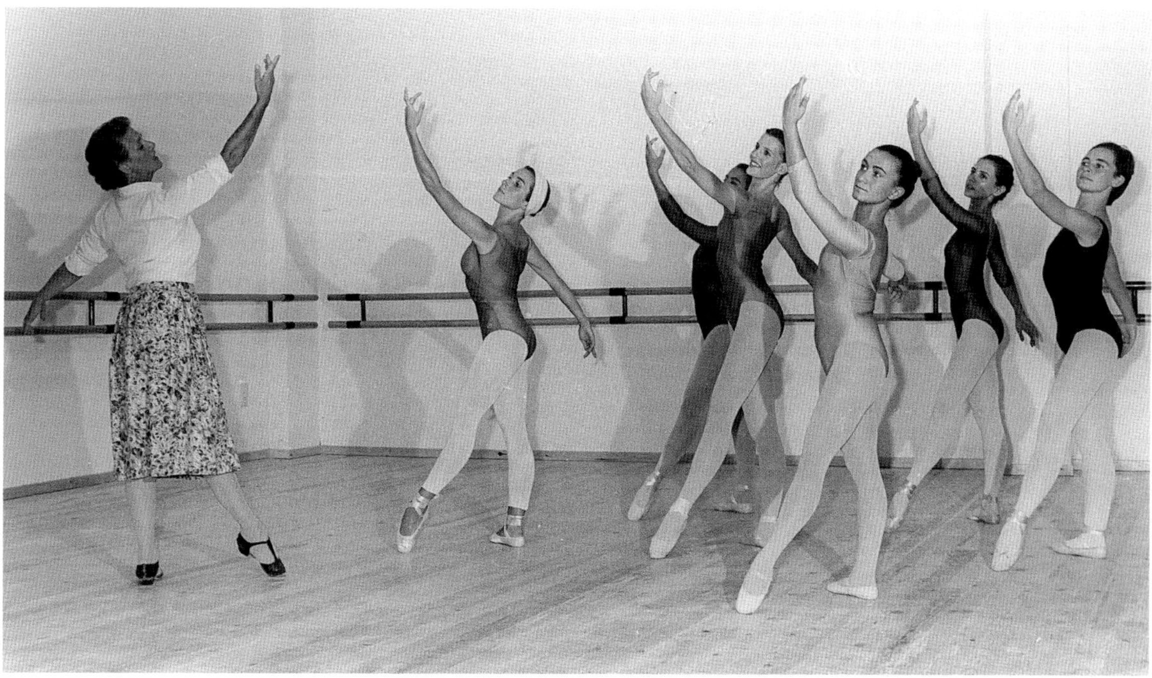

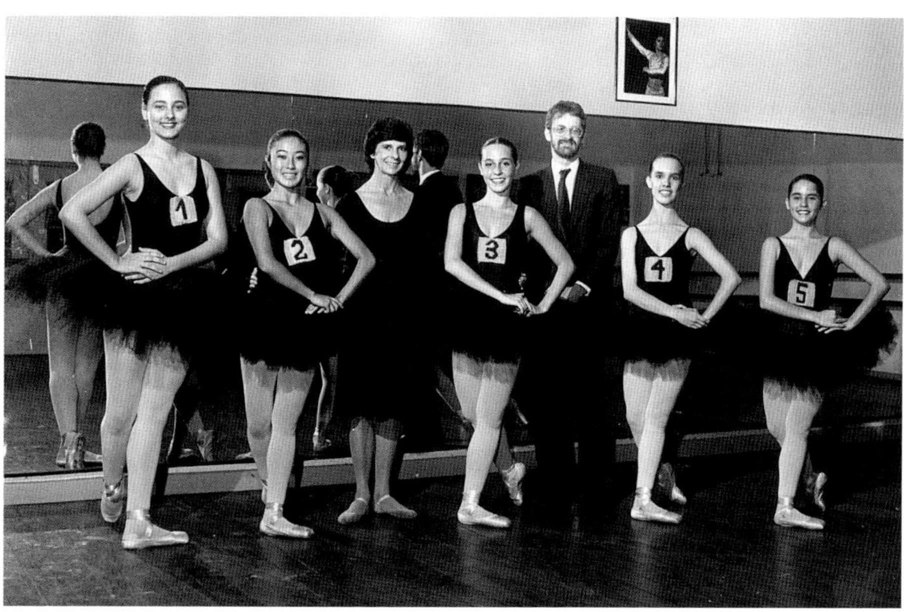

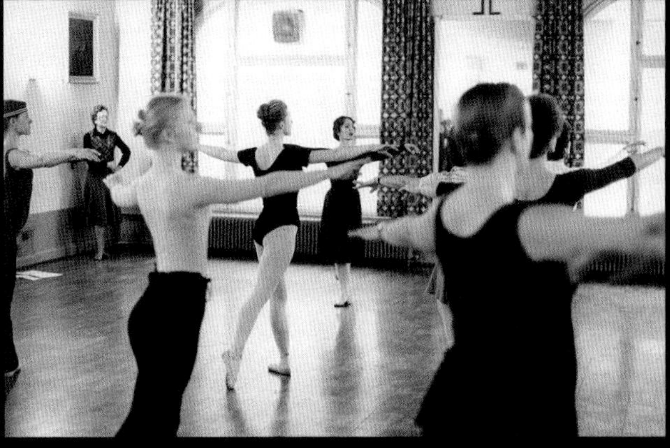

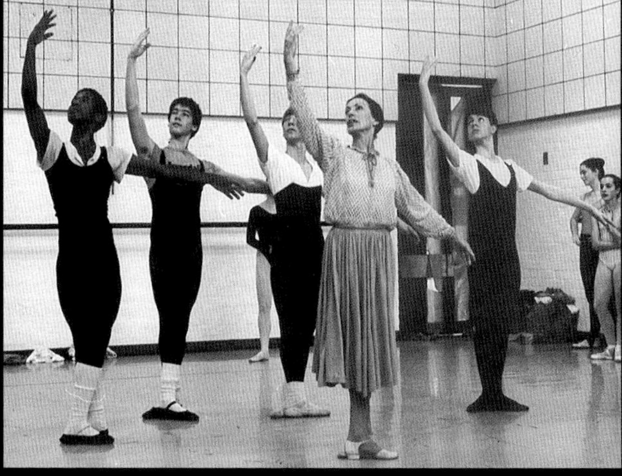

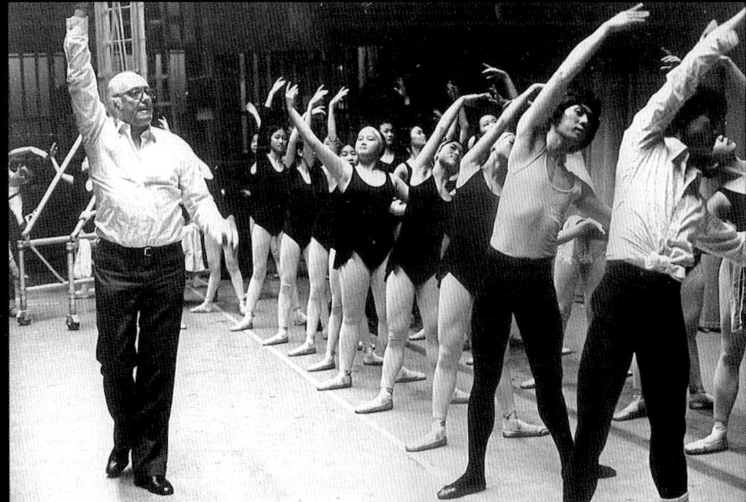

ABOVE, LEFT
June Christian teaching in Norway, 1977.

ABOVE, RIGHT
Sara Neil teaching at the International Winter School in Cape Town, South Africa, July 1985.

LEFT
John Field giving a master class to Intermediate and Advanced RAD students. The visit was part of the 1976 Hong Kong International Festival.

BELOW
Julia Farron teaching Intermediate students at the International Summer School in Mexico, 1988.

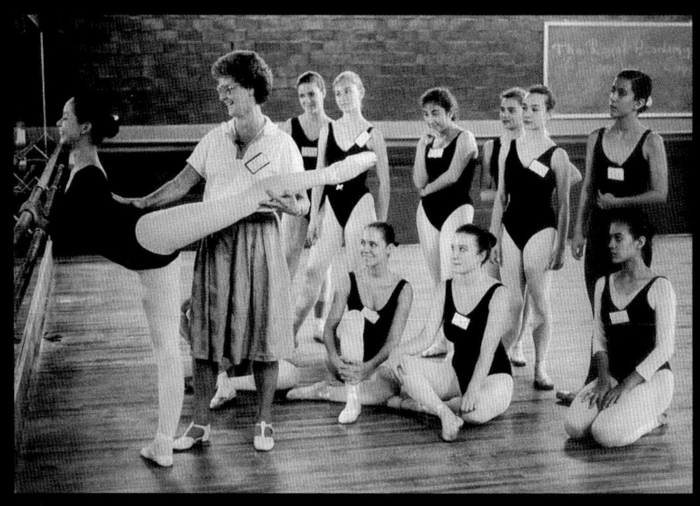

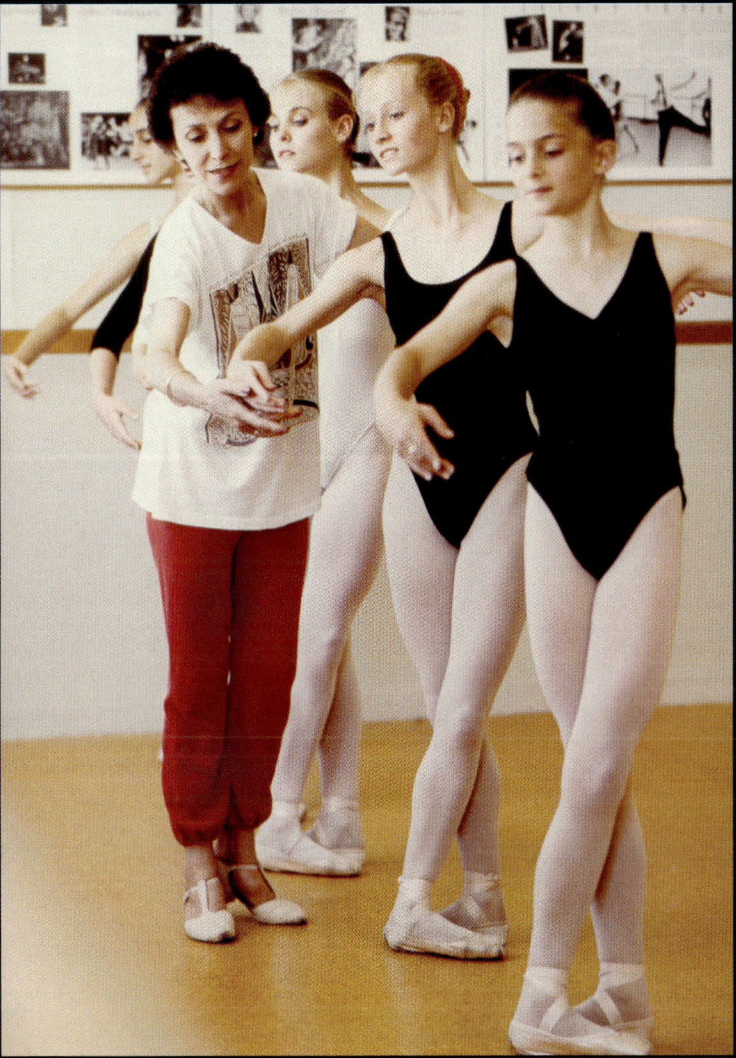

LEFT
Alfreda Thorogood teaching
at a summer school in New
Zealand, 1989.

BELOW
Alan Hooper teaching
male students in Manila,
Philippines, 1981.

FOLLOWING PAGES
LEFT
IRELAND, 2018

RIGHT
PORTUGAL, 2014

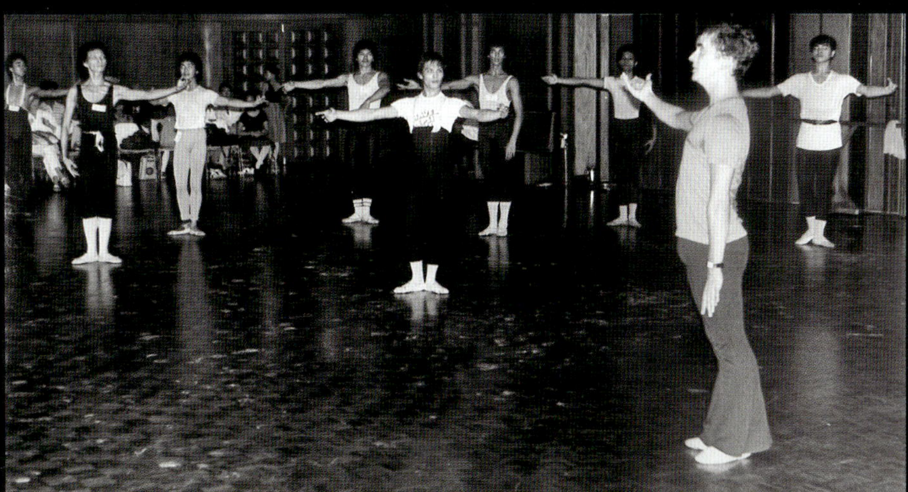

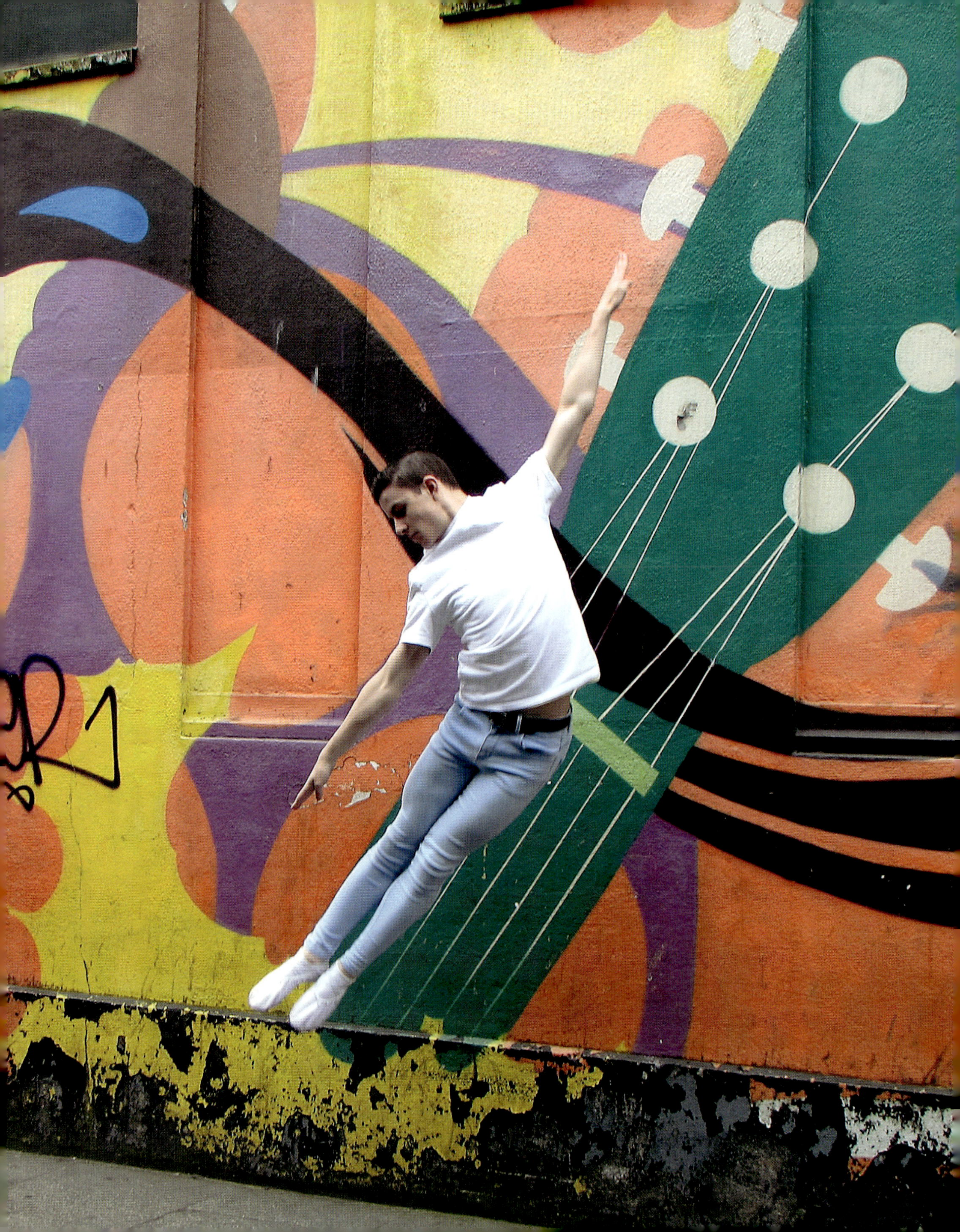

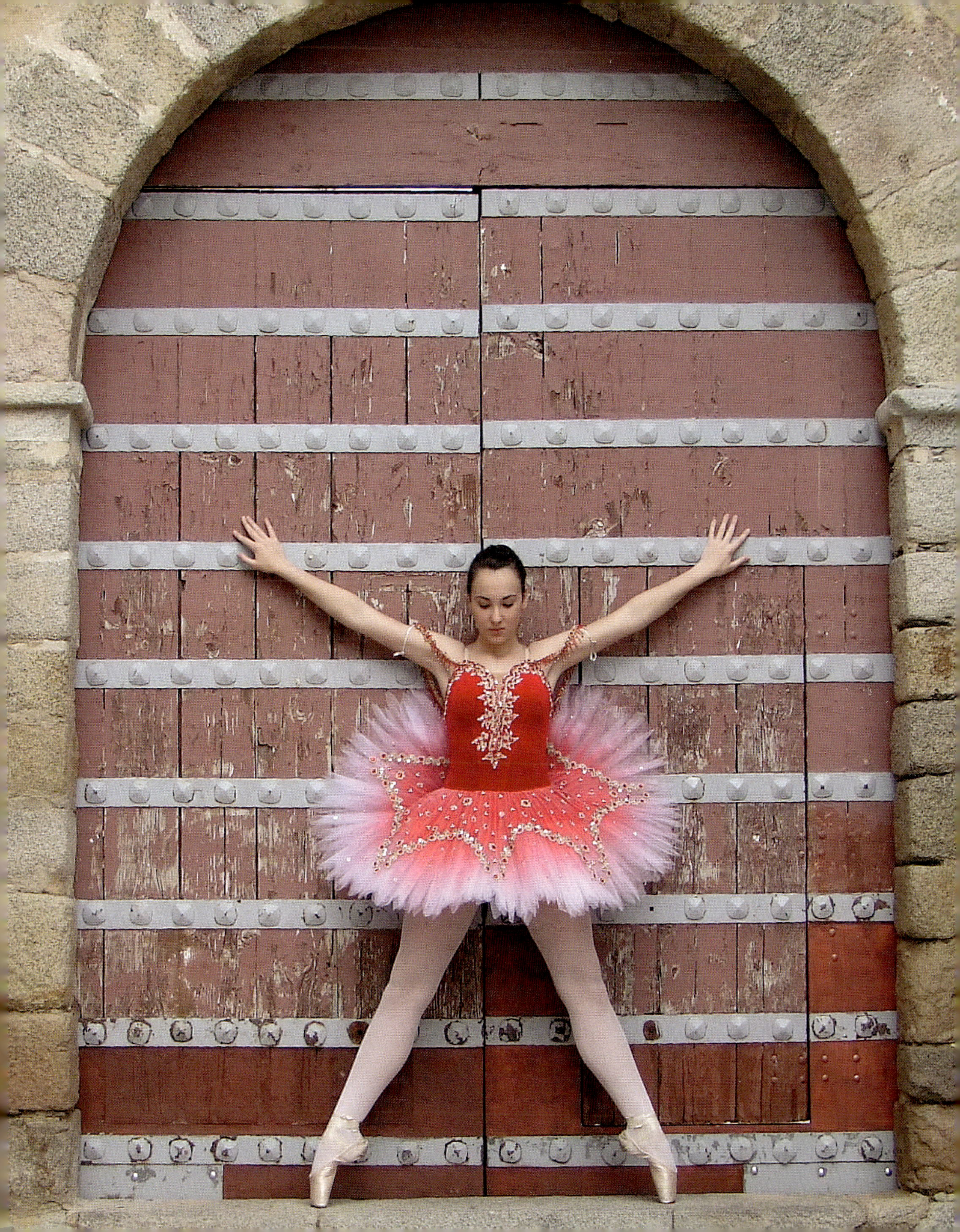

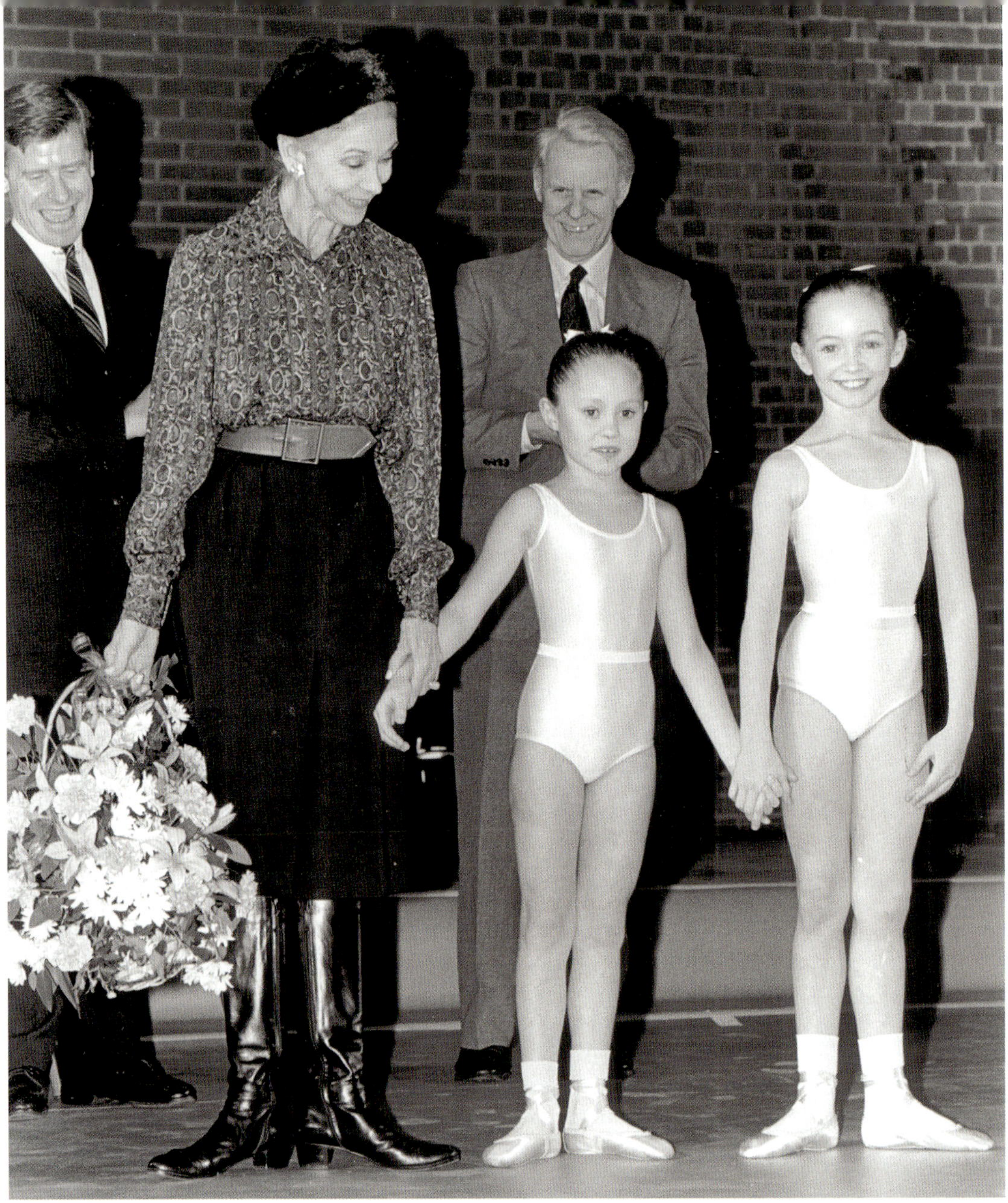

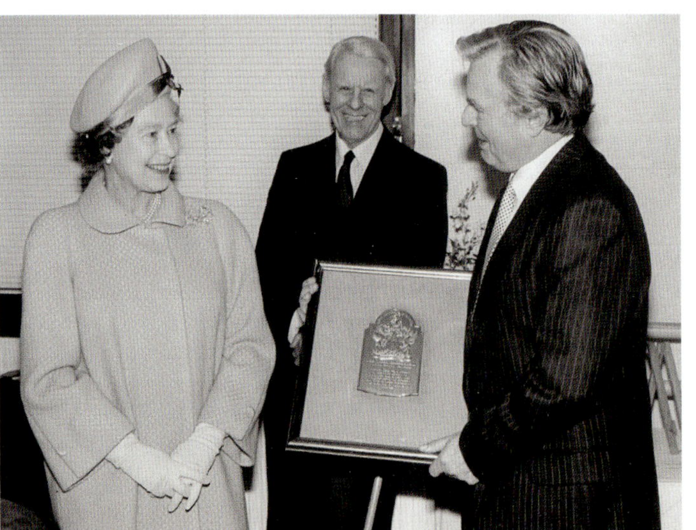

ASSEMBLY, 1986
Dame Margot Fonteyn with young RAD students in first position at Assembly in 1986. David Wall and Ivor Guest look on.

CORONATION AWARD, 1990
Peter Wright CBE receives the Queen Elizabeth II Coronation Award from HM The Queen. The award was made during the Queen's visit for the opening of the Fonteyn Centre on 5 December 1990.

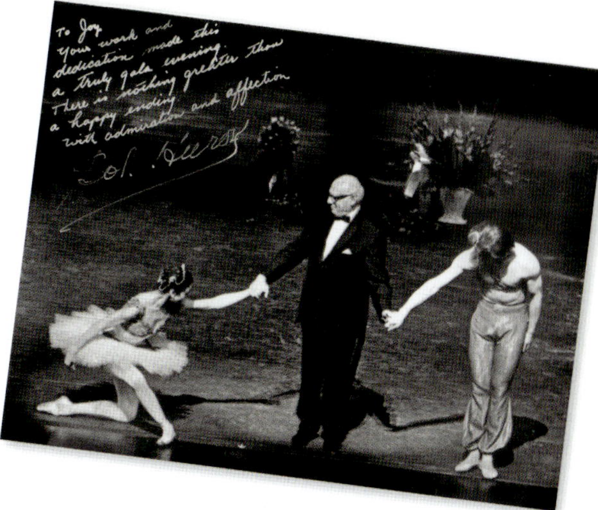

HAPPY ENDING, 1969
Margot Fonteyn, Sol Hurok and Rudolf Nureyev at the 1969 gala in New York. The photo is inscribed by Sol Hurok to Joy Brown.

The 1970s also saw international expansion, particularly in Brazil and Japan, with the first RAD examinations being held in Greece (1973), Spain (1975), Switzerland (1975), Portugal (1976) and Cyprus (1977). Other notable developments included Keith Lester's Dance Education syllabus, which encapsulated the French Romantic ballet era and was later joined by a Character dance syllabus created by Maria Fay.

The Artistic Director role proved to be contentious. John Field resigned after only a few years and was replaced by Alan Hooper, a much-loved dancer who was to make an enormous contribution to the RAD before his tragic, accidental death in 1983. Writing in *Dance Gazette*, the Chairman, Ivor Guest, commented, 'He has left the Academy an enduring legacy', citing the new impetus and energy that Hooper had brought, both in and outside the UK, as well as the greater prominence he had given to the training of male students.[3] Hooper was succeeded by Julia Farron and, a year later, David Wall was appointed Co-Director along with Priscilla Yates.

In 1986 the RAD introduced a new teacher Registration Scheme to provide official recognition of the standard of work of dance teachers. The scheme was rolled out first in the UK, Australia, Hong Kong, Japan, New Zealand, South Africa and Zimbabwe and, later, around the rest of the world. At the same time the RAD faced a number of challenges, which led to restructuring and other measures that created a leaner, fitter organisation.

The Fonteyn Centre was opened by HM The Queen in 1990, just a year before Fonteyn died. While her death was not unexpected, it was a sad loss not just to the RAD but to the wider ballet world.

NOTES

1   Bedells 1971, p. 21.
2   Parker 1995, p. 36.
3   Ibid., p. 40.

Joy Brown remembers the 1969 gala at the Metropolitan Opera House in New York

On 23 May 1969 a gala performance by The Royal Ballet took place at The Metropolitan Opera House in New York. It was a triple celebration for Margot Fonteyn's 50th birthday, her 35th year with the company and the 20th anniversary of her historic debut in New York in 1949. The beneficiary was The Royal Academy of Dancing (now The Royal Academy of Dance), and the programme included Margot Fonteyn and Rudolf Nureyev at the height of their international celebrity.

Margot and I met for the first time in Paris in 1948 and became life-long friends. I knew Margot was president of the RAD, but as a Balanchine dancer, trained at The School of American Ballet, I knew little about it. One evening, after a performance in New York, Margot asked me casually about running the RAD in America. I said yes, because no one ever refused Margot anything.

In late 1968 Margot, noting her various anniversaries coming up, thought we might put together a gala to benefit the RAD. Margot took me to discuss the idea with Sol Hurok, the pre-eminent impresario in America since the 1920s. He had first brought The Royal Ballet (then Sadler's Wells) to New York in 1949. Like everyone else, Sol Hurok too couldn't refuse her anything. Margot said we would make the gala 'the place to be in New York on that particular night' – and it was.

The programme was a mixed bill of Royal Ballet repertoire concluding with Fonteyn and Nureyev in their crowd-pleasing *Le Corsaire* pas de deux, which brought down the house. It was a memorable evening in every way. Sol Hurok was beaming. The gala's net profit, sent to London, was $87,000.00, a considerable sum in 1969. At the time, I was led to believe, it saved the RAD.

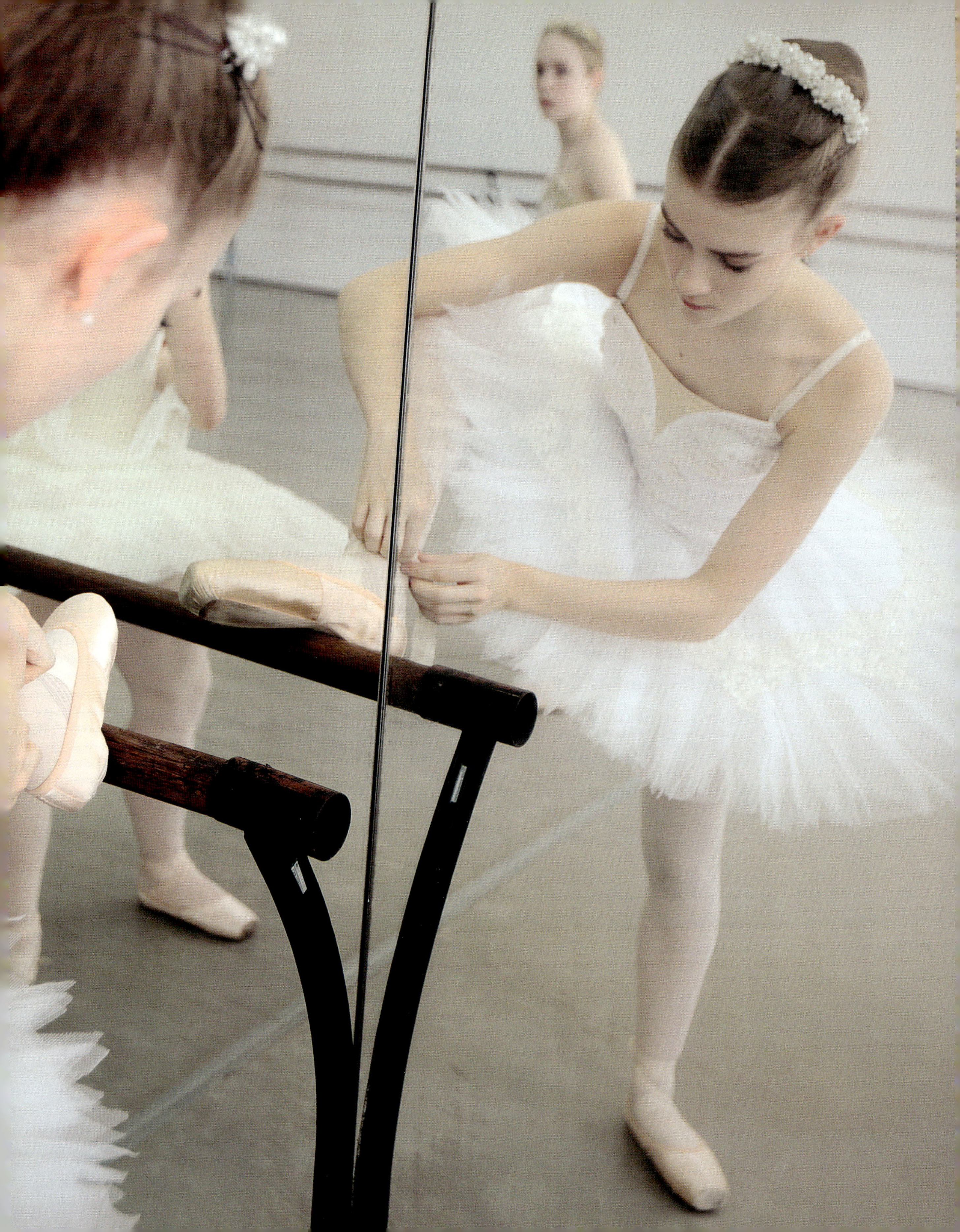

4

LEADING THE PROFESSION

1991 to the present day

F ONTEYN was succeeded as President by
Antoinette Sibley, former Principal of The Royal
Ballet, whose legendary partnership with Anthony
Dowell was admired around the world. Sibley had
long shown her commitment to the RAD as a Vice
President and member of the Executive Committee.
Her appointment was a popular choice. In the same
year (1991), the RAD appointed David Watchman as
Chief Executive, a newly created role in recognition
of the Academy's rapid expansion and financial
challenges. Watchman had no background in dance
but ample experience in business and was ready to
face the challenges at 'a particularly exciting time
for the Academy with the launch of the new Grades
Syllabus, the opening of the Fonteyn Centre and so
much happening in the Academy's affairs around
the world'.[1]

'A Service of Thanksgiving for the Life and
Work of Dame Margot Fonteyn de Arias (1919–1991)'
took place at Westminster Abbey on 2 July 1991.
Jointly organised by the Academy, the University
of Durham (where Fonteyn was Chancellor) and
The Royal Ballet, the service was attended by

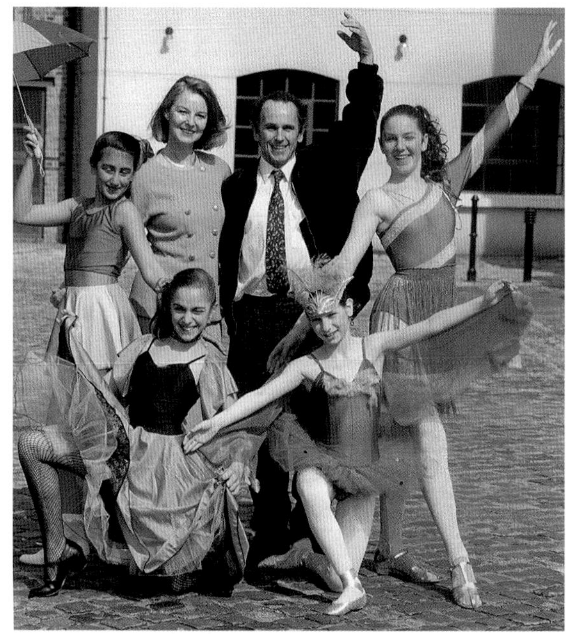

DANCING FOR DREAMS, 1992
Antoinette Sibley and Wayne
Sleep at the launch of Dancing
for Dreams, a project that invited
dance and stage schools to
help raise money for the Family
Holiday Association.

ROYAL VISIT, 2018
HRH the Duchess of
Cornwall visited the
London headquarters
in February 2018 and
observed a Discovering
Repertoire class
with Chief Executive
Luke Rittner.

PREVIOUS PAGE
In the rehearsal studio at
the Lisbon Genée, 2017.

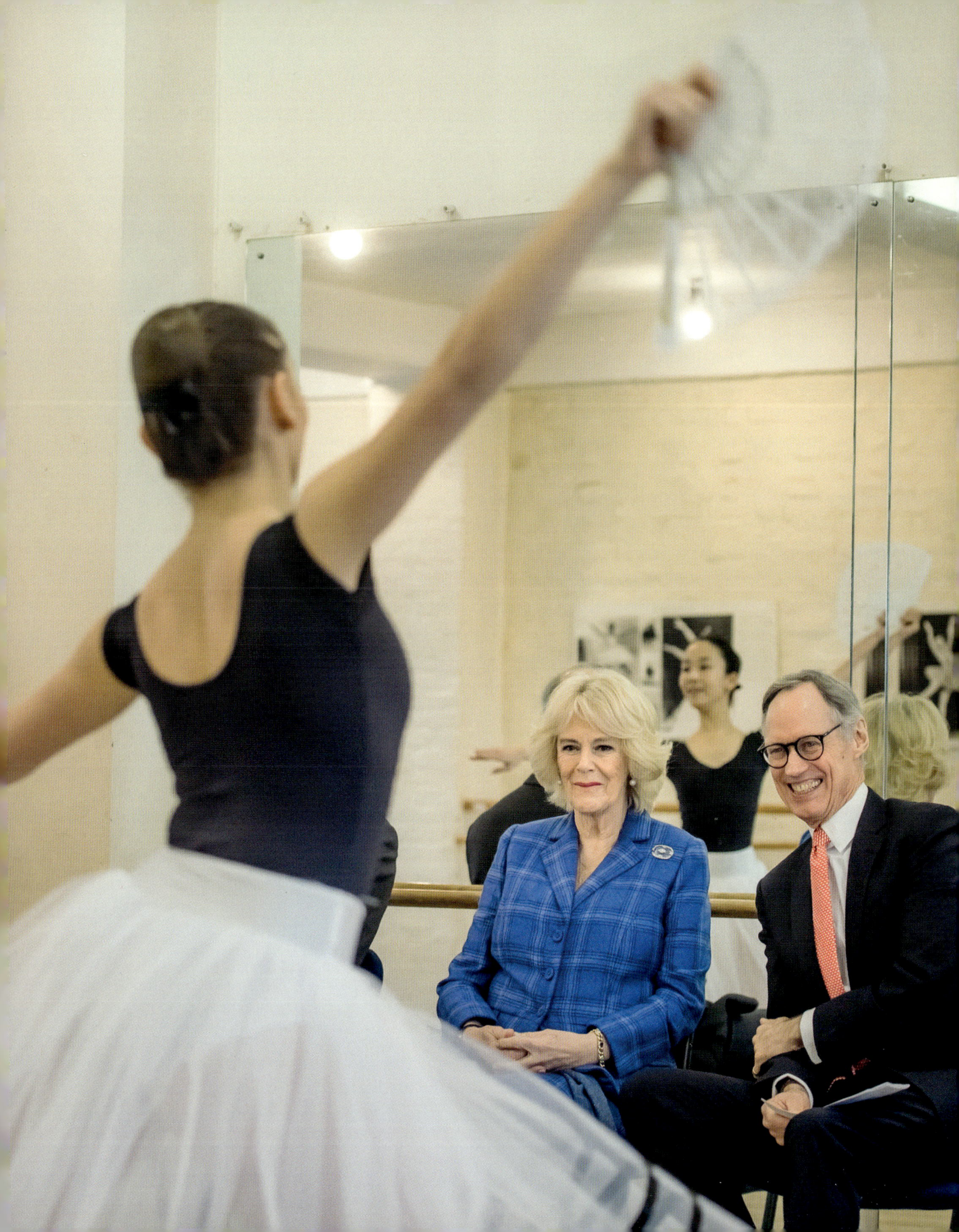

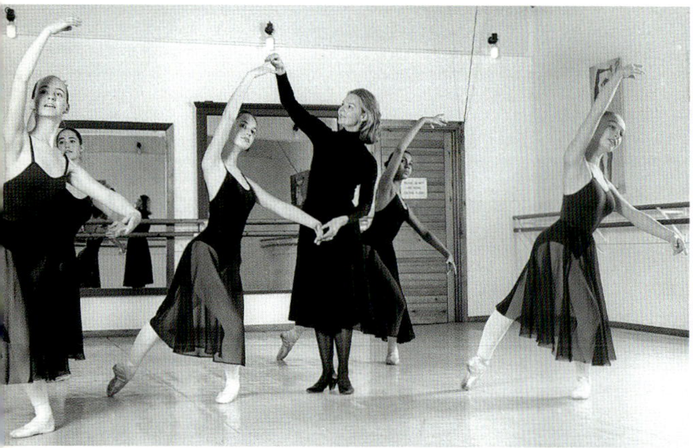

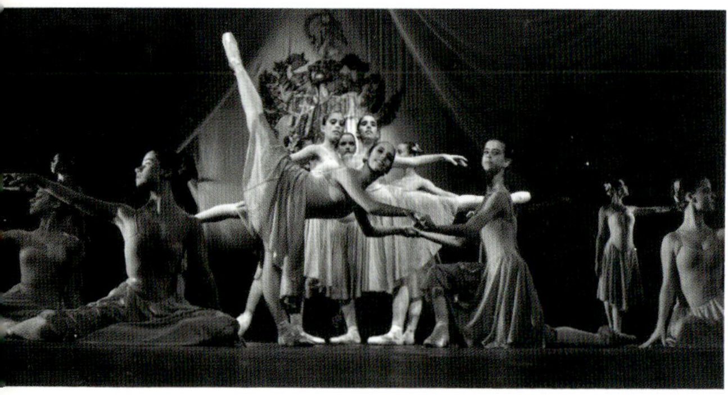

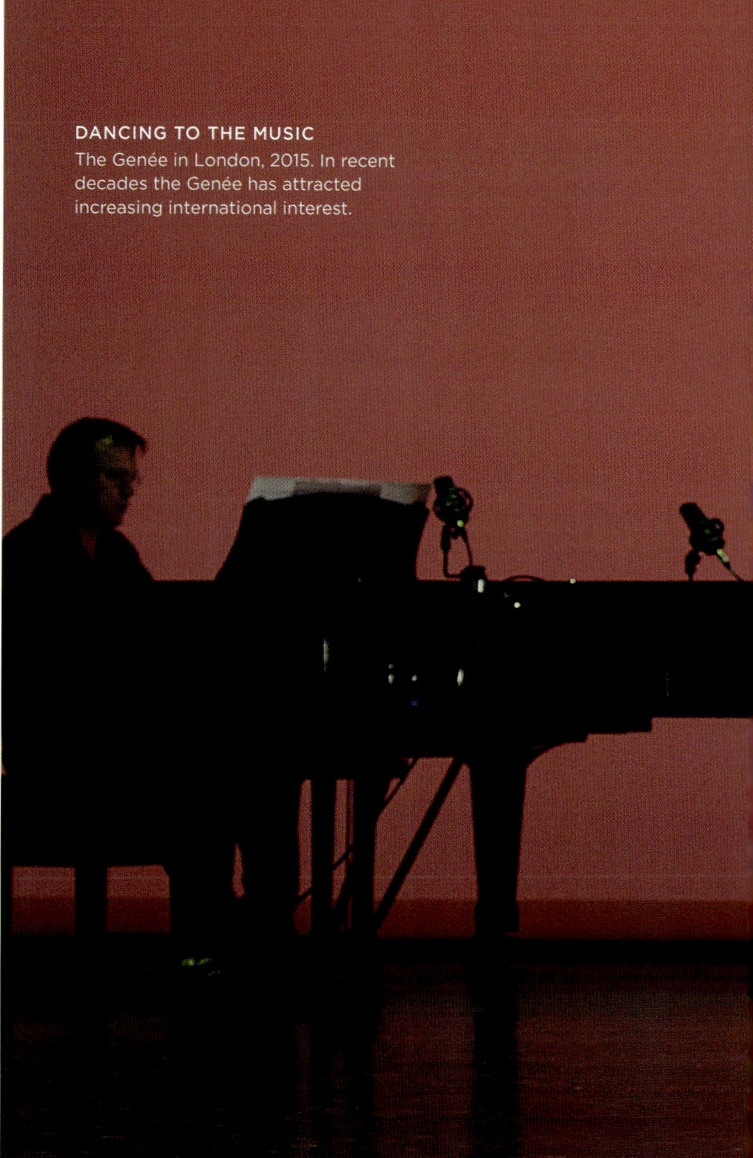

HRH Princess Margaret as well as some 2,000 guests. Concluding her review in the *Dancing Times*, the Editor, Mary Clarke observed that 'A great lady had been greatly celebrated'.[2]

The early 1990s saw a much-needed boost to the Academy's finances following heavy investment in the Fonteyn Centre. The New Grades syllabus (which replaced the 1968 'Fonteyn' syllabus) prompted a series of national and international courses for teachers. The new work, with its combination of classical, Character and 'Free Movement', had been created by an experienced panel comprising Alfreda Thorogood (Chair), Noreen Chisholm, June Christian, Susan Cooper, Jacqueline Ferguson, Valerie Hitchen,

Peggy Olden, Heulwen Price and Valerie Sunderland. The schedule for the launch of the new Grades 1 to 5 reflected the increasingly international Academy membership. In 1991 alone, courses were scheduled in Australia, Belgium, Brazil, Canada, Italy, Japan, Malaysia, Malta, Mexico, United Arab Emirates, Netherlands, New Zealand, Norway, Peru, Philippines, Portugal, Spain, Singapore, Switzerland, Thailand, Taiwan, the USA and Zimbabwe. In that year more than 153,000 candidates were examined across 47 countries. Higher Grades were added from 1992, providing an alternative to the vocational training route and prompting another worldwide roll-out of courses for teachers.

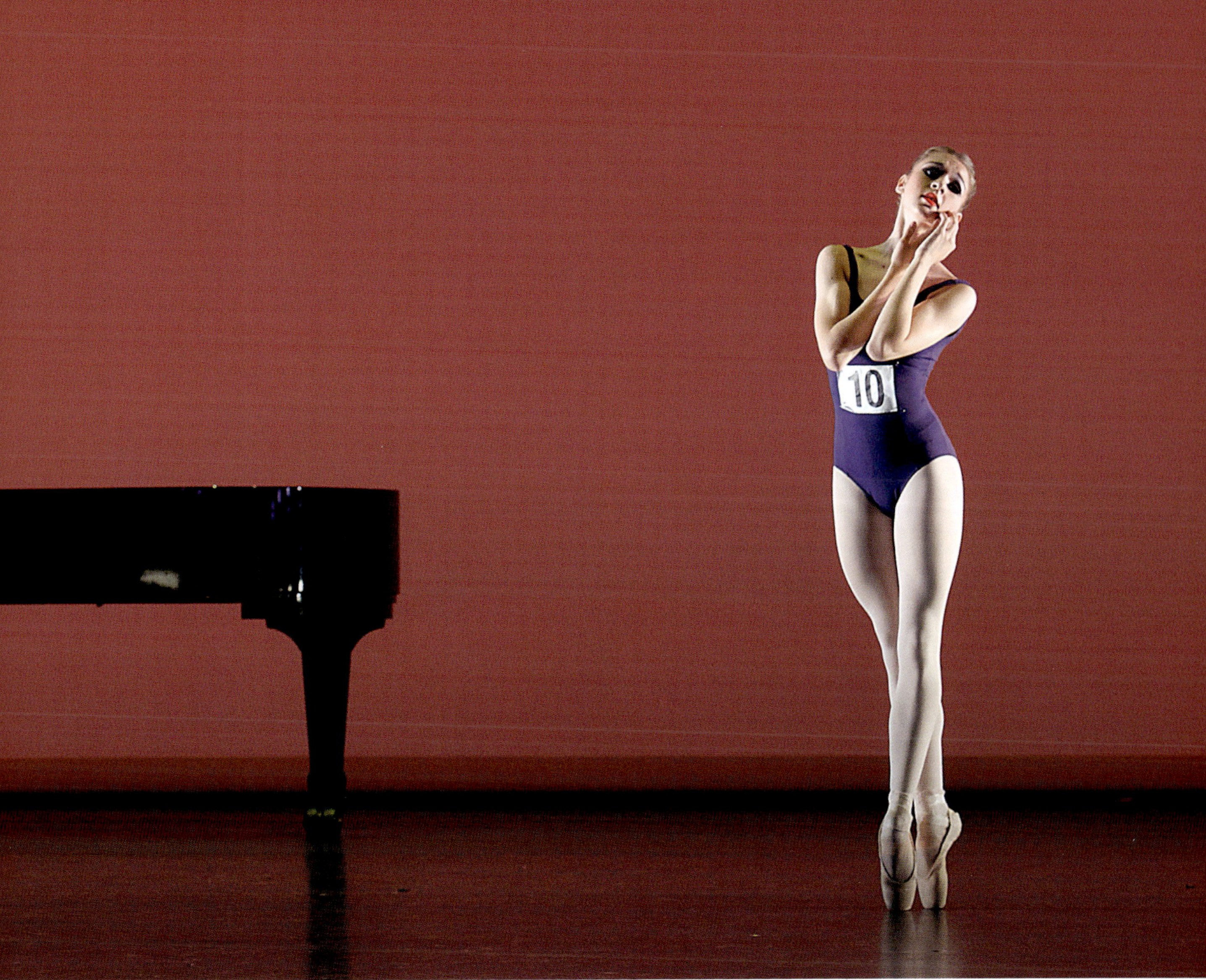

Another financial boost came from the Digital Equipment Company, which sponsored the Genée International Competition for much of the decade. The Digital Genée Awards, as they became known, offered significant prize money and attracted growing numbers of participants from around the world. In the same year (1991) the Academy's pioneering work with children with special needs was rewarded with a £15,000 annual grant from the Ward Blenkinsop Trust.

The decade also saw a series of changes in management roles, departmental structures, membership categories and the teacher registration framework. David Wall served the Academy as General Secretary from 1984 to 1990 and, following his retirement, John Byrne was appointed as Artistic Director in 1991. In the same year Richard Thom was created Director of Finance, a post he was to hold for the next 25 years. In 1994 Lynn Wallis replaced John Byrne as Artistic Director, a post she was to hold until her retirement in 2016.

Under David Watchman, rectifying the Academy's unstable financial footing became the number one priority. The February 1992 issue of *Dance Gazette* carried a clear 'wake-up call' for an organisation which, arts-oriented or not, needed to exist in the 'real world'. Watchman's opening statement set the tone, emphasising that the

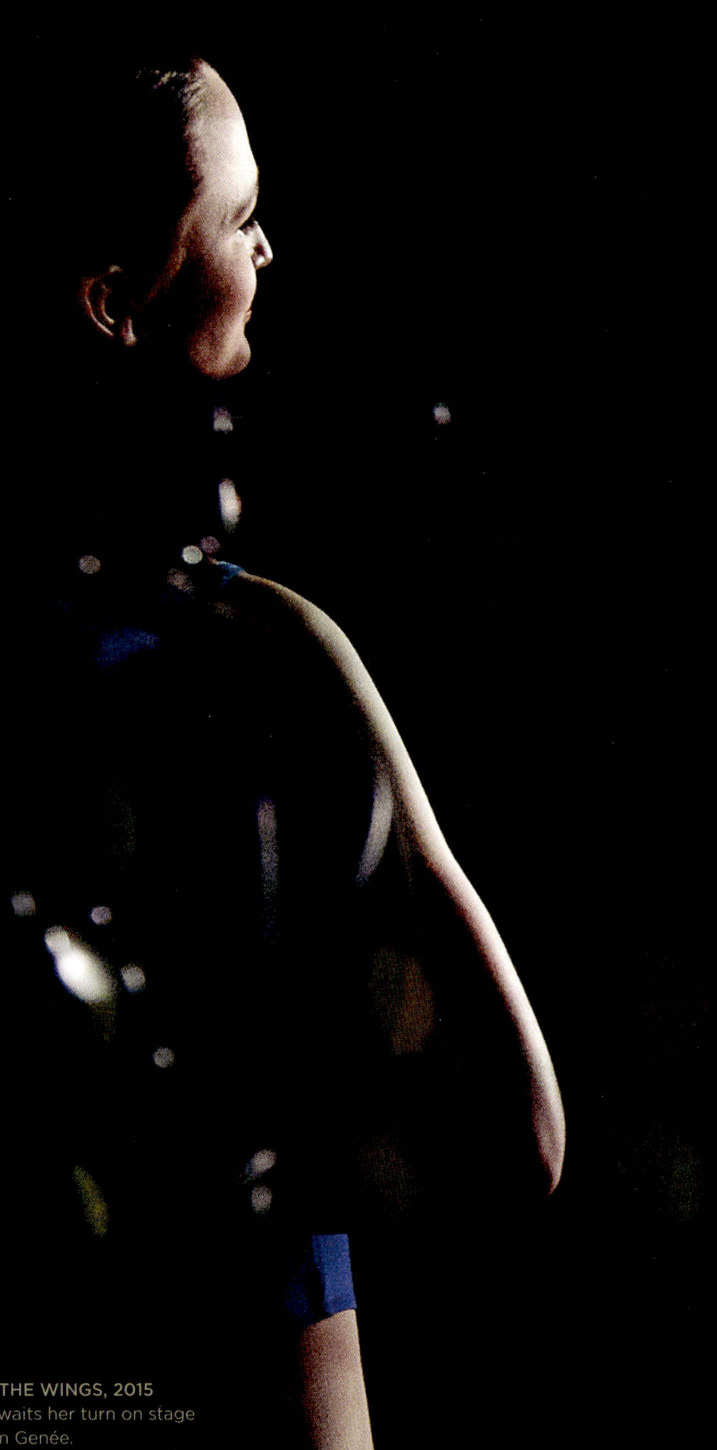

WAITING IN THE WINGS, 2015
A candidate waits her turn on stage
at the London Genée.

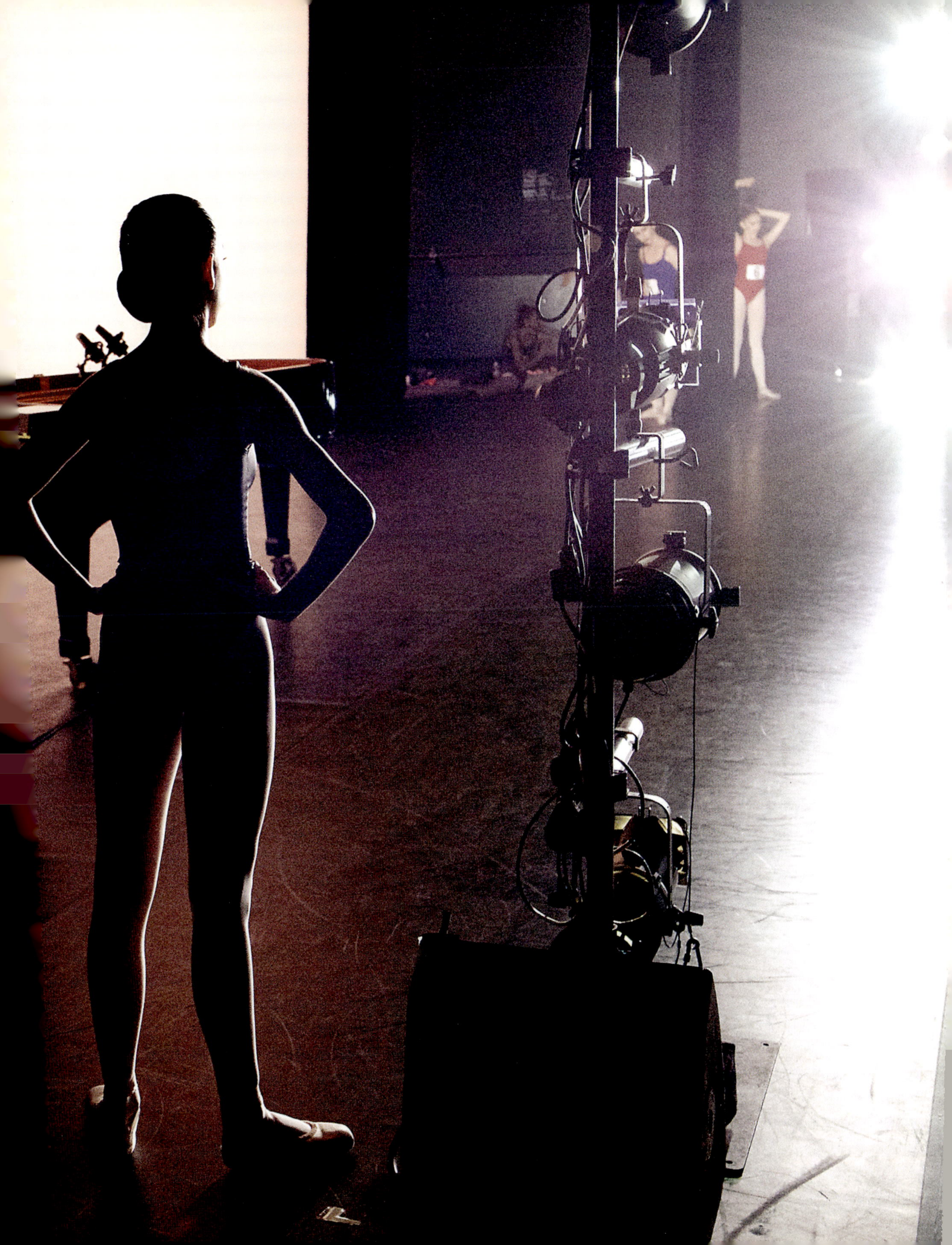

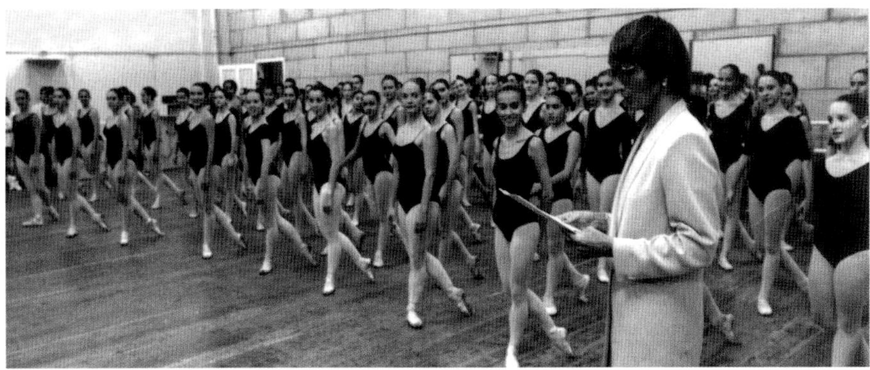

organisation's activities would now be conducted in 'a more business-like way', adding that 'we have managed to balance the books for the first time in several years' but that another appeal would be launched to clear the costs of the Fonteyn Centre.[4] Of interest too is a reference to impending legislation by the European Union (EU) and its potential impact on the Academy's Registration framework.

In 1993, following the tradition set by her predecessors, Antoinette Sibley organised a gala at the Royal Opera House, which raised an outstanding £125,000 for the Academy's funds. Sibley also introduced the President's Award and was a regular Guest of Honour at the annual Graduation Day at the College, where plans were already under way (led by Dr Mollie Davies) for a degree programme.

Regional development within the UK was another dominant feature of the 1990s, as was the growing popularity of UK and international summer schools. In 1992 the RAD ran three summer schools in London, with others held in Australia, the United States, Canada, Italy and Japan; some of the international summer schools, such as in Trento, Italy, have continued regularly until the present. Numbers of students attending increased steadily throughout the decade and, together with the annual Assembly (which concluded with the Digital Genée Awards), provided the backbone of the Academy's calendar.

In 1997 the Benesh Institute (now Benesh International) was incorporated within the RAD. The occasion was marked by 'Stars of the Night', a royal gala held in November at Her Majesty's Theatre, London. Organised by Andrew Ward

(Benesh Director), Wayne Sleep and Lady Sainsbury, the event brought together a host of international stars from The Royal Ballet, Paris Opéra Ballet, Stuttgart Ballet, Dutch National Ballet, Birmingham Royal Ballet, Rambert Dance Company, Phoenix Dance Company and the Jiving Lindy Hoppers. The evening included the memorable performance in which comedienne Dawn French 'mirrored' Darcey Bussell in a ballet class, as well as appearances by Royal Ballet and RAD students.

In March 1998 David Watchman and Lynn Wallis led a delegation of international dance professionals on a trip to Russia. Organised by the American Citizen Ambassador Program, the visit was to discuss Russian and Western traditions in classical ballet. The trip included a visit to the Bolshoi Ballet in Moscow and an evening performance of *Swan Lake* at the Moscow State Theatre, followed by a train to St Petersburg to meet the company based at the famous Maryinsky Theatre and see an 'unforgettable' performance of *La Bayadère*.

By the end of the 1990s the RAD had done much to consolidate its infrastructure and develop its 'products'. The last year of the twentieth century was marked by three milestones: the appointment of Luke Rittner as the new Chief Executive; the creation of a Faculty of Education to replace the former College; and the appointment of Professor Joan White as Dean of Faculty and Director of Education. As the millennium approached, Rittner launched an all-encompassing Strategic Review of the Academy's activities as preparation for the twenty-first century.

DON QUIXOTE GALA, 1993

Viviana Durante and Irek Mukhamedov in the Royal Ballet production of *Don Quixote* at the Academy's Royal Gala (top).

ANTOINETTE SIBLEY

At the Fonteyn Phenomenon Conference in 1999; Sibley and Anthony Dowell during filming of the Mime Matters video in 2002.

LUKE RITTNER

Chief Executive of the RAD since 1999.

STARS OF THE NIGHT, 1997

A royal gala was held to celebrate the amalgamation of the RAD and the Benesh Institute in 1997. The programme cover photo shows Viviana Durante as the Grand Duchess Anastasia, *Anastasia*, Act II.

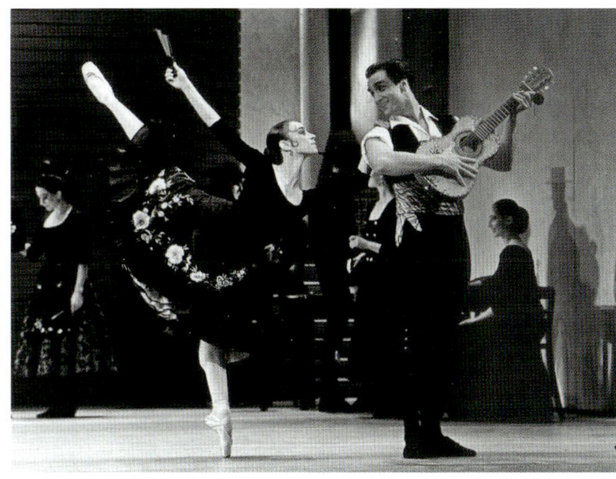

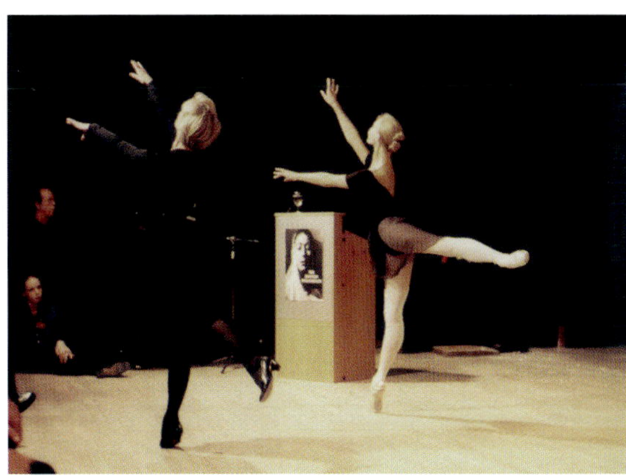

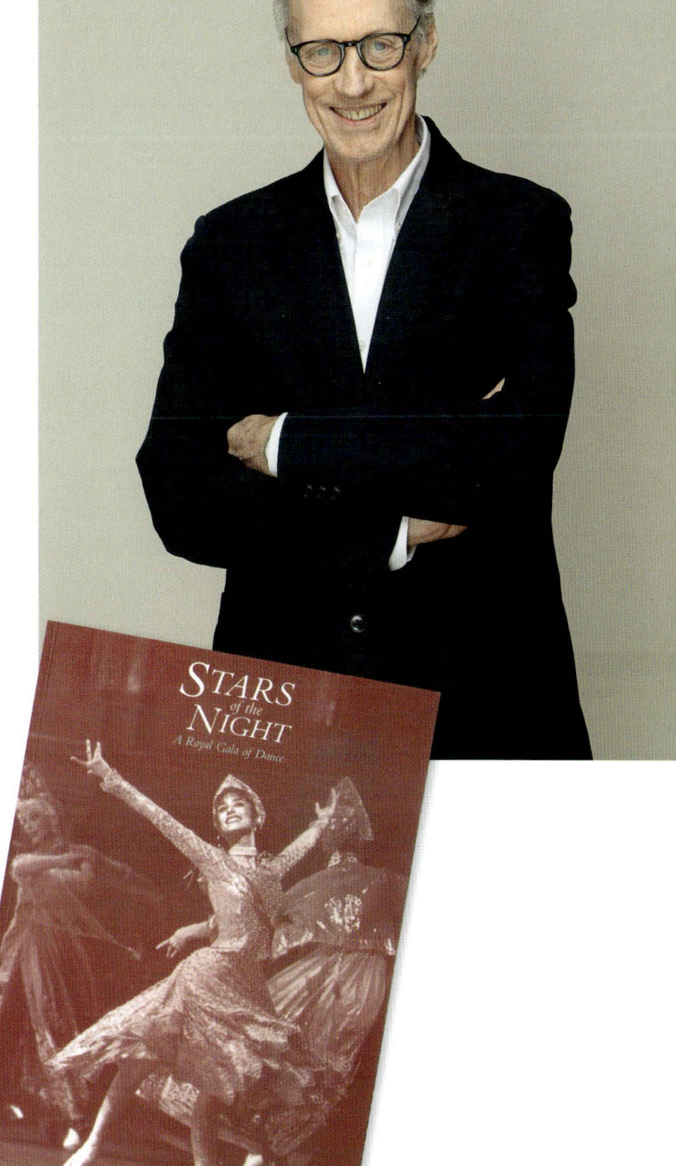

STRATEGIC REVIEW

The Review was designed to identify the RAD's strengths and weaknesses; to give members an opportunity to voice their opinions and contribute to the shape of the Academy in future; and to identify areas for change and opportunities for development. Focus groups were held in Australia, Brazil, Canada, Italy, Germany, Greece, New Zealand, South Africa, the USA and other countries, as well as in the UK, while an international focus group was held in April 2000. In his first interview, Chief Executive Officer Luke Rittner identified a series of fundamental questions that were to shape the Academy's strategic development for the decade and beyond.

Noting that his predecessor, David Watchman, had saved the organisation from financial disaster, Rittner, nonetheless, acknowledged 'some potentially serious "clouds" on the horizon', which would entail 'a radical overhaul' for the Academy's future survival.[5] Foremost of his concerns was the organisation's tendency to look inwards and ignore some of the social and cultural shifts that were, and would continue to be, intrinsic to its core activities. These included changing attitudes to the 'control and discipline' of ballet (and other classical traditions), to the value of examinations and to the elitism implied in maintaining standards of excellence. In addition, Rittner identified the distinctions between children attending dance classes for enjoyment and those wishing to pursue a career in dance, concluding that a 'two-tier' system was the most logical answer.

Other concerns were changes within the dance profession, in particular the breaking-down of barriers between different dance genres. Noting the historical enmity between the ballet and modern dance worlds, Rittner concluded that ballet professionals could learn from modern and contemporary dance. At the same time, the increasing popularity of 'commercial' dance genres would force the Academy to reconsider and 'redefine its purpose in the context of today's conditions – international, multicultural, experimental, inclusive, educational'. Fundamental to this modernising process would be for the RAD to have a closer relationship with the dance profession rather than being seen as 'museum curators'. In this context, the recent incorporation of the Benesh Institute (now Benesh International) was a welcome development.

One of the first outcomes of the Strategic Review was the decision to change the name from the Royal Academy of Dancing to the Royal Academy of Dance, bringing it into line with its sister Academies of Music, Art and Drama. The Review also prompted a completely new syllabus in response to members' concerns, as well as a Continuing Professional Development scheme for dance teachers at every stage of their careers.

The story of the RAD in the twenty-first century has been one of rapid evolution and forward thinking, supported by the embrace of new communication technology and the power of marketing and social media, driven by Melanie Murphy (Director of Marketing and Communications). The RAD website and *Dance Gazette* both underwent radical changes in search of wider relevance and new markets. The *Gazette*, under the editorial guidance of David Jays, was transformed beyond an internal, information-sharing newsletter exclusively for members to a dynamic, international and inclusive publication in its own right.

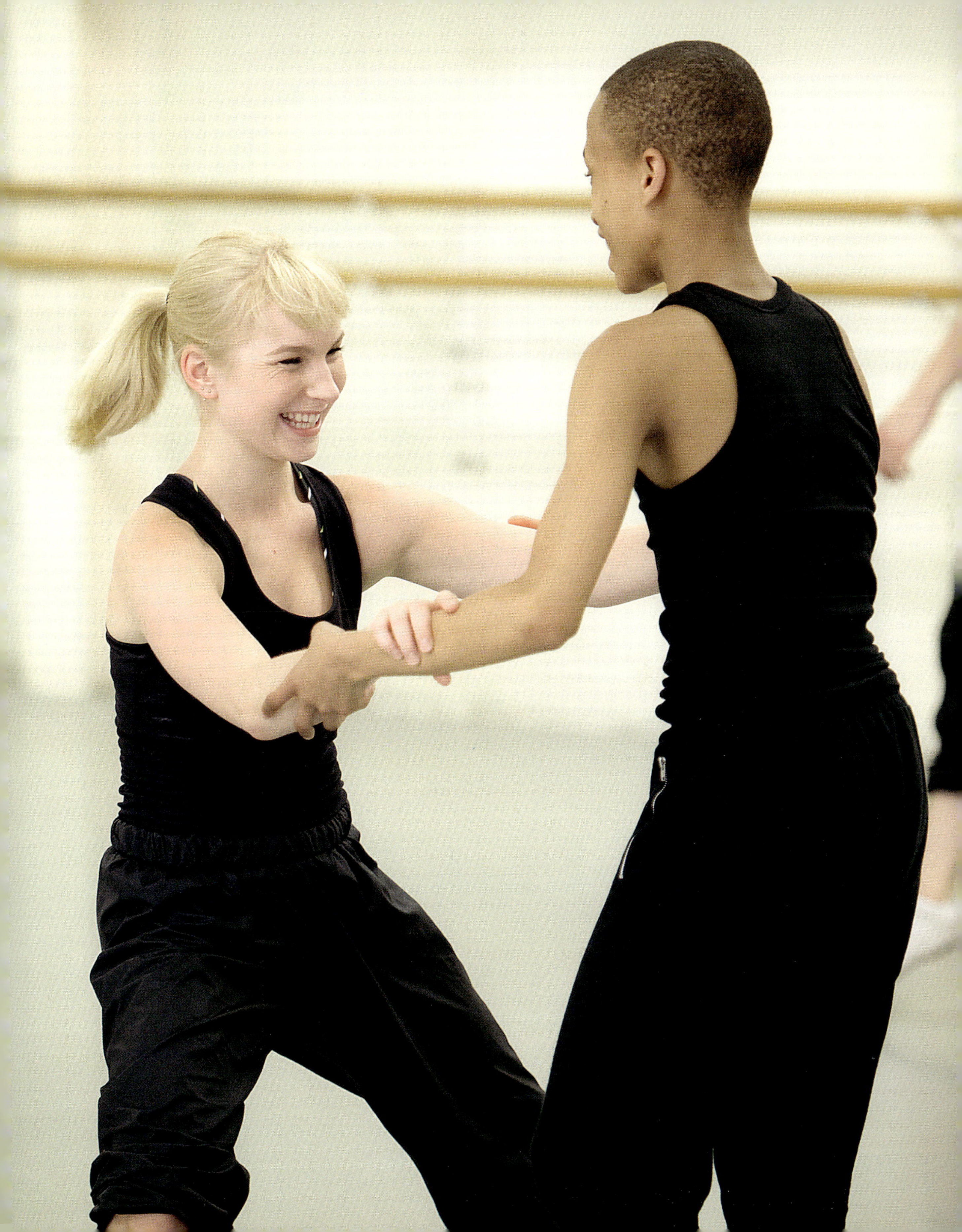

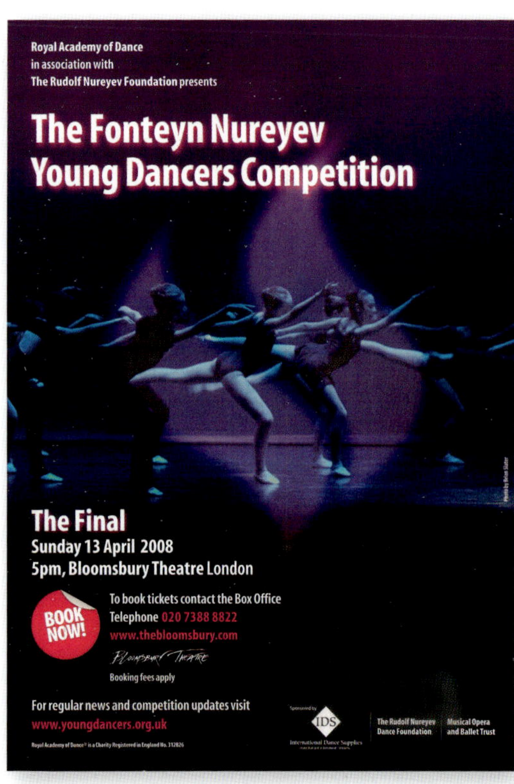

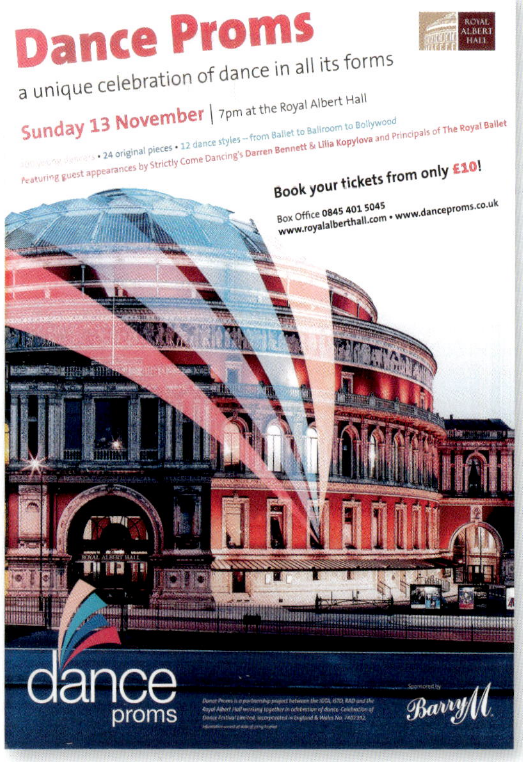

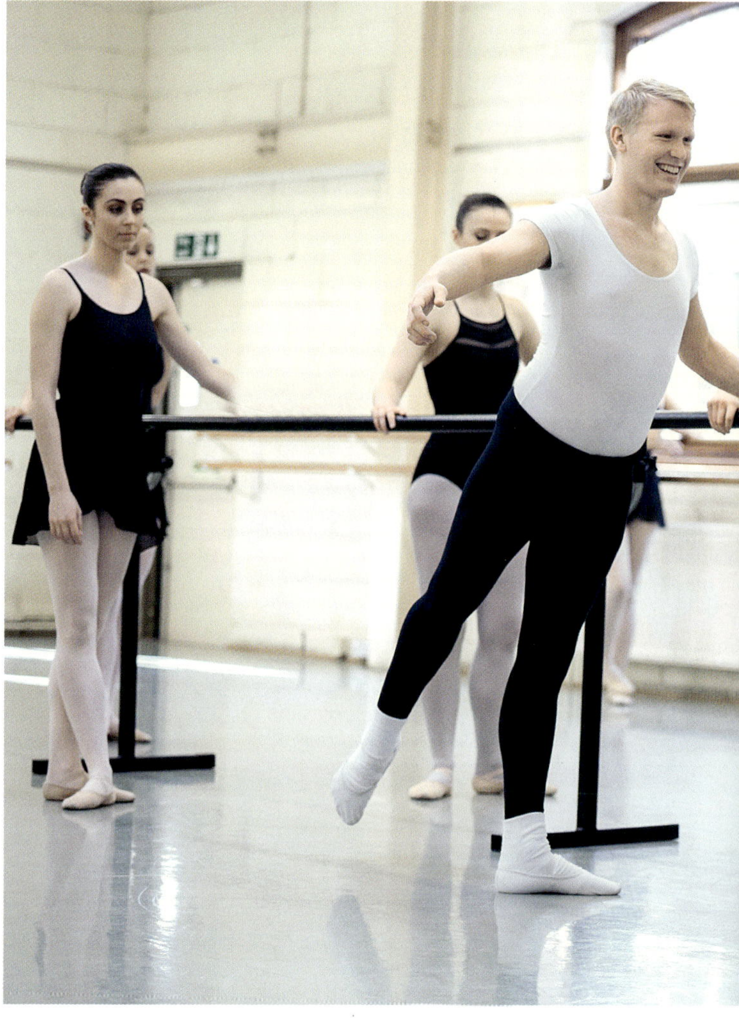

FACULTY OF EDUCATION

The appointment of Professor Joan White, together with the motivating force of Rittner's Strategic Review, was to inspire a new era of teacher education within the newly created Faculty of Education (FOE). From 2000 until 2010 the Faculty produced no fewer than nine different programmes for teachers, moving beyond the traditional parameters of ballet teaching to the ever-increasing contexts of dance education: state sector education; community dance; the health and leisure industries; higher and further education; and the vocational training sector. As the Academy celebrated its 90th anniversary, its founders could hardly have foreseen the expansion in

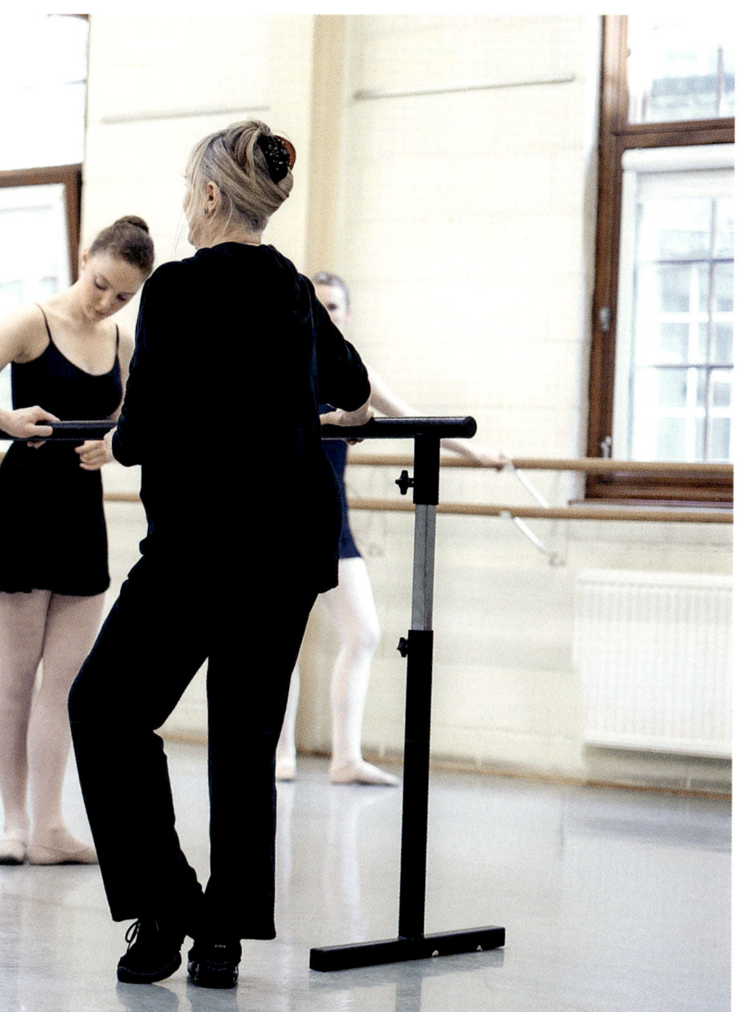

NEW BEGINNINGS

Sibley was succeeded by another legendary ballerina, Darcey Bussell. Like her predecessors, Bussell had travelled widely and proved an inspiring ambassador for the RAD around the world. In addition to her sparkling career with The Royal Ballet, Bussell had become a household name as a judge on the BBC's popular *Strictly Come Dancing* television show. Indeed, her diverse interests in all forms of dance reflected the 'new' Academy without diminishing its classical ballet roots and heritage. In the 2018 New Year's Honours List Darcey Bussell was made a Dame of the British Empire in recognition of her services to dance.

The expansion of the RAD in the twenty-first century led, inevitably, to the question of finding a new home. Increasing numbers of staff and students at the Battersea headquarters prompted plans for a renovation of the existing site but these were eventually abandoned in favour of finding a new building. It was considered important to keep the RAD's headquarters in London and, if possible in the Borough of Wandsworth, as this had been the RAD's home since the early 1970s. In 2017 a deal was agreed with developers Avanton to 'swap' the Battersea Square building for space within a new development on York Road, about a mile from the current site. The new headquarters will occupy the ground floor and part of the first floor of the development site, with residential space in three towers above it. It will include state-of-the-art studios, offices, a library, a café and a dedicated performance space. The move to the new building is scheduled to

teacher education, much less the vast and changing landscape of qualifications and regulatory frameworks. In line with Rittner's call for a more outward-looking and professionally connected Academy, the FOE pioneered programmes for dance teachers in secondary education and for dance professionals approaching the end of their performance career, as well as models of distance learning that were to serve the organisation's increasingly international membership profile.

Joan White retired in 2011, her knowledge, drive and experience leaving an enduring legacy. After 22 years of dedicated service, Dame Antoinette Sibley retired as President in 2012.

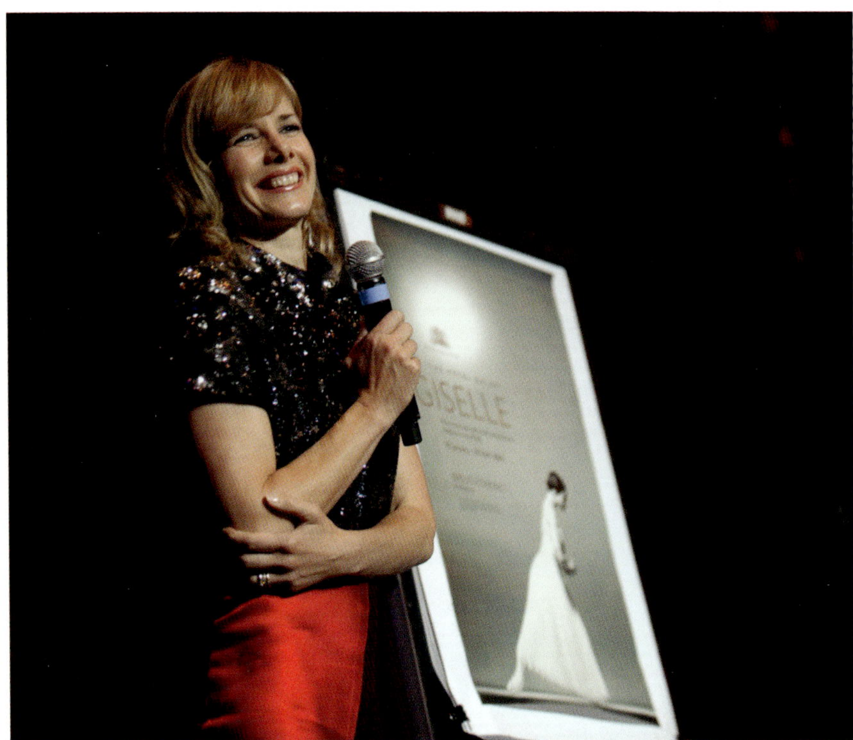

take place in 2020. The new building will offer enormous advantages to the RAD, not only in terms of better facilities, but also in enabling the Academy to open its doors to the wider community in a way that was never possible before. The move will be a landmark event for the Academy and an appropriate one in the centenary year.

The Academy also outgrew St Mary's Church, Battersea, where the annual Graduation Ceremony was traditionally held. Since 2016 the ceremony has taken place at a new venue, Imperial College, to accommodate the increasing numbers of graduates and their guests.

The years since 2010 have also seen numerous changes and developments in the regulation of examinations. The demise of the Qualifications and Curriculum Authority (QCA) and the emergence of its replacement, the Office of Qualifications and Examinations Regulation (Ofqual), prompted a new quality assurance structure and qualifications framework, and the inevitable workload involved in steering the RAD's examinations through the change. In the Faculty of Education, the change of

validating universities, from the University of Surrey to the University of Bath, created similar challenges. The international recognition of RAD qualifications has continued to grow in complexity, the Brexit dilemma adding another layer of potential change and uncertainty. Nonetheless, RAD qualifications currently enjoy greater recognition than at any point in the Academy's 100-year history and undoubtedly exceed the expectations of its founders.

The RAD now operates internationally via a network of 35 branch offices, representative offices and subsidiary companies. Its primary sources of income are examination fees, education and training fees, membership subscriptions, trading and licensing. In total these activities account for 95 per cent of the RAD's income, while the remaining 5 per cent comes largely from funding for special programmes and a small amount from donations and legacies, and other activities.

The retirement of Finance Director Richard Thom (2015) and Artistic Director Lynn Wallis (2016) marked the end of an era; collectively they had given almost fifty years of loyal service to the

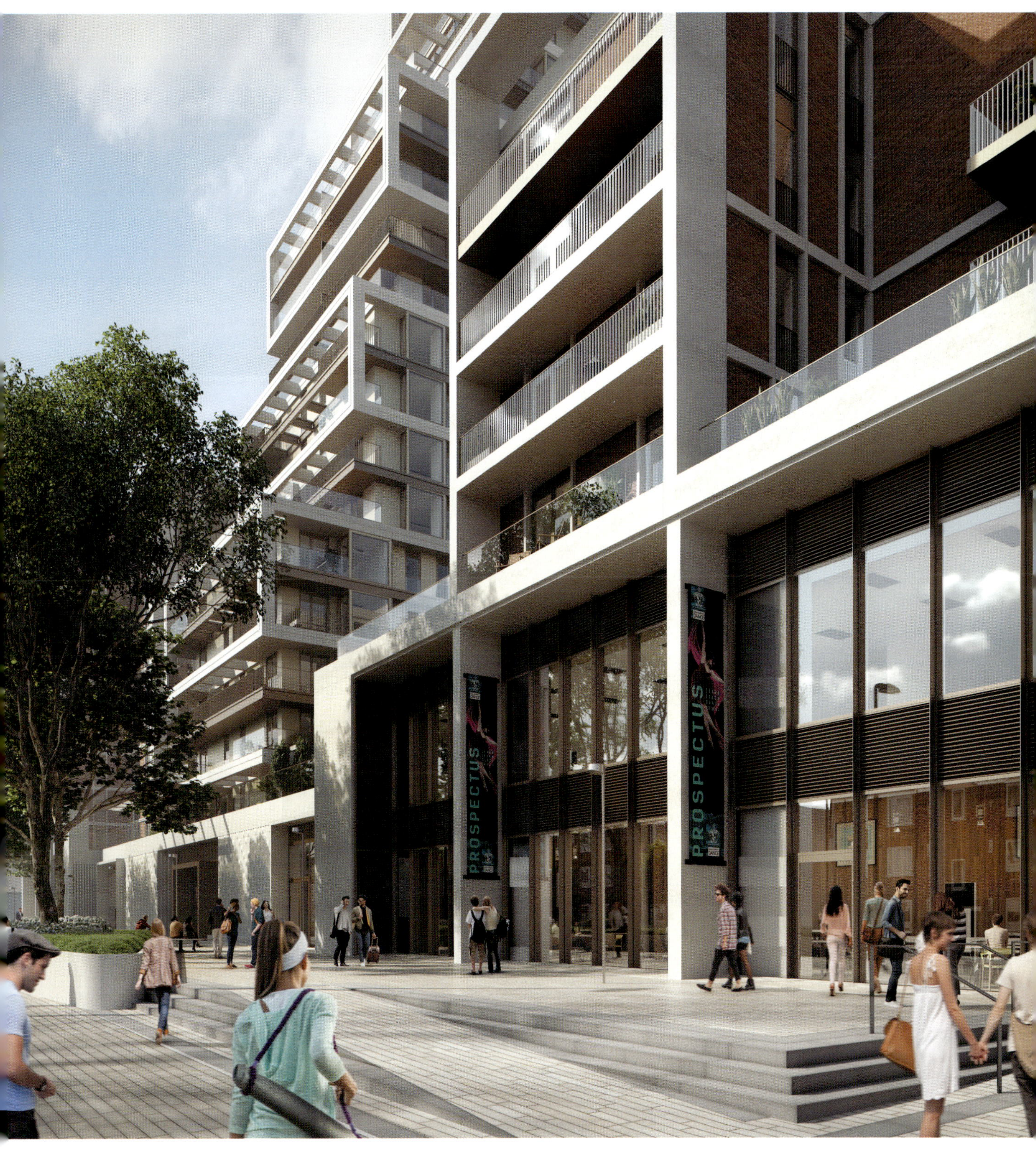

PROSPECTUS
PROSPECTUS

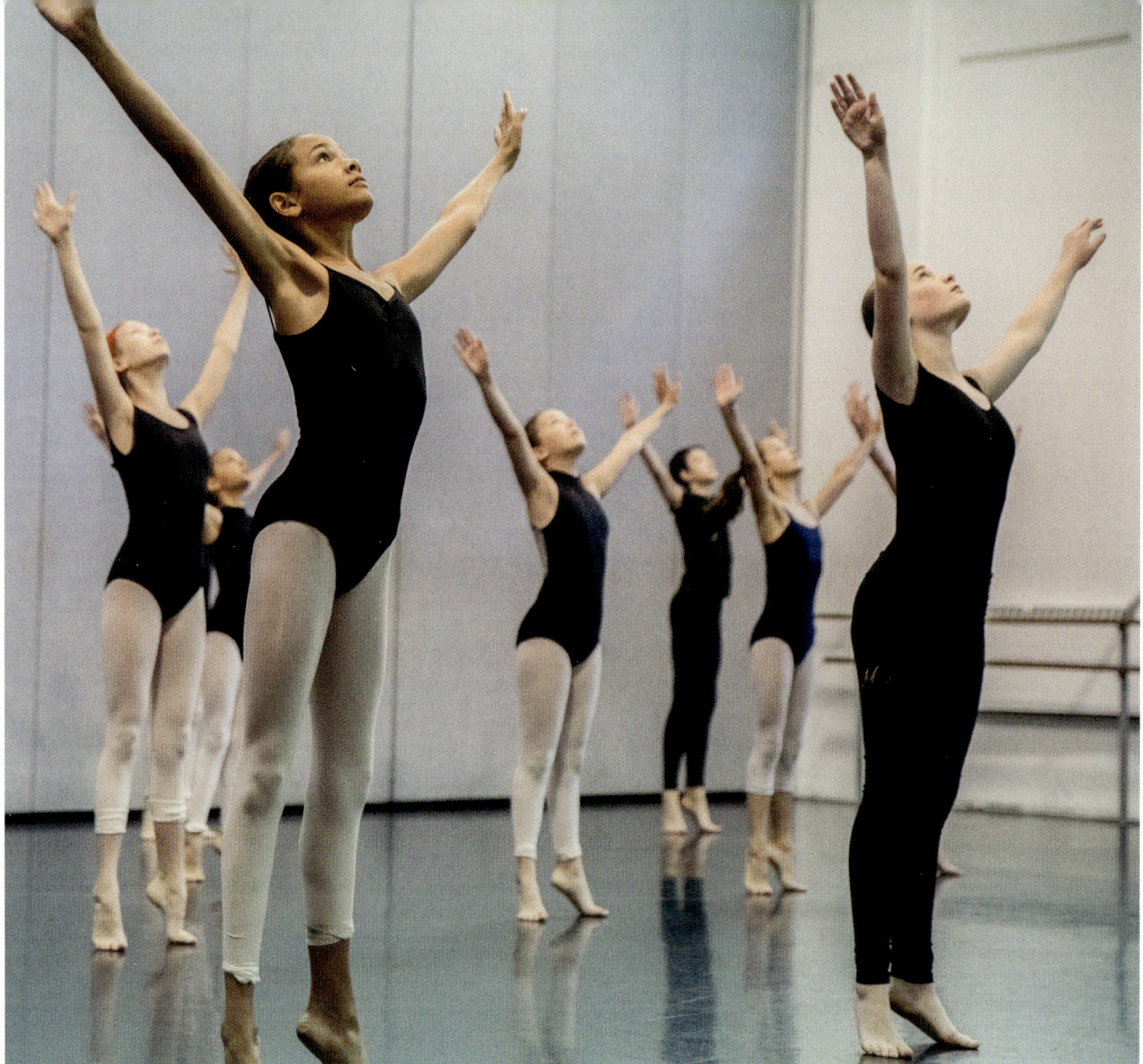

Academy and were intrinsic to its transformation through and beyond the new millennium. Thom's successor was Ian Pogue (current Director of Finance and Operations), while Paula Hunt held the role of Artistic Director in 2017 and 2018. In 2016 Michelle Groves was appointed Director of Education and in 2018 Gerard Charles became Artistic Director. In their hands lie the artistic and educational future of the Academy's work.

Through it all, Luke Rittner has continued to steer the ship as the RAD prepares to move to its new London home, celebrate its centenary and look ahead to the unknowable and limitless opportunities that lie ahead. Rittner once said 'adapt or die'; the RAD has mastered the art of change and, like a well-trained dancer, can tackle any 'unseen *enchaînement*' ahead.

NOTES

1   Royal Academy of Dancing 1991, p. 38.
2   Clarke 1991, p. 1023.
3   Rittner 2000, p. 26.
4   Watchman 1992, p. 14.
5   Rittner 2000, p. 26.

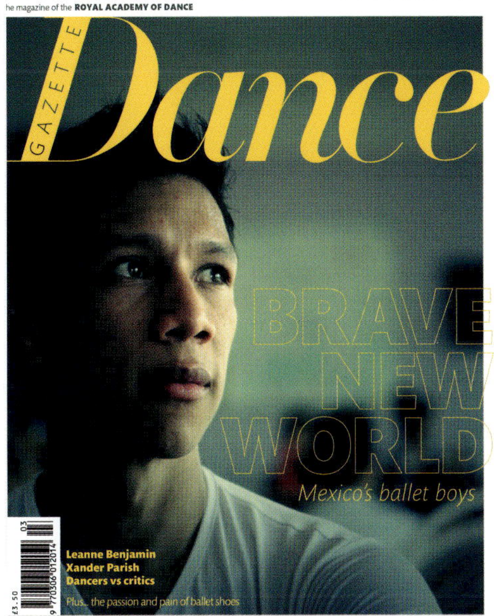

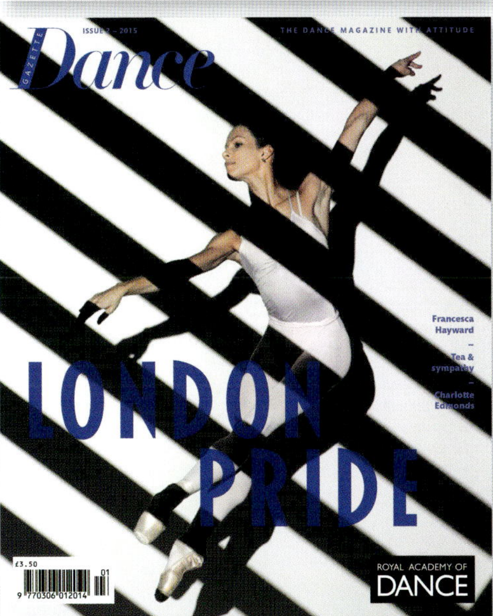

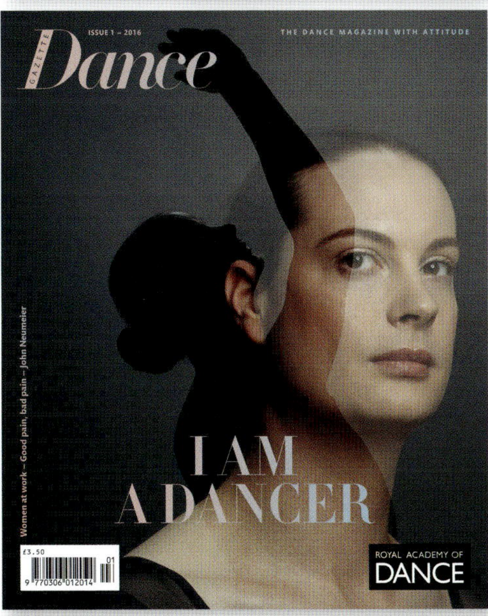

David Jays, editor of *Dance Gazette* since 2005

Dance Gazette has long been the public voice of the RAD, and keenly valued by members. As the RAD began to renew its syllabus, competitions and other aspects of its work, we wanted to reflect these changing attitudes in the magazine, which led in 2011 to a new format and a fresh approach. *Dance Gazette* became even more international and outward-looking – we feel there is almost no subject that we can't make relevant to the lives and interests of our members.

RAD members frequently tell us how much they treasure the magazine, which is a real source of pride. One of the changes was to make it even more visually appealing, and we commission sumptuous photographs and illustrations to accompany the stories. Dance and dance training touch so many aspects of people's lives – at all ages, all levels of expertise. It's a constant source of inspiration. We have worked with leading writers to report from Baghdad, Hong Kong and the Amazon. We have investigated such sensitive subjects as transgender ballet students, the ways in which religious Muslim dancers approach their training, and sexual harassment in professional dance. We are based in the Academy but look out at the world – sharing the RAD's work with a wider public, and retaining our passion for dance and a constant sense of discovery.

DRESSING FOR DANCE

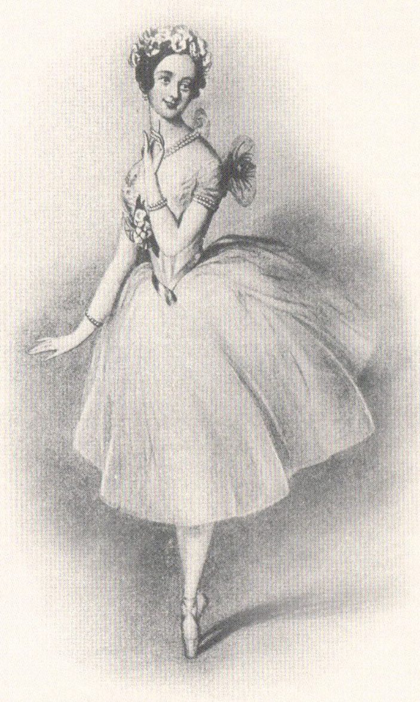

TUTUS

Costume design is an essential feature of dance as a theatre art, and in classical ballet the tutu remains an iconic symbol of the ethereal and elusive ballerina. In the early part of the nineteenth century the Romantic ballet saw the development of the longer, bell-shaped 'romantic tutu', which revealed the lower leg and accentuated the growing complexity of technical footwork. It was during this era that the other icon of ballet costume emerged: the pointe shoe.

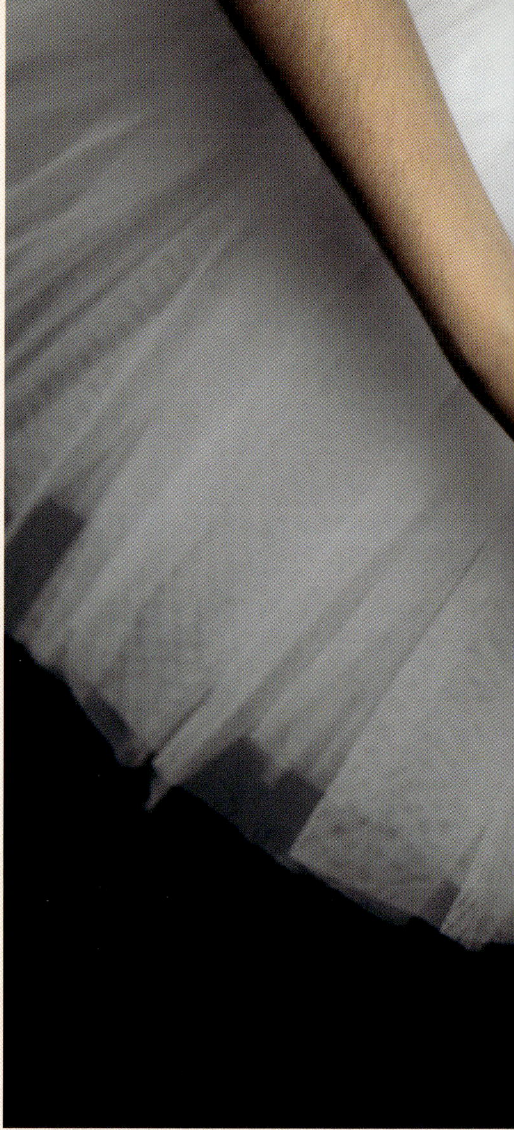

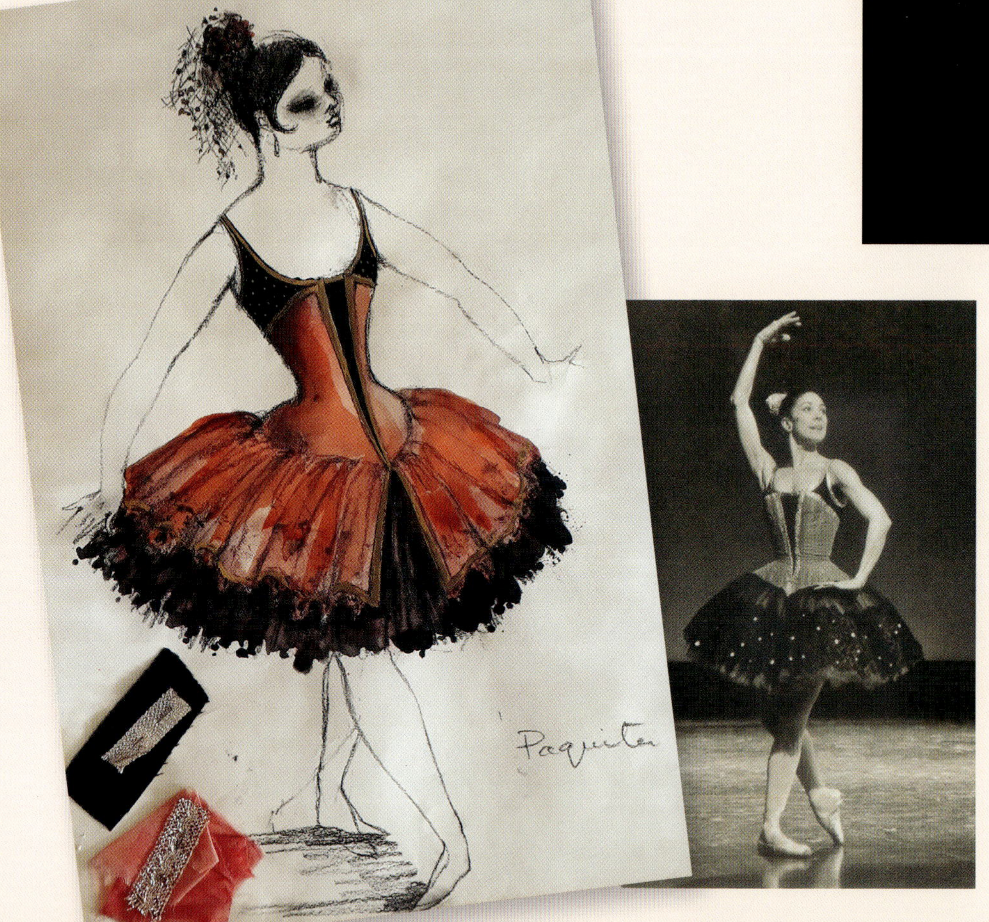

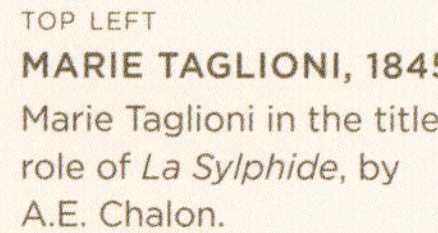

TOP LEFT
MARIE TAGLIONI, 1845
Marie Taglioni in the title role of *La Sylphide*, by A.E. Chalon.

PAQUITA, 1964
Margot Fonteyn in Rudolf Nureyev's production of *Paquita* at the RAD Gala Matinée, wearing the costume designed for her by Philip Prowse (far left).

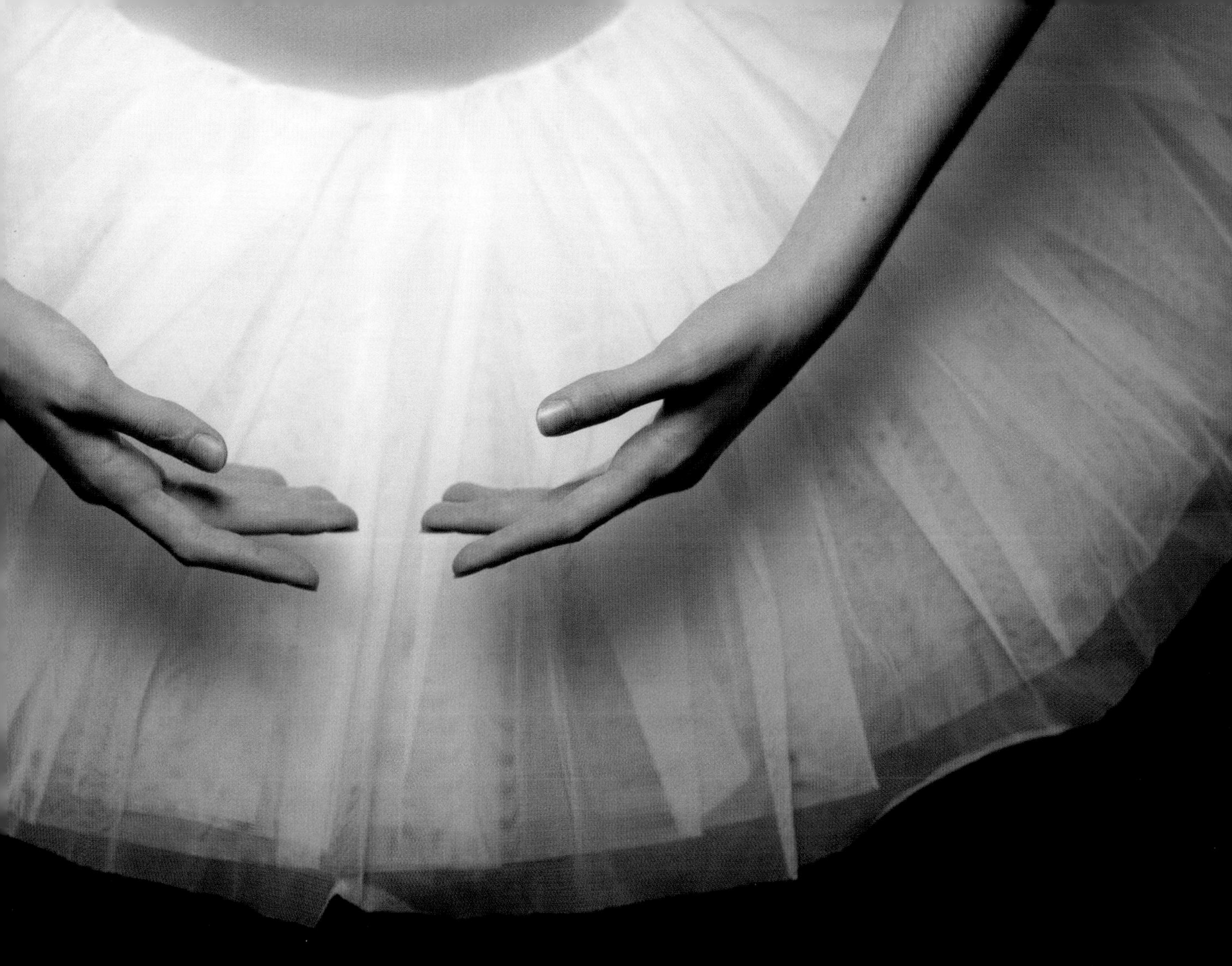

Reinforced with extra layers of fabric and glue, the early pointe shoe allowed the ballerina to rise momentarily onto the tip of her toe, adding to the traditional storyline of supernatural sylphs, nymphs and apparitions who seemingly defied gravity as they 'floated' across the stage. The corps de ballet scenes in *La Sylphide* and *Giselle* epitomise the dramatic effect of the romantic tutu en masse: the sculptural quality when dancers are still and the soft, fluid movement of the net skirt when they alight from jumps.

By the end of the nineteenth century the tutu skirt was shortened to allow greater freedom and visibility of the ballerina's legs. The great classical ballets produced in Imperial Russia from the 1870s onwards, *The Sleeping Beauty*, *Swan Lake* and *The Nutcracker* among them, were created with the shorter tutu in mind. The famous 32 fouettés in Act III of *Swan Lake* (for example) would be difficult, if not dangerous, to perform in a longer romantic net skirt.

In the twentieth century the skirt gradually became shorter: today a traditional tutu is made using up to 12 metres of net, with a narrow steel hoop that supports the top layer of skirt. There can be as few as ten graduated layers of net or as many as twenty, with an increasing variety of net and tulle fabrics. The skirt is attached to a basque that fits smoothly between the waist and hip. The point at which the skirt sits has varied considerably according to fashion and, in some instances, the individual preferences of dancers. Whilst the mid- to late twentieth-century tutu skirt started at the level of the crotch/upper thigh, the twenty-first century has seen a preference for a skirt that sticks out from high on the hips.

BALLET SHOES

The shoes worn by ballerinas have also evolved since the Romantic ballet era. In the early twentieth century the famous ballerina Anna Pavlova was to influence developments in ballet around the world with her performances in roles such as *The Dying Swan*. Less well known is the fact that her feet made pointe work extremely problematic: a combination of her high insteps, slender feet and tapering toes created excessive pressure on her big toe and left her vulnerable to injury when dancing en pointe. Pavlova had her shoes redesigned to include a toughened leather sole for extra support with a toe area that was flattened ('squared') and hardened to form a box. All pointe shoes today incorporate a box to encase and support the dancer's toes, as well as a stiffened sole (known as a shank) that provides support for the arch of the foot.

It is essential that a pointe shoe fits an individual dancer's foot perfectly. For this reason, pointe shoes come in a vast array of widths, shank strengths and other variations of fit. Some dancers have their pointe shoes handmade, ensuring the ultimate fit on repeat order. The colour of the shoe may also vary, from bluer shades of pink to more flesh-coloured or nude tones. Generally the aim is for tights and pointe shoes to match, so that the dancer's foot appears as a seamless extension of the leg. In some instances pointe shoes are dyed to match the exact colour of the tights. On occasion, the costume design may specifically require a different coloured pointe shoe, a notable example being Moira Shearer's character in the classic 1948 ballet film *The Red Shoes*.

Pointe shoes have a short life, softening with the heat of the foot and the pressure of pointe work. Some dancers may get through several pairs in a single performance, particularly if performing in a long, three-act ballet. Over the years dancers have developed a number of methods for prolonging the life of pointe shoes. In her book *The Ballet Lover's Companion* (1949), Kay Ambrose recommended that students 'soak the interior with *straw hat dye*' and then leave them to soak overnight. Ambrose's book also contains tips on darning pointe shoes and the making of tutus, which she concludes are rarely constructed properly and are either 'depressing and untidy' or 'too short and bulky'.

Soft ballet shoes are available in canvas, leather or satin and are most commonly used in graded examinations, prior to

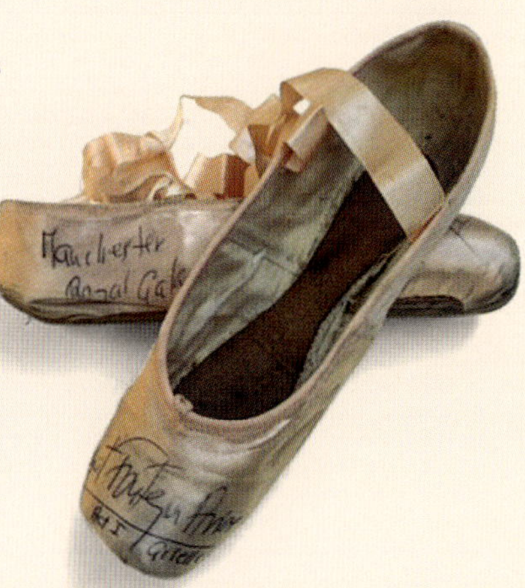

progressing to pointe shoes. Even at entry level it is important that the shoe is correctly fitted, so they are available in various widths and with elastics to secure the foot, which are now pre-sewn by many manufacturers. Traditionally these shoes have a single length of leather that forms the 'full sole', which offers stability and resistance when articulating the foot; this in turn may aid in strengthening footwork. More recently the 'split sole' shoe has been developed. Ribbons may also be used on soft ballet shoes and are advised as part of the uniform for the Intermediate Foundation examination.

Today, the making of shoes (and other items of dancewear) for dancers and companies is a global business and an integral part of a wider ballet culture. What to wear, whether on stage or in the dance studio, has always been an important aspect of a dancer's life, whether the preference is for neatly groomed, artfully dishevelled or comfortably functional. Such changing trends are reflected in dance magazines and journals over the last one hundred years, which reveal a huge number of dancewear suppliers, many of them now defunct. Companies such as Freed of London have a long and successful association with the ballet world, having made shoes for Pavlova and Margot Fonteyn. Setting up in London's Covent Garden in 1929, the shoemaker Frederick Freed and his wife went on to create one of the biggest dance shoe suppliers in the world. Freed shoes are now available in over fifty countries, and two thirds of their classic pointe shoes are 'made to measure' for individual dancers.

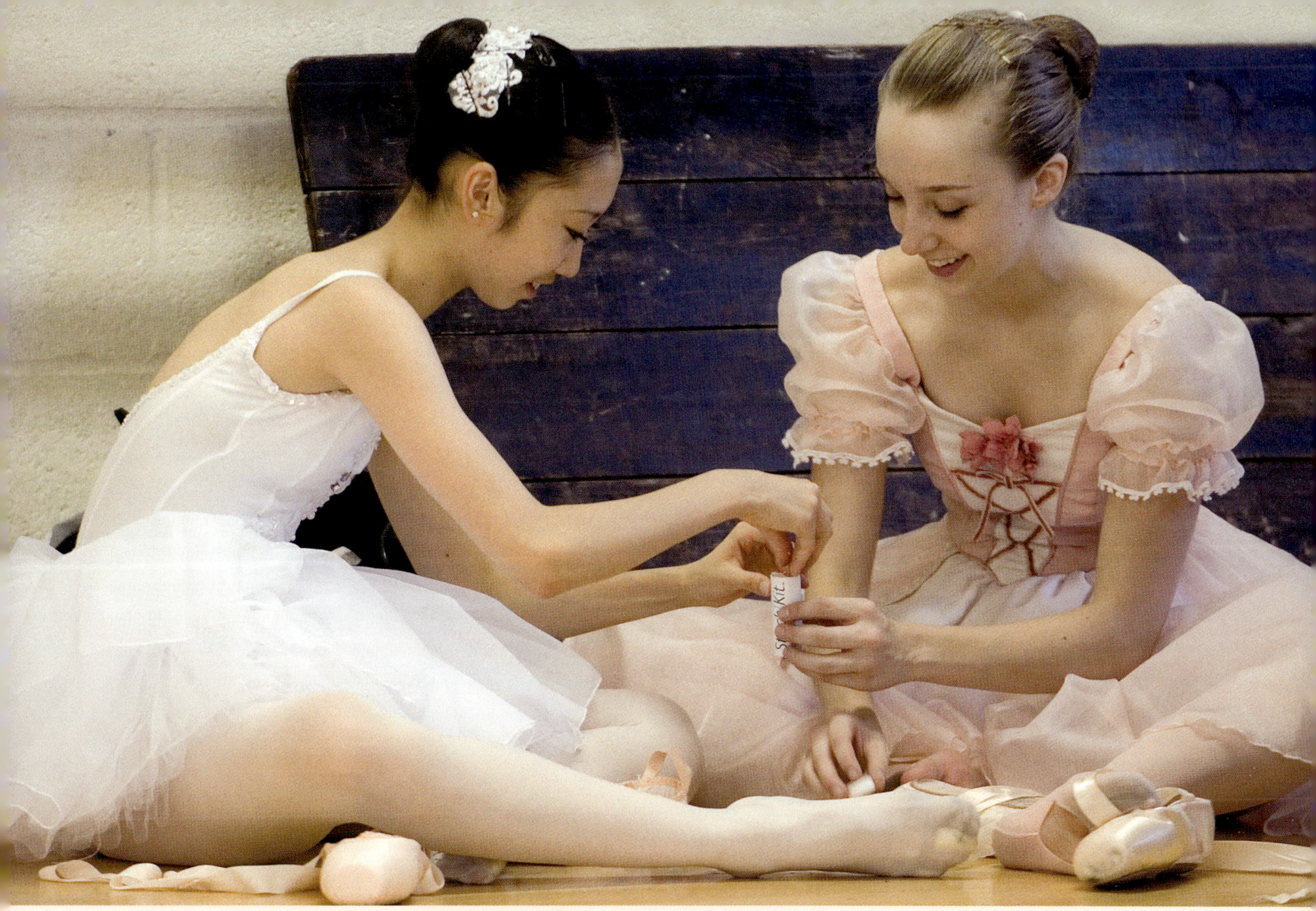

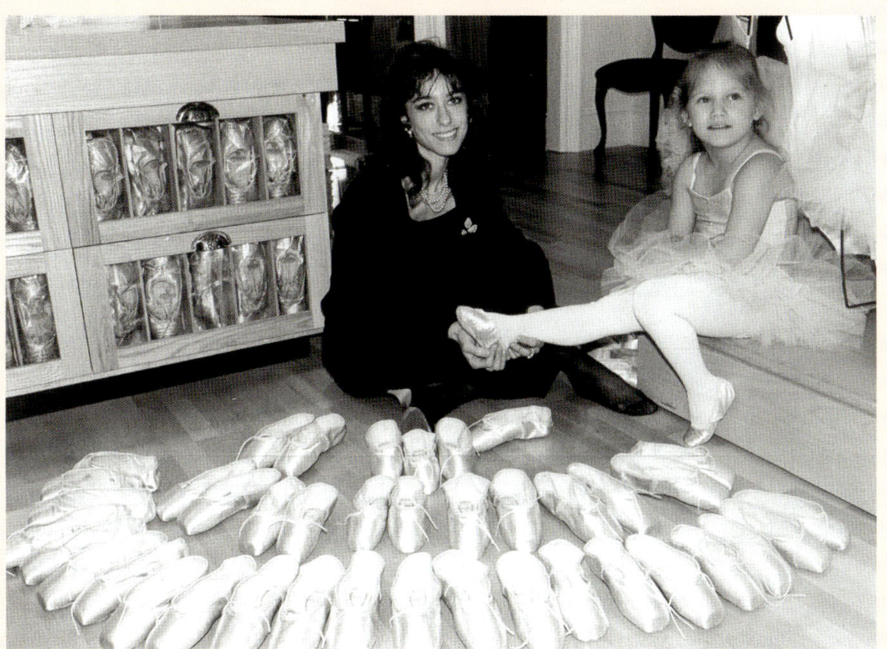

LEFT

BALLET SHOES, 1989
Royal Ballet dancer Viviana Durante
with an RAD Junior Friend at the
opening of the new Freed store in
London, 1989.

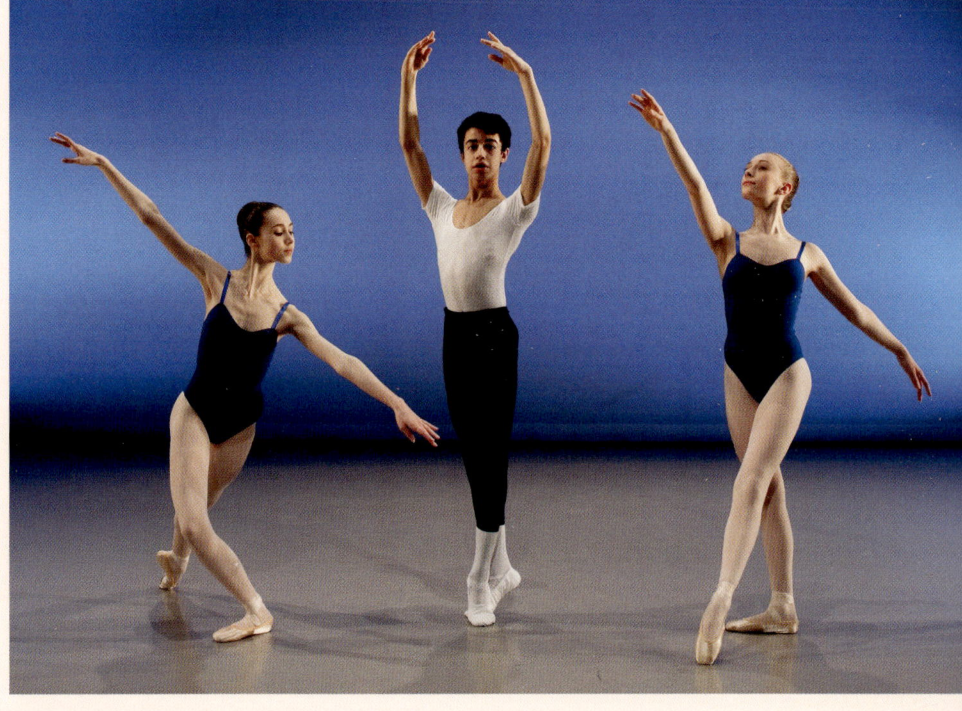

EXAMINATION UNIFORMS

Dance examinations are another context in which costume plays a role. Traditionally, candidates for RAD examinations (and those of other dance teaching societies) were required to wear a regulation uniform. Candidates for the first RAD exams held in 1921 were asked to present themselves in practice dress – dark gym wear being deemed most suitable – but after one candidate turned up dressed as a butterfly, strict uniform regulations were introduced the following year. In 1922 female candidates were required to wear ballet skirts with pink satin shoes and stockings or tights, and in later years they wore full ballet dress, laced and boned at the back with full net skirts which, as Pat Beadle remembers, 'sprang to life when you danced … it was a dream'.

In the 1920s and 1930s ballet tights were made from silk, which wrinkled at the knee on the first plié. The tights were dipped in water, put on while still wet and secured with a couple of pennies twisted into the material at the waist to stop the legs sagging as they dried. For her Elementary examination in 1938, Jacqueline B'nay wore a new white ballet dress (with a compulsory rose attached to the bodice) and pink stockings (held up with pennies and tape), which made her feel 'like a trussed chicken'.

Examination uniform for early male candidates comprised a white, short-sleeved shirt with black woollen tights and white ankle socks. Male candidates traditionally wore

TUTU, 1937

Pat Beadle wearing the regulation uniform in 1937, when she passed her Intermediate examination. A pupil of Madame Judith Espinosa, Beadle was awarded an RAD Scholarship in 1938.

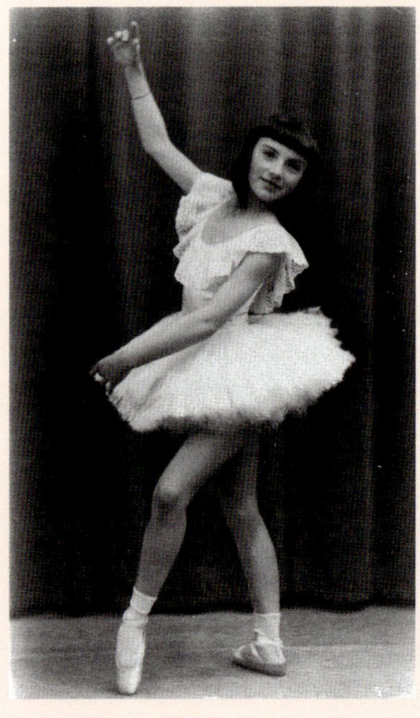

black leather ballet shoes secured with elastic rather than ribbons. Following the commercial availability of synthetic fabrics such as nylon (in the 1940s) and Lycra (in the 1960s), dancewear underwent a transformation with seemingly unlimited designs for items such as leotards, all-in-ones (body stockings), leggings, leg warmers, ankle warmers, sweatpants, teaching skirts and crossover cardigans, to name a few. While the demand for ballet wear continued, the introduction of new dance genres such as Modern, Jazz, Tap, Street Dance, Disco and Musical Theatre saw a boom in dancewear and leisurewear.

Today the RAD continues to recommend specific uniform for each syllabus, examination or award. Tutus may be worn by female students for Vocational Graded examinations, as well as by students who are following the Discovering Repertoire programme, in which they may choose to wear a romantic or classical tutu skirt for the individual variations. For the Solo Seal examination, the RAD's highest

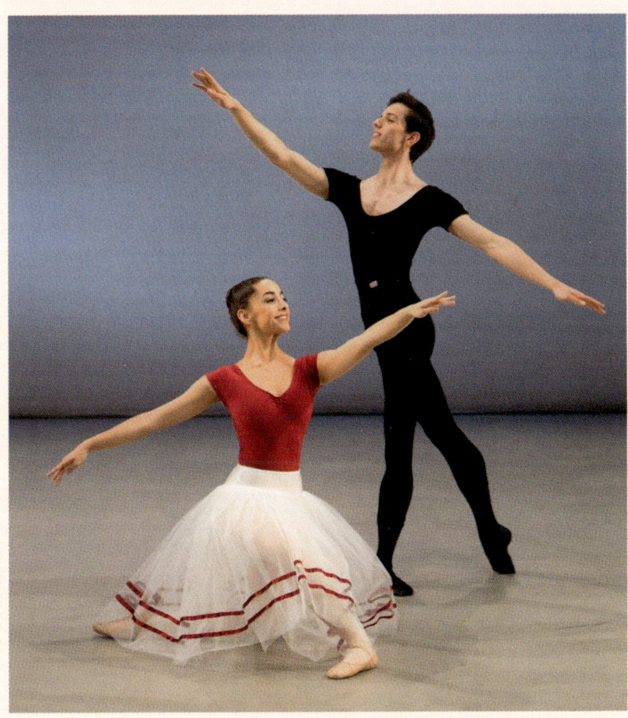

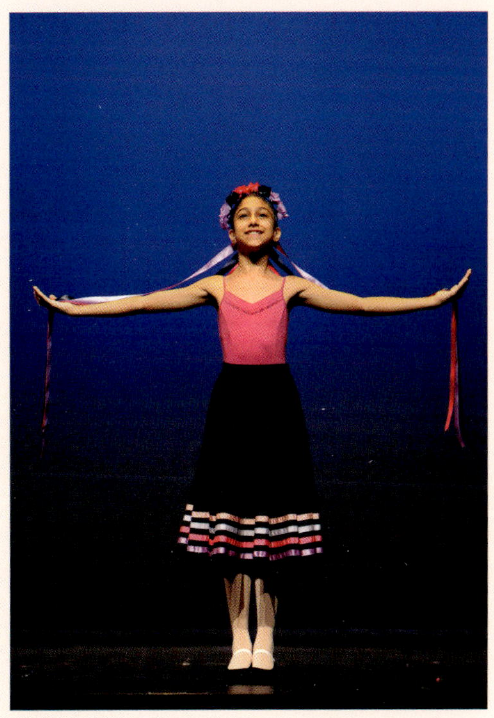

executant award, a different costume is required for each of the different variations: a soft chiffon mid-calf-length skirt for the Genée port de bras, a shorter chiffon skirt for the twenty-first-century variation, and a tutu for the classical variation and finale. For male candidates the recommended uniform consists of a white short-sleeved leotard or T-shirt, with black tights or shorts, dependent on the level.

National costumes worldwide provide us with a wealth of information about the character of the people and their ethnic origins. 'Costume, dance, music, folklore and the decorative arts … are closely linked' (Robert Harrold, *Folk Costumes of the World* [1978]). In stage productions these costumes provide a contrast to the more muted colours and styles of those for ballet. Historically, national dances became very popular in both opera and ballet as they were often used in narrative pieces to establish the settings – a useful device for the audience to follow the story and a

wonderful opportunity for the dancers and costume designers to flourish. For the purposes of exams, the recognised Character dance garment for females is a full or circular skirt to below the knee attached to a waistband, with rows of ribbons or braid added towards the bottom. Low or Cuban-heeled shoes are worn by both male and female candidates for most of the Character dances in the RAD syllabus because the technique calls for flexed feet, stamps and heel beats.

Royal Academy of Dance Enterprises Ltd, the trading arm of the RAD in the UK, is authorised to sell products using the RAD brand, and gift-aids its profits to the RAD. RAD Enterprises has established relationships with selected manufacturers who develop uniform wear for use in examinations. Its approved suppliers under license worldwide are Bloch Australia, Freed of London, International Dance Supplies, Little Ballerina and Mondor Canada.

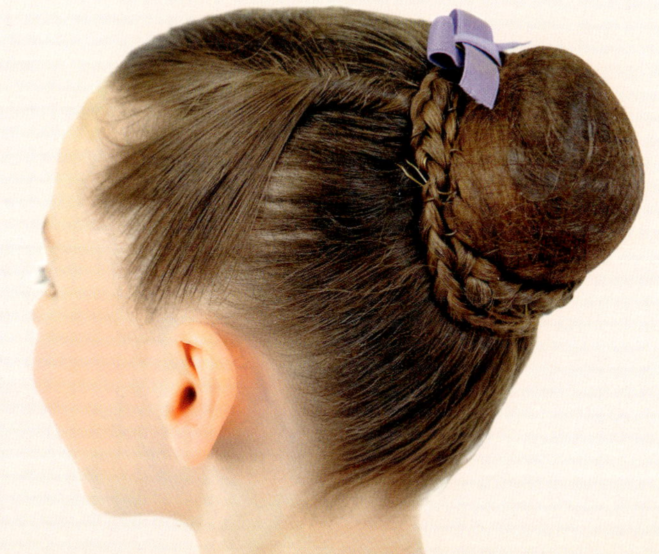

HERITAGE COLLECTIONS AT THE RAD
AND THE VICTORIA AND ALBERT MUSEUM

THE history of the RAD is preserved to a great extent through the documents and photographs housed in the Academy's own archives. In view of the historical context in which the RAD was founded, and its relationship with the wider ballet scene, additional relevant material can also be found in collections elsewhere.

The collections at the Victoria and Albert Museum in London are a particularly rich source of material on the RAD's five elected founders. For Lucia Cormani there is information on, and photographs of, her productions at the Alhambra, just as there is a very good collection on the Empire Theatre, where Adeline Genée and later Phyllis Bedells were ballerinas. There is a collection on the Espinosa family and substantial holdings on Tamara Karsavina, particularly with the Ballets Russes and her independent activities, including designs for her own productions by Alexandre Benois and Claude Lovat Fraser. But the V&A's collection is not limited to the genesis of the RAD, for it includes Ivor Guest's papers, designs by Ralph Koltai and Nadine Baylis for Rudolf Nureyev's *Raymonda* (1965), John Cranko's album documenting his early creations, and a wealth of photographs and drawings.

The RAD has received many gifts over the years from members and friends, ranging from souvenir programmes and photographs to paintings, objets d'art, costume designs and costumes. Many examples can be seen on display at the RAD headquarters. Sometimes it is deemed that one institution is better able to handle specific material,

V&A

Adeline Genée

Centenary of the Edwardian Ballerina

An Exhibition arranged by Philip Dyer for the Royal Academy of Dancing at the Theatre Museum · Victoria & Albert Museum · 2 May - 3 September 1978

Weekdays 10.00-17.50   Sundays 14.30-17.50   Closed Fridays

which is what happened with the collection of costumes left to the RAD. Without proper textile storage facilities, these fragile items were in danger, and they are now housed in the Theatre & Performance Department of the V&A. The costumes include C. Wilhelm's designs for Genée's danced history of ballet, *La Danse* (1912) and the second version of her tunic made for *The Dryad* (1907). There is also a collection of costumes designed and made for Karsavina, including her white and ice-blue *Russian Dance* dress, designed by Natalia Goncharova. Karsavina's costumes relate to her independent tours in the 1920s when she was supported by young graduating dancers, just as she later enabled RAD students to serve as the opera-ballet at Covent Garden.

In 1978 the RAD and the V&A collaborated on an exhibition to commemorate the centenary of the birth of Adeline Genée. The material displayed included costumes and artworks alongside photographs, programmes and other memorabilia. The RAD Centenary in 2020 provides another opportunity to exhibit material from the collections of both institutions, which run in parallel and together preserve the RAD's heritage.

Jane Pritchard, Curator of Dance,
Victoria and Albert Museum

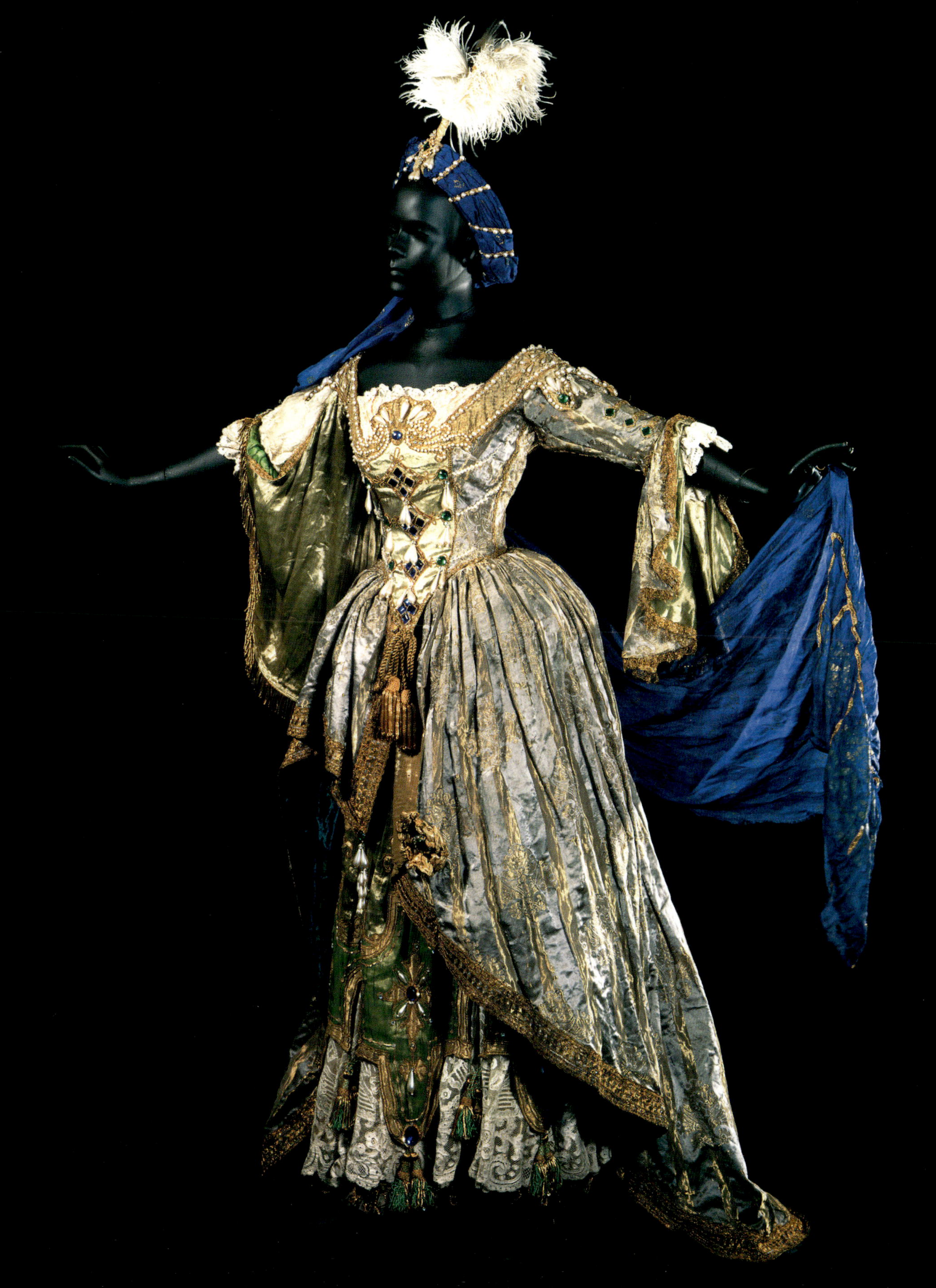

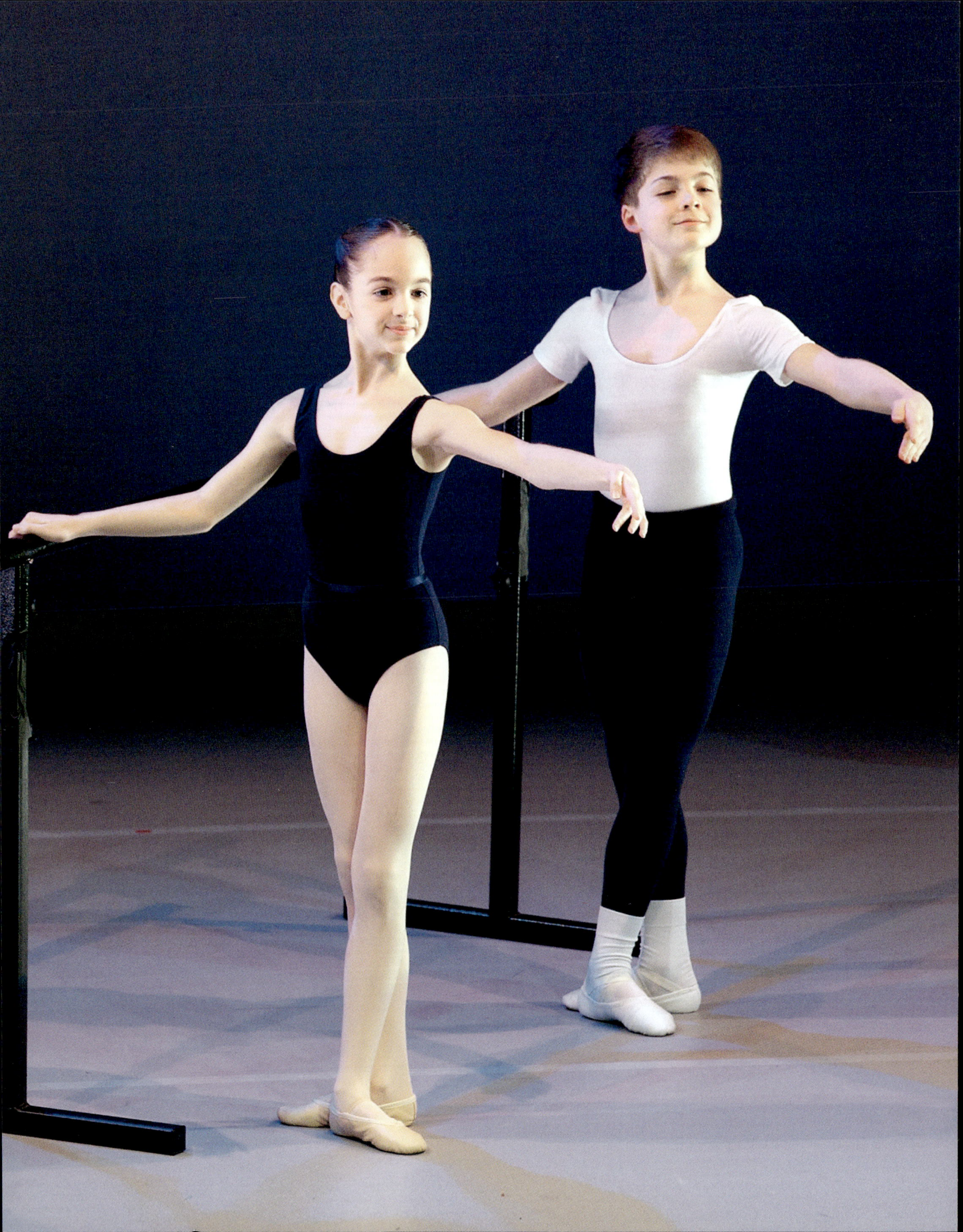

5

SYLLABI AND EXAMINATIONS

A S early as 1916, Edouard Espinosa
had proposed a dance syllabus in a *Dancing Times*
article entitled 'What Every Teacher of Operatic
Dancing Ought to Know and Be Able to Teach'.
Espinosa's syllabus was the basis for the Elementary
syllabus agreed by the first committee of the
Association of Teachers of Operatic Dancing of Great
Britain, after much discussion in December 1920.
Announced in *The Dancing Times*, it was described
as 'An Official List of the Exercises and the Steps
with which every Teacher of Elementary Operatic
Dancing should be acquainted'.

Membership of the Association was dependent
on passing this Elementary examination. More than
160 candidates put themselves forward for the first
examinations, held in 1921; 107 passed and were
accepted as members. These may have been the

hundred or so competent dance teachers said to
have been operating before the foundation of the
Association. Certainly by the next year standards
seemed to have fallen dramatically; in Genée's
words,

> I do not wish to hurt people's feelings but the
> standard of knowledge shown at the recent
> Examination was most decidedly poor....
> On one occasion a single simple question had
> to be repeated to twelve or more candidates
> before a correct answer was given, and many
> could not say how many open and how many
> closed positions of the feet there are.

Espinosa was no more impressed. He took some
satisfaction in noting that the enormous number
of candidates, far too many for comfort, as the
committee all agreed, proved that teachers
recognised the value of the Association and how
important it could be in their careers. But too many
of the candidates for the May 1922 examination had
been 'merely mediocre'. Espinosa defended the high

THE ELEMENTARY
Operatic Syllabus

An Official List of the Exercises and the Steps with which every Teacher of Elementary Operatic Dancing should be acquainted.

This list was prepared and approved of by the Committee appointed to initiate the movement for the founding of an English Association of Teachers of Operatic Dancing: Mesdames ADELINE GENEE, TAMAR KARSAVINA, LUCIA CORMANI, PHYLLIS BEDELLS, and Mr. ESPINOSA.

Positions.

Five positions in which the weight of the body is evenly distributed on both feet.

The fourth position may be *ouverte* or *croisée*.

Exercises: Side Practice.

Pliés, grand battements, battements tendus, battements en rond, ronds-de-jambe à terre, assemblés soutenus, battements frappés and battements sur le cou-de-pied, ronds-de-jambe en l'air, developpés, fouetté ronds-de-jambe en tournant, and exercises on the demie pointe.

Arms.

First, second, third, fourth, and fifth position.

Centre Practice.

Same as Side Practice with alternate feet and the use of both arms.

Adage.

Degagés, chassés, coupés, posés, attitudes, arabesques, detournés, fouettés, relevés, rotations, assemblés soutenus en tournant, preparations for pirouettes, pirouettes sur le cou-de-pied, exercises on the demie point and ports de bras.

Steps.

Pas marchés, glissades (devant, derrière, dessous, dessus, en avant, en arrière), assemblés (as glissades), jetés, échappés, ballonés, temps levées, pas de basque, pas de chat, pas de cheval, fouetté movements and fouettés, pas de bourrée, emboités, deboités, temps de flèche, temps de cuisse and elementary temps de pointes.

Simple Steps of Elevation.

Changements, soubresauts and sissones.

Petite Batterie.

Simple royale and entrechat quatre.

standards of the judges: 'The future of good dancing in England is in the hands of the younger generation, and these *must* be *good* to carry forward the banner of the art.'

The correct positions of the arms seemed to have been a particular point of contention. While the five positions of the feet had been fixed for many years, there was no agreement about the arms, and the differing traditions were clearly a source of difficulty for the first candidates. Writing in *The Dancing Times* in 1922, Genée explained that the committee had discussed the matter and by studying the methods used in Denmark, Russia, Italy and France, as well as in England, for the purposes of the examination they

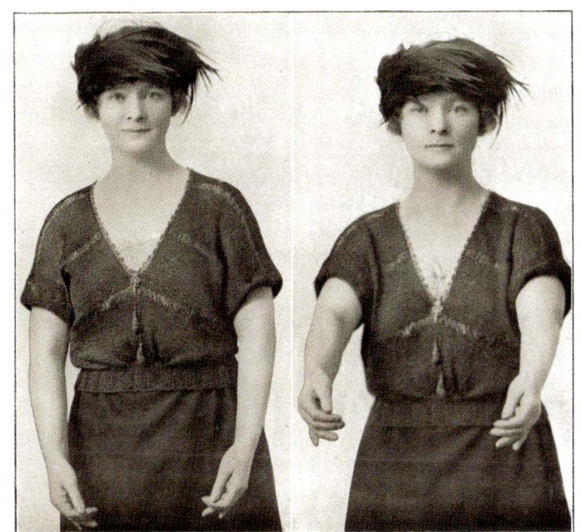

PREPARATORY POSITIONS.

On the left the preparatory position (bras bas), from which the arms are raised through the position shown on the right (demi bras) to the FIRST POSITION.

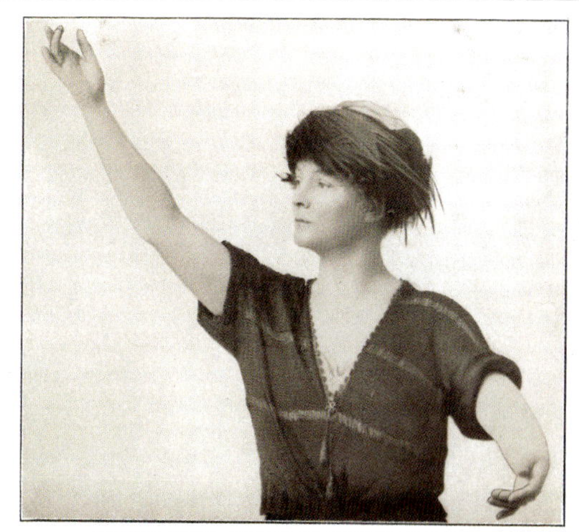

MOVING DOWN FROM THE FOURTH POSITION.

When moving down from one position to another care should be taken to always move them downwards first to bras bas and then up again through demi bras into the required position. In the above photograph it is shown how they should commence to move downwards from the fourth position.

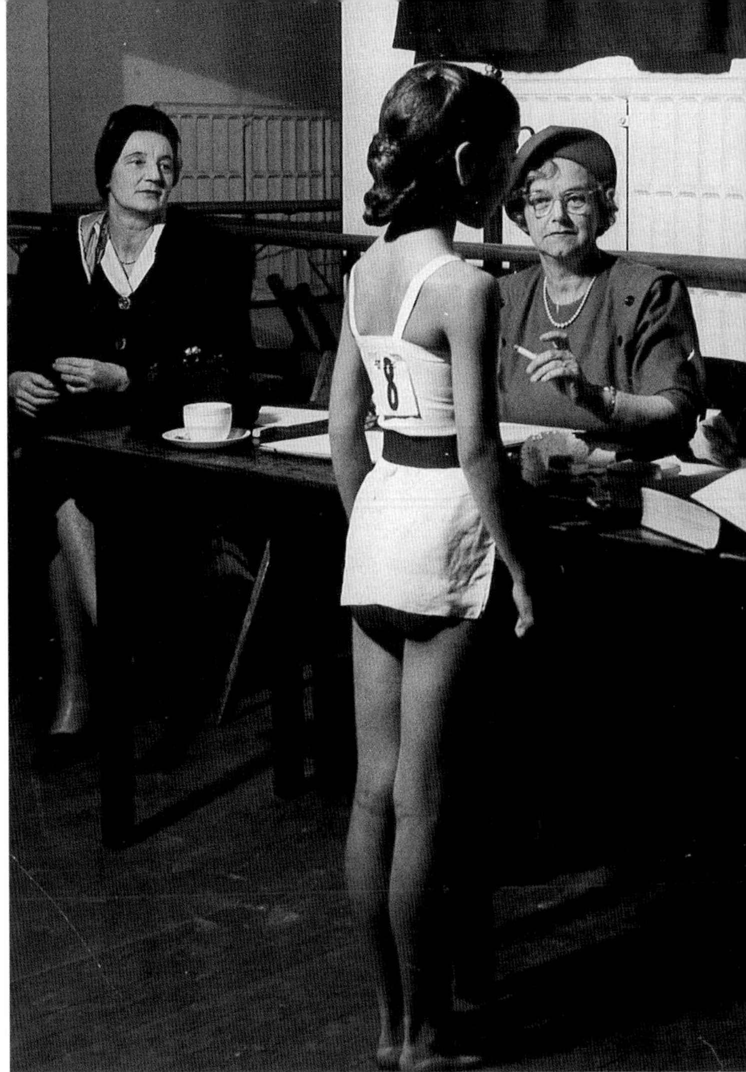

agreed on a set of five arm positions, illustrated in the same edition with a series of photographs of Genée herself, 'so that candidates will not be hopelessly confused'.

This did not prevent more disappointments in Elementary examinations held in spring that year. The judges' markings, in most instances, showed low marks or no marks at all in barre work, and yet good marks in steps. 'This is all wrong!' an exasperated Espinosa wrote in the examiner's report. 'The point to look for is many good marks in side practice and elementary adage and arms, the rest is less important.' Even those candidates who managed to perform certain steps well were, he said, 'quite at sea in executing the easier *enchaînements* given them'.

An Intermediate syllabus was introduced in 1922. As with the Elementary syllabus, it was printed in *The Dancing Times* so that everyone knew what was expected. The candidates for the Intermediate examination, having already passed the Elementary, fared much better than the Elementary candidates: writing in *The Dancing Times*, Espinosa commented that their 'carriage, dress, style, appearance and work were all to be praised'. The following year an Advanced syllabus was set out as the next stage in a dance teacher's development, but it was evidently so daunting that it had to be simplified six months later. By 1928, however, there were enough candidates with sufficient performance ability to justify the introduction of an additional 'solo examination' – a forerunner of the Solo Seal.

Membership of the Association grew steadily and by 1923, having ensured a standard for dance teachers, the committee turned its attention to what members should teach their pupils. A syllabus was designed with the needs of the majority of the members' pupils in mind, the 'one-lesson-a-week' child. These children were not destined to be professional dancers but could, nonetheless, progress through four graded examinations. The syllabus was intended to give pupils an incentive to work upon correct lines, while at the same time providing a focus for the teacher and evidence for parents of their child's progress.

The children's examinations were immediately successful. More than 600 pupils entered for the first sessions held in London and the regions to show that they knew the four foot positions, how to bend their knees in first and second position, how to 'walk on their toes' and demonstrate the Greek Walk, Mercury and Bacchante balance, and form 'athletic, sorrowful and joyous' friezes. By 1930 that figure had risen to more than 3,000 and a fifth grade had been added to link Grade 4 with the Elementary examination, which only the most talented students would be able to enter.

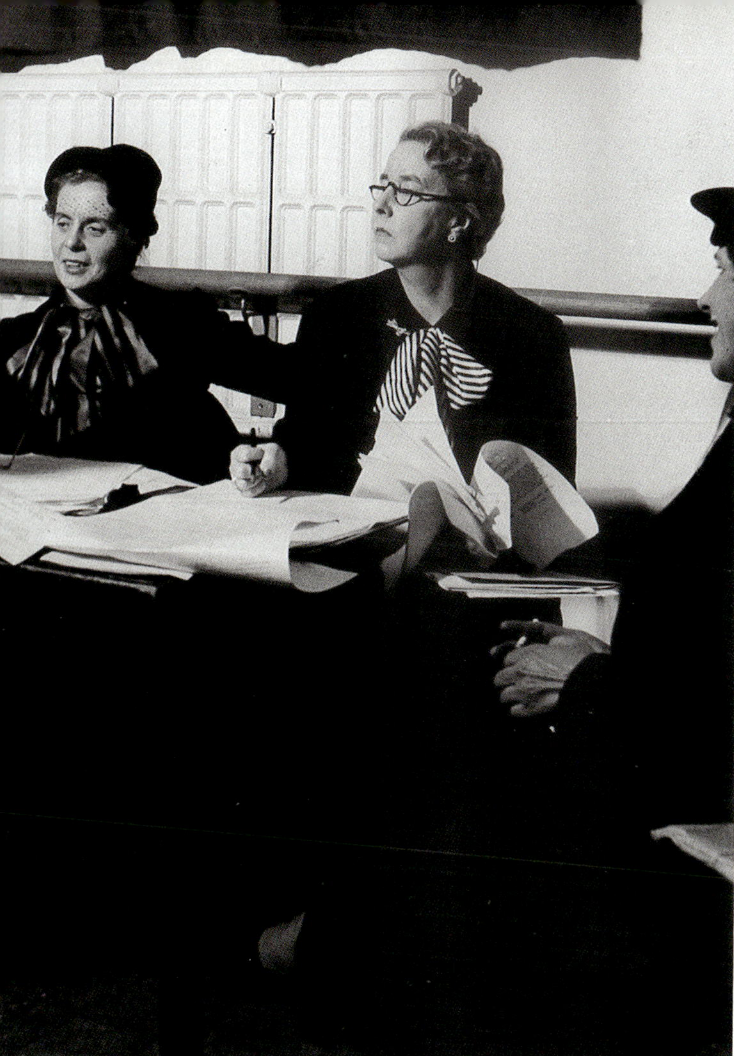

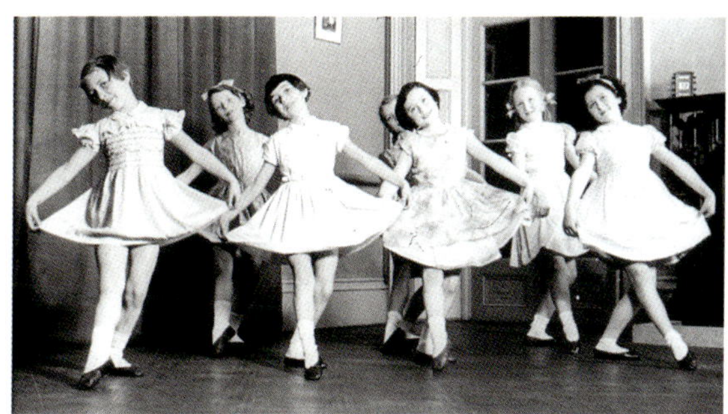

Demonstrations for the Ballet in Education syllabus. In the 'step and point' exercise (top) for Primary Grade, children begin to balance on one leg. Grade 2 children use mime (centre) to express a moment in the story of Cinderella, while Grade 4 pupils (bottom) demonstrate Character with the Friss step from the Hungarian Czardas.

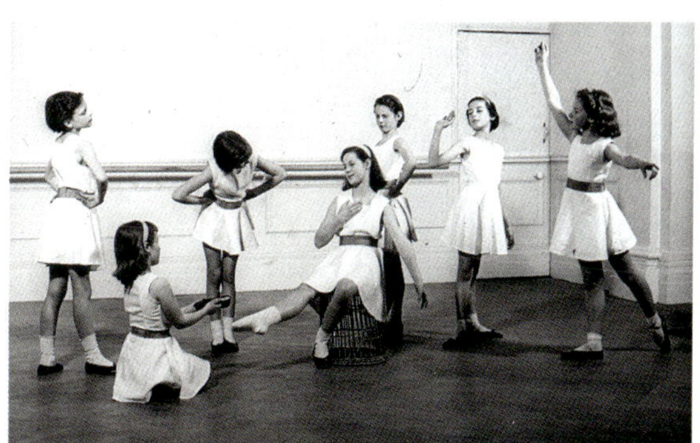

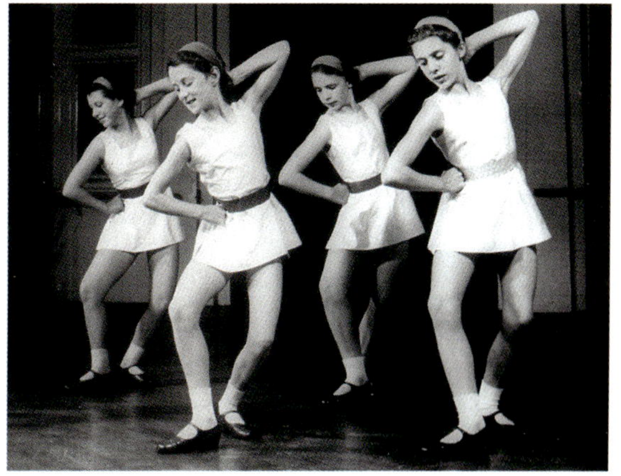

CHANGING SYLLABI

As teaching practices have changed over years, so the Academy's syllabi have changed with them. A new children's syllabus was announced in 1946. Known as 'Ballet in Education', the syllabus was intended to bring the teaching of ballet in line with modern educational development. It was designed to provide boys as well as girls with a basic vocabulary of steps, while encouraging self-expression and musicality in performance, and included an element of mime as well as national and historical dances, which allowed links to be made with the teaching of geography, history and art.

The 'Ballet in Education' syllabus was revised several times before it was replaced in 1968 by a new Children's syllabus, promoted by Dame

ARABESQUE, 1952
Patricia Ashworth
demonstrates an *arabesque*
for audition judges seated at
the table: Phyllis Bedells (left)
and Ninette de Valois (right).

AT THE BARRE, 1952
Candidates for the Major
examinations performing an
attitude à terre at the barre
watched by RAD examiners
Phyllis Bedells (left) and
Adeline Genée (right).

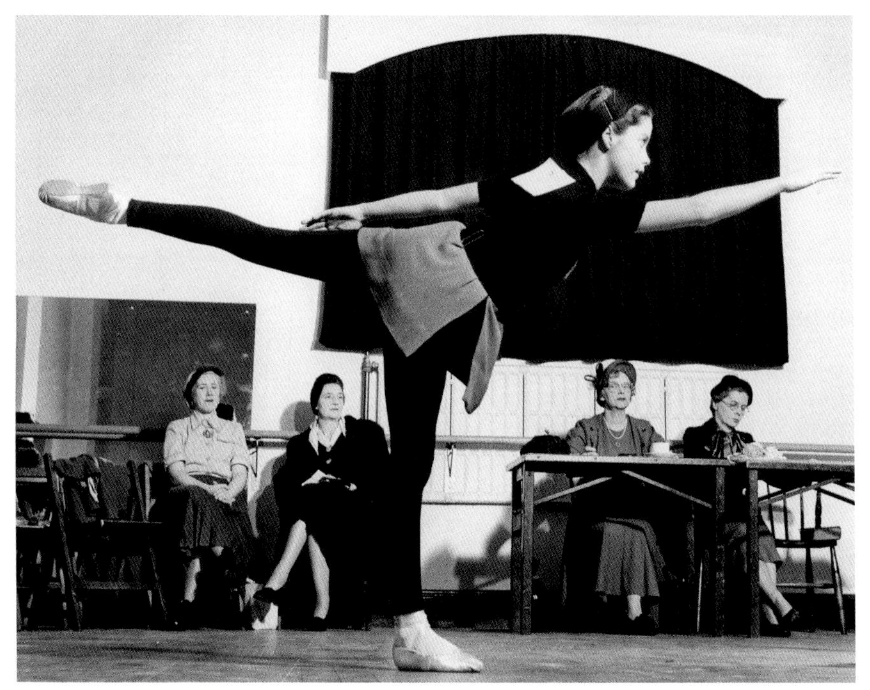

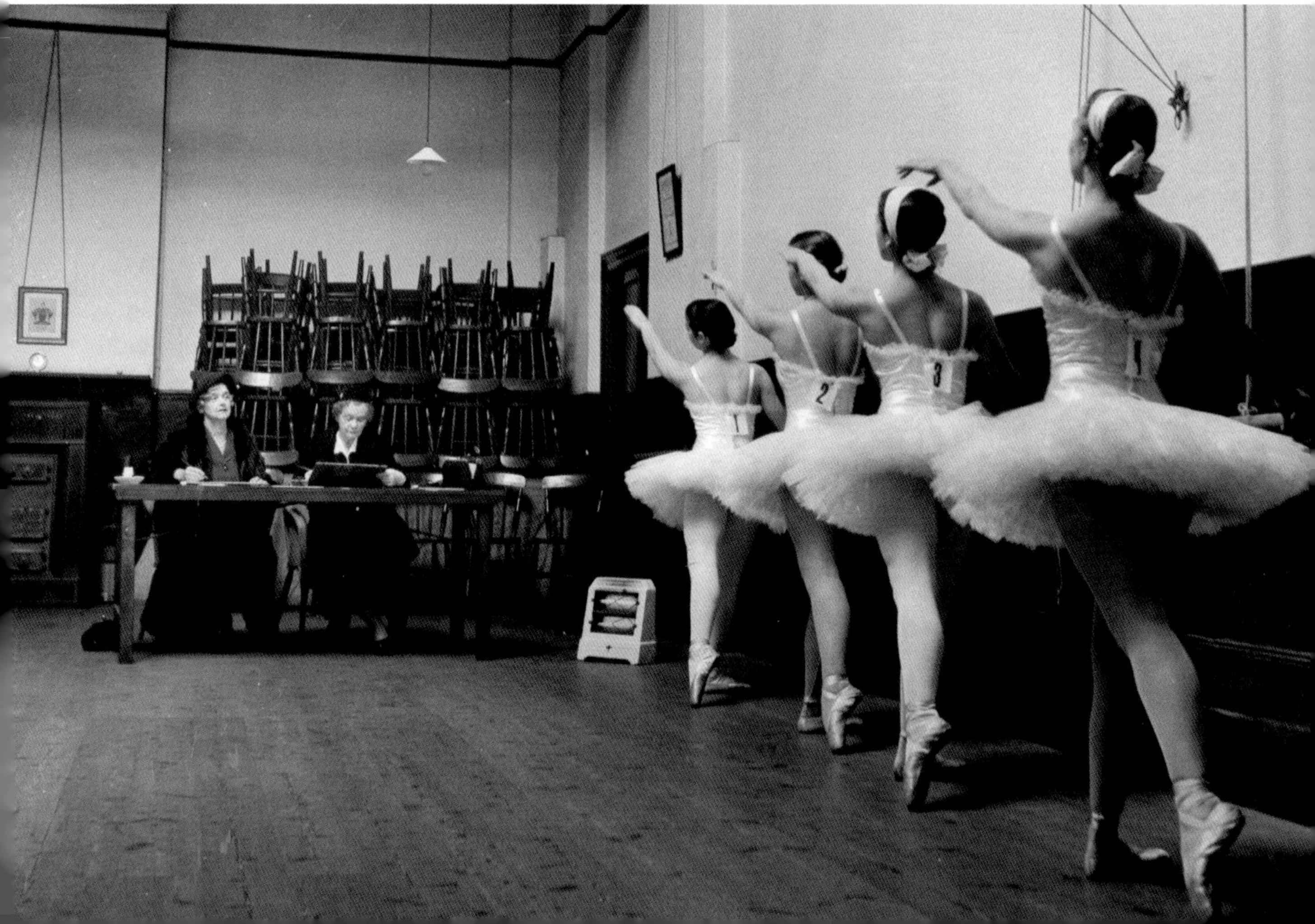

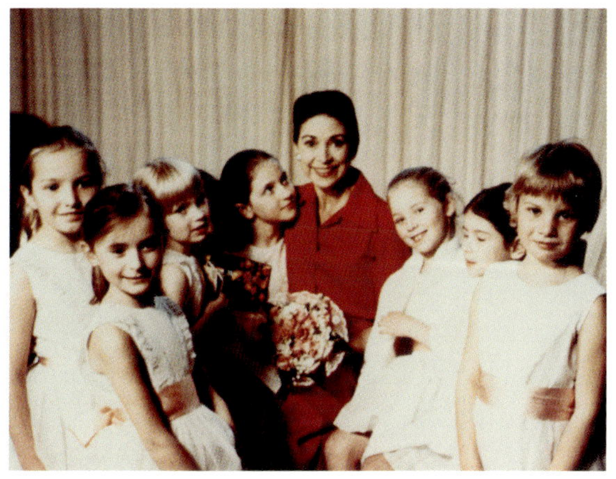

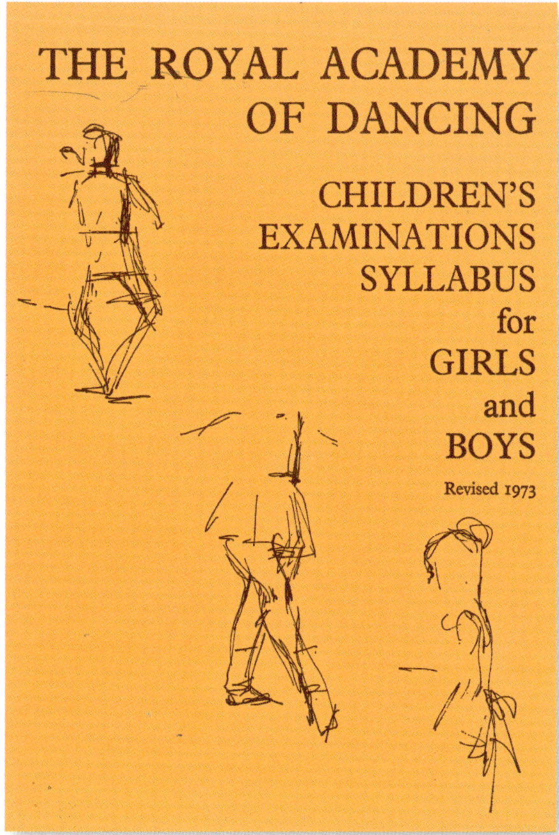

Margot Fonteyn, then President of the RAD, and often referred to as the 'Fonteyn syllabus'. The new syllabus was designed to meet the needs of all children (to the age of 12) attending dancing class once or twice a week, while also providing a sound preparation for those who were planning to progress to serious ballet training from the age of nine.

The new work abolished unnecessary attention to technical details that had characterised 'Ballet in Education' and concentrated instead on the essentials of position and placement. Historical deportment and mimes were removed, while national dances were maintained. Age limits were streamlined and the pass mark lowered in order to 'help children and encourage their dancing, not to make them fail'. In her foreword to the revised edition of the syllabus in 1973, Fonteyn emphasised the importance of encouraging the spirit of dancing, which, she wrote, 'should be freely felt as enjoyment of movement and its use to express story or character'.

Over the next 20 years additional grades and levels were added, until in 1991 the Fonteyn syllabus was replaced by the New Grades syllabus, which offered a fresh approach with an emphasis on dance and the joy of movement. For the first time 'Free Movement' was introduced to help encourage musicality and a 'natural' feeling for movement outside the confines of ballet technique. National and Character dances were maintained. The training exercises in the New Grades syllabus helped teachers to concentrate on essential parts of the technique.

By the end of the twentieth century, however, it was felt that the RAD syllabus should offer even greater opportunities for individual creativity, artistry and enjoyment. The Artistic Director, Lynn Wallis, proposed a complete overhaul of the syllabus. A Creative Panel was set up to design an entirely

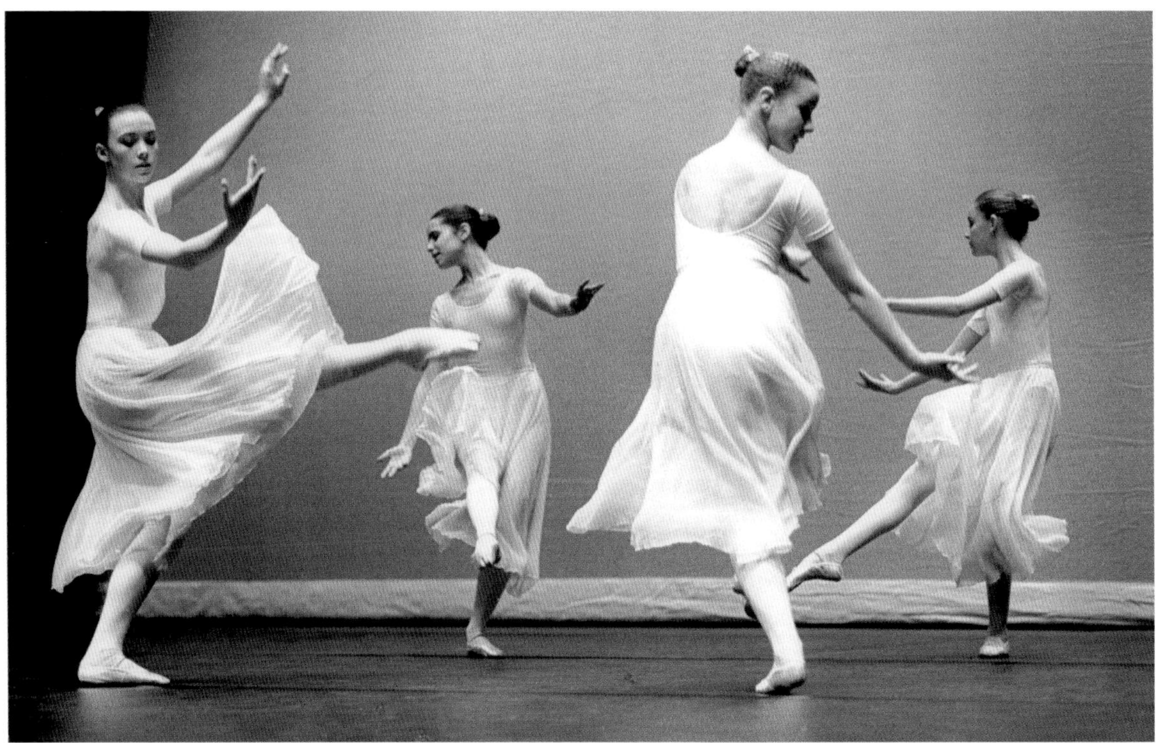

new syllabus for the new millennium, including
Wallis, Paula Hunt (Chair of the Panel of
Examiners), Jonathan Still (Music Development
Manager) and other experienced teachers. Their aim
was to design a syllabus that would not only be
'educationally sound, internationally relevant and
attractive to both teachers and students', but one
that would also align with the requirements of the
National Qualifications Framework (NQF), on
which the Academy's exams were placed in 2001,
and the proposed move towards a mandatory
Continuing Professional Development (CPD)
scheme for RAD teachers. A new marking and
grading system was also introduced, to comply
with NQF requirements and to address concerns
about inconsistency.

Dance To Your Own Tune, a dance curriculum
for pre-school children, was first launched in 2003,
followed by Pre-Primary in Dance and Primary in
Dance in 2009. Aware that its members were looking for a commercially viable package that would
appeal to children, teachers and parents alike, the
Creative Panel ensured that the content of the new
foundation syllabi was fresh and fun, embracing
children's curiosity and their natural desire to move,
and providing them with opportunities to develop
their physical skills, stamina, creativity, expression
and musicality. These syllabi promoted the idea
that children at the early stages of learning dance
should be 'feeling the movement' rather than simply
dancing the steps. This emphasis on creativity and
on 'feeling before form' typified the syllabi that were

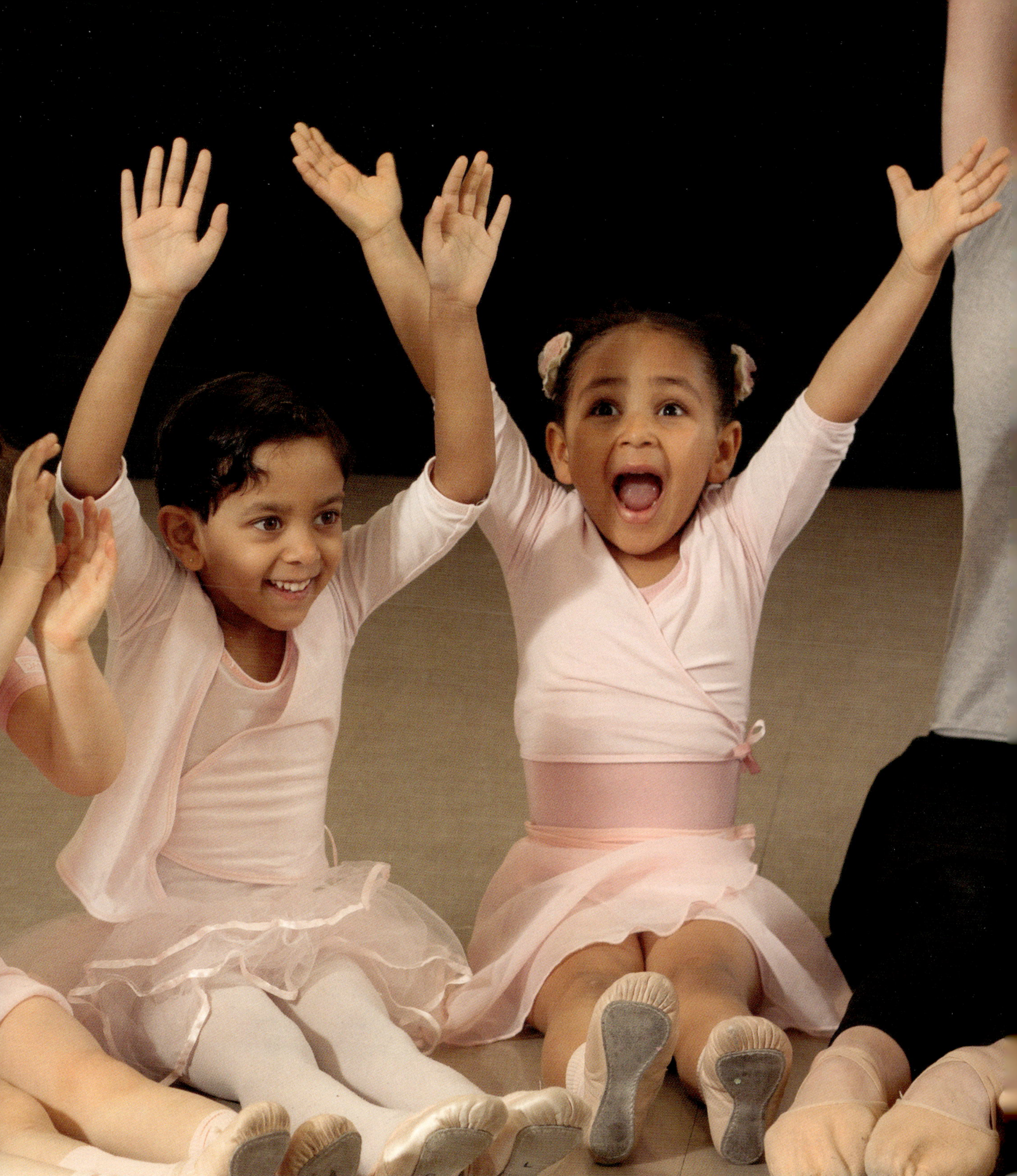

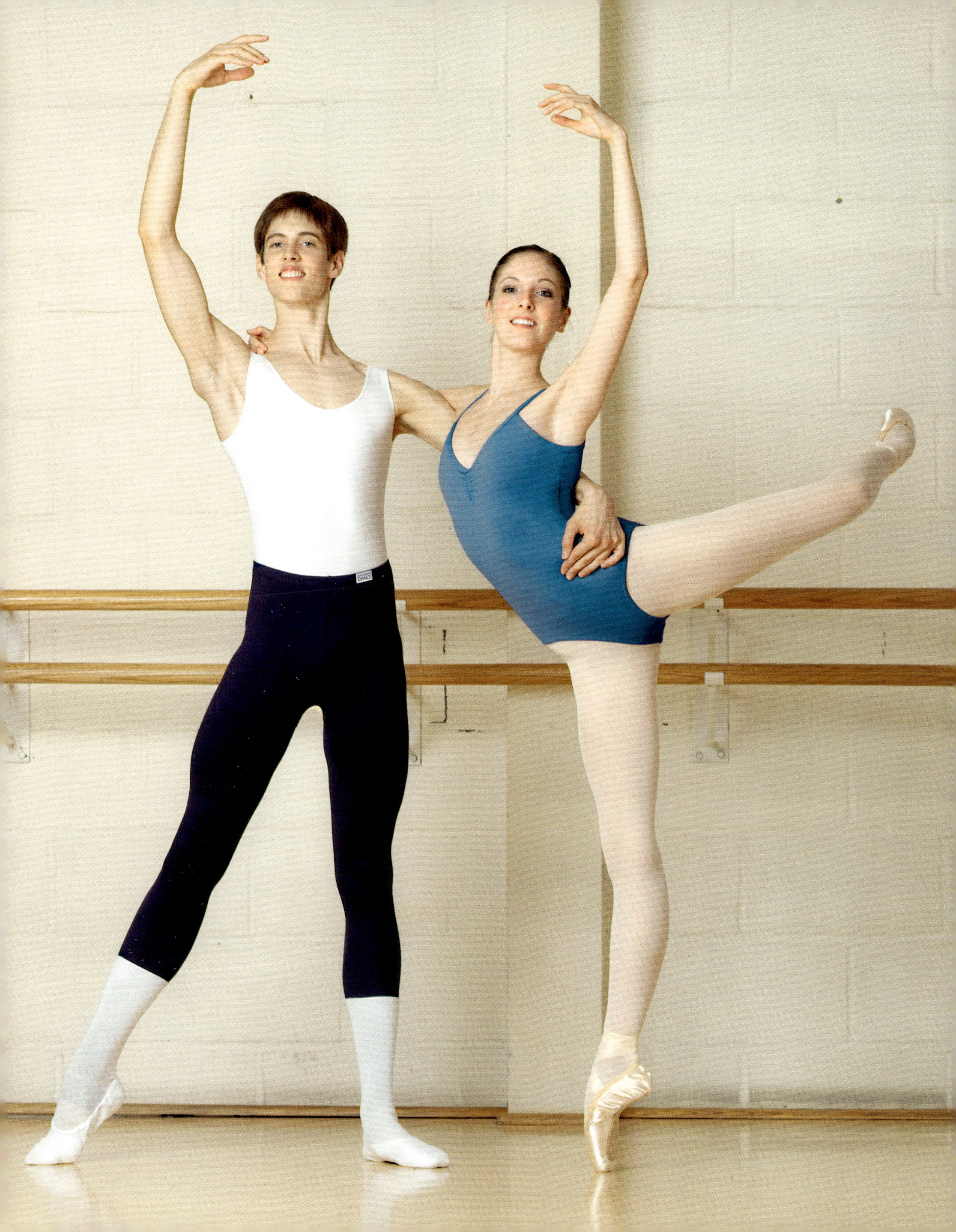

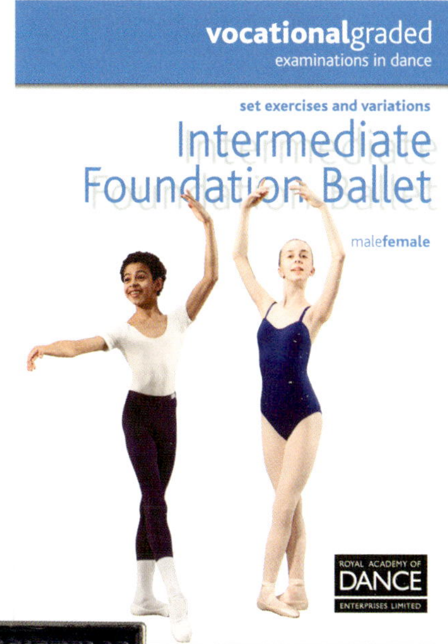

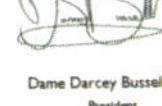
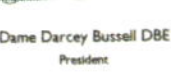
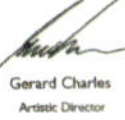
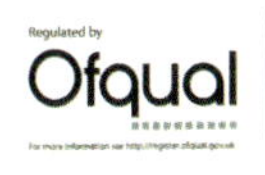

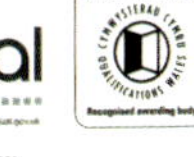

ROYAL ACADEMY OF DANCE

RAD Level 1 Award in Graded Examination in Dance: Grade 2 (Ballet)

Carrie Revere

DISTINCTION

Date of Examination : 23/04/2019

Date of Award : 03/06/2019

The candidate has been awarded 7 credits
Unit: Graded Examination in Ballet: Grade 2
European Qualifications Framework Level 2

Dame Darcey Bussell DBE
President

Luke Rittner CBE
Chief Executive

Gerard Charles
Artistic Director

Regulated by
Ofqual

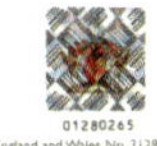

developed over the next few years across the range of grades and levels, from Pre-Primary in Dance, through the Graded and Vocational Graded syllabi, to Solo Seal. The Creative Panel wanted learning dance to be enjoyable while at the same time maintaining the rigorous standards for which the RAD had been noted since its foundation.

Today the Academy continues to support the highest standards in performance through its syllabi and examinations, culminating in its highest award, the Solo Seal. The format of the Solo Seal Award dates back to 1928. A candidate had to have already passed the Advanced Examination and would dance 'a purely operatic solo arranged by herself to music of her own selection' as well as a character or demi-character dance and an impromptu variation set by the judges. Candidates for the Solo Seal today are assessed in front of not only the examiner and an external judge but also a small

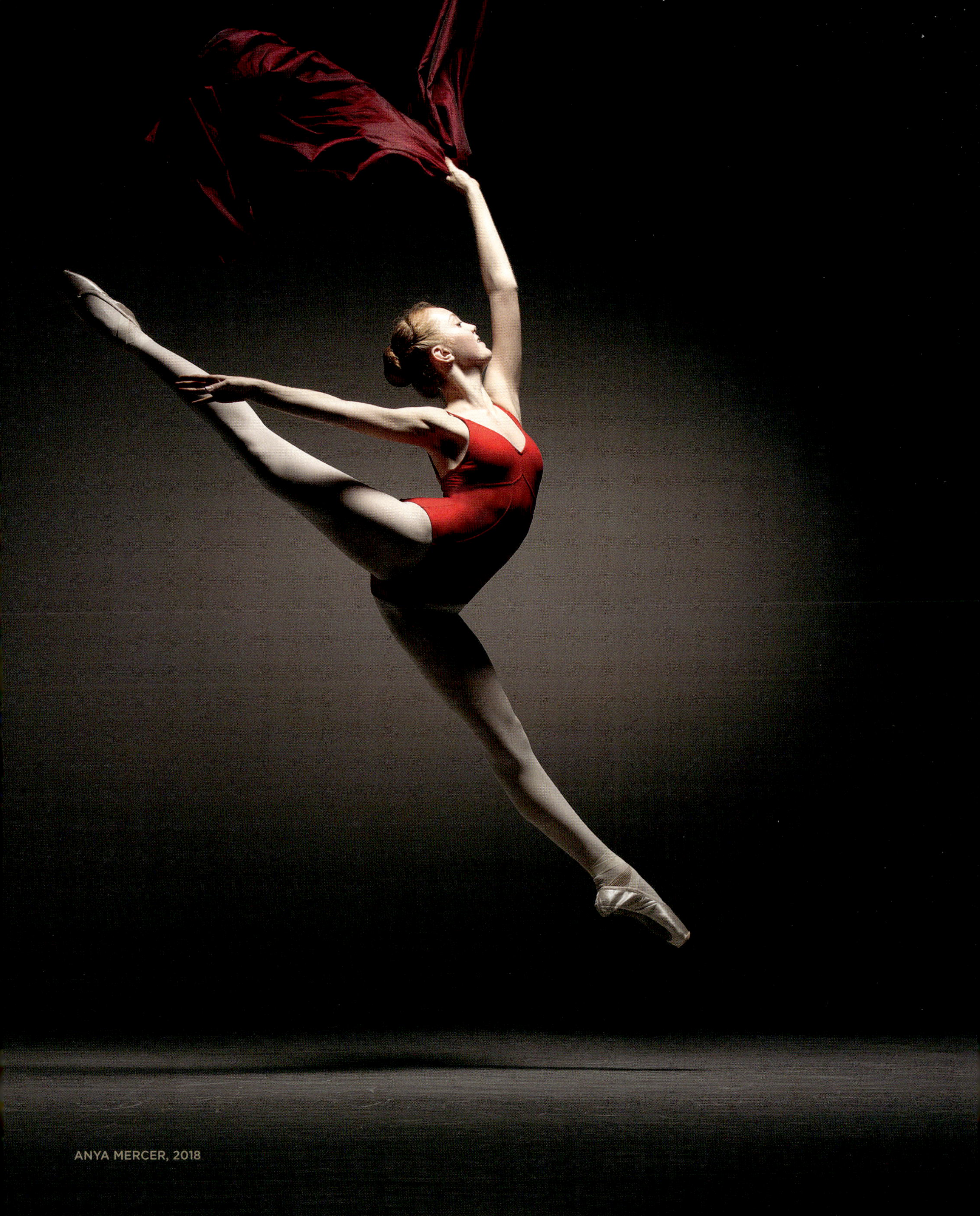
ANYA MERCER, 2018

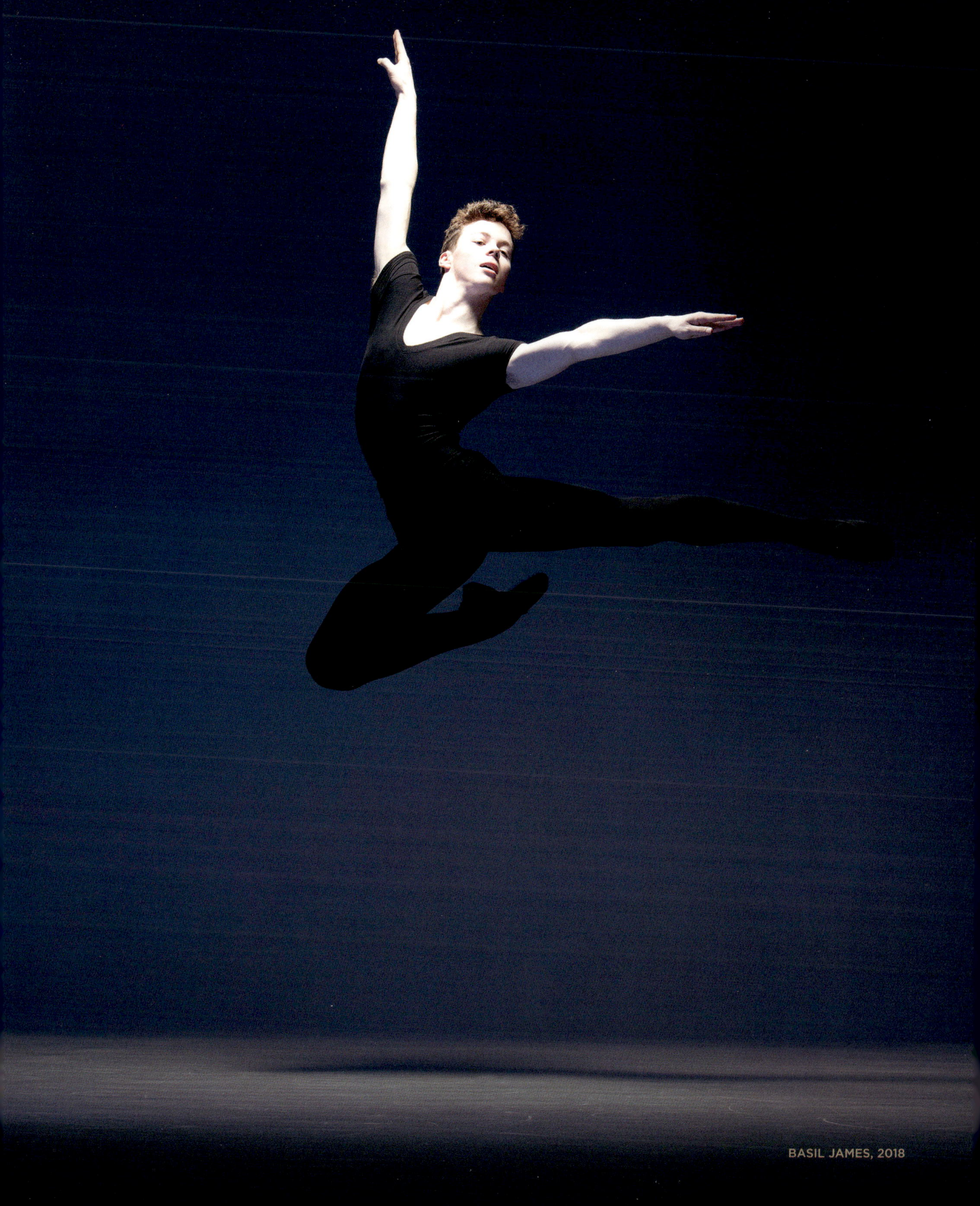
BASIL JAMES, 2018

audience, which may include members, students and relatives.

The process for creating each syllabus has been long and complex, beginning with the careful selection of dance vocabulary and choice of music for each level. The choreography or 'settings' followed. In recent decades these elements were trialled by teachers around the world, with feedback taken into account before the final package was developed using the latest technologies. This involved filming the content for a DVD, recording the music, writing notes and providing Benesh Movement Notation, as well as working with other departments in the RAD such as Marketing and IT, who set up the technology for the successful virtual launch of the new Advanced syllabi in 2013. A host of individuals contributed to the landmark syllabus renewal project: creative panels; trial teachers; musicians and filmmakers; choreographers; students at the Elmhurst School of Dance, who tested out the new syllabus; the young dancers from Wellington Dance in New Zealand, who worked closely with the creative team; and many others.

The syllabus project as a whole marked a milestone in achievement for the world of dance and for the RAD in particular. As Andrew McBirnie, Director of Examinations, commented in 2014, it has enabled the Academy to 'lead the way in defining the standards and expectations of ballet education globally' and to create a cultural heritage of dance that continues to evolve and reflect the vision of its founders a hundred years ago.

More recently, a different kind of performance programme was launched. Since 2017 Discovering Repertoire has offered an imaginative addition to the RAD's examination opportunities and gives students the opportunity to learn and to dance extracts from well-known ballets such as *Swan Lake*, *The Sleeping Beauty* and *Giselle*.

EXAMS AND EXAMINERS

Each year nearly a quarter of a million candidates around the world take an RAD examination. Great care is taken to ensure that the experience is the same for every candidate, no matter who or where they are, so an RAD examination can only take place in two kinds of venues: an Approved Examination Centre, which is provided by a teacher entering candidates, or at a venue run and provided by the RAD.

The very first RAD examinations were held in May 1921 at the studio of Lucia Cormani, one of the founders of the Association of Teachers of Operatic Dancing, as the RAD was then known. The work was set by Edouard Espinosa and judged by the rest of the committee: Adeline Genée, Tamara Karsavina, Lucia Cormani and Phyllis Bedells. As some of the most celebrated dancers of the day, they must have been a daunting panel for those first candidates.

The day began at 9.30am and lasted until 5.00pm and numbers were so great that there were 42 entries in a day, with the four judges and Espinosa, all numbered back and front. Many of the teachers taking the examination were, as Bedells tactfully put it, 'no longer really young' but were 'willing to undergo the ordeal' and wore the regulation ballet skirts, boned bodices, pink tights and shoes. Although the examination was not particularly demanding, some candidates struggled with balance and several actually fell over. After the second examination in 1921, Espinosa was blunt about those teachers 'of more mature years' who insisted on entering the examinations in the hope that their knowledge of theory would be enough to get them through. Unless they could also perform the exercises accurately, he told them, they would not pass and should send up a junior assistant instead.

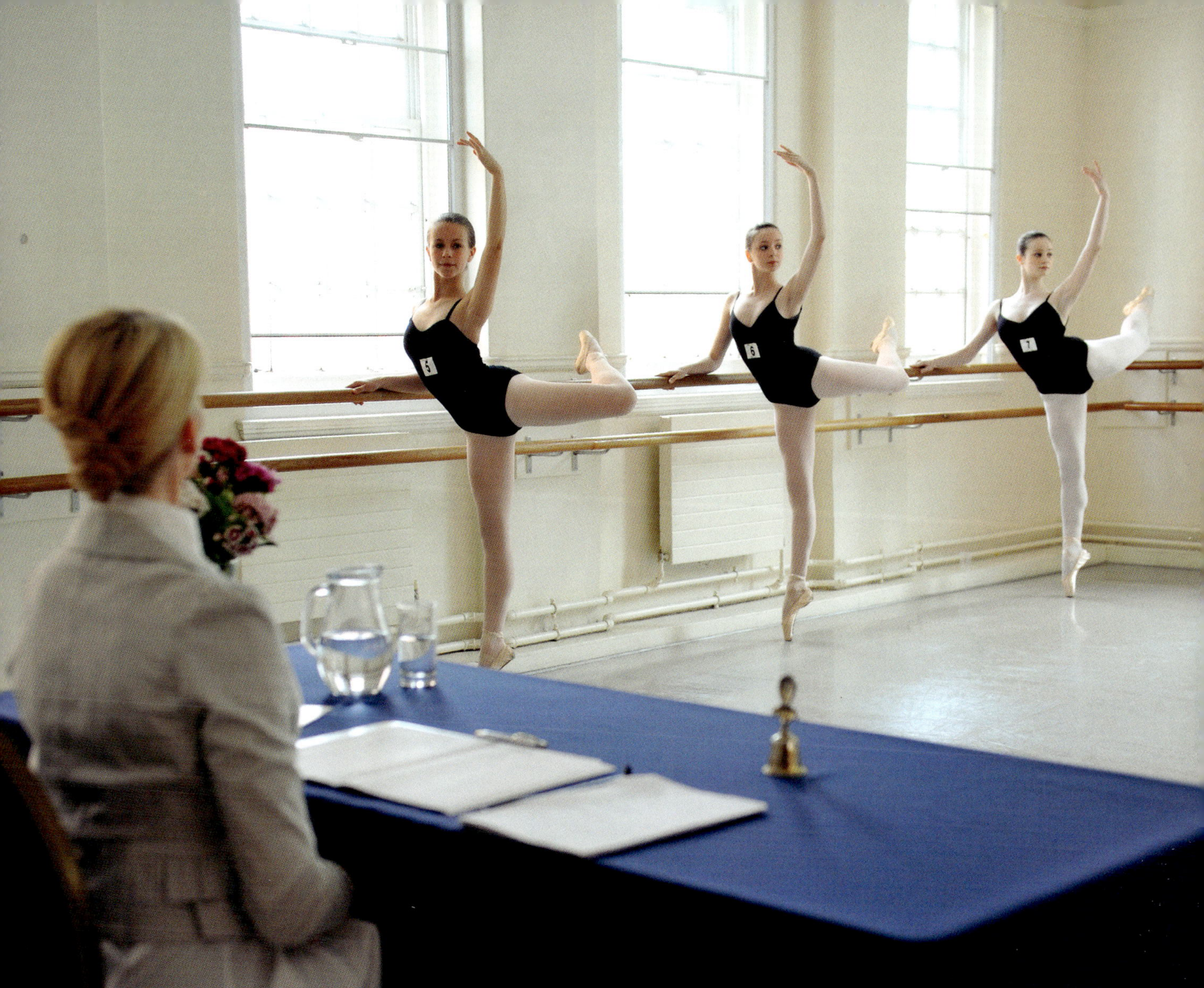

The early instructions seemed to have assumed that those entering the examinations would be female but there were male candidates, too, who objected to being told 'to wear pink tights and pink satin ballet shoes'. However, it was not until 1931 that specific arrangements were made for male candidates, who were to be examined together under a new system that allowed no more than four candidates to be examined at a time. At the same time, the committee acknowledged a growing male membership by proposing a free class for them, in addition to the existing classes for female members. In 1932 the information for candidates that was published in the *Operatic Association Gazette* in advance of the exams included for the first time a regulation dress for males: black woollen footless tights, white socks and a short-sleeved white shirt.

Today wherever an examination is taken, the room is set up as it has been for as long as anyone can remember. The examiner sits behind a table on which is placed a jug of water, a glass, and a bell used to summon the candidates. In earlier years a pianist was always present to accompany the candidates, but more recently many examinations are held using recorded music.

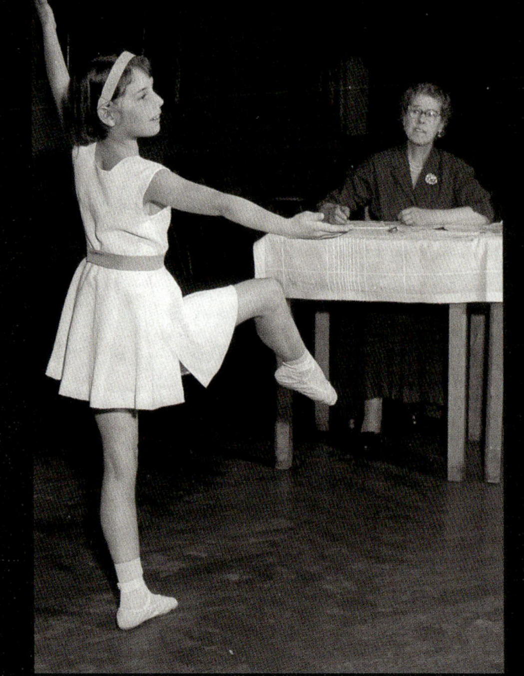

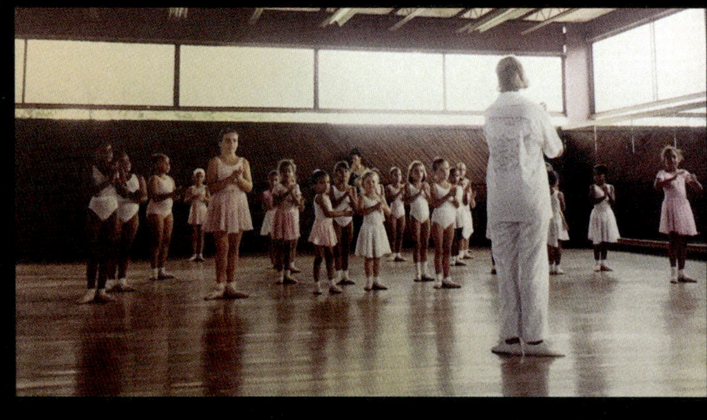

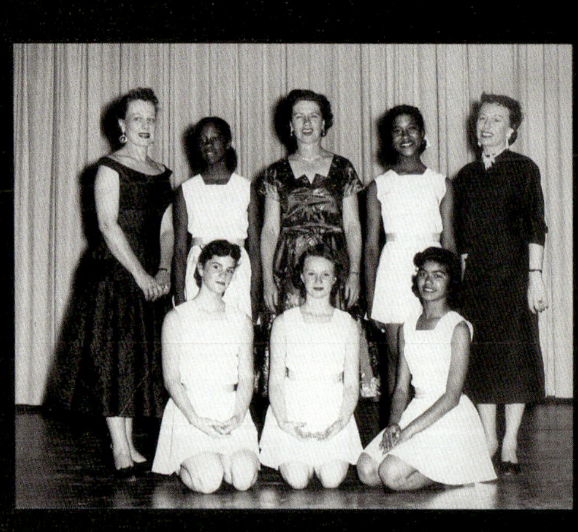

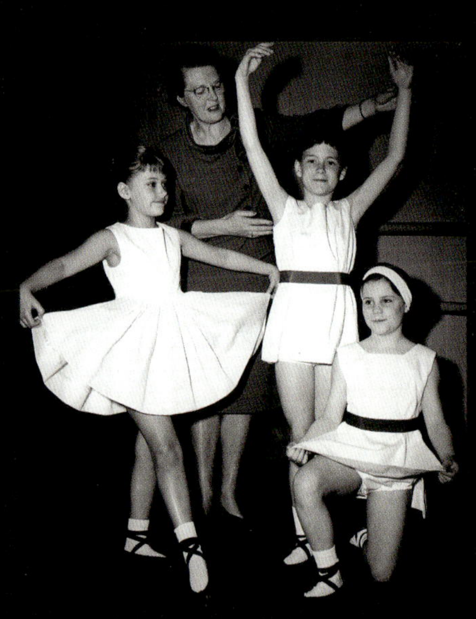

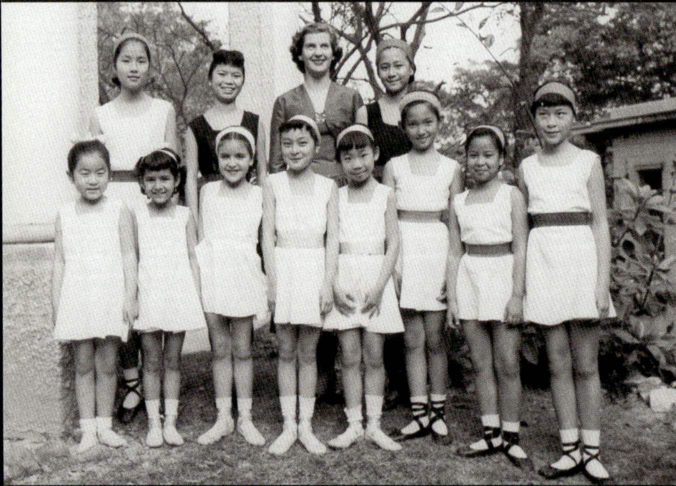

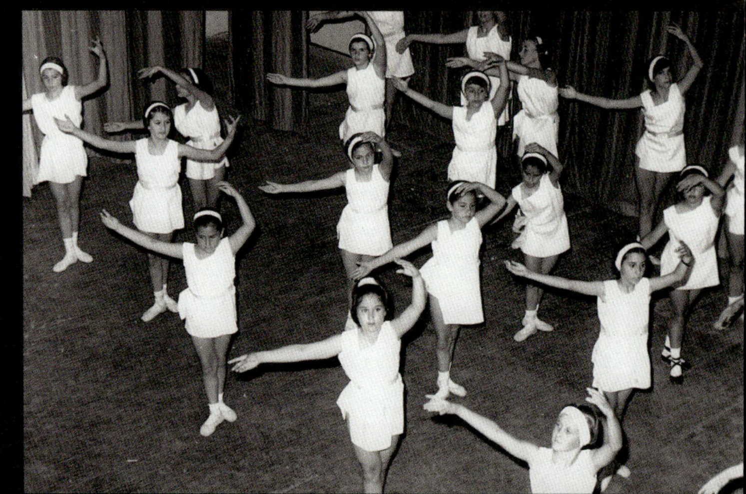

Although much has changed in the last one hundred years, a candidate's nerves are much as they always were. Jacqueline B'nay took her Elementary examination in 1938 and remembers:

I was absolutely terrified, because during the previous weeks rumours had been going around the school that if one was unfortunate enough to have Miss Grace Cone or Mr Felix Demery as examiners one did not have a hope of passing…. We were ushered into the studio, did our salutations and as I looked up there was Grace Cone and Felix Demery. I could have died on the spot. My legs turned to jelly as I walked to the barre, and I am sure I did a dreadful exam, and I think I was in total shock for hours after.

Happily, B'nay did pass but her sense of occasion will no doubt be familiar to many candidates today. Few of those taking an examination may realise, however, that examiners have to undergo a rigorous selection process of their own. Those wanting to be examiners for the RAD first submit an application with details of their experience, followed by an interview. If accepted, they take part in an intensive three-week training course, followed by a tour 'shadowing' an experienced examiner.

Almost from the outset, the Academy sent examiners overseas, often on gruelling trips to some very remote areas in countries such as South Africa, Australia, New Zealand and Canada, until these countries were able to appoint their own examiners. Edouard Espinosa travelled widely in the 1920s, as did Felix Demery in the 1930s. The work of both men was seminal in ensuring consistency of examining and raising standards of dance around the world.

Examiners continued to travel from the UK to Australia and New Zealand for many years. Visiting

International challenges

Even today, some exam venues can prove testing for the examiner as well as for the candidates. Audrey Nicholls, an Australian RAD examiner and tutor, sometimes found herself in some very isolated areas. An examination tour to a small dairy farming area in mid New South Wales did not go entirely to plan:

I arrived at the small airport manned by only one person to find the teacher not there to meet me. The one taxi had departed as I was the only passenger to arrive. The airport official was also a dairy farmer and had to leave for the 4pm milking. He gave me instructions of how to lock up the airport and told me not to answer the phone while I awaited the arrival of the tardy ballet teacher. The phone rang continuously. I finally answered 'Tarcutta Airport?' to hear a frantic mother of the ballet teacher needing to speak to a Miss Nicholls and explaining that her daughter had forgotten to collect me for the examinations and was now on her way to her other ballet school 50 miles away. If I could wait for one hour when their milking would be completed she, the mother, would collect me!

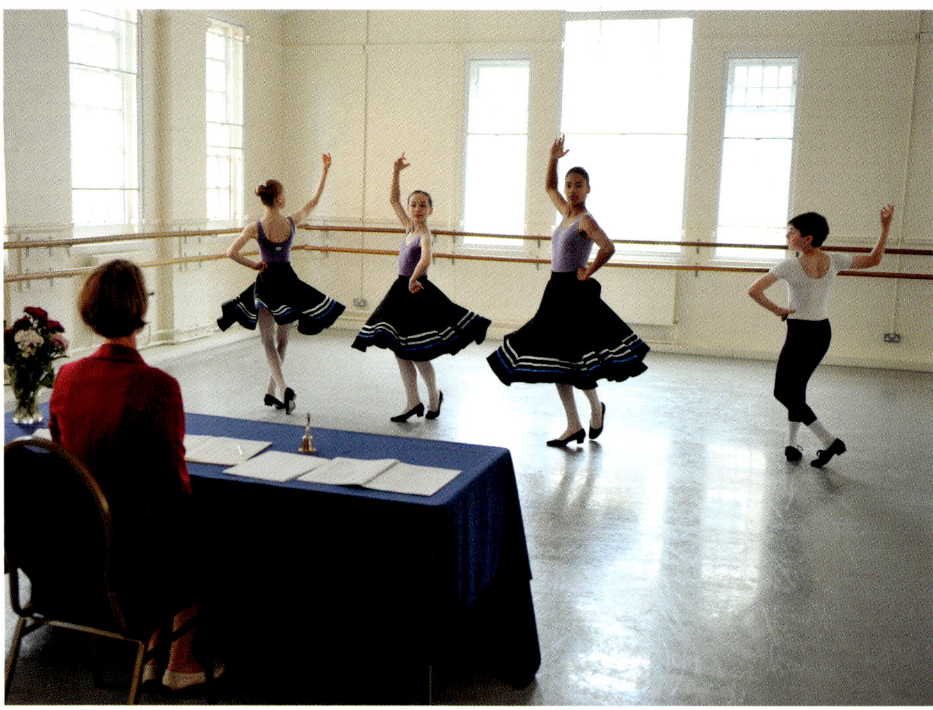

Canada in 1940, Adeline Genée wrote to the RAD in London and insisted that Kathleen Danetree should go out there and examine, regardless of the Blitz! In spite of the enormous difficulties of travelling at that time, Miss Danetree did indeed make it to Canada to conduct the first Royal Academy examinations there, and went on to New Zealand, Australia and eventually to South Africa. The work of the RAD overseas expanded hugely during the 1950s, and by 1960 exams were also being held in Mexico, the Caribbean, the USA, Belgium, the Netherlands, Norway, Germany, Italy, Malta, Malaysia, Singapore, India, Sri Lanka, Rhodesia (now Zimbabwe) and Hong Kong.

Many examiners still travel extensively, both within their own countries and internationally. There are currently about 230 examiners resident in over 25 countries, so the earlier pattern, which relied on sending out examiners from the UK, has long been superseded. The RAD examination model is a truly global one: examiners cover the world, examining dance to the same standard regardless of whether they are in Brazil or Japan, New Zealand or the Netherlands, the UK or Mexico.

Character dance

In the late 1950s the Hungarian dancer and teacher Maria Fay choreographed five solo national dances for the Children's syllabus of the time. At that time children were examined singly. Fonteyn retained two of these dances, with the addition of some new dances, for her syllabus in 1973. The Dance Education syllabus followed, for which Fay devised a Character section for each of the three Levels. From 1991 onwards the grade levels were gradually extended to Grade 8, which meant that the national dance work could be developed and expanded into Character dance (the theatrical presentation of national dances). Some of the styles chosen were Russian, Hungarian and Polish, which were the styles most often used in traditional productions of the classic ballets. Exercises and *enchaînements* were examined, as well as the solo dances. The exercises provided knowledge of the rudiments of music, essential for developing good rhythm. The use of mime and props was introduced in the dances, developing attributes necessary for stage performance. The current syllabus from Grades 1 to 5 has a choice of two new Character dances at each level, maintaining the overall aims of the previous syllabus and giving candidates an opportunity to experience the joy of dance.

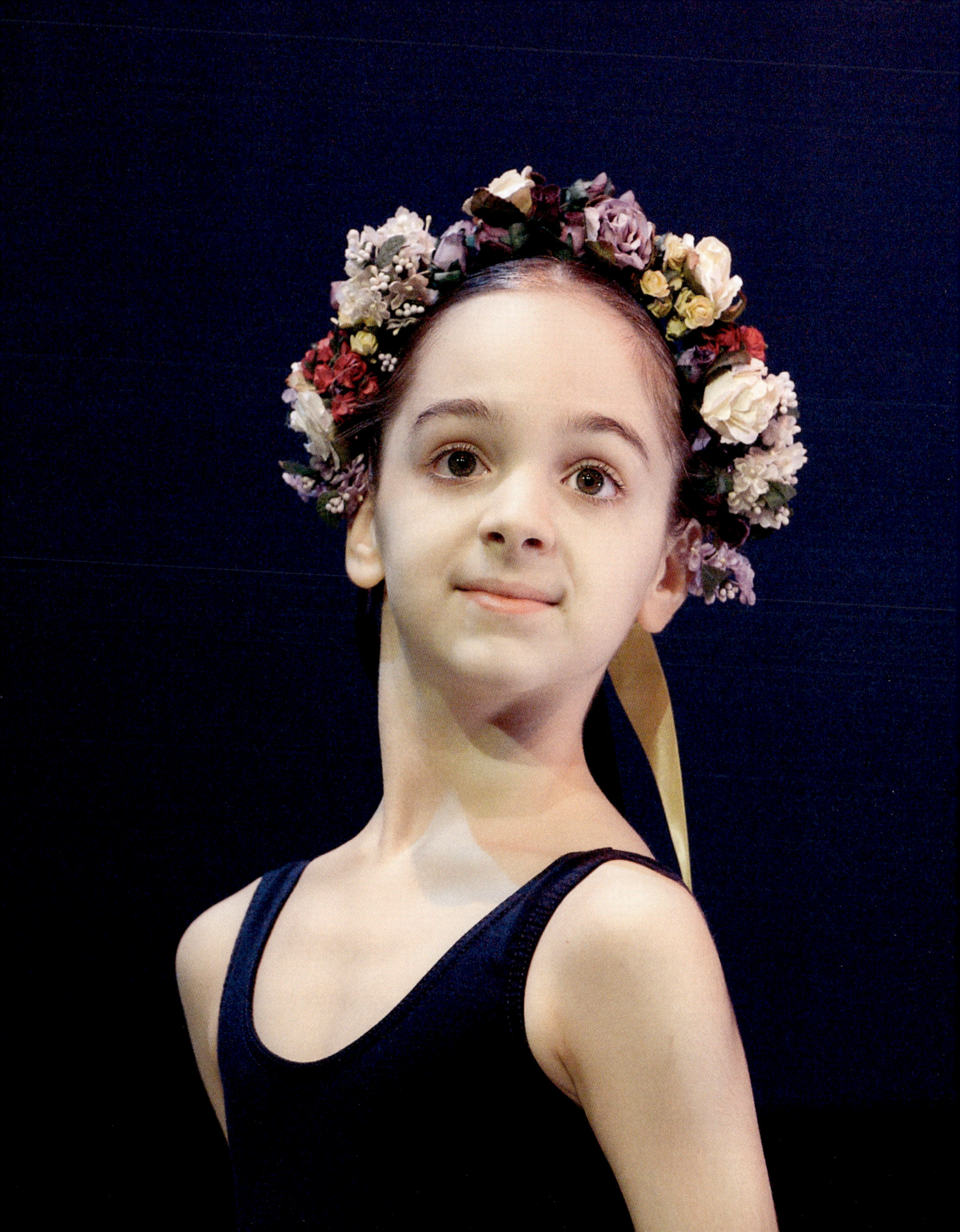

MUSIC

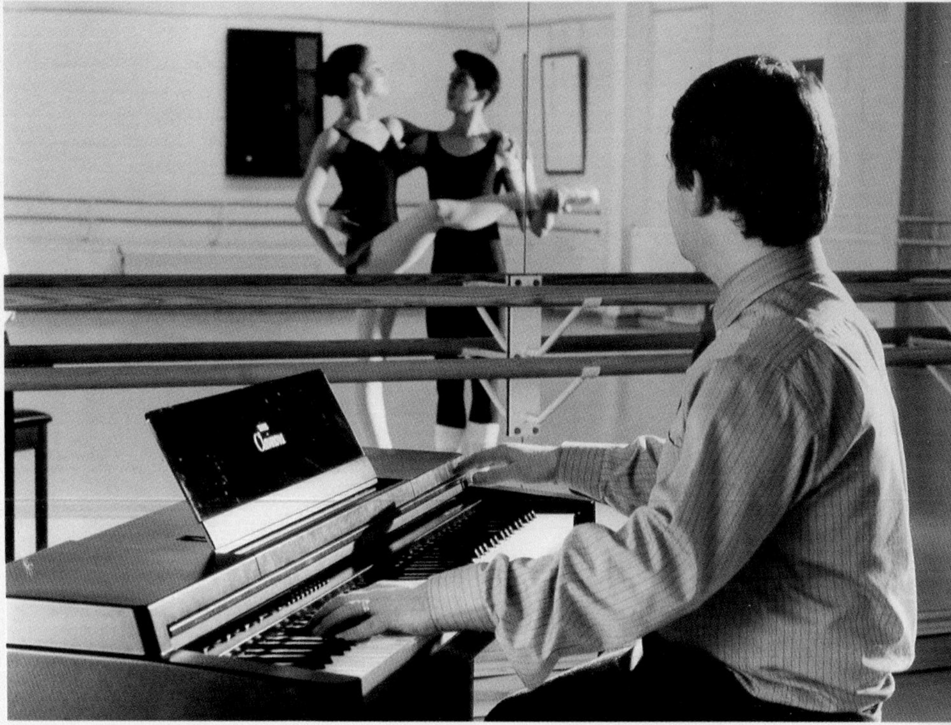

ELECTRIC PIANO, 1991
Mike Concah playing the Yamaha Clavinova with Clair Thomas and Justin Meissner in the mirror reflection. Thomas and Meissner were gold medal winners at the 1991 Genée competition. At Assembly in 1991 it was announced that the Academy would allow the use of digital pianos for examinations (the Clavinova was the recommended model).

THE musical conventions of the ballet class can be traced back over 200 years and, in many respects, have not changed substantially in that time. For many dancers the sound of the piano is inextricably entwined with the experience of a ballet class and the ways in which a teacher conveys rhythm, tempo and style when marking exercises. While vocational schools and ballet companies still commonly use live music, today many dance teachers around the world opt for recorded music in their classes, often because good musicians are unavailable or unaffordable. Live or recorded, music continues to play a key role in inspiring and motivating dancers.

When the Royal Academy of Dance was founded, people had to create more of their own amusements than they do today. At the time it was common for women of the more leisured classes to learn to play the piano as a social skill to entertain at gatherings in the home. Although many women and men also worked as professional musicians, dance teachers in the early years of the Academy may well have called on friends or family of students to play for local dance classes, perhaps as a favour or for a modest payment.

Gradually, however, the cost of live music increased as music students or professional musicians replaced the amateur pianists who had been the mainstay of those early dance classes. Regardless of who was playing, from its inception the Academy has emphasised the importance of providing musical materials for pianists. As a result, generations of pianists around the world have learned what it means to play for ballet from RAD publications, and continue to do so today.

Over the years a number of different approaches have been taken to the sourcing of music for the Academy's examination syllabus. In the early days, extracts from the classical repertoire were selected by Caroline Bedells, mother of the Academy's English founder Phyllis Bedells, and then adapted to suit the exercises concerned. The idea of selecting and adapting music from the existing repertoire was repeated later in the 1960s for the Fonteyn syllabus, when much of the music was personally chosen by the then President, Margot Fonteyn.

Professional composers have also been engaged from time to time: Thomas Pitfield, who specialised in small-scale works; Leighton Lucas (himself a dancer with Diaghilev's Ballets Russes), who had success with concert works as well as film scores, working with the likes of Alfred Hitchcock; and John Lanchbery, composer for the ballet *The Tales of Beatrix Potter*. Many of the Academy's own pianists have had the opportunity for their music to be published by the RAD for use in classes and examinations, thus giving their compositions the potential of being performed all over the world – surely the dream of any composer!

For a century now, music for examinations has cycled between bespoke improvisations, the classical repertoire,

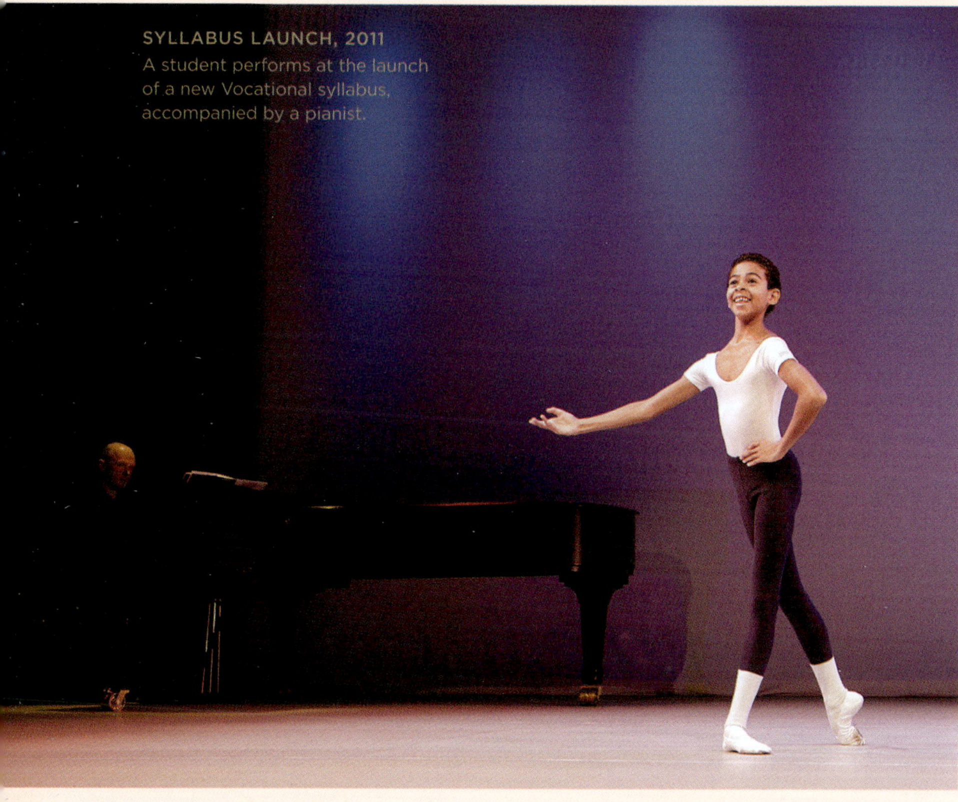

new compositions and the concert repertoire, between music that 'tells you what to do' in an exercise and music that celebrates and refers to the musical world of the ballet stage.

With the full-scale review and development of the RAD's syllabi, including the Dance To Your Own Tune curriculum, Pre-Primary in Dance and Primary in Dance, and Graded and Vocational Graded syllabi from 2003 to 2014, the musical resources developed in unprecedented new directions under music development manager Jonathan Still and producer Andrew Holdsworth.

Music of many different styles and periods was arranged for small instrumental ensembles rather than only solo piano, including for the first time the human voice in a song by Schubert, and the Welsh lullaby *Suo Gân*. Character dance expert Valerie Sunderland directed the production of a CD of music for Character work from Russia, Hungary and Ukraine using a specially formed folk group. But most adventurous of all was the collaboration with the English National Ballet Philharmonic, conducted by Gavin Sutherland, to produce custom-made recordings for Grades 1 to 5, the Vocational Graded syllabus and the Discovering Repertoire programme, which included some of the greatest classics of the ballet repertoire. To have such extracts specially tailored – with suitable introductions, at the right length, and the right speed for dancing – and played by a leading ballet orchestra and conductor, is a luxury the original founders of the Academy could scarcely have imagined.

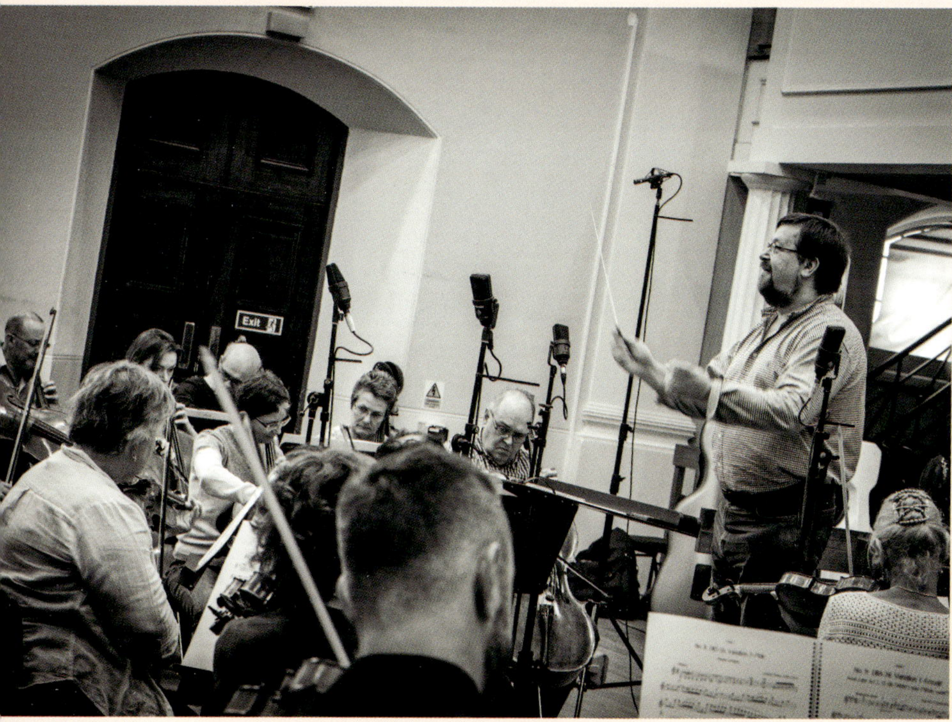

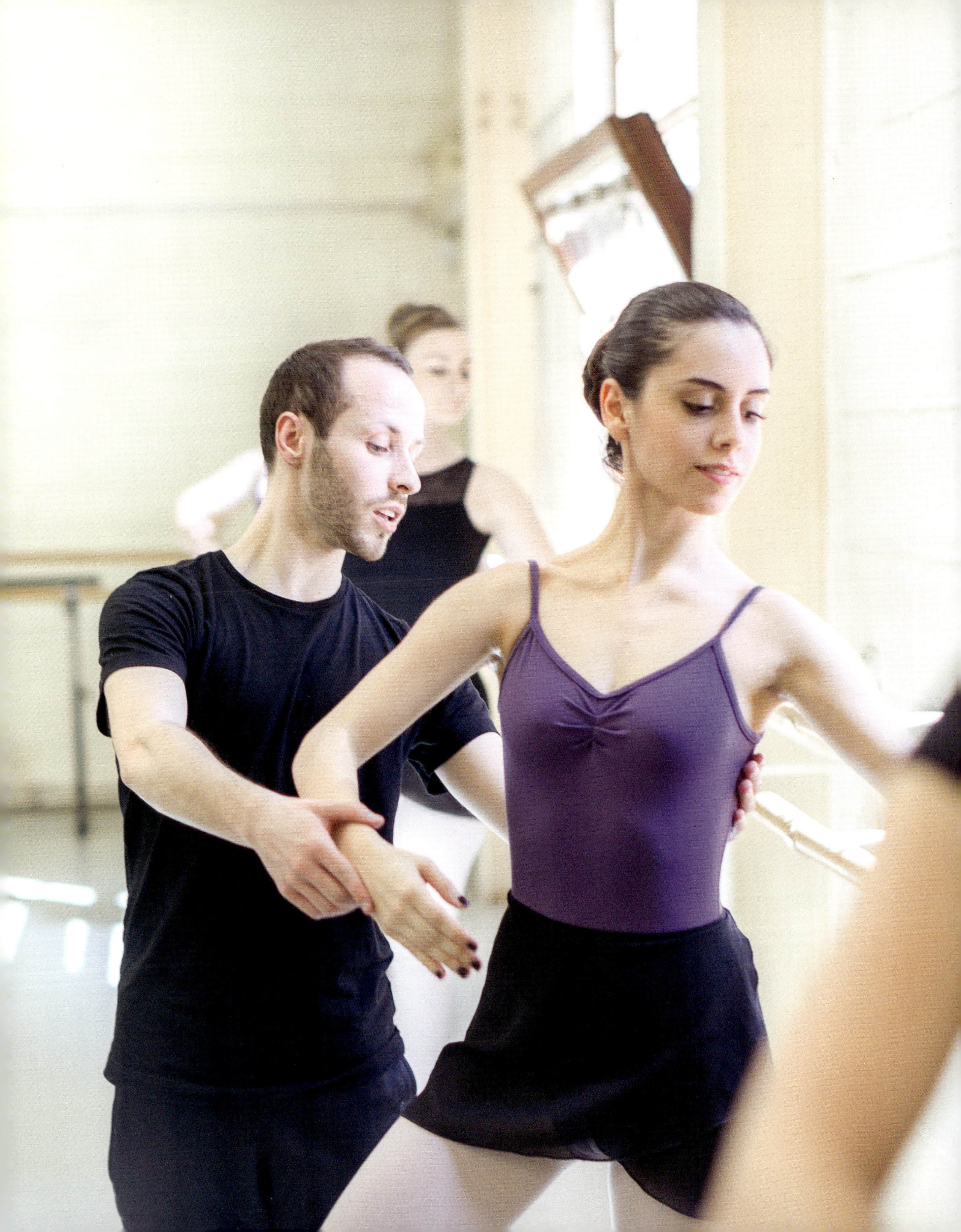

6

TEACHER EDUCATION

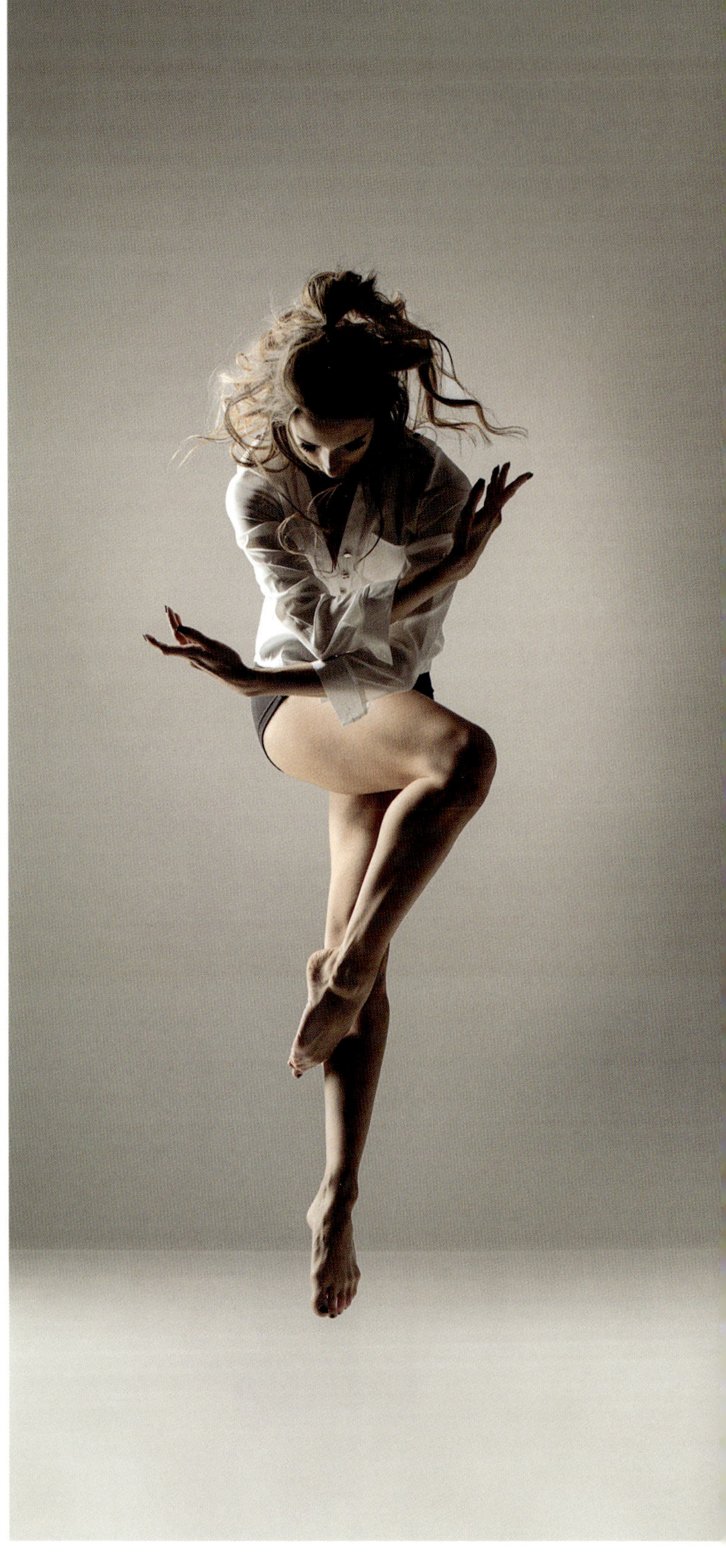

T HE heart and soul of the Academy's work'
is how Chief Executive Luke Rittner described dance
education in 2009. Education has been at the core of
the RAD's activities since it was founded a century ago
to improve the standards of dance teaching in the UK.
Membership of the original Association of Operatic
Dancing was dependent on teachers demonstrating
that they had mastered the techniques and knowledge
required to teach to what the founders of the
Association considered an acceptable standard. Soon
examinations were introduced to examine proficiency
in teaching as well as in performance, and as the
Academy developed and adapted to changing ideas
about teaching practice, new syllabi were developed in
tandem with courses specifically designed to train dance
teachers. A College awarding teaching certificates, and
the teachers' and professional dancers' examinations
offered by the Academy, were combined in 1999 into
the Faculty of Education (FOE). Today the FOE
awards undergraduate degrees, postgraduate degrees
and teaching qualifications validated by the RAD under
its Royal Charter, as well as devising courses and workshops as part of Continuing Professional Development.

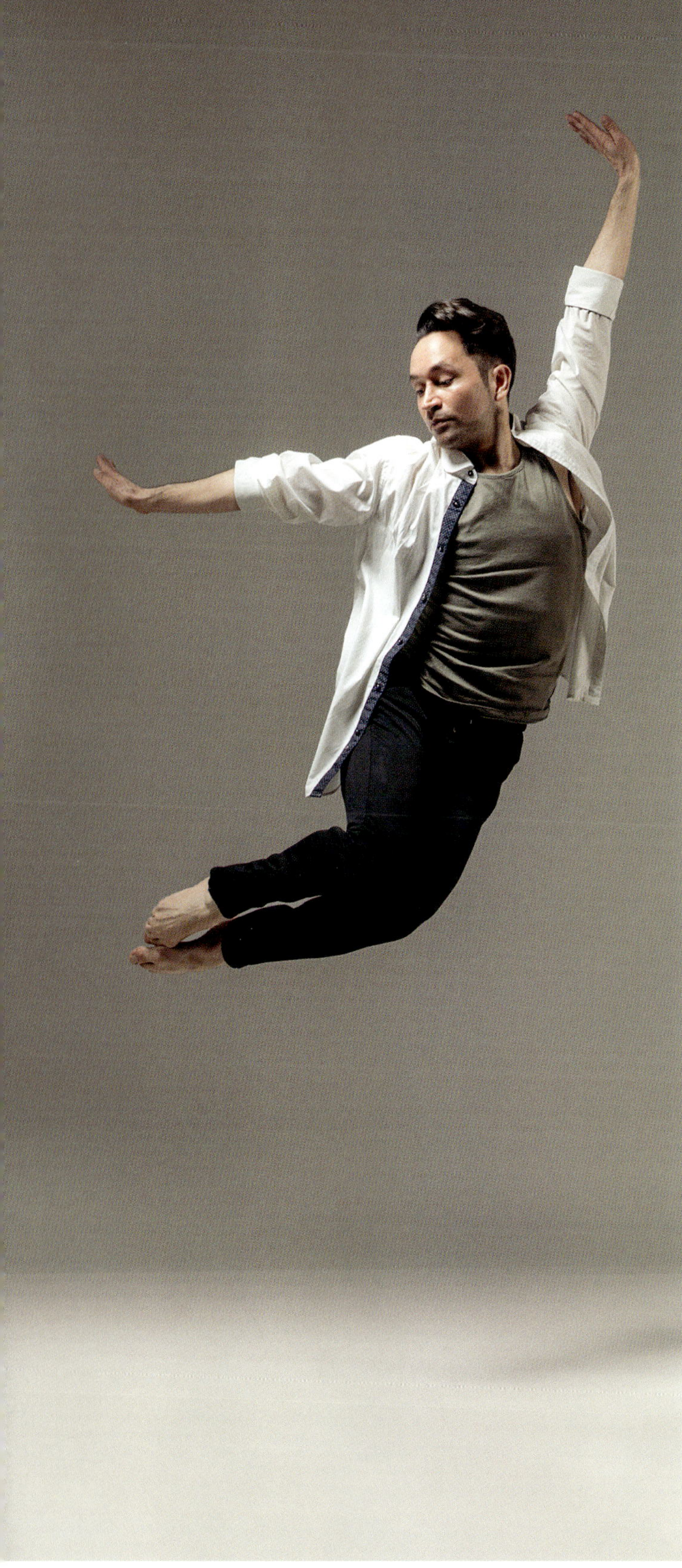

In many ways, raising standards in dance teaching has remained the primary focus of the Academy's work but, as with so many things, perceptions of what constitutes 'good teaching' have varied according to time and context. Clearly a good teacher is more than someone who knows and can demonstrate the 'correct' technique. In search of answers, the dance teaching profession has forged much closer links with the wider world of education but this is not a new phenomenon. From the first full-time Teachers' Training Course (TTC), launched after the end of the Second World War in 1945, the Academy has sought the guidance and input of education experts, beginning with E.R. Gwatkin and Professor Winifred Cullis who, along with Arnold Haskell, led the first TTC (ably supported by Kathleen Gordon). The course culminated in the award of a diploma and the Licentiate of the Royal Academy of Dancing (LRAD), bestowed at a prestigious Diploma Day ceremony with a guest of honour. In 1957 Lilian Charlesworth was elected to replace Professor Cullis and in the 1960s, the considerable educational expertise of Peter Brinson (appointed Director of the RAD in 1968) was a significant (if short-lived) influence on both the TTC and the organisation as a whole. During the 1970s it was Robin Howard, the pre-eminent crusader for British contemporary dance, and a committed educator, who gave TTC students a home at 'The Place' (the location of the newly established London Contemporary Dance School) when the Academy could not house them. By the early 1990s, when the idea of a degree programme seemed a realistic proposition, the guidance of Dr Mollie Davies (awarded FRAD in 1996) was inestimable.

In terms of curriculum, student teachers have always been offered a broad programme of study encompassing both practical and theoretical components. Daily technique classes and the

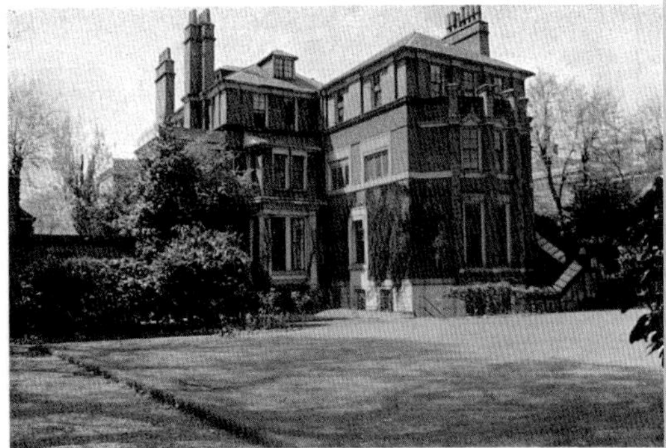

SPECIALISED SCHOOLS—GREAT BRITAIN

London   Map Ref. T.21

FAIRFIELD LODGE FROM THE GARDEN.

THE ROYAL ACADEMY OF DANCING

Patroness :—HER MAJESTY QUEEN MARY.

President :—DAME ADELINE GENÉE, D.B.E., D.Mus., M.I.etA., B.M.

Directors :—

PROFESSOR WINIFRED CULLIS, C.B.E., M.A., D.Sc., LL.D.

ARNOLD HASKELL, M.A.

A POST Educational Training for girls wishing to become Teachers of Dancing.

The curriculum includes Anatomy and Physiology, History of Period Costume and Practical Design, Musical and Art appreciation, Voice Production, Ballet Technique (Intermediate and Advanced), Ballet in Education Syllabus, National and Character work, Principles of Education, French, etc.

Length of training, three years.

Open to girls of 17 years of age and over who have passed Elementary (R.A.D.) and School Certificate or an equivalent examination. Residence arranged.

For particulars apply to :—THE DIRECTOR, The Royal Academy of Dancing, 154 Holland Park Avenue, W.11. Tel. : Park 7402.

706

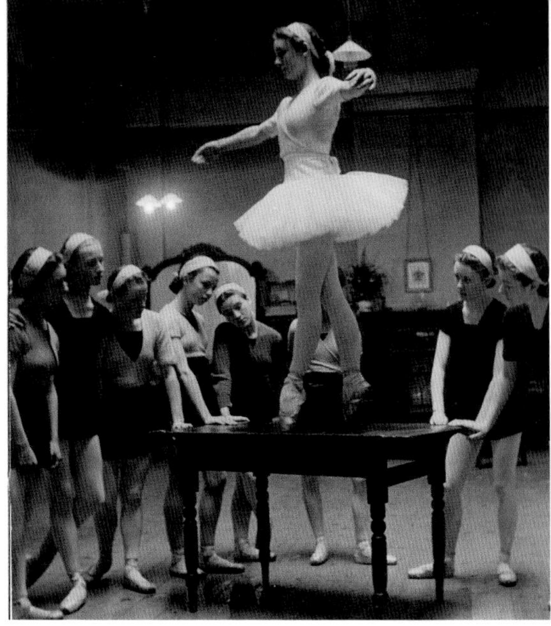

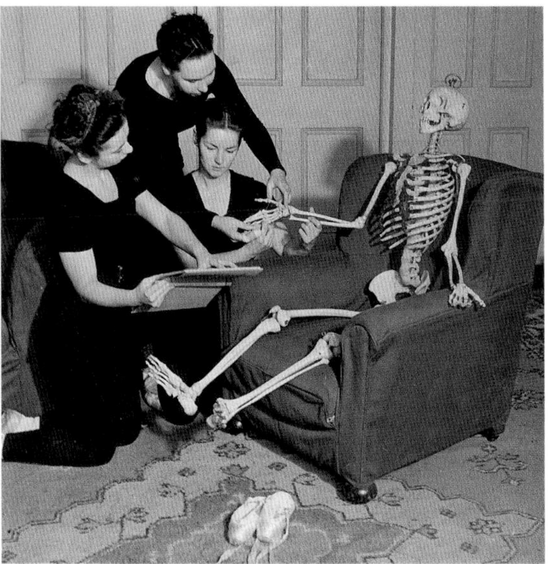

intensive analysis of RAD syllabi were the backbone of teacher training through the decades before and after the establishment of the College of the RAD, in 1976. The wealth of dance expertise available to the Academy ensured that the art of dance remained the motivating force. Early TTC students had the honour of being taught by some of the greatest dancers of the early twentieth century, including Adeline Genée, Phyllis Bedells, Tamara Karsavina, Stanislas Idzikowski and Keith Lester. Senior examiners were also an indispensable asset to the training of future teachers and regularly formed part of the TTC teaching faculty.

THE COLLEGE

The College, which occupied the third floor of the Battersea headquarters for nearly 25 years, produced generations of highly qualified LRAD teachers, recruiting from across the UK and, increasingly, from overseas. Led by a series of Principals, Keith Lester, Patricia Mackenzie, Valerie Taylor and Susan Danby, the College served the Academy well in ensuring excellence in teaching and equipping its graduates to forge successful careers within the private sector, many of them establishing their own

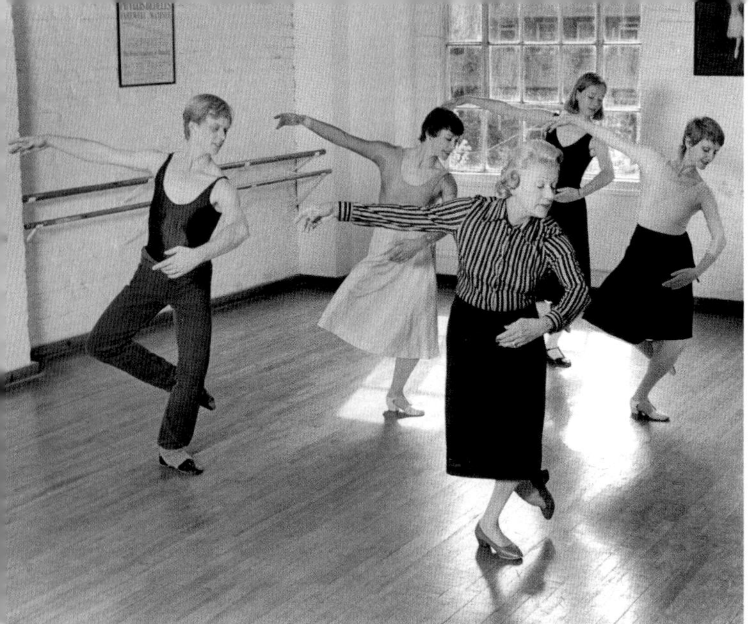

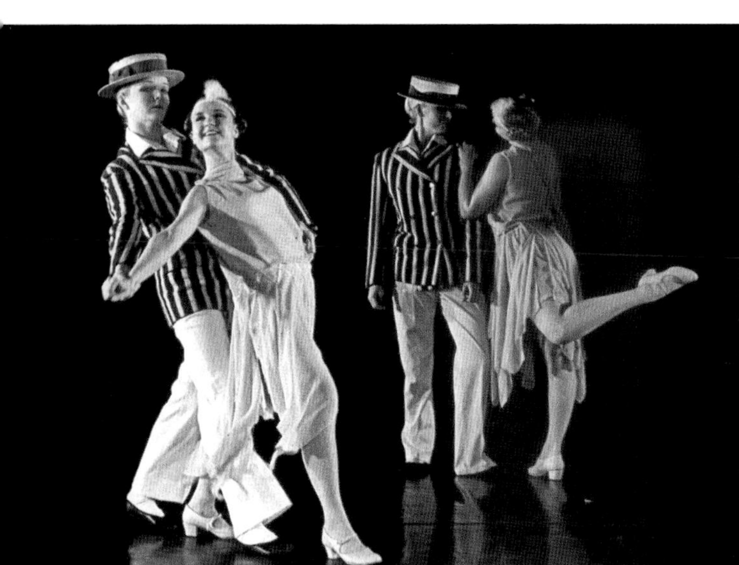

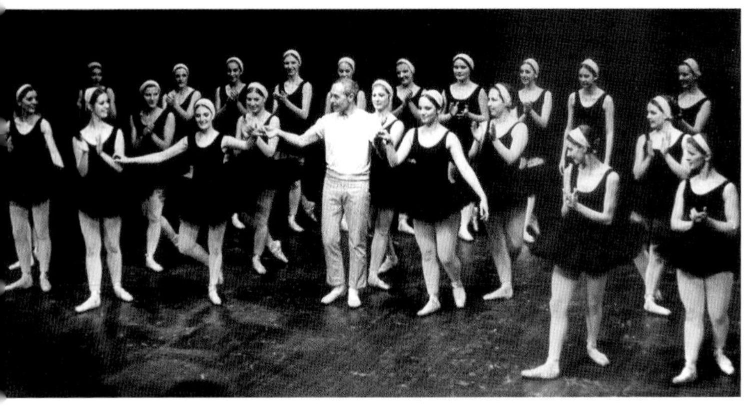

RAD schools, becoming examiners, joining syllabus development panels or becoming members of the College staff.

During the 1970s and 1980s the College was able to attract local council funding for some of its UK students. As one graduate remembers,

> in those days if you got a place at a top vocational school or college, and you were from a low-income family, you could get a full grant. I lived in Surrey, who were pretty good and gave me a grant for the full three years, fees and maintenance included.

Not everyone was so lucky and as council funding became harder to obtain, reliance on international students who could pay full fees increased. By the beginning of the 1990s, numbers on the three-year training course had declined considerably and the College faced new competition from the first university degree courses in dance (notably at Bedford and the University of Surrey). In addition, graduates of the College were getting very little recognition for their LRAD and diploma qualifications and, in some instances, being made to start undergraduate degree programmes from scratch, alongside post-A Level students.

The development of the first BA (Hons) degree programme, delivered by the RAD and validated by the University of Durham (in 1994), remains a

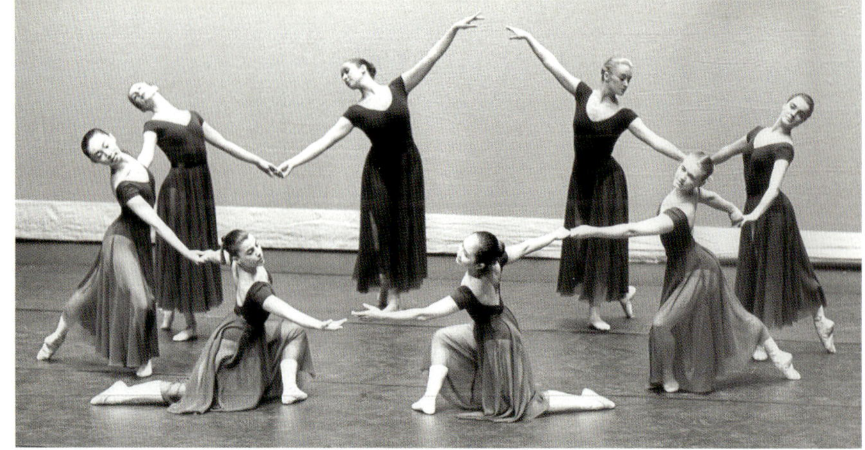

milestone in the Academy's history. The first cohort to complete their degrees (in The Art and Teaching of Ballet) joined other Durham students for the conferring of degrees in 1996. The partnership with one of the oldest and most prestigious universities in the UK surprised many in the dance world but the link was just one of many parting gifts from Dame Margot Fonteyn, who was both President of the RAD and Chancellor of the University of Durham until her death in 1991. As University and Academy representatives set about organising her Thanksgiving Service at Westminister Abbey, the seeds of a future collaboration were being sown. Somewhat fortuitously, the incoming Chancellor, Sir Peter Ustinov, was a man of artistic sensibilities and a committed ballet lover.

Degree status for College graduates was a well-earned victory but it did not solve the problem of funding: students were still self-financing, so recruitment was still limited by financial barriers. Nonetheless, the relationship forged between the College and the University of Durham prompted some optimistic longer-term plans for other degree programmes, including a distance-learning option for international teachers (particularly LRAD holders) to upgrade their qualification to a degree. The BPhil (Hons) Ballet and Contextual Studies, introduced in 1995, fulfilled a much-needed pathway and attracted significant numbers of RAD teachers from all continents. Before the advent of information technology and virtual learning environments, the RAD modelled a distance learning process using telephone and fax, with a week spent at London headquarters that brought learners and staff together.

THE FACULTY OF EDUCATION

The appointment of Joan White in the summer of 1999 was to prove another milestone in RAD teacher education. Her background in mainstream education, higher education and the private dance sector, combined with her phenomenal energy and drive, made her the ideal Dean of the new Faculty of Education and the Academy's first Director of Education. Shortly after her appointment she was made a Professor of the University of Durham and forged closer ties with the University's management team. Supported by an ever-growing number of

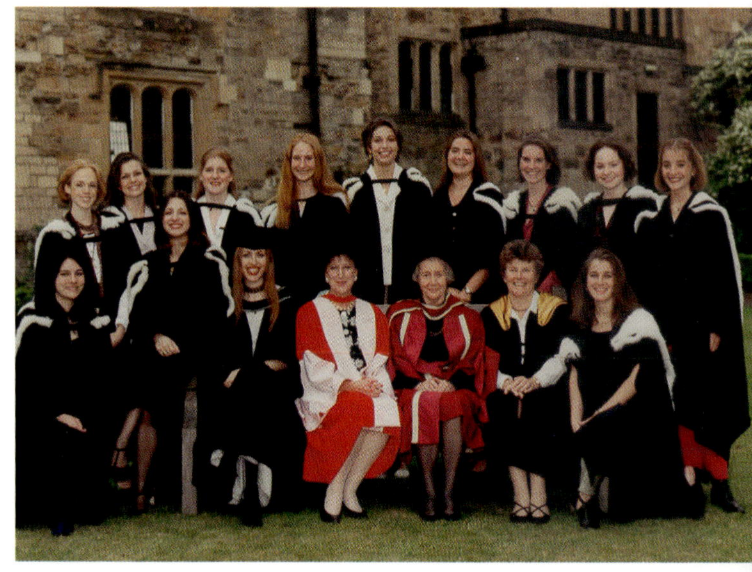

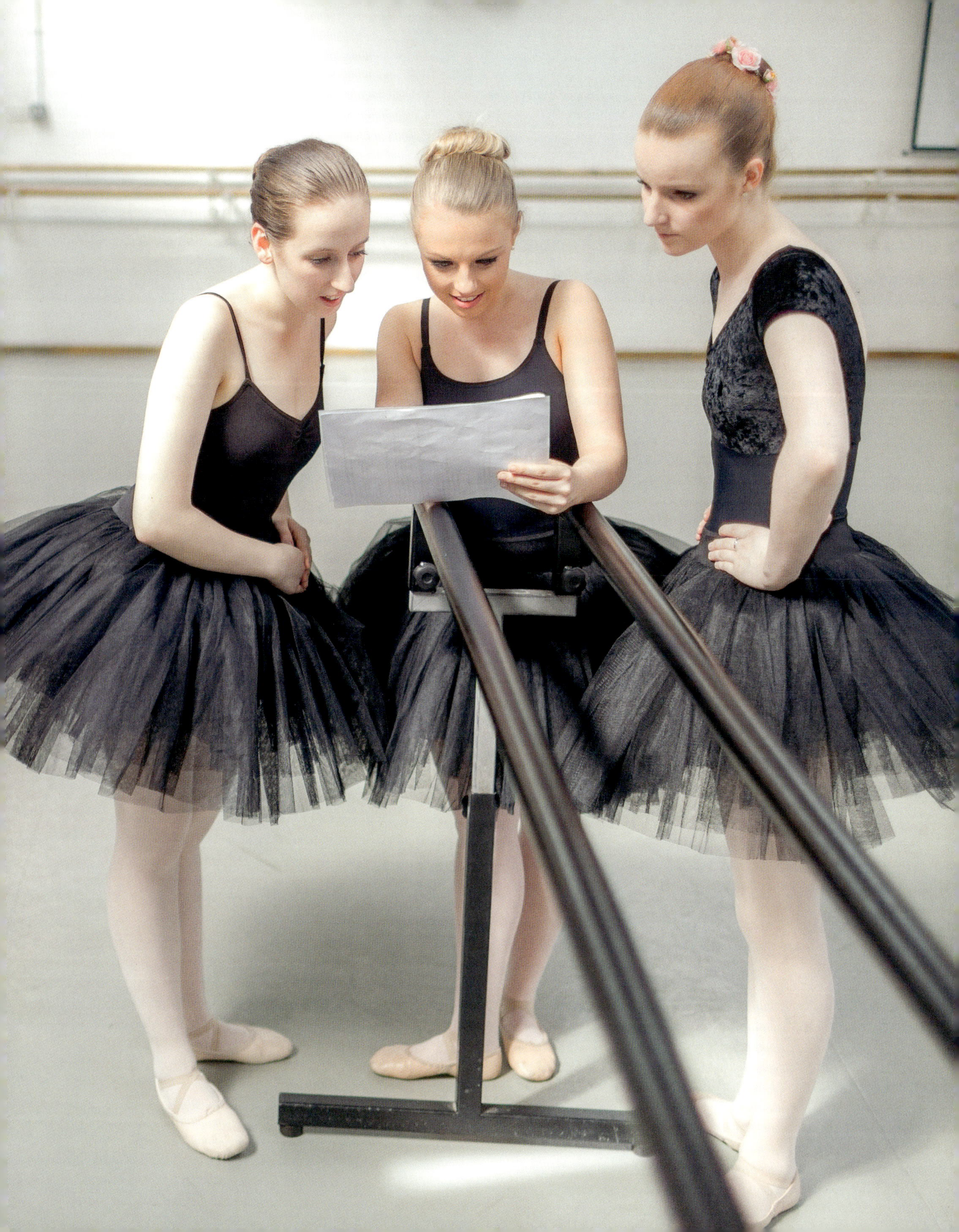

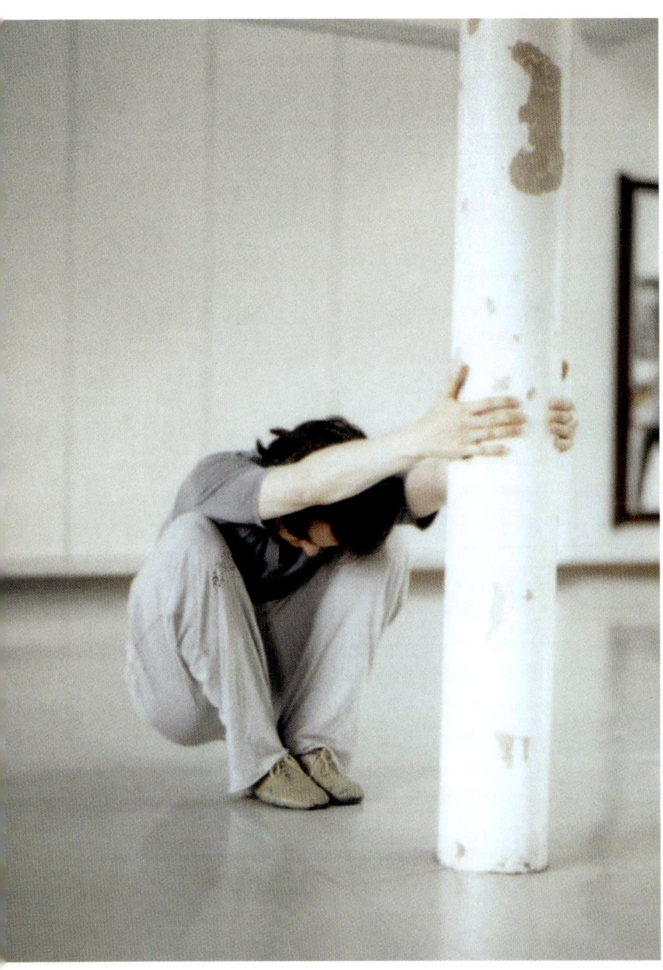

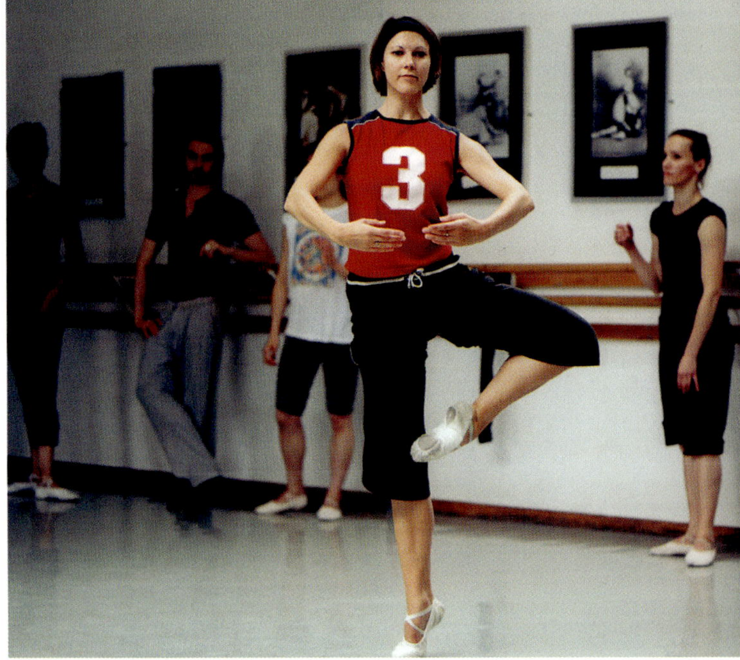

staff, White led the FOE through a series of reviews, validation and revalidation panels for the next 12 years. The price of external recognition is, of course, external accountability but the rewards were considerable. In 2002 the Academy gained Accredited Provider of Initial Teacher Training status and was able to offer a fully funded PGCE in Dance Teaching (from 2003), simultaneously gaining access to funding for full-time students on the BA (Hons) Art and Teaching of Ballet programme. In the same year the RAD changed university partners from Durham to the University of Surrey, and in 2008 launched its first post-graduate degree, the Master of Teaching (Dance).

In addition to university-validated programmes, the FOE developed a group of RAD-validated professional awards, recognising the needs of the private sector and vocational training. The year

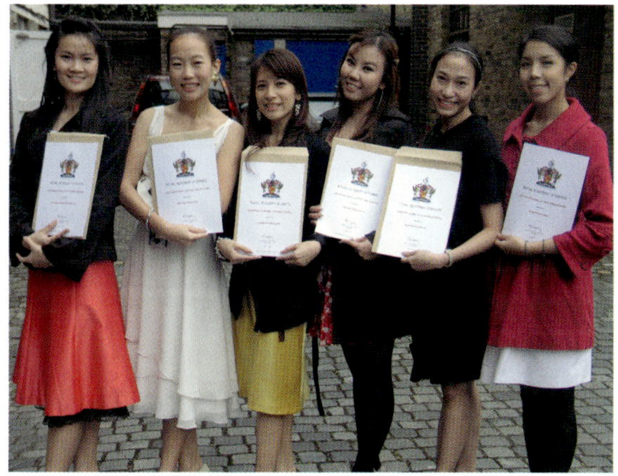

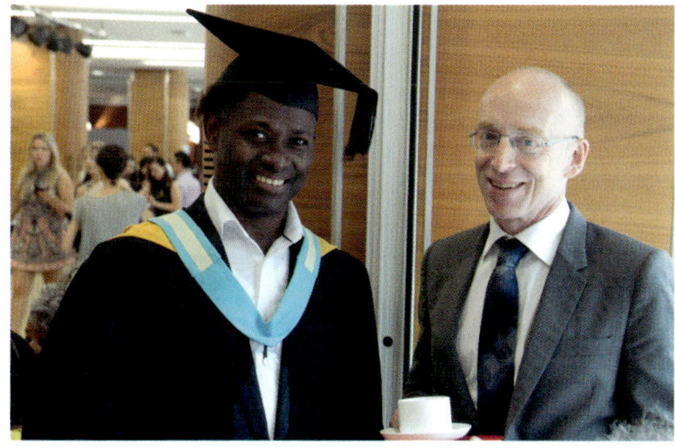

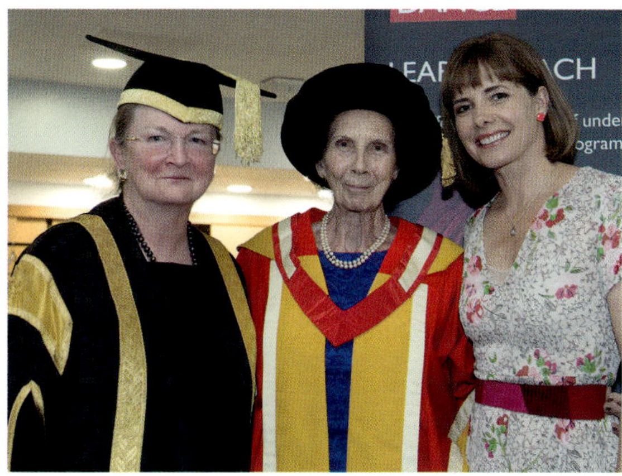

2004 saw the new Certificate in Ballet Teaching Studies (CBTS) and the Diploma for Professional Benesh Movement Notators (the Certificate in BMN having been available since 2002). A revised Licentiate (LRAD) programme was introduced in 2005, which allowed BA (Hons) students to undertake additional studies in order to gain their LRAD status. Opportunities for professional dancers to retrain as teachers were also a focus, with a revised Professional Dancers' Teaching Diploma introduced in 2002. The intensive three-month course (which replaced the Professional Dancers' Teaching Certificate, studied full-time over nine months) allowed dancers to gain their qualification between June and August and begin employment in September of the new academic year. By 2012, under the new Director of Education Anne Hogan, the Professional Dancers' Postgraduate Teaching Certificate (aligned to Masters-level study) was delivered in Berlin and is now also available in Australia. In the same year CBTS graduates were offered an upgrade option in the Diploma in Dance Teaching Studies.

Since September 2015 RAD degrees have been validated by the University of Bath and the current prospectus reflects the diversity and inclusivity of its programmes and awards. The FOE is currently in the safe hands of Michelle Groves, Director of Education since 2016 and a member of Faculty staff since its beginning. More than anyone else, she has witnessed the continuity and change that have shaped the Faculty over nearly two decades and will continue to do so. 'An ongoing challenge for dance teacher educators, and for dance teachers themselves, is keeping abreast of current educational and artistic thinking and practices to ensure dance teaching is "fit for purpose"', says Groves. 'This challenge will become even more paramount in an ever-changing, globalised world.'

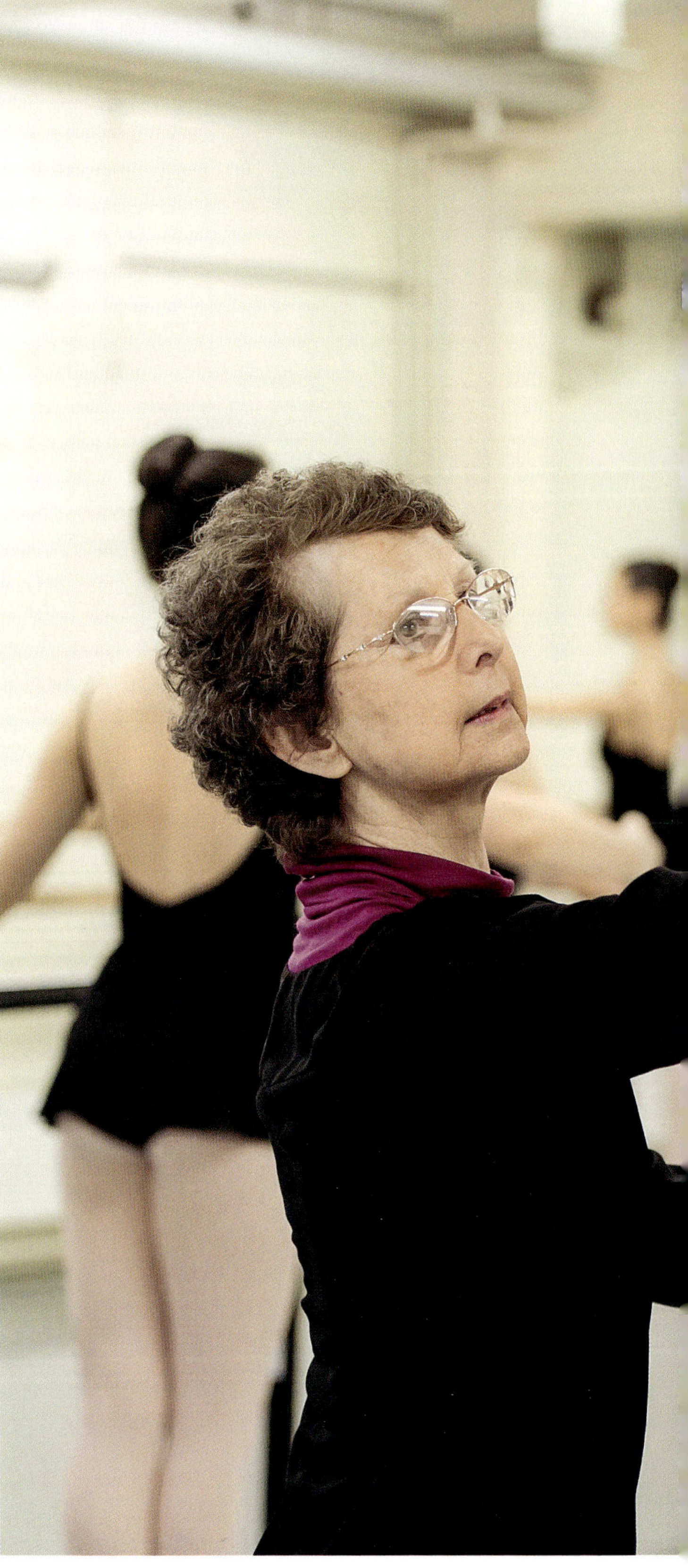

TEACHER REGISTRATION AND CPD

It is, perhaps, fair to say that the issue of teacher registration has continued to provide the Academy with a challenge, with no clear consensus on how any formal registration scheme should be structured. Early attempts to 'match' higher education qualification levels were not popular and highlighted the fundamental issue of how practical knowledge and experience are valued in comparison to formal qualifications. It is an issue that concerns the dance education and teaching sectors more widely and is, no doubt, a relevant topic for future conferences. It is worth noting that throughout a century of RAD history, the contributions of so many women and men demonstrate that practical and professional experience are paramount: from Presidents to summer school and gala organisers, from Artistic Directors to Secretaries and College Principals, from teachers and examiners to Genée panel judges, the list is endless.

Nonetheless, it is equally fair to say that we live in an age when teaching is recognised as a profession, a definition that implies the achievement of qualifications and continuous learning. The Continuing Professional Development scheme, tailored to the needs of RAD teaching members, is a crucial element in maintaining standards of teaching and giving teachers more flexibility and increased employment opportunities. 'Lifelong learning' may be a new catchphrase but it is not a new concept to the dance world, where performance careers have always been relatively short and dancers have been forced, or have sought, to reinvent themselves in numerous ways: the principle was as true for Dame Adeline Genée in the 1920s as it is for our current President, Dame Darcey Bussell, today.

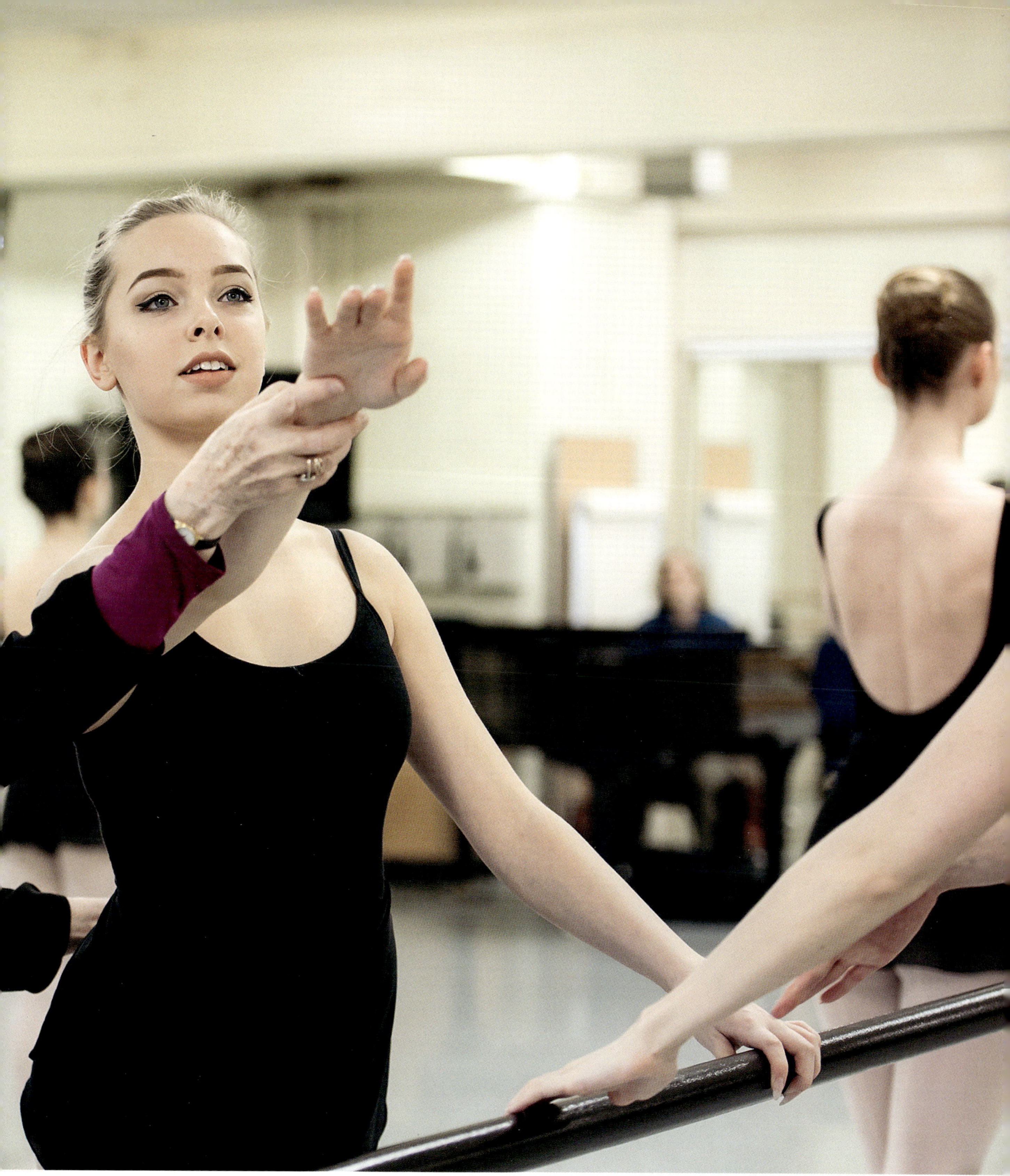

BENESH INTERNATIONAL

THE steps in the formal court dances of the eighteenth century were written down, but the dancing masters of that time were mainly concerned with the placement of dancers' feet and the patterns made as dancers moved across the floor. By the late nineteenth century a more sophisticated system of notation (named after its creator, Vladimir Stepanov) had been developed and used to record the great classical repertoire of Marius Petipa and Lev Ivanov. However, it was not until the twentieth century that systems of dance notation could record human movement in all its complex detail. In the 1920s Rudolf Laban devised a system that became known as Labanotation. A few decades later Rudolf and Joan Benesh developed an alternative system of notation, which became known as Benesh Movement Notation (BMN).

BMN is written on a five-line stave (similar to a music score) that is read from left to right and from the top of the page to the bottom, recording the dancer's position as viewed from behind. The stave lines correspond to visually distinctive features of the body: the top line shows the height of the top of the head, the bottom line the floor. The middle line indicates

TEACHING BENESH, *c.*1957
Joan Benesh teaching Royal Ballet School students in the Pavlova studio at White Lodge.

LEARNING BENESH, *c.*1955
Royal Ballet School students learning to read Benesh Movement Notation in the Salon at White Lodge.

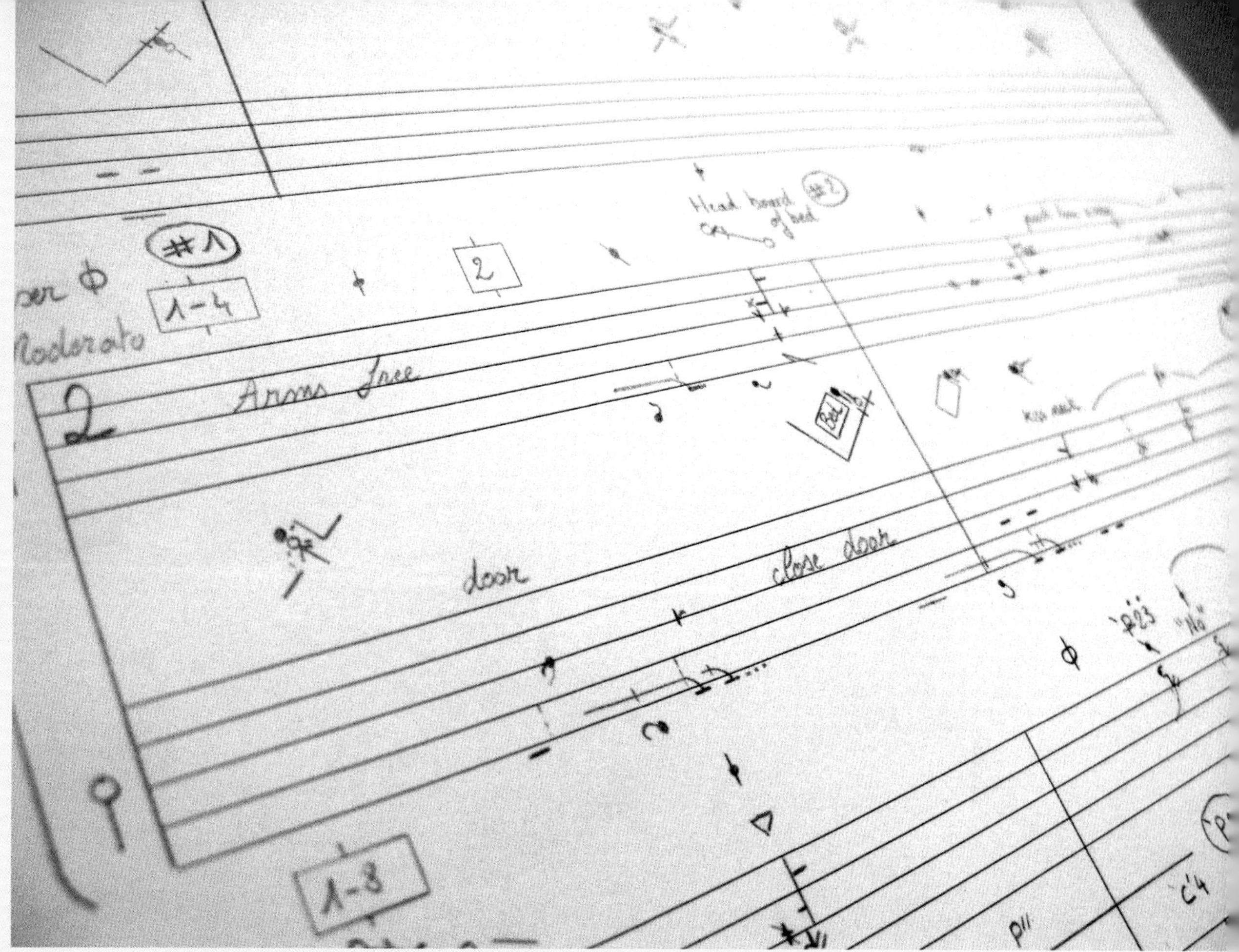

the height of the waist and the inter-vening lines the heights of the knees and shoulders. A series of 'frames' records the positions of the hands and feet relative to the body and of bent elbows and knees, while movement lines describe the paths taken by the limbs from one position to the next and locomotion lines link the posi-tions of the feet, indicating whether the dancer steps, jumps or slides. Rhythm, phrasing and movement quality are shown above the stave, and the direction faced, location within the working space and paths of travel are shown below the stave.

Since 1997 the Benesh Institute has been incorporated within the RAD and was renamed Benesh International in 2018. BMN is used by dance companies to record new works and restage existing works with precision. Notation assists in accurately transferring ballets in current repertoire from one company to another, and in the revival of older works that would otherwise be lost: the RAD holds a unique collection of notation scores of ballets from the nineteenth century to the present day. For dance academics, BMN allows for the in-depth analysis of choreographic structure and style, whilst teachers can also benefit from being able to record their classes in notation and analyse dance tech-niques in greater depth. Most RAD syllabi are published in BMN, which enables teachers to study the work in more detail than is possible from word notes or videos alone.

Benesh International has continued to expand its activities. In 2002 the pioneering Benesh Notation Editor software programme was released. The RAD has hosted a number of

international conferences on the work of Rudolf Benesh, including those in London (2005) and Paris (2017); another conference is planned for London in 2020. *The Encyclopaedia of Benesh Movement Notation* (released in 2017) is the first-ever comprehensive reference work on BMN. It addresses both dance and clinical usages of the notation and, where appropriate, explains the usage for each discipline separately. Benesh International has also developed a range of courses and qualifications in dance notation, most recently the Professional Award in BMN (2018) and the Postgraduate Diploma in BMN (2020).

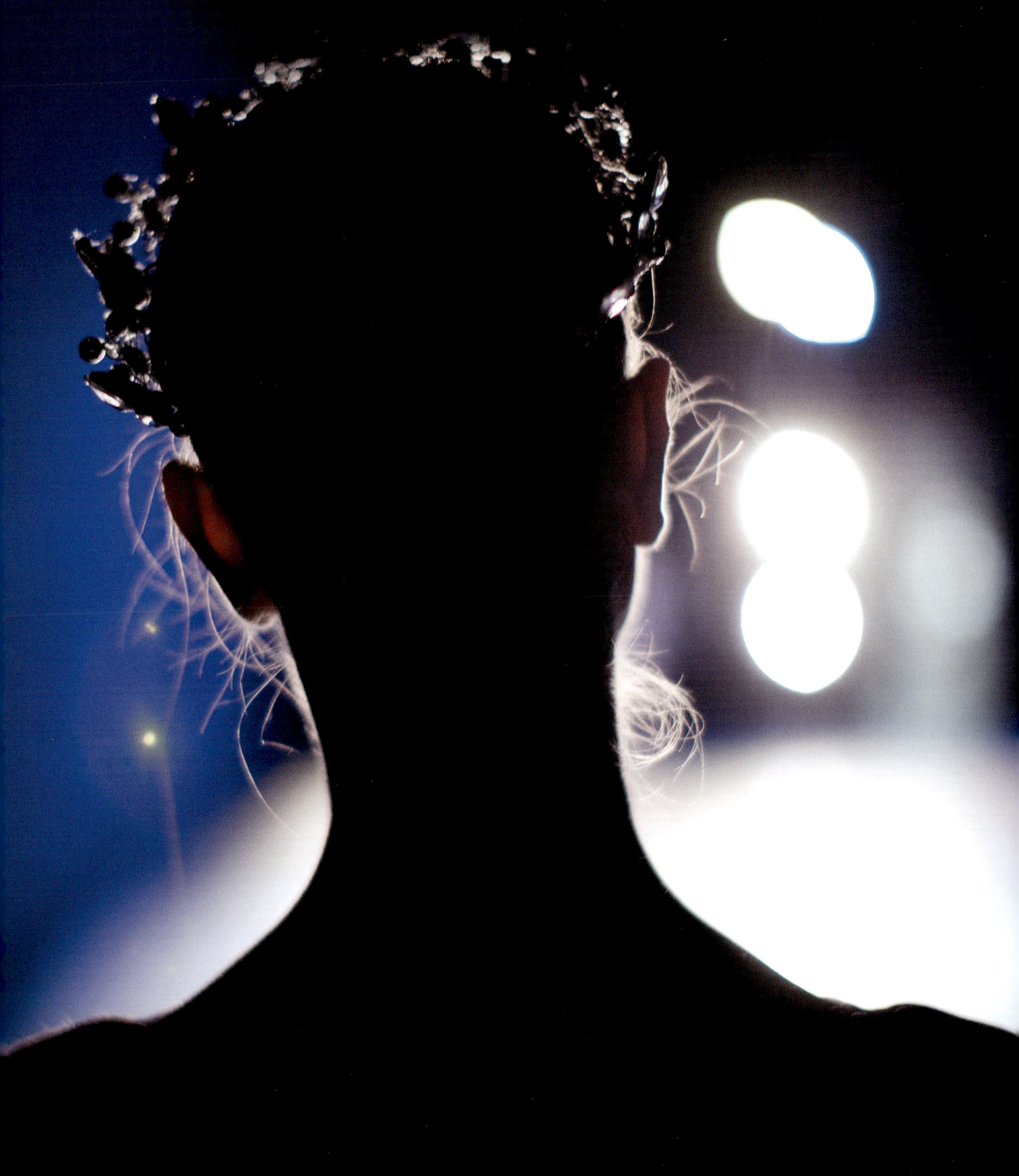

7

GALAS, COMPETITIONS AND AWARDS

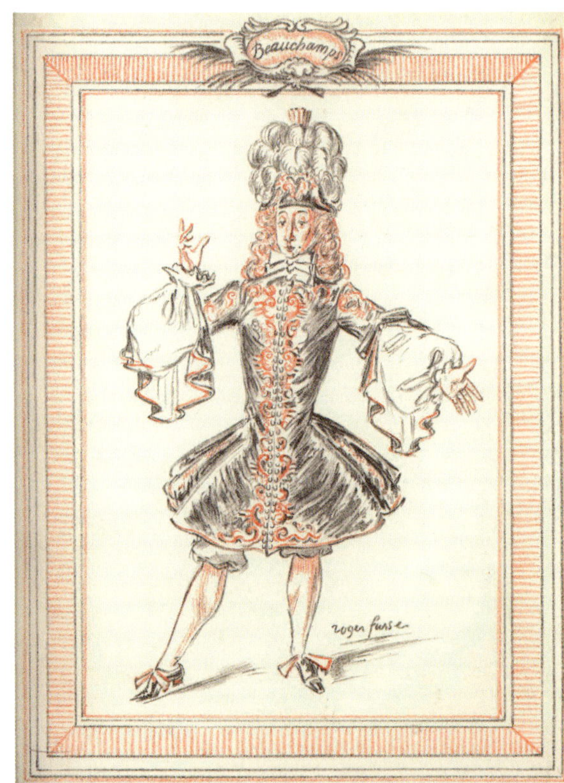

F ROM its earliest years the RAD has been keen to demonstrate the performance abilities of its members. In November 1923, a mere three years after it was founded, a public matinée was held at the Gaiety Theatre, at which Adeline Genée danced in public for the first time in seven years. It was a tremendous success and was the first of many such events that not only helped to raise the profile of British ballet generally but also to draw attention to the work of the Association and the talents of its members. Some of the biggest names of the day danced the principal parts, and their performances were much admired; but *The Dancing Times* also noted, in 1929, the 'solid technical excellence of dozens of young dancers', which offered proof that the Association's efforts to improve the standard of dance teaching were working.

GALAS

With a membership of so many talented dancers, performance was also an effective way of fundraising. A ball in aid of the Building Fund was held in June 1939 and was to be one of the Academy's last great social occasions before the outbreak of war. The entertainment was a 'Grand Fête de Ballet' devised by Ninette de Valois with a setting conceived by the ballet designer Roger Furse. Described as a 'gorgeous extravaganza of two centuries of the history of ballet', it featured the great dancers of the past being played by leading dancers of the time, including the Russian ballerina Irina Baronova with Anton Dolin, who rushed from Southampton where their ship had docked only that morning, to dance the pas de deux from *Les Sylphides*. The entertainment ended with Adeline Genée dancing a polka with Phyllis Bedells and her daughter, Jean, after which 800 people danced until dawn.

The brilliant social success of that occasion was revived in style between 1958 and 1965, when a spectacular series of galas took place to raise funds

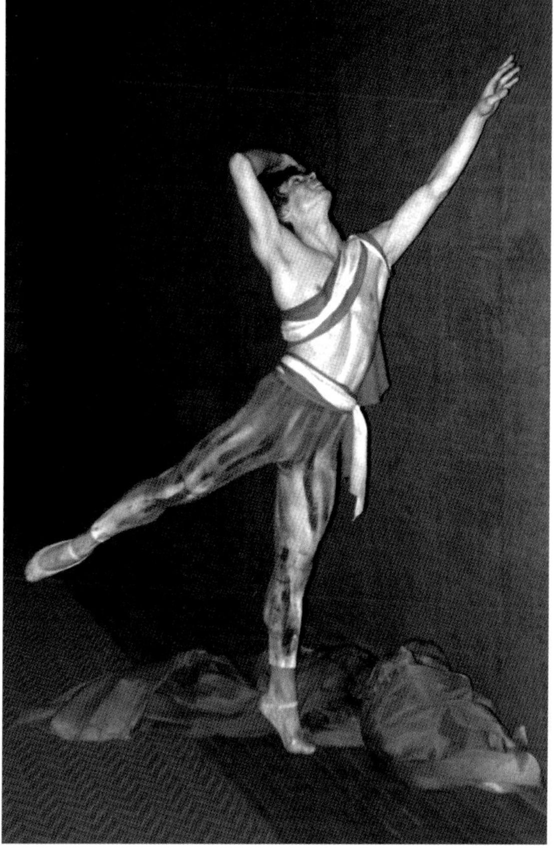

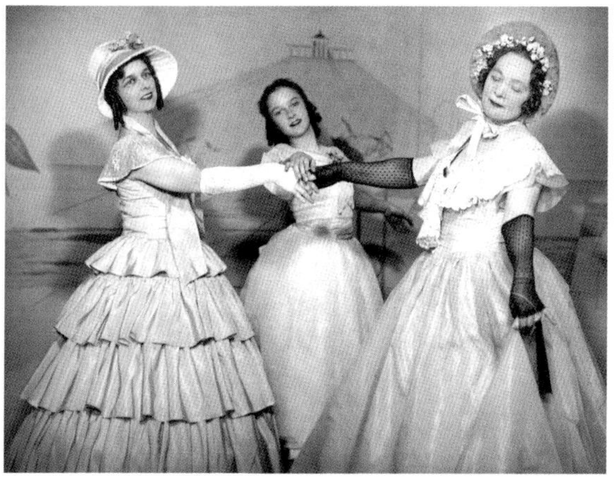

LENA KING,
A Member of the Association who has passed the Intermediate Examination.
She appears in "No English Need Apply."

for the Academy. These were usually held at Drury Lane and featured performances by the most celebrated dancers of the day. Organised by Margot Fonteyn in her role as President of the RAD, they were extraordinarily glamorous affairs, attended by members of the royal family, and always created a buzz of excitement, most notably at the gala held in 1961 when Rudolf Nureyev made his first stage appearance in London. That memorable performance was described by Jane Pritchard (Curator of Dance, Theatre & Performance at the Victoria and Albert Museum) in *Dance Gazette* in 2003:

> The curtain rose on a distant figure swathed in a red cloak. In a burst of energy he flung aside the cloak and, with a bare torso draped with a sash, and streaked grey tights, rushed to the footlights. Forgetting most of the choreography that Frederick Ashton had created for him, Nureyev hurtled around the stage, surging like a force of nature, evoking an heroic figure by Delacroix.

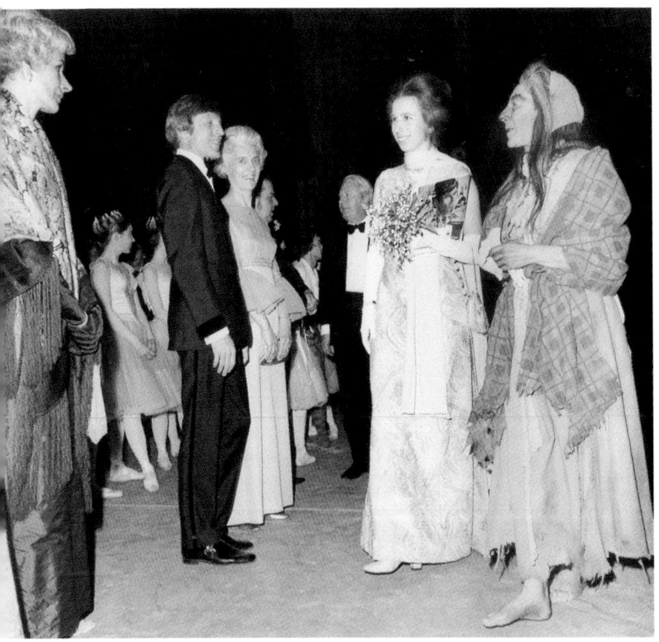

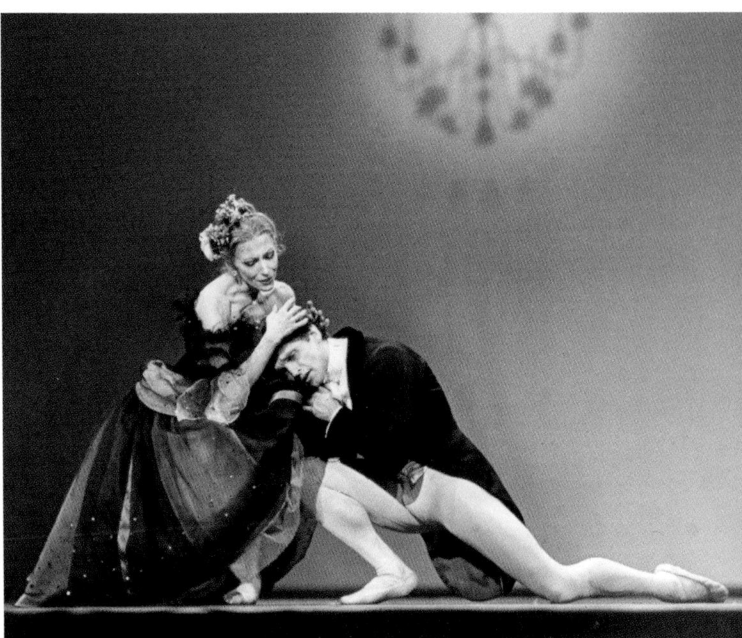

While the galas of the 1960s are particularly well remembered, similar events also took place in the following decades. In 1972 and 1975 the National Ballet of Canada organised galas at the London Coliseum in aid of the RAD, also attended by royalty. Proceeds from these events helped the RAD to purchase several high-quality pianos. At a fundraising gala in 1987, also held at the London Coliseum, Peter Schaufuss and Natalia Makarova danced Frederick Ashton's *Apparitions* and the London Festival Ballet presented the British premiere of Maurice Béjart's *Bolero*. In 1993 a gala was held in aid of the RAD and the Royal Opera House, while the amalgamation of the RAD and the Benesh Institute, in 1997, was also celebrated with a gala. The RAD hosted a further gala performance of *Billy Elliot* with the Royal Ballet School in 2006, and used its share of the proceeds to fund a series of dance workshops aimed at encouraging boys to dance.

COMPETITIONS

Whereas the focus of the Academy in its earlier days was on improving standards of technique, one of the earliest competitions was for dance arrangement, or choreography. Following the death of Anna Pavlova (in 1931), Philip Richardson bought a casket from the sale of her effects. He had this mounted on an ebony plinth and enclosed in a glass case and donated it as the prize for a dance arrangement by a member of the Association. The dance had to be 'strictly demi-character in nature (that is, based on the Operatic technique)' and was to tell, if possible, a short story. Props were allowed but had to be 'of an easily portable nature' and able to be quickly placed and removed. A synopsis of the story in 75 words was read out before the dance was performed. The first 'Pavlova Casket' competition

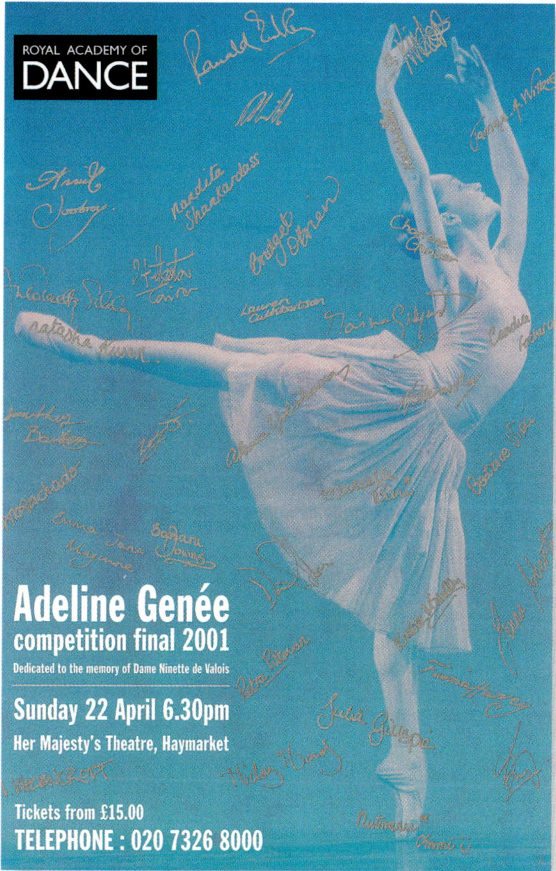

ADELINE GENÉE COMPETITION FINAL POSTER, 2001

The Genée marked its 70th anniversary in 2001 and was dedicated to the memory of Dame Ninette de Valois. Dame Antoinette Sibley judged it 'a vintage year of talent' and Sir Peter Wright 'the best year yet'. The poster is signed by many of the candidates, faculty and judges.

history, and that year the Sydney Opera House played host to a record number of candidates. Since then the Genée has been hosted in Birmingham, Athens, Hong Kong, Toronto, Singapore, Cape Town, Wellington, Glasgow, Antwerp and Lisbon as well as London, with repeat visits to Australia, Hong Kong and Canada.

Candidates at the Genée may come from a wide range of cultures and countries, but they have much in common. All are aged between 15 and 19, all have passed the RAD's Advanced Level 2 examination with Distinction and all are passionate about dance. The competition involves five days of intensive coaching and two days of semi-finals before the candidates compete for gold, silver and bronze medals by performing in three categories: Classical Repertoire, Commissioned Solo and Dancer's Own Variation.

The Genée gives candidates a unique opportunity to work with renowned choreographers and teachers, and for many of those who take part the coaching they receive as part of the competition is one of the most valuable parts of the whole experience. The focus of coaching ranges from improving technique, music and performance to stagecraft and the ways dancers communicate their personality to the audience. Other sessions might concentrate on entrances and exits, or advice on bows that are in keeping with the role just performed. The Genée is also an opportunity for candidates to think about presentation in more detail: tying back hair to accentuate the line of a cheekbone, adjusting a ribbon to avoid a gap between the shoe and the foot, choosing the right costume and headwear to enhance character. The coaching at the Genée forms a bridge between technique and artistry, and between rehearsal and performance – between practising and performing live.

was held on 16 July 1932; the competition ran until the 1950s, after which, sadly, the casket was stolen.

The Genée International Ballet Competition – renamed the Margot Fonteyn International Ballet Competition from 2020 – is the Academy's flagship event. The RAD's first President, Adeline Genée, proposed an annual award of a gold medal, donated by her husband, Frank Isitt, the first of which was awarded in 1931. Other medals were added in the years that followed: the silver in 1934, bronze in 1956, and gold and silver for male dancers in 1938. In the 1960s the Gold Medal competition was held in public and became a popular annual performance, attracting large audiences to Her Majesty's Theatre or the Festival Hall in London.

Today the Genée is truly international, attracting some of the finest young RAD dancers from around the globe. In 2002 it was decided to hold the Genée outside London for the first time in its 70-year

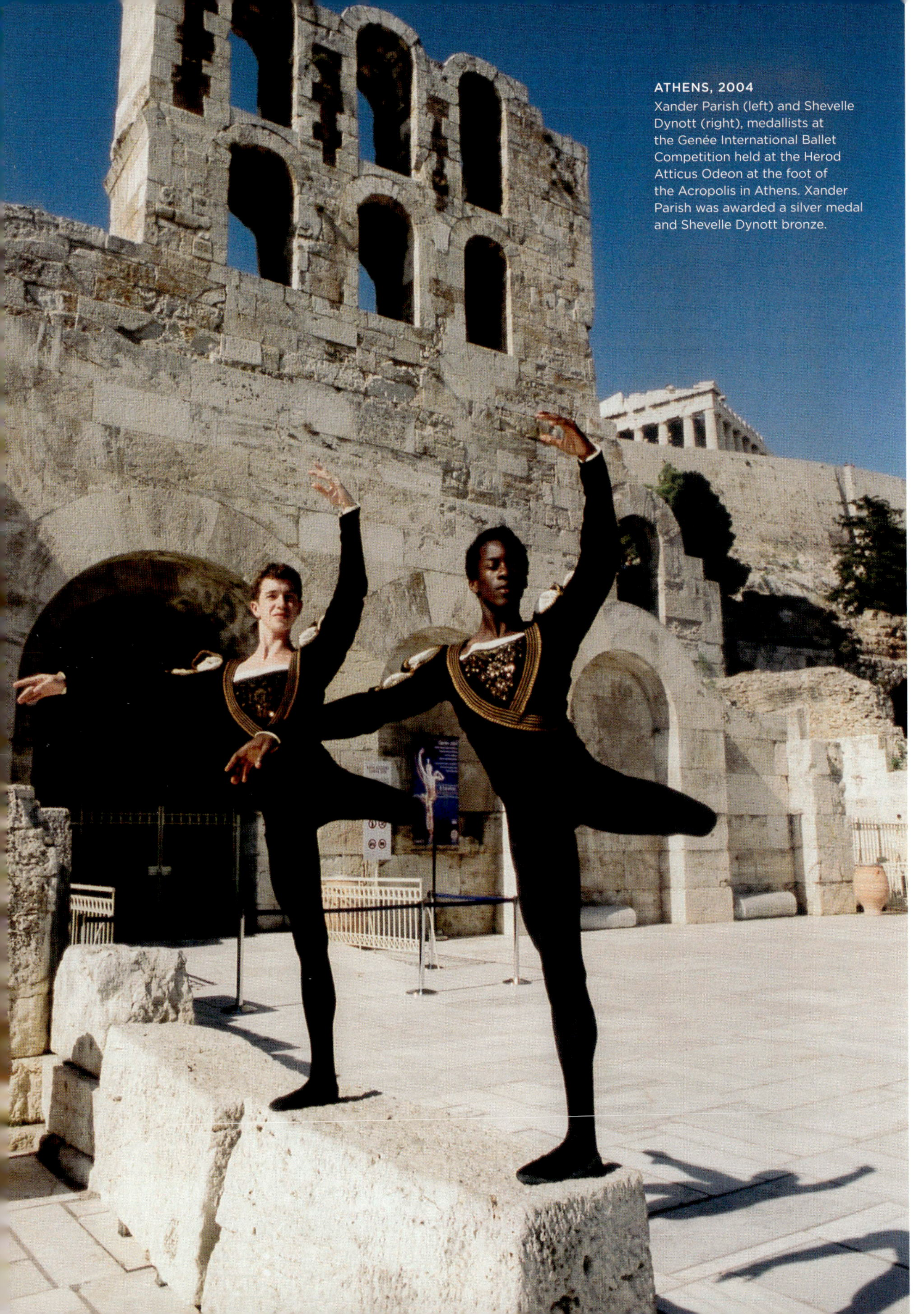

ATHENS, 2004
Xander Parish (left) and Shevelle
Dynott (right), medallists at
the Genée International Ballet
Competition held at the Herod
Atticus Odeon at the foot of
the Acropolis in Athens. Xander
Parish was awarded a silver medal
and Shevelle Dynott bronze.

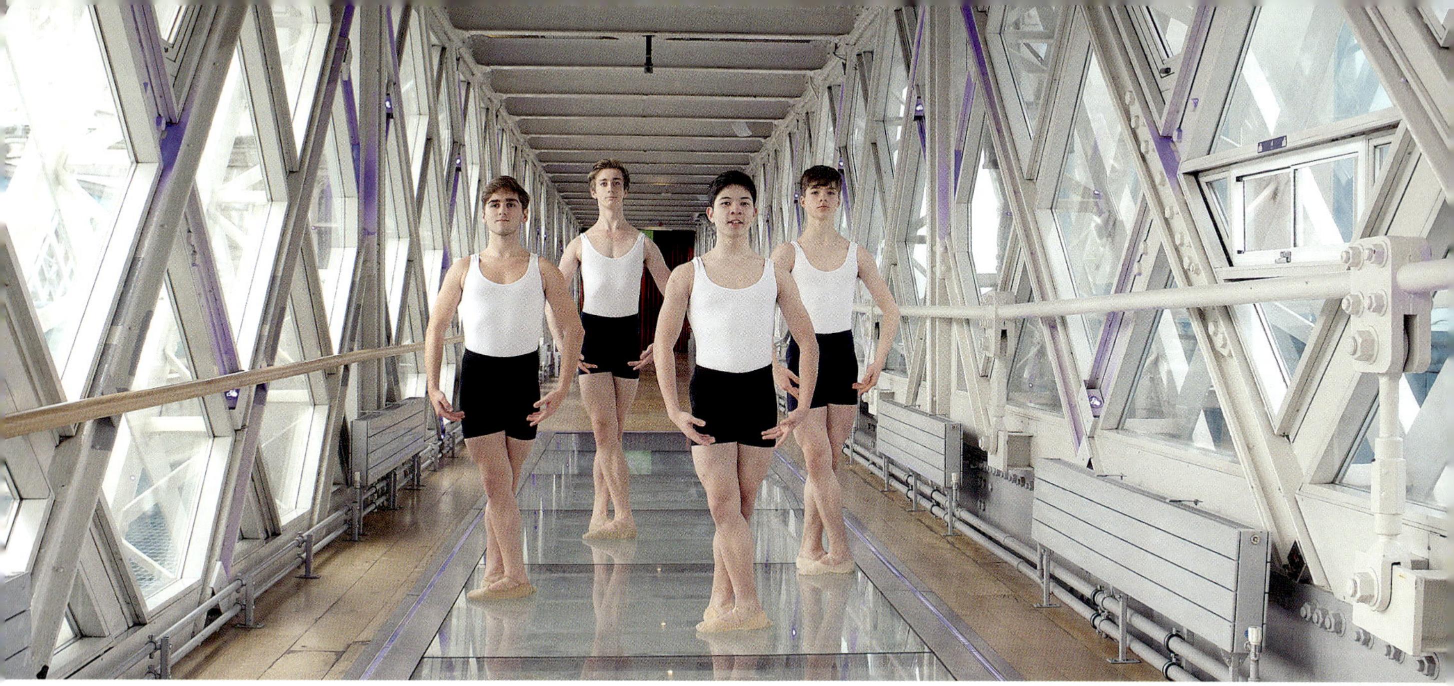

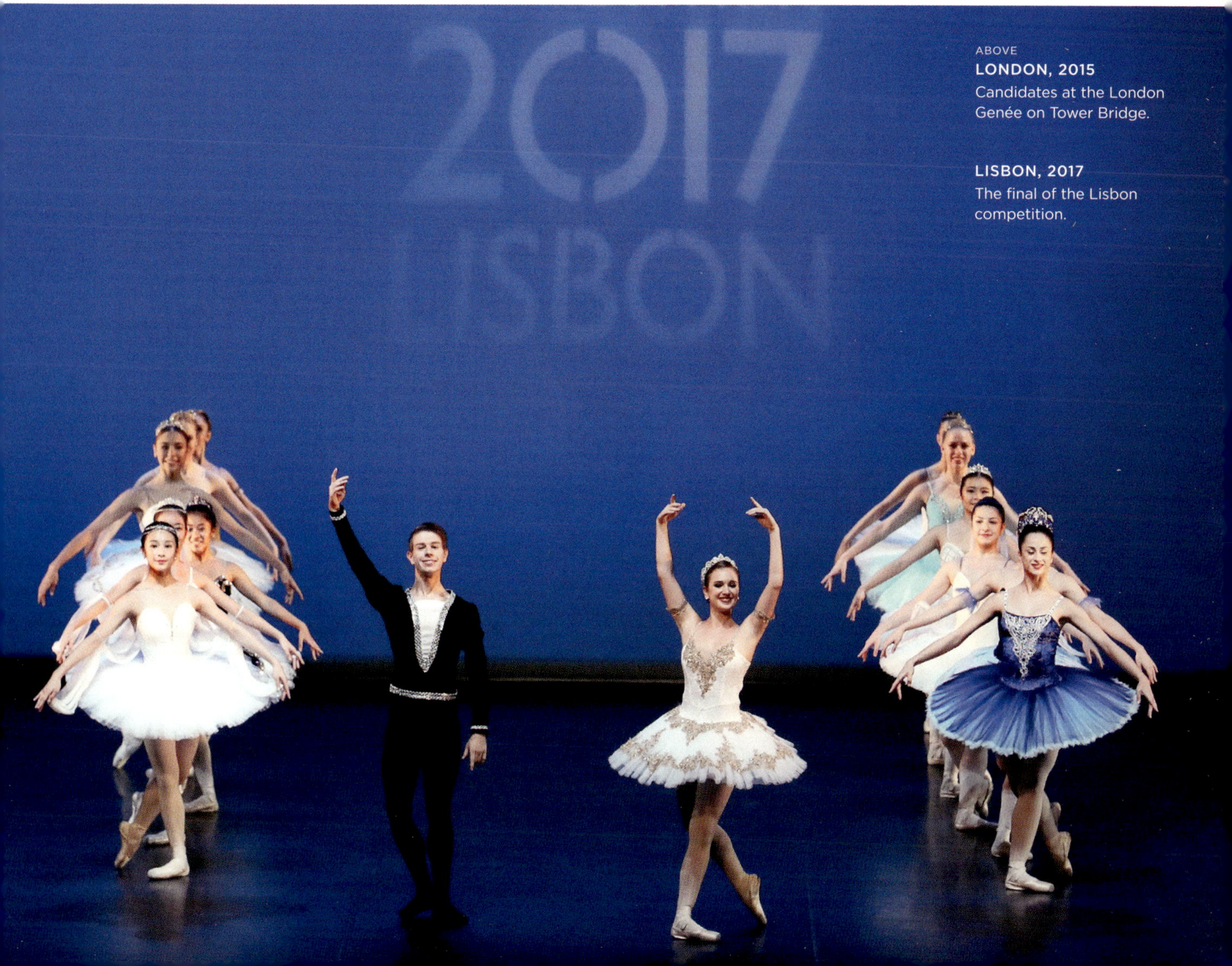

ABOVE
LONDON, 2015
Candidates at the London
Genée on Tower Bridge.

LISBON, 2017
The final of the Lisbon
competition.

TEACHING, 2017
Hilary Clark teaching at the Genée in Lisbon.

COACHING, 1981
Artistic Director Alan Hooper coaches David Yow.

DIGITAL GENÉE AWARDS, 1993
John Byrne gives a class to Darren Goldsmith and Shimon Kalichman at the 1993 Digital Genée Awards. John Byrne was the Academy's Artistic Director at the time. Darren Goldsmith won a bronze medal and Shimon Kalichman won a silver medal.

COACHING, 1996
Valerie Adams conducts a class at the Genée, 1996.

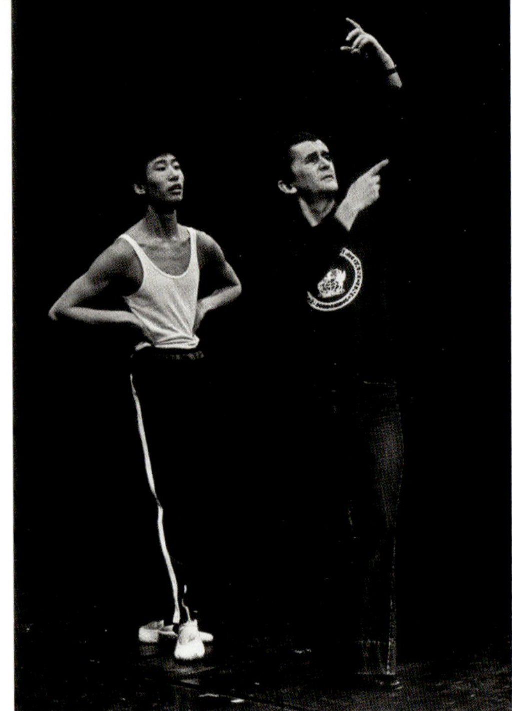

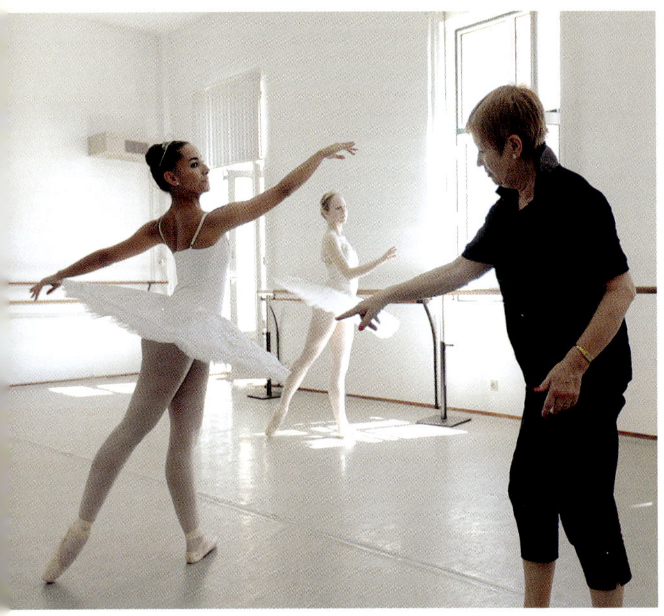

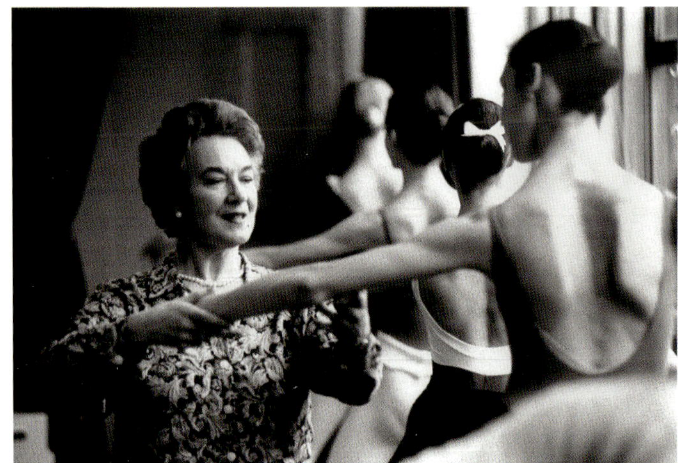

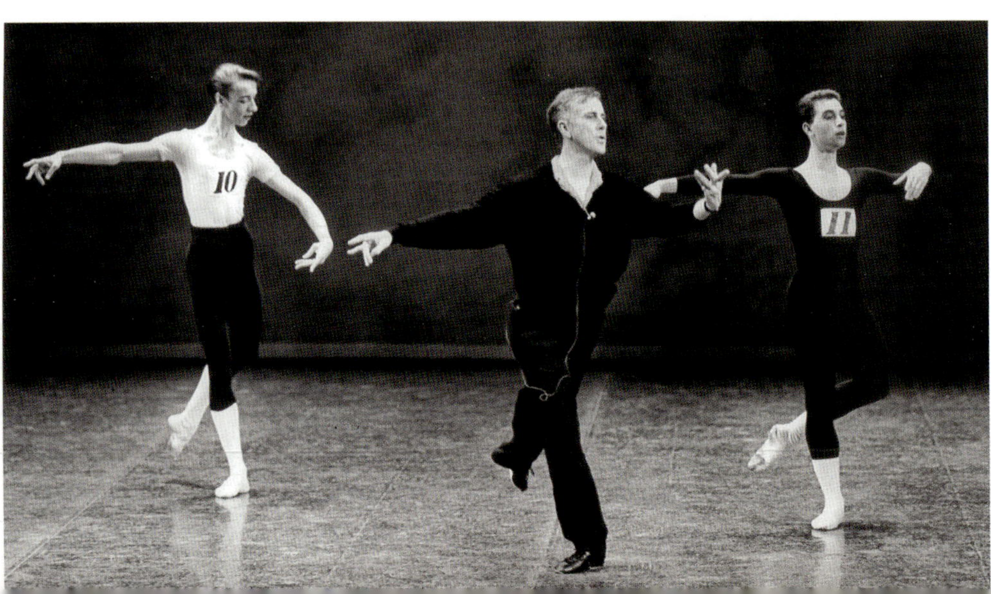

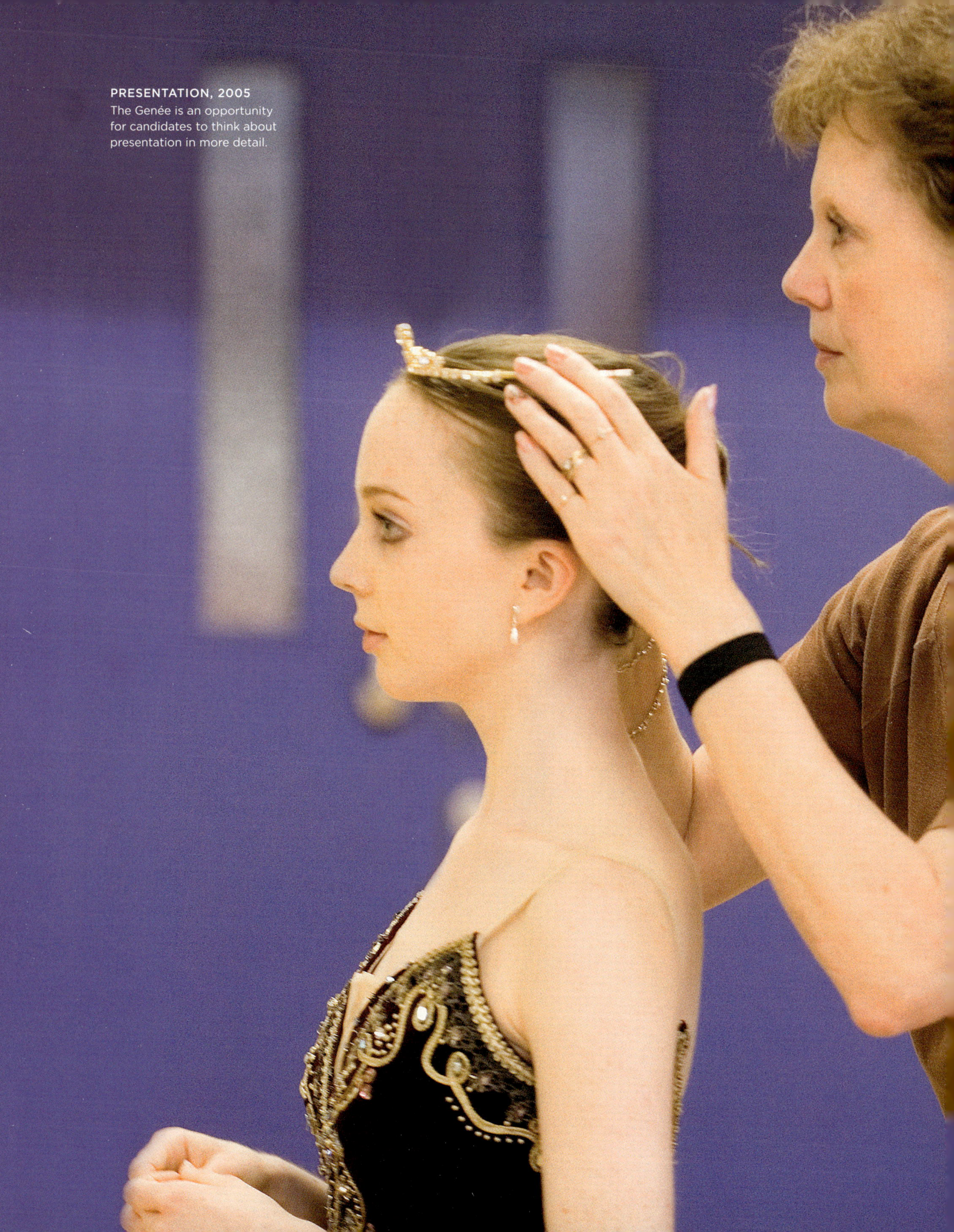

PRESENTATION, 2005
The Genée is an opportunity
for candidates to think about
presentation in more detail.

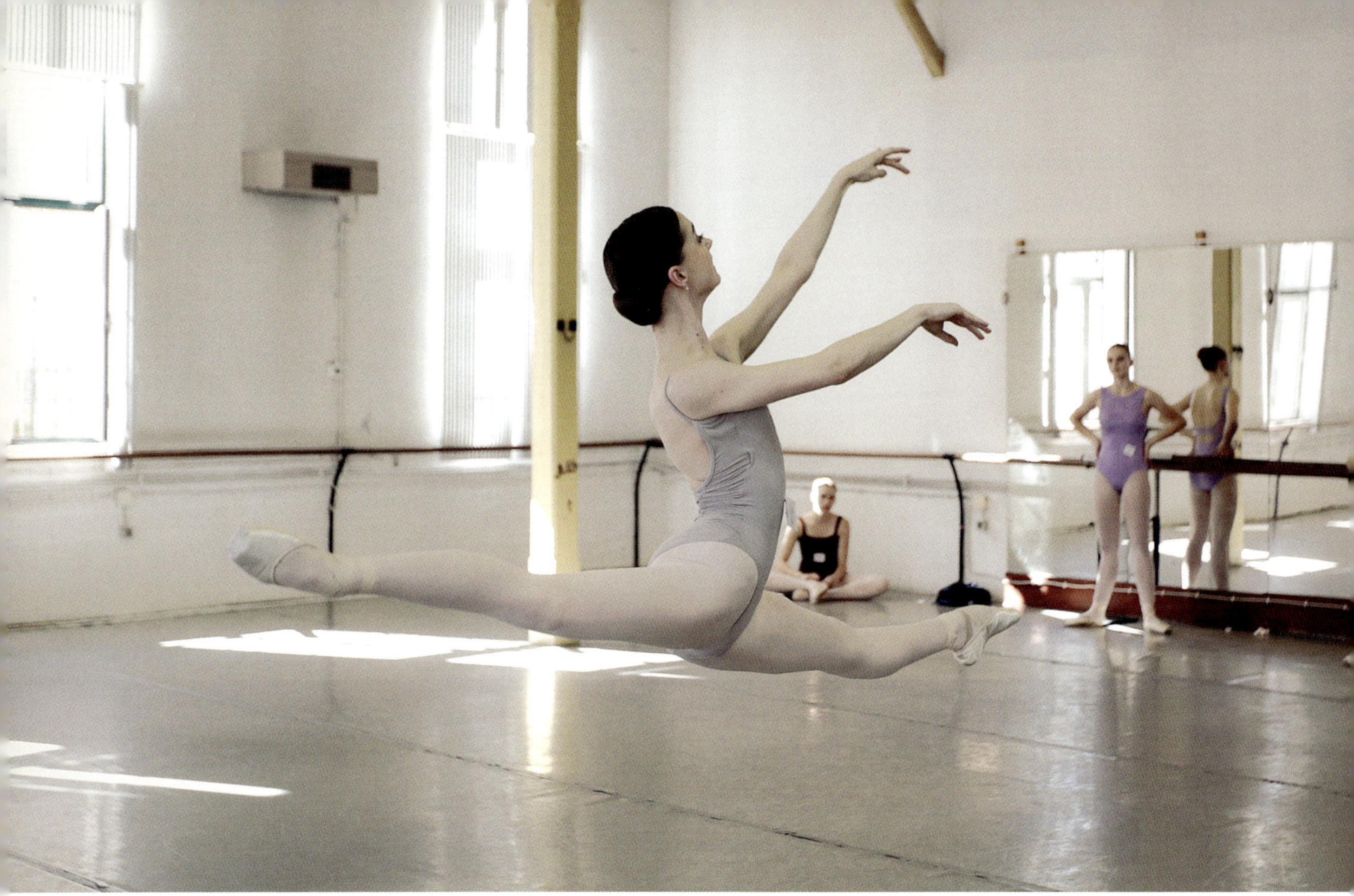

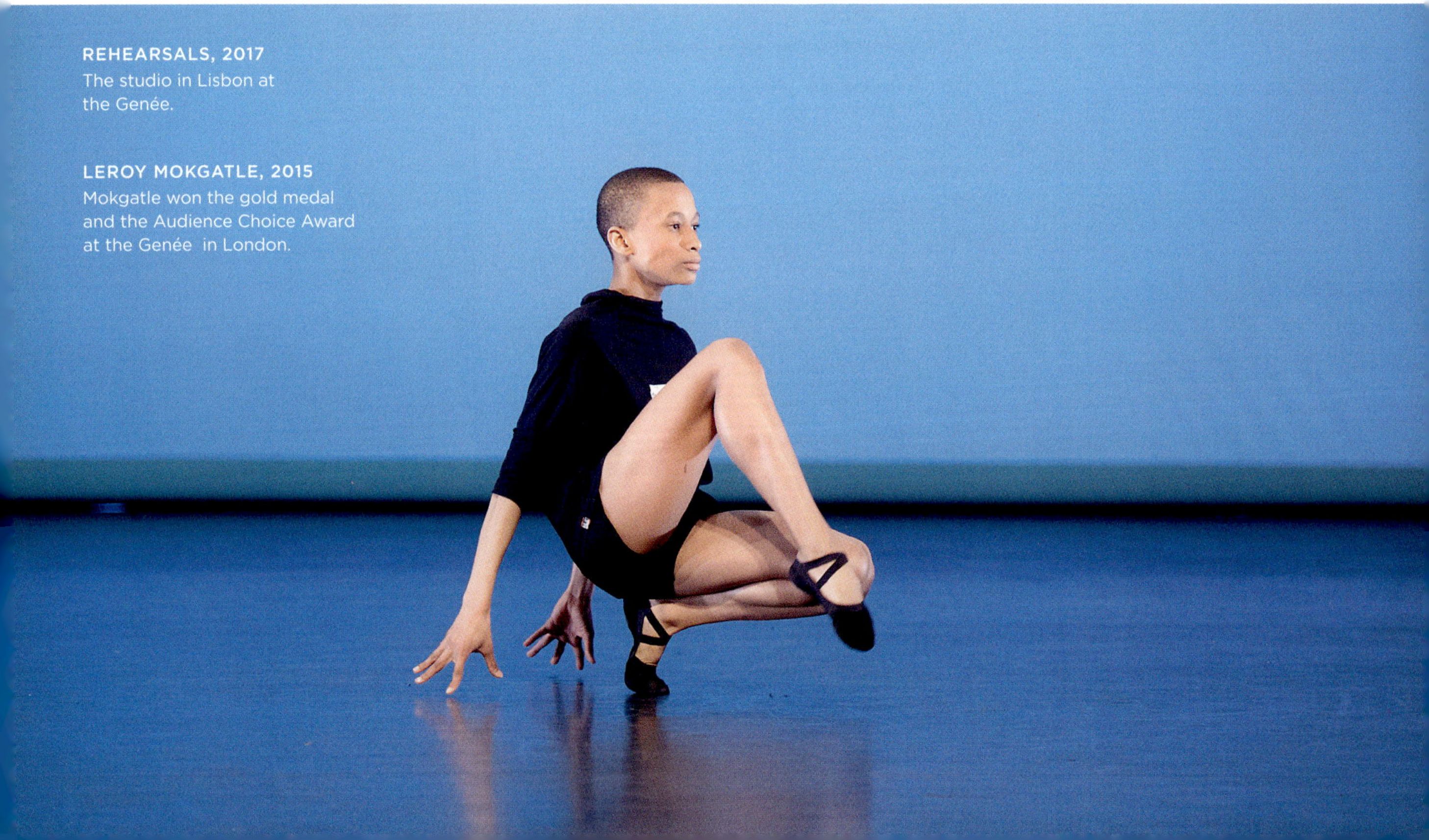

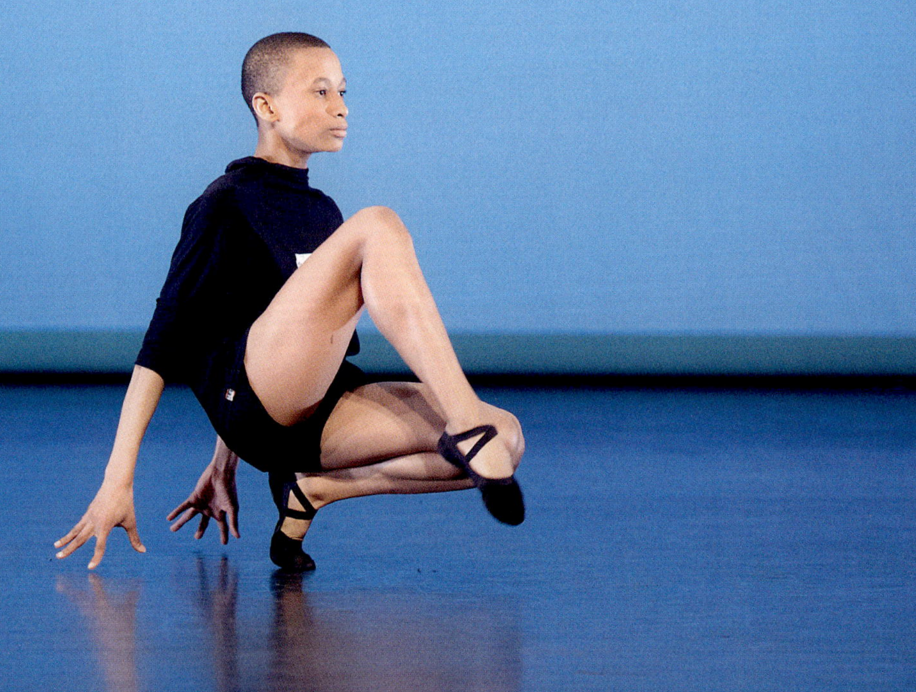

REHEARSALS, 2017
The studio in Lisbon at
the Genée.

LEROY MOKGATLE, 2015
Mokgatle won the gold medal
and the Audience Choice Award
at the Genée in London.

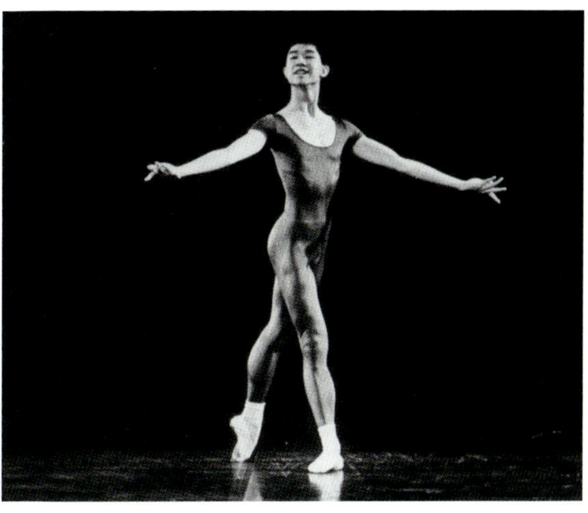

Each year the RAD commissions a choreographer to work with the candidates and create a variation that they all learn in addition to a variation from the classical repertoire, while creativity is encouraged in the solos, which are choreographed by the candidates themselves, by a teacher or by a peer, to a piece of music of their choice. The chance to work with a professional choreographer is popular with the young dancers. Canadian Alexandra MacDonald, a finalist in 2006 and now First Soloist with the National Ballet of Canada, remembers the 'eye-opening' experience of learning a variation from the Commissioned Choreographer (2006) and former gold medallist Yuri Ng: 'It was a piece that I truly loved, as it allowed me to play with the musicality, dynamics and intentions of the dance, something that I had never experienced before.' Other Commissioned Choreographers for the Genée have included Christopher Hampson (2003), Antony Dowson (2004), Michael Corder (2005), Sabrina Matthews (2008), Liam Scarlett (2010), Kirsten Isenberg (2011), Adrian Burnett (2009 and 2012), Robert Binet (2013), Ricardo Amarante (2014), Charlotte Edmonds (2015), Tim Harbour (2016), César Augusto Moniz (2017), Carlo Pacis (2018) and Gioconda Barbuto (2019).

Genée candidates often go on to successful careers with some of the world's leading ballet companies: since the year 2000, for example, 14 Genée medallists have gone on to join The Royal Ballet. Many participants comment on the friendliness of the competition. 'It felt like you were part of a little family for the week leading up to the final competition', British dancer Tierney Heap remembered. Winner of a bronze medal in 2010, Heap is now a soloist with The Royal Ballet, where Australian Steven McRae is Principal Dancer. McRae won gold in Sydney in 2002 and describes

> *'It was a piece that I truly loved, as it allowed me to play with the musicality, dynamics and intentions of the dance, something that I had never experienced before.'*

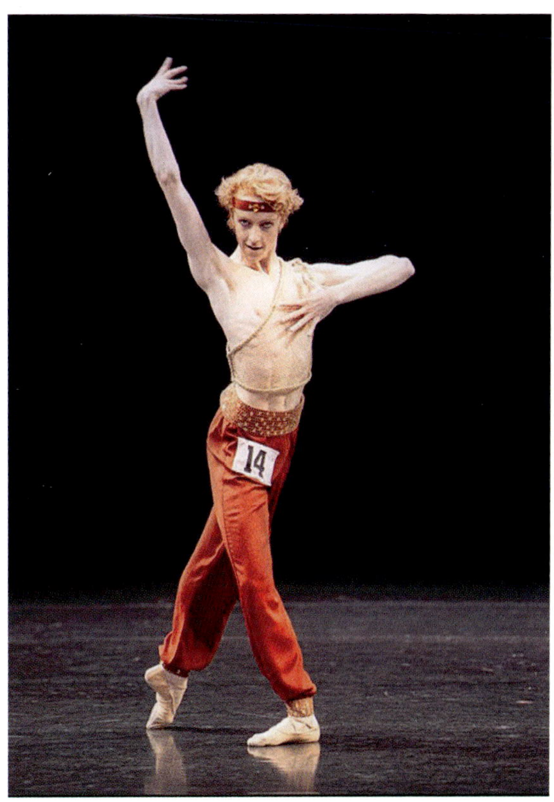

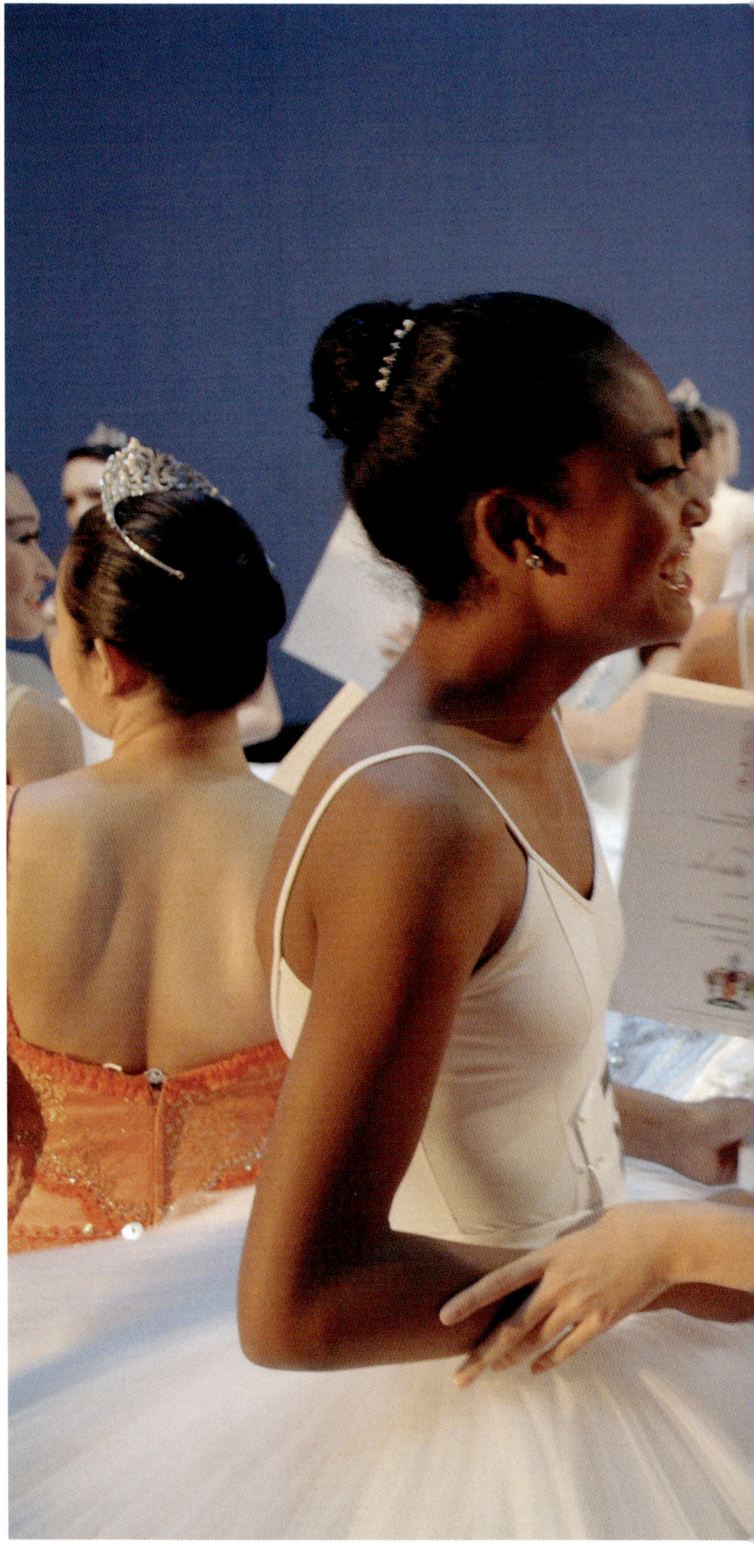

the Genée as less a competition than 'a celebratory workshop highlighting the achievements of everyone involved'.

Other finalists, like Alex Wong, Canadian winner of a bronze medal and the Audience Choice Award in 2003, talk about the friendliness and fellowship that led to a 'summer camp feeling', while Isabelle Brouwers from Germany, now First Artist with the English National Ballet, felt that she took away much more than the silver medal she won in 2013: 'it felt like a wonderful week of workshops, a unique opportunity to take class with world-class teachers and work directly with an amazing international choreographer!'

Trinidadian ballerina Céline Gittens is Principal Dancer with Birmingham Royal Ballet. She won a gold medal and the Audience Choice Award at the Genée in 2005. Her fondest memory of the competition, she recalls, 'was walking through the doors of the RAD headquarters in Battersea, London. I had been doing my RAD exams since the age of 5 and now being in the building, with dancers from all around the world who studied the RAD syllabus just like I did, was very exciting.' Mlindi Kulashe, who is from South Africa and is now a First Soloist with Northern Ballet in Leeds, first went to the Genée in Singapore in 2009. His teacher Dianne Cheesman recalls: 'I will always remember how his smile spread broadly across his face as he proudly wore his South Africa tracksuit, on the plane travelling to Singapore.' Kulashe later won the bronze medal at the 2011 Genée in his home town of Cape Town.

In addition to the Genée International Ballet Competition, the Academy encourages performances through competitions at other levels. For some years it worked in association with the Rudolf Nureyev Foundation to provide encouragement to young dancers in Great Britain and Northern Ireland. Launching the Fonteyn Nureyev Young

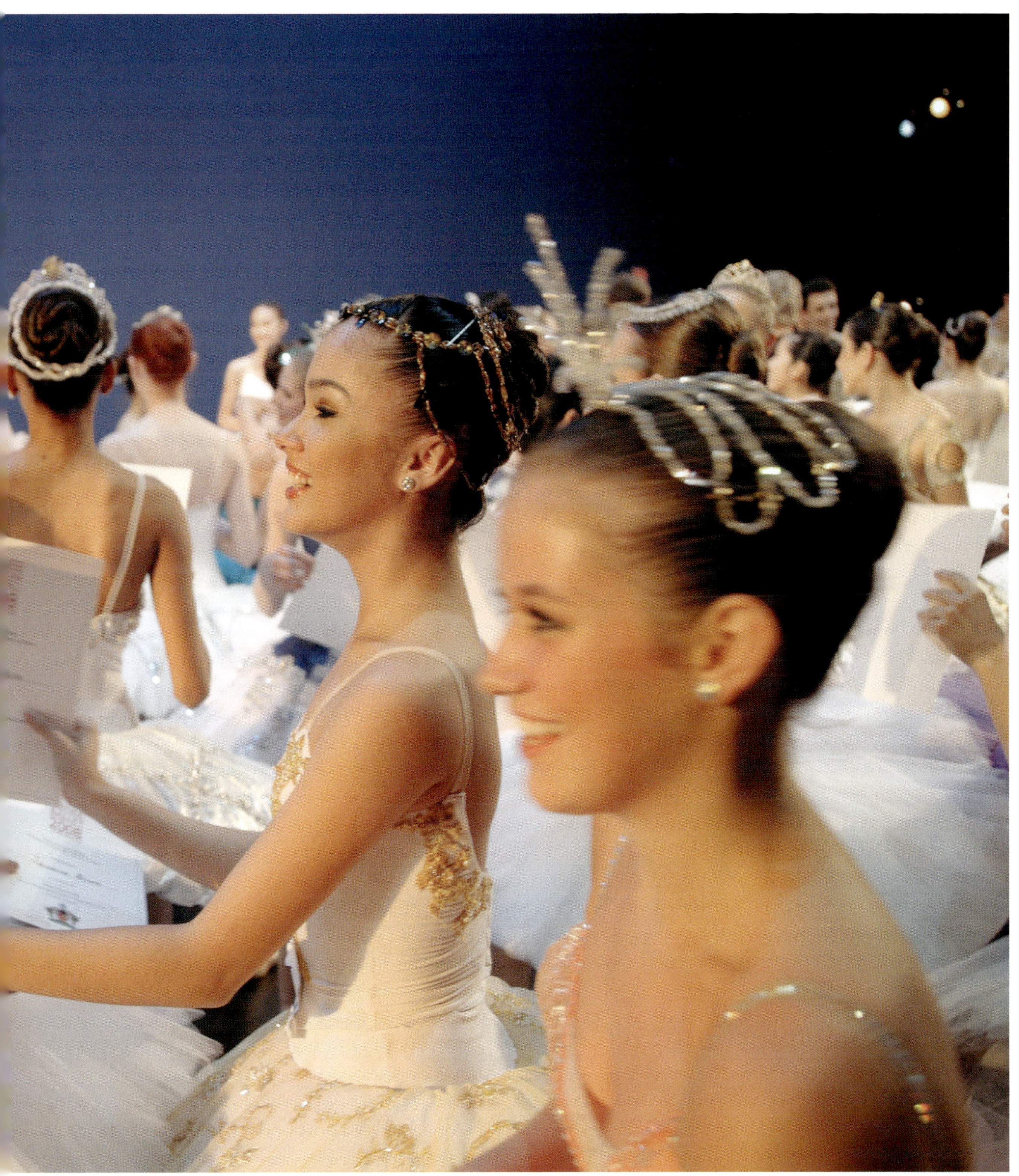

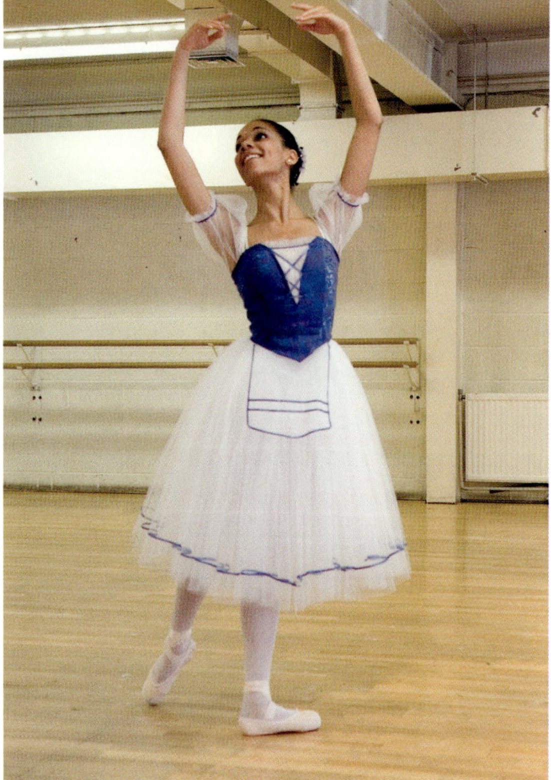

'I had been doing my RAD exams since the age of 5 and now being in the building, with dancers from all around the world who studied the RAD syllabus just like I did, was very exciting.'

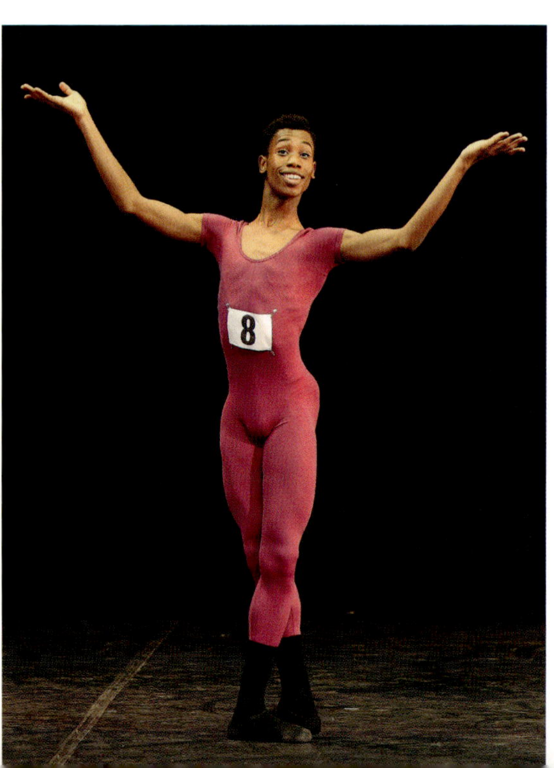

Dancers Competition in 2005, Antoinette Sibley explained that it was intended to provide dancers in the often-overlooked age group of 10 to 13 years with the opportunity 'to experience the thrill of performance and a taste of theatre for themselves'. Four variations, two for males and two for females, were created for the competition by the renowned choreographer Gillian Lynne.

Recently the RAD has provided additional opportunities for its UK members to perform in public through a variety of pop-up events. These have taken place at a number of locations in London, including King's Cross Station, where the RAD provided a stage, technology and administrative support for members who were invited to bring along a group of dancers of any ability and perform for two minutes. These events are hugely popular and, as well as being enjoyed by those taking part, promote the RAD and the wide range of its members and activities. Similar pop-up events have been organised overseas, often in conjunction with the Genée International Ballet Competition.

Many of the other activities organised by the RAD in the UK, and increasingly in other countries too, are geared towards supporting performances. A number of summer schools take place around the world in countries as varied as Norway and Japan, Malaysia and Canada or Australia and Italy, where as many as a thousand students a week attend a range of classes on dance and related disciplines. Summer schools give students the opportunity to make new friends and to feel part of the dance community, and a performance can provide the highpoint of the week when they have a chance to share what they have learned in front of an audience.

Throughout the year, RAD workshops and masterclasses inspired by famous ballets or musicals often conclude with a performance.

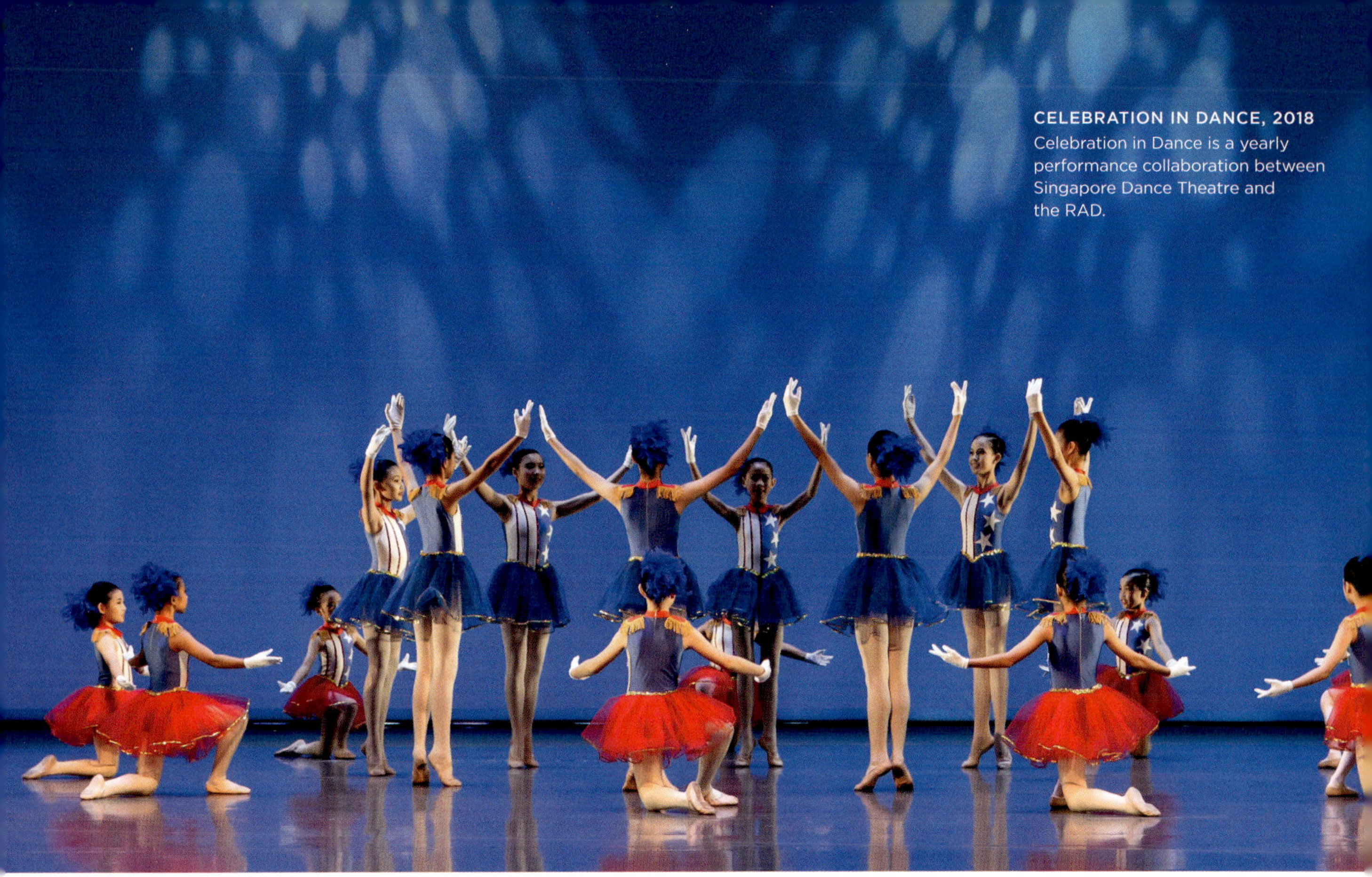

CELEBRATION IN DANCE, 2018
Celebration in Dance is a yearly performance collaboration between Singapore Dance Theatre and the RAD.

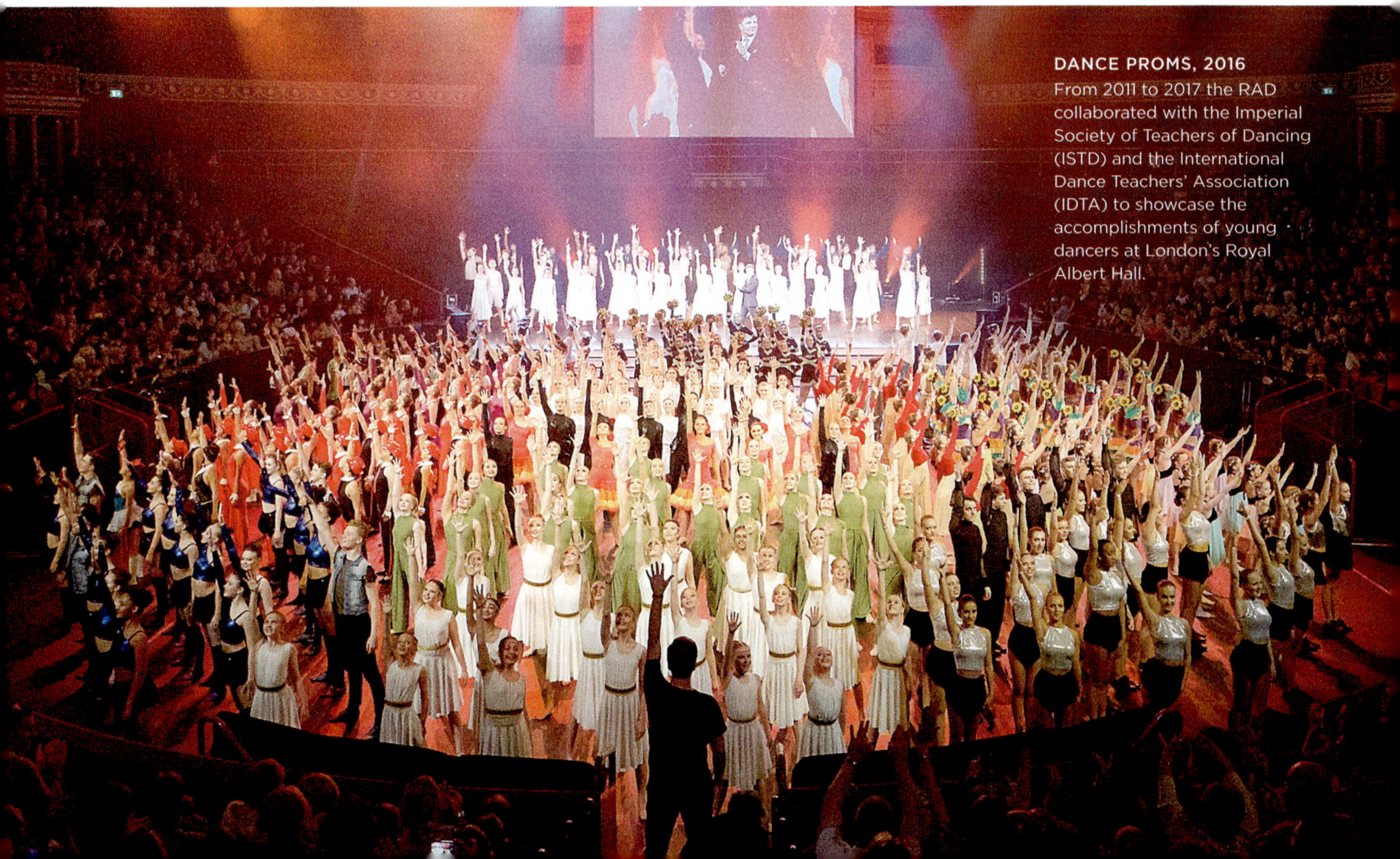

DANCE PROMS, 2016
From 2011 to 2017 the RAD collaborated with the Imperial Society of Teachers of Dancing (ISTD) and the International Dance Teachers' Association (IDTA) to showcase the accomplishments of young dancers at London's Royal Albert Hall.

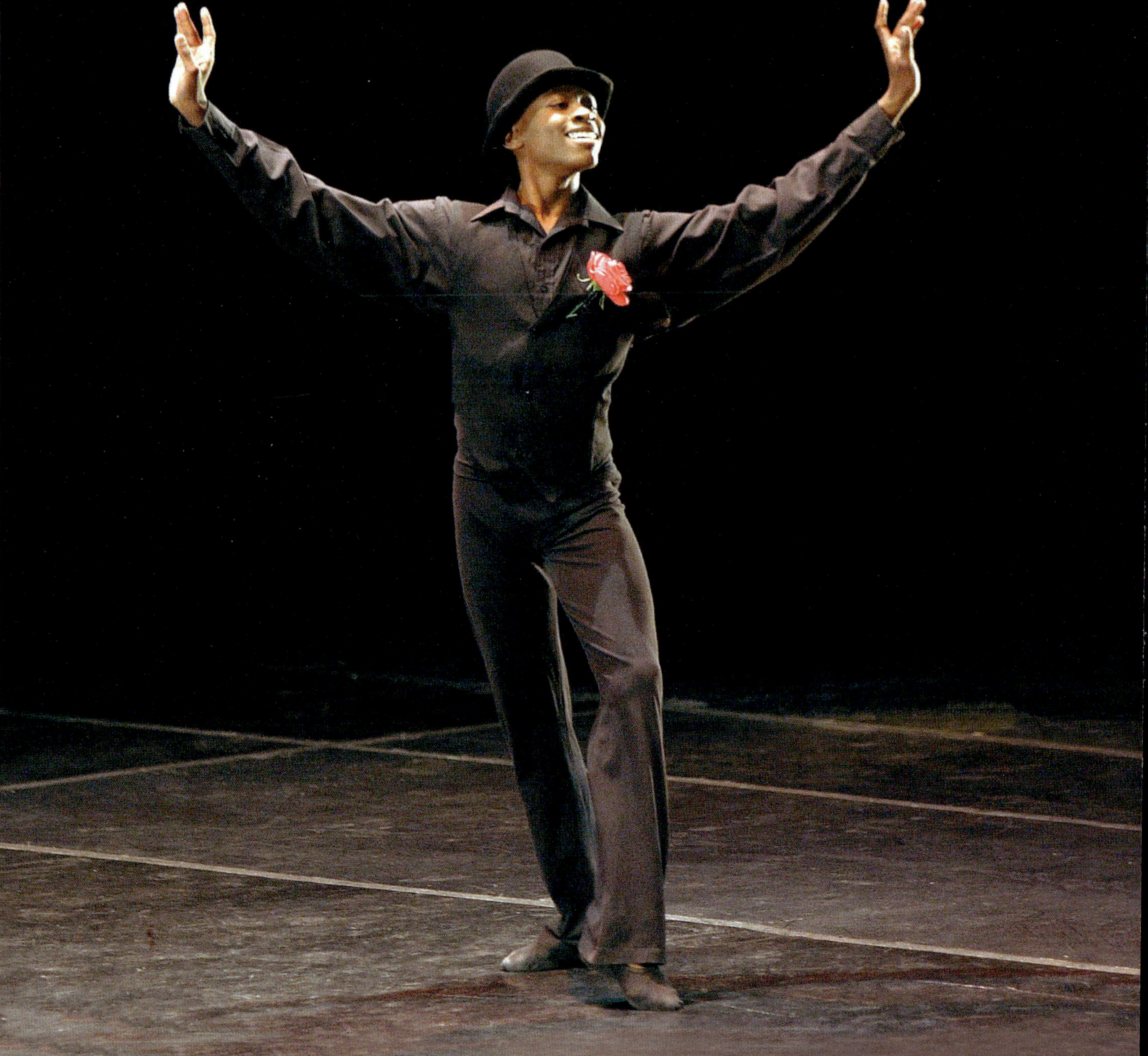

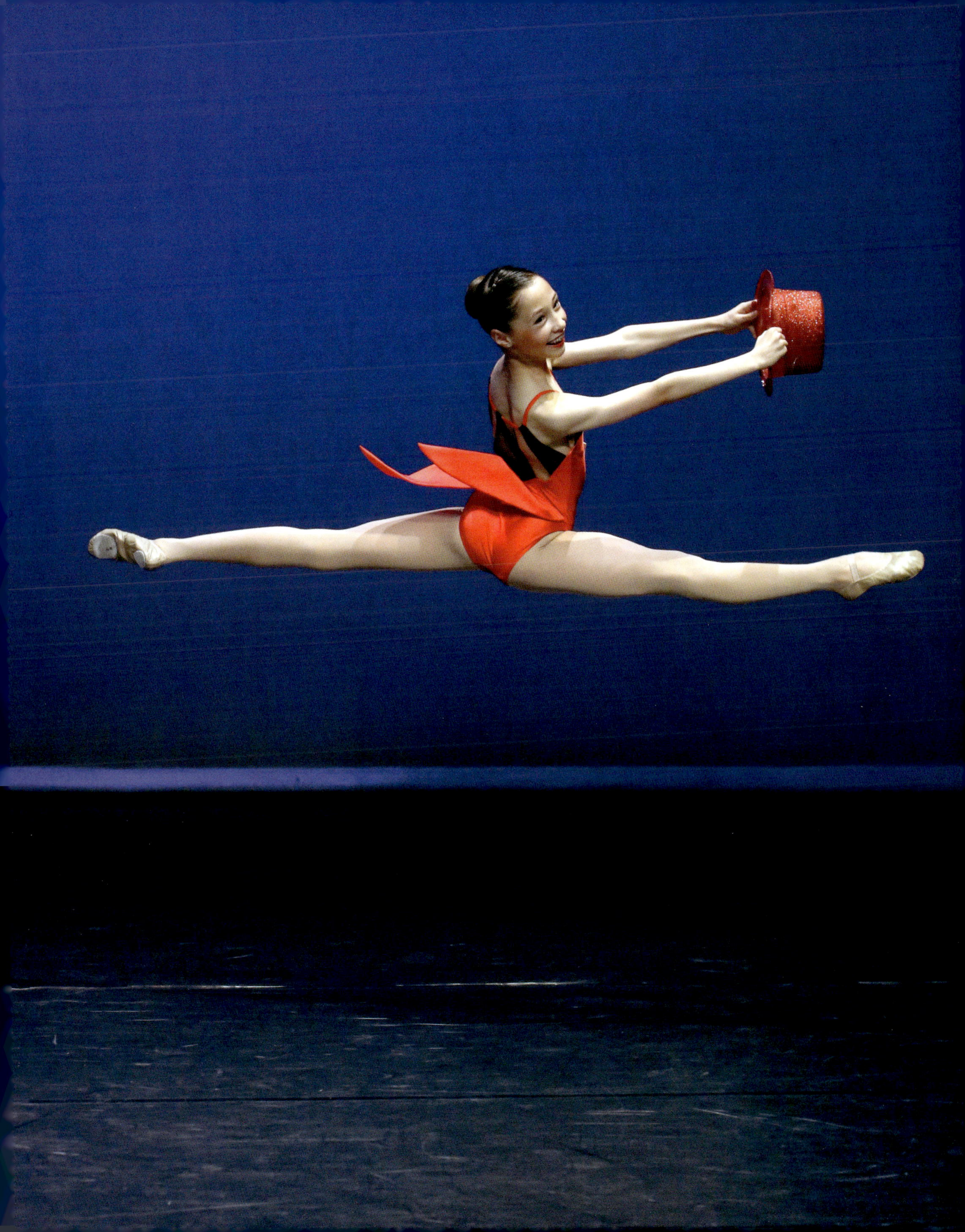

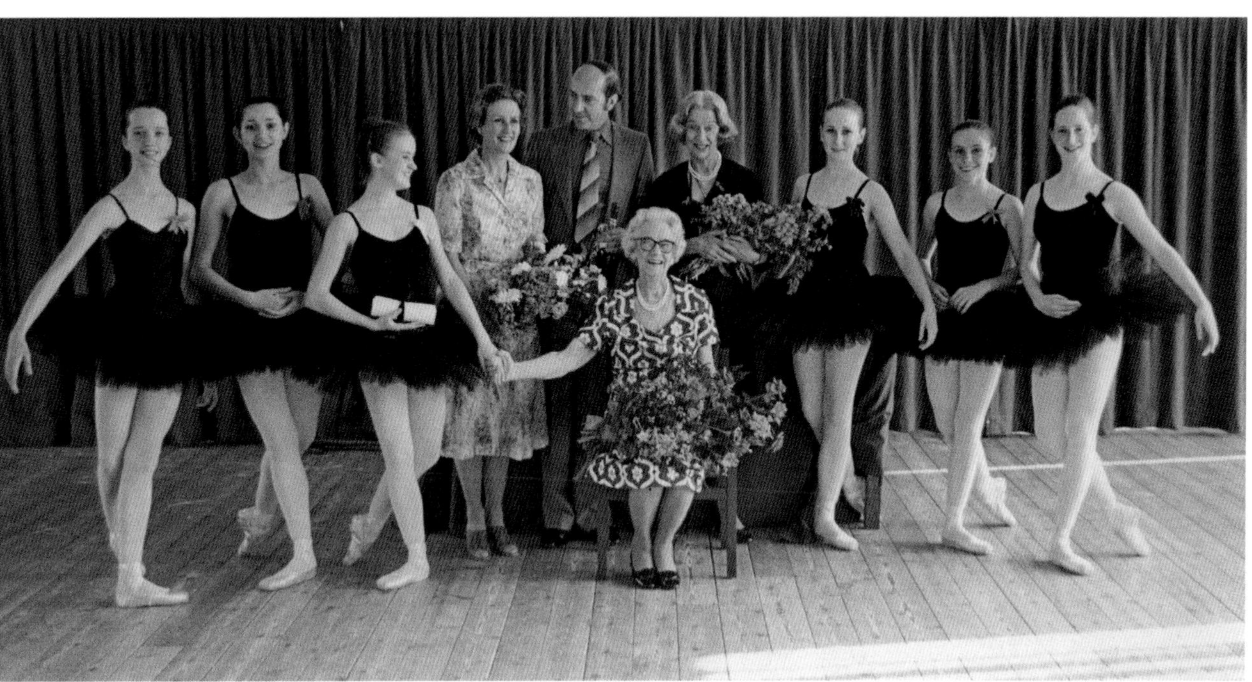

The Academy is also building partnerships with organisations such as the Mandarin Oriental Hotel Group, where, for instance, members and their students performed as a backdrop to an 'afternoon tea' themed around dance. Under the direction of Matthew Cunningham, Director of Strategic Development and Fundraising, the RAD has increased its focus on collaborations that allow the RAD to extend its reach, deliver more and demonstrate the impact of its work across diverse communities.

In 2016, as part of the Ashton Workshop Programme, the RAD was given permission by the Frederick Ashton Foundation to teach Ashton's choreography to non-professionals and vocational students, aged 10 and over. This was the first time the choreography was made widely available to dance students other than those enrolled at The Royal Ballet School. Students developed their performance skills by studying and rehearsing scenes from *La fille mal gardée* and *The Dream*, as well as learning how to apply stage make-up.

Around the world, the Academy's international branches have their own awards, prizes, medals and cups, which provide opportunities for student performance and reward achievement. The Genée competition itself provides inspiration for a whole series of other awards and events, giving students around the world the chance to perform on stage and compete for awards. The RAD's Dance Challenge, for example, takes place in Australia, the US, Canada, the UK and Singapore. Modelled on the Genée, the Dance Challenge is aimed at a lower age group, and although there are some variations between the different countries, essentially it follows the same format.

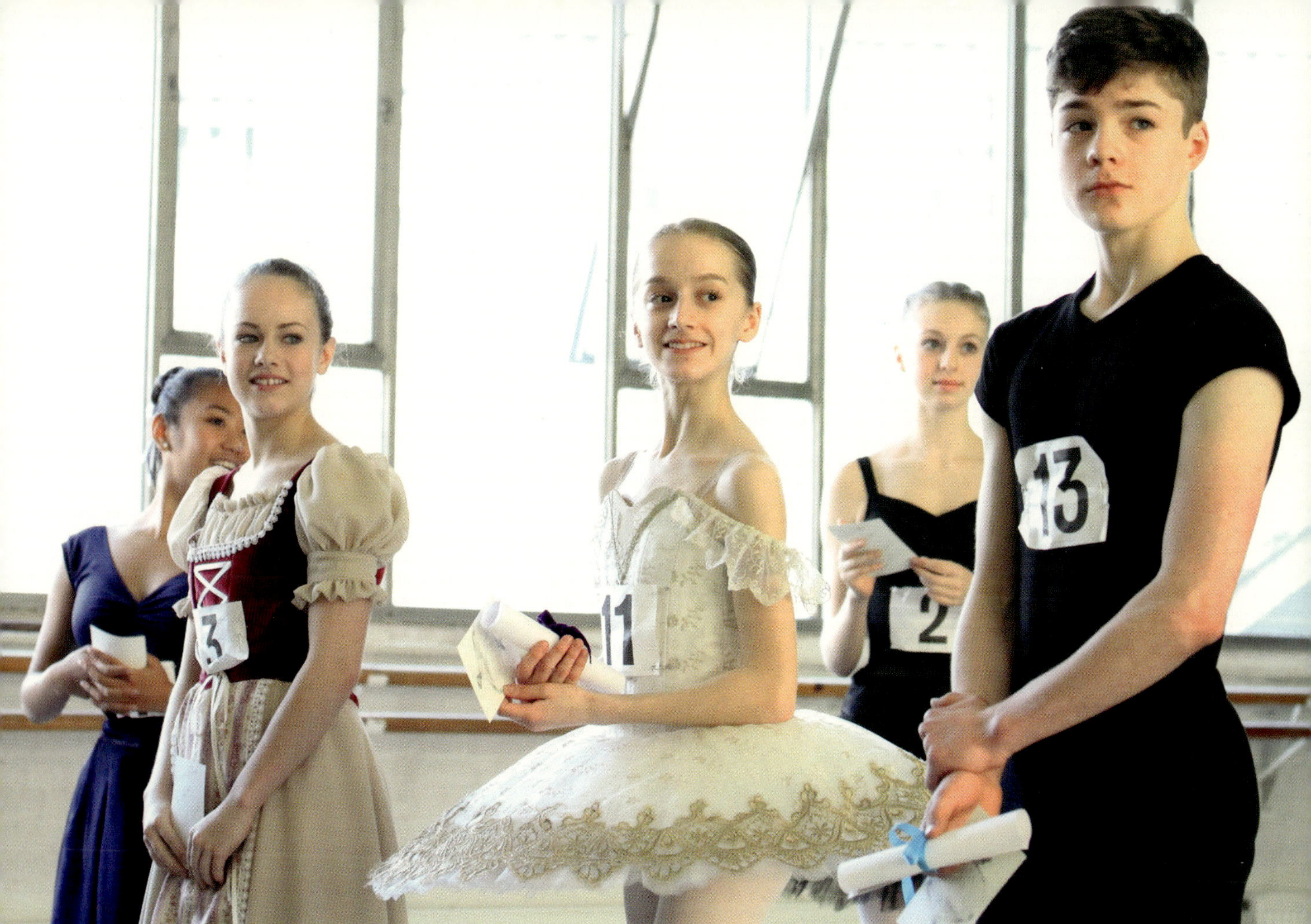

BURSARY AWARDS

The RAD offers a number of bursaries for talented students in need of financial assistance. The Phyllis Bedells Bursary, named after one of its founding members, is for young dancers (male or female) under the age of 17, who have passed the Advanced 1 examination but have not yet entered for Advanced 2. The bursary, made possible by the Mary Kipps Bequest and worth up to £1,000, attracts applicants from across the UK and culminates in a performance before an audience and panel of judges. Since 2015 the Bursary has followed the 'Dancer's Own' format of the Genée competition, with students required to perform their own solo or one that has been created by their teacher or a peer. A choreographic award has also been added, 'to promote and reward choreography as a distinct part of the creative process'.

In the latter 2010s Genée candidates have been eligible for two bursary schemes thanks to an annual contribution from the Dame Margot Fonteyn Scholarship Fund (which was set up following Fonteyn's death, in 1991) and a glittering evening held in 2014 when the Queen Elizabeth II Coronation Award was awarded to The Royal Ballet. The £70,000 raised that evening towards Genée bursaries was named in honour of current President Dame Darcey Bussell, and both schemes offer support to students from any country, male or female. Other schemes, such as the Project B Student Activities Bursary and the Project B Dance Schools Boys' Bursary, are further evidence of the Academy's commitment to rewarding achievement and supporting talented students.

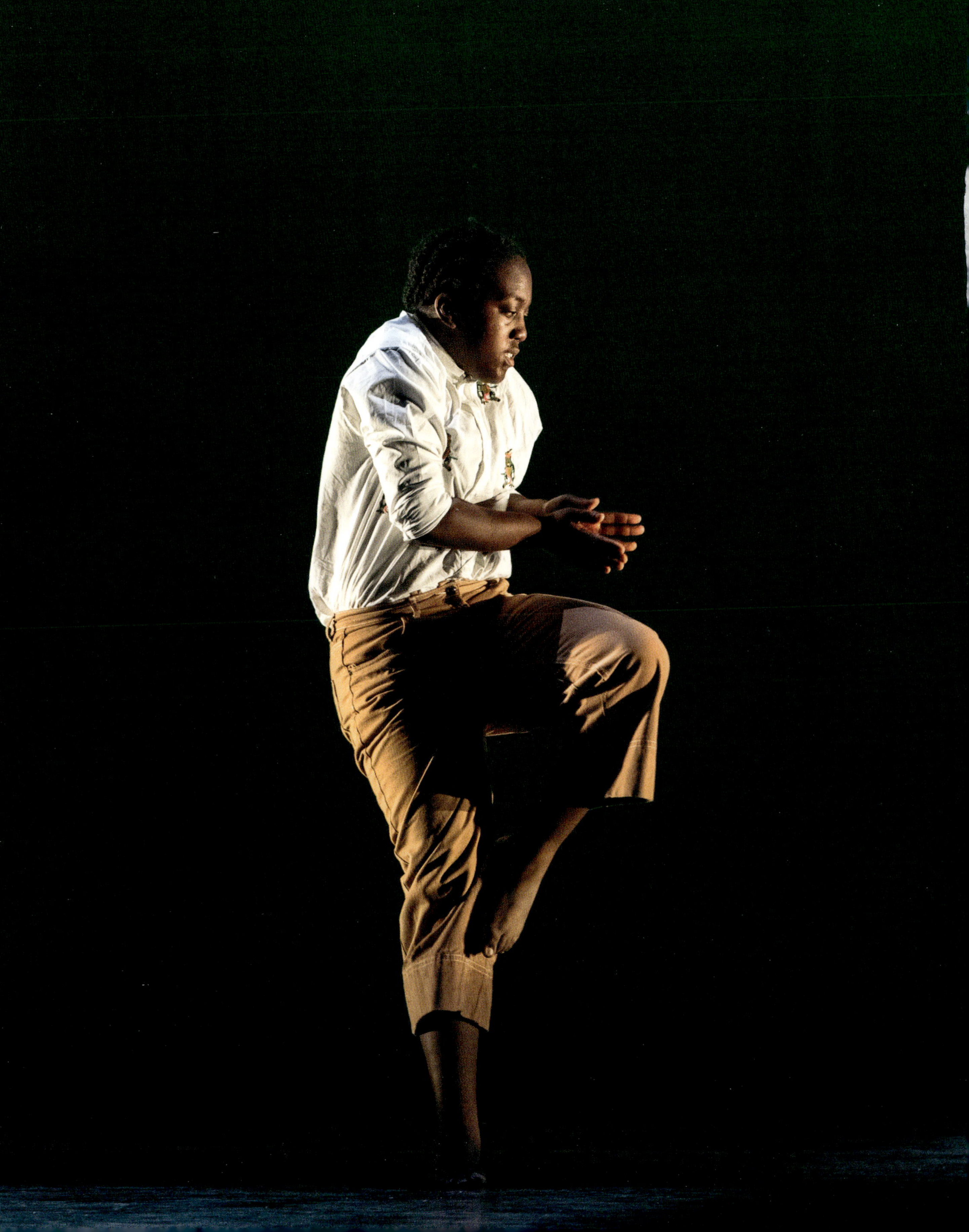

8

———

EVERYONE'S ACADEMY

Widening participation in dance

THE Academy has always sought to include wider participation in its core activities. Both the earliest Ballet in Education syllabus and the Dance Education syllabus of the 1970s sought to make dance more relevant and accessible to a wider cross-section of students, while the more recent Discovering Repertoire programme offers a fresh alternative to the core syllabi. Other strategies, such as Presentation Classes and Class Awards, as well as Special Considerations and Reasonable Adjustments, help to make the Academy's examinations accessible to candidates with disabilities or special needs. In addition, the RAD has increasingly initiated and developed numerous projects, nationally and internationally, to bring dance to people of all ages and from all backgrounds, reducing or eliminating some of the barriers that have traditionally limited participation.

The idea of taking ballet to new audiences was promoted as long ago as 1954, when the RAD was approached by the Whip and Carrot Club to provide a series of experimental ballet classes aimed at athletes. The Whip and Carrot Club was an association of high-jumpers, and its members were intrigued at reports from the Soviet Union and the USA that their athletes had benefited from ballet exercises. After a number of meetings, a series of experimental classes for athletes was set up and, following a successful demonstration, the Amateur Athletics Association (AAA) joined the project. In 1960, in collaboration with the AAA, the Academy published a booklet called *Ballet Exercises for Athletes*, describing those exercises that were deemed to have benefited high-jumpers, hurdlers and other athletes.

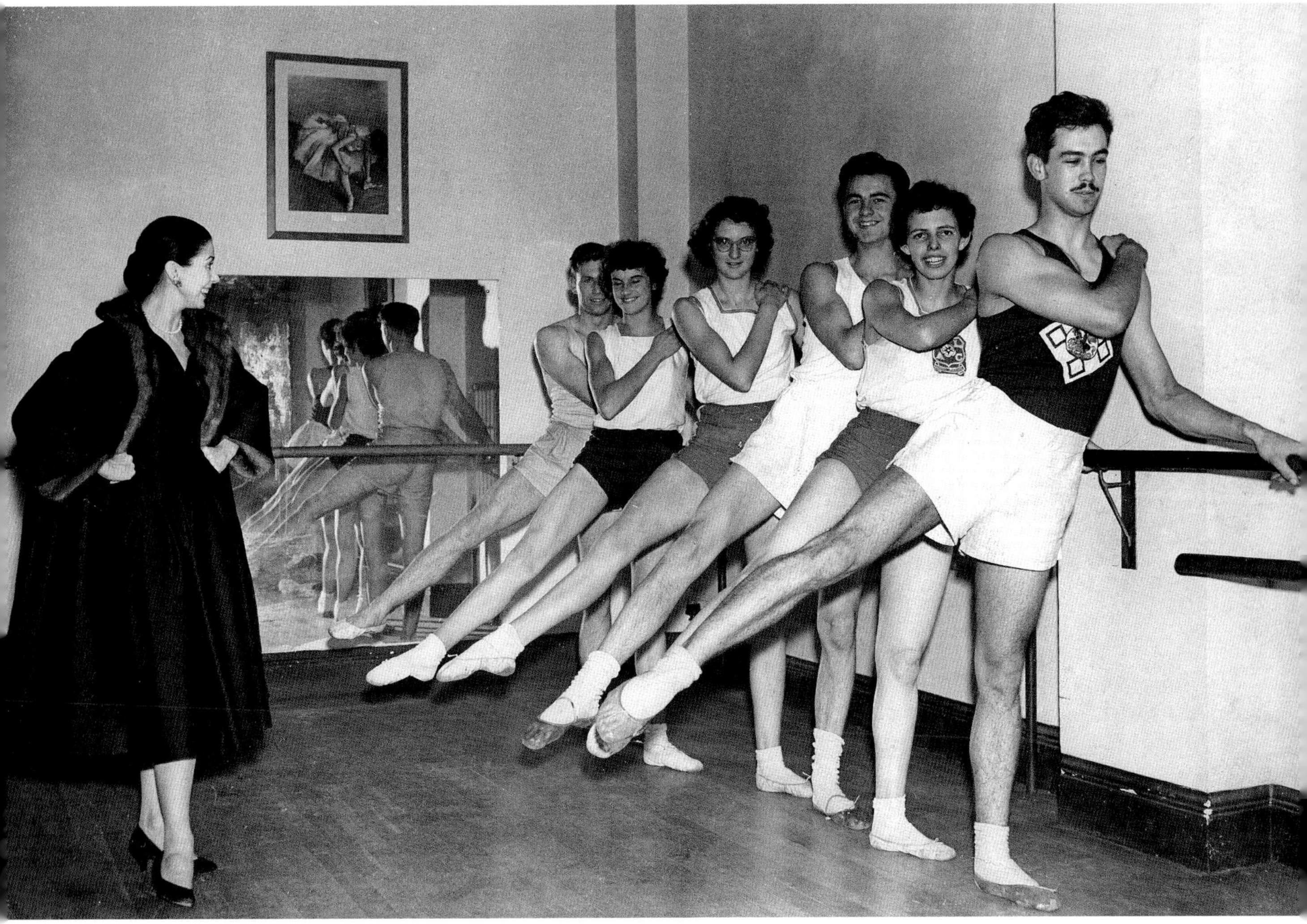

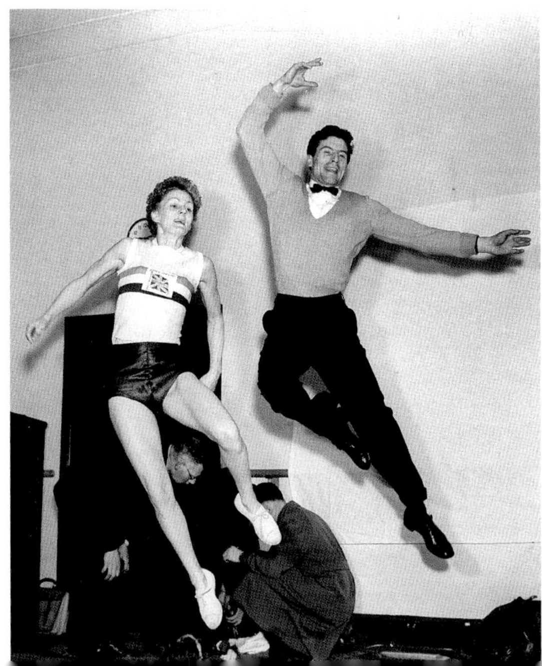
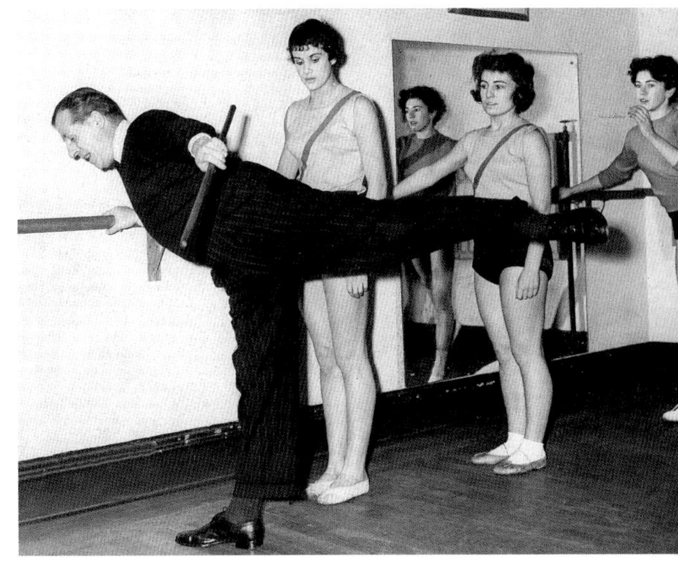

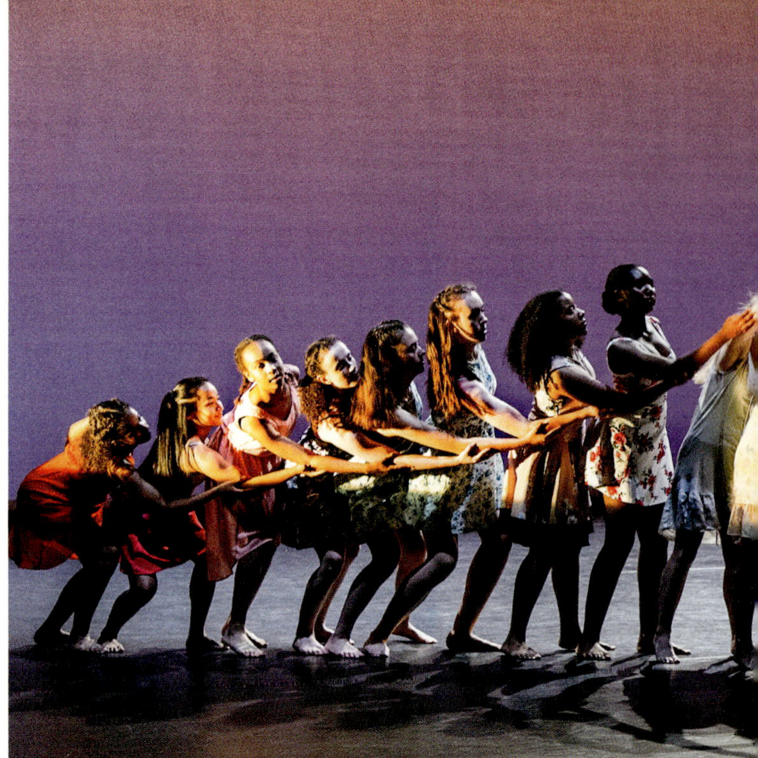

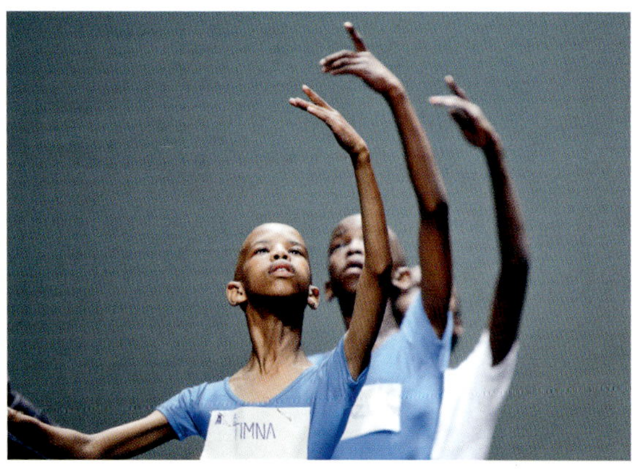

DANCE IN THE WIDER COMMUNITY

The twenty-first century has seen a real growth of RAD programmes introducing dance to the wider community. The Step Into Dance programme, for instance, was piloted in 2007 in partnership with the Jack Petchey Foundation. The programme offers regular dance classes to secondary school children across London and Essex and aims to reach students who might not otherwise experience dance. Taught by professional dancers, Step Into Dance provides a range of ways in which children can engage with dance through different dance styles, from street dance and hip hop to ballet, and encourages them to grow as dance performers, artists and leaders.

Step Into Dance reaches approximately 6,000 students in mainstream and special educational needs schools in London and Essex every year through weekly classes and workshops. A programme of shows runs throughout the year, culminating in a showcase performance by all the separate groups in a professional theatre.

The idea of introducing young people, many from disadvantaged backgrounds, to the theatre was the springboard for the RAD's outreach project Sizodanisa, or Let's Dance, when South Africa hosted the Genée in Cape Town in 2011. In association with Cape Town City Ballet, Sizodanisa brought together children from dance groups and different communities and townships across Cape Town for two days of workshops at which they learned a variety of different dance forms, including ballet, hip hop and mime. On the third day they performed in front of a live audience at the Artscape Theatre, demonstrating work inspired by the Genée Commissioned Choreography and music. For some of the children, including those living in townships, it was their first experience of visiting a professional theatre, let alone performing in one. The project had a lasting impact on how local children from the townships interacted with Cape Town City Ballet.

In recent years the Academy has also put much effort into challenging the stereotype of ballet as something that only girls do and in promoting the philosophy that dance is for everyone, regardless of age, gender, ethnicity or ability. In particular, the RAD has targeted three groups that have traditionally been less associated with dance: older adults, boys, and children with special educational needs.

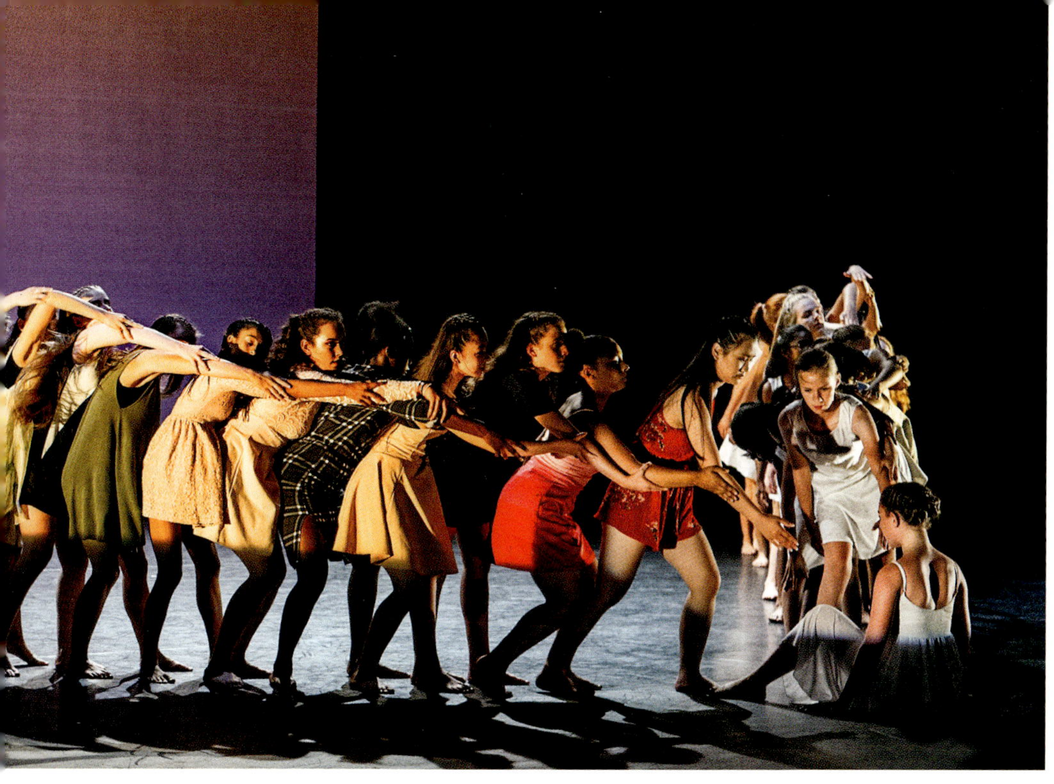

STEP INTO DANCE, 2018
The programme offers regular dance classes and culminates in an annual performance at a professional theatre.

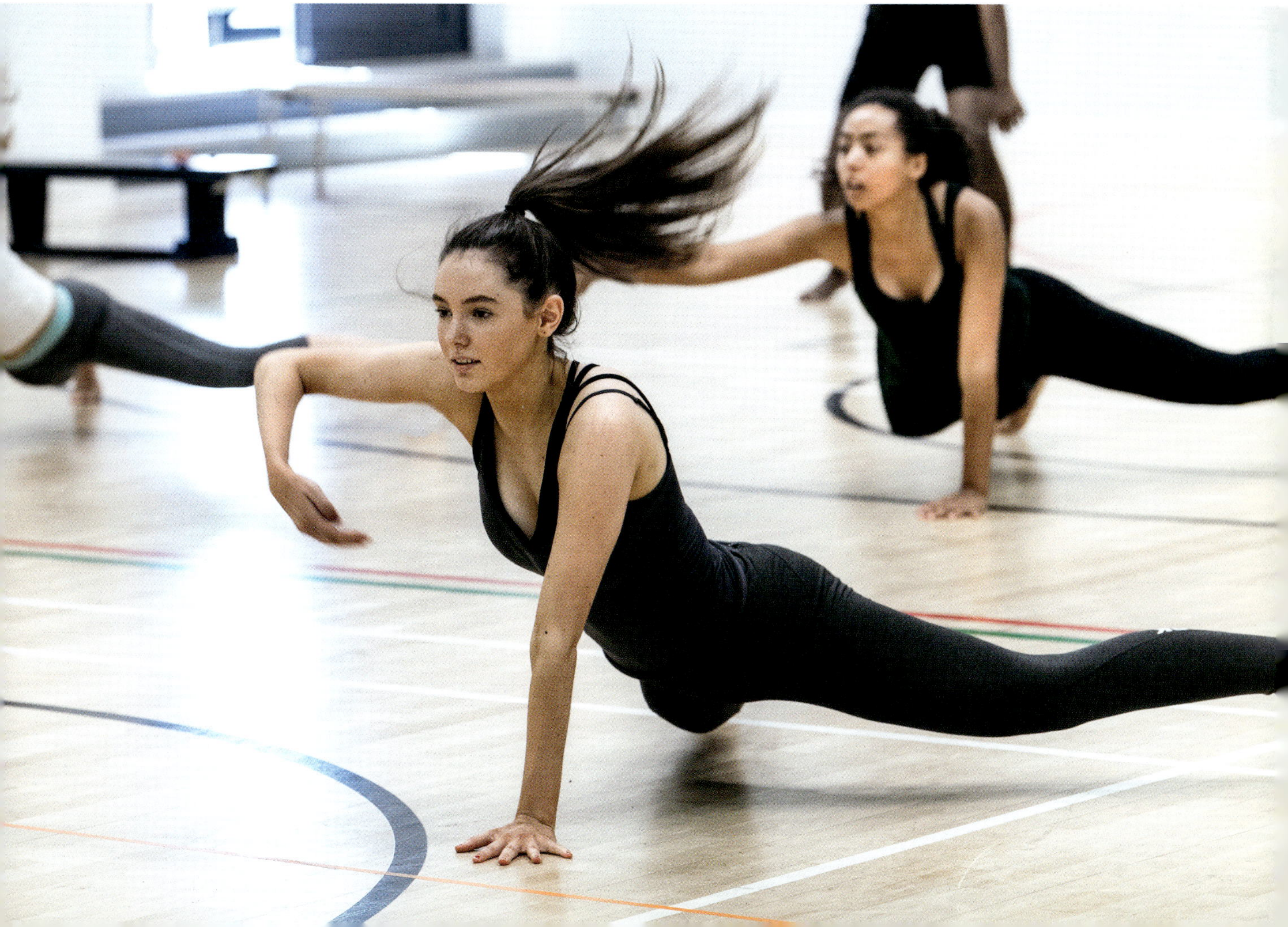

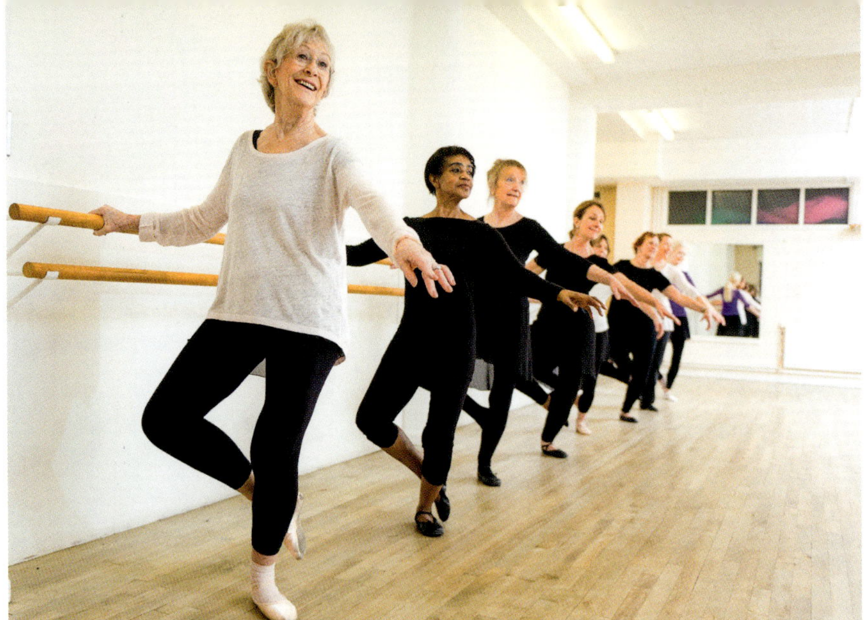

SILVER SWANS

The Silver Swans initiative – currently available in Australia, the US, the UK, Ireland, New Zealand, Mexico and Canada, with more territories planned for future years – challenges age barriers by providing dance classes for adults over the age of 55. Research on the benefits of ballet for older adults undertaken by Queensland Ballet and the Queensland University of Technology (QUT), as well as by the Academy's own researchers, has underlined the vital role that dance can play in ensuring a long and healthy life. Research has found that dance helps to reduce the incidence of diabetes, heart disease, dementia, high blood pressure and high cholesterol levels, and can also help to improve bone density and cognitive skills such as balance and coordination.

The benefits of Silver Swans classes, which are open to people of all abilities and designed to be inclusive, fun and accessible, are obvious to Angela Rippon, the RAD's Silver Swans Ambassador in the UK: '[dance] keeps you supple, it's an aerobic exercise, it gives you spatial awareness, it makes you use your brain, and it gives you some kind of social contact as well.'

The reflective element of ballet appeals to older learners, particularly when it combines music, movement and the sheer beauty of classical line. 'There is still a beauty of feeling and movement in people even when they are older', one Silver Swan explained. 'The feeling of the movements with the particular pieces of music can really take you to another world; you can feel elegant and spiritual again. The classes not only help me connect with my body but they raise me up – they are incredibly good for your soul.'

Many Silver Swans studied ballet as children and the classes are about rediscovering sometimes long-forgotten memories: 'we were all working at the barre', one remembered, 'and everyone was in step when we realised the "swish" sound of the feet and ballet shoes together … it took us back instantly to those days in class when we were much younger!' For others, the benefits are physical and a way to combat the effects of ageing. One Swan described joining a class as 'a protest against getting old and a bid to seize the day' but soon discovered other advantages to ballet: 'core strengthening, grace and subtleness', as well as improved coordination. Even better, the classes do not feel like an exercise class: 'It's a joy, not a boot camp.'

The early success of the scheme, which was piloted in early 2017, is being built on as the programme matures. The aim is to give even more older adults, men as well as women, the 'freeing and exhilarating' chance to express themselves to music. It is a class, one participant noted, 'where you can work at your own humble level but dance as if you were a pro'.

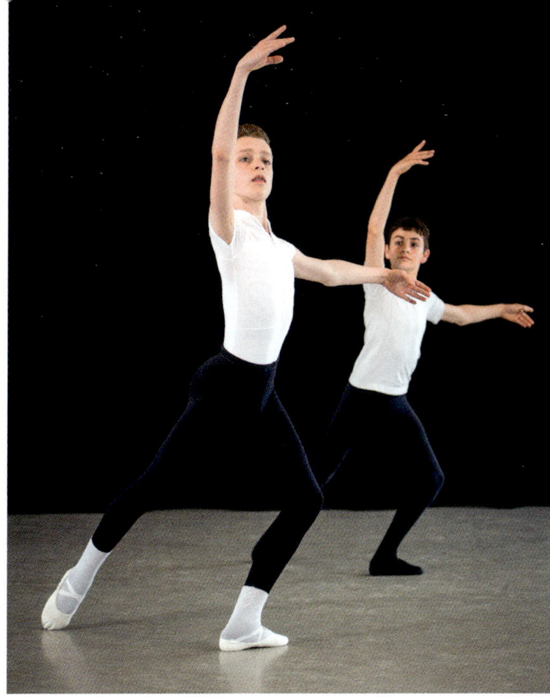

BOYS ONLY! AND PROJECT B

In 2006, when the musical *Billy Elliot* premiered, the RAD and the Royal Ballet School hosted a joint gala performance and dinner as a fundraiser. The RAD used its share of the proceeds to create a programme of weekend workshops entirely for boys and young men, called Boys Only!, based on a proposal by an RAD Regional Manager, Mandy Wix.

As part of a centennial aspiration to bring dance to more people in more places – and building on the Boys Only! concept – the RAD in 2017 launched Project B, a range of initiatives to widen access to dance for boys and to encourage them to take up ballet.

In 2017 Iain Mackay, then Principal at Birmingham Royal Ballet, was appointed the RAD's Male Dance Ambassador. He drew on his experience as a dancer, a teacher and a father to create Project B choreography that appeals especially to boys and gives them the opportunity to share in the benefits that all ballet dancers enjoy: fitness, confidence and imagination.

In his Project B workshops, Mackay aims to harness the energy and imagination of boys, often forgoing the rituals of barre and centre to engage the boys first with movement-based games or imagery from computer games or films. 'I try to grab their imagination first', Mackay explained in *Dance Gazette* in 2016; 'then when it comes to technique, they know where it's leading. Instead of starting with the plié and telling them it leads to jumping, I get them jumping first. Then I'll say: how can we help you jump like a superhero? Let's work on this plié.'

Alongside ballet and contemporary dance classes, and creative workshops that are designed with boys in mind (often taught by male teachers),

Project B aims to promote more male role models and make explicit the links between dance and sport so that ballet can be seen as complementary to football or tennis, for example. Bursaries and financial support for male dancers, financial support to encourage more men to train as dance teachers, and new resources for existing teachers are all part of the Project B mix.

Project B also entails ventures such as Dance Down the Wicket, a primary school project delivered in 2017 in partnership with Marylebone Cricket Club, which aimed to cross the stereotype gender divide by encouraging more boys to do ballet and more girls to play cricket. This six-week project used dance and sport to explore how the teaching of dance can be used to enhance the coaching of cricket, and vice versa. Strategies included thinking about coordination and respect in connection with fielding; about agility and balance for batting; and about bowling as an exercise in communication and teamwork.

The success of the project has led to a further pilot programme in India, supported by the British Council: Changing Moves, Changing Minds is evidence of the RAD's determination to take dance not only to new people within the UK but also to places with no established tradition of ballet and British dance.

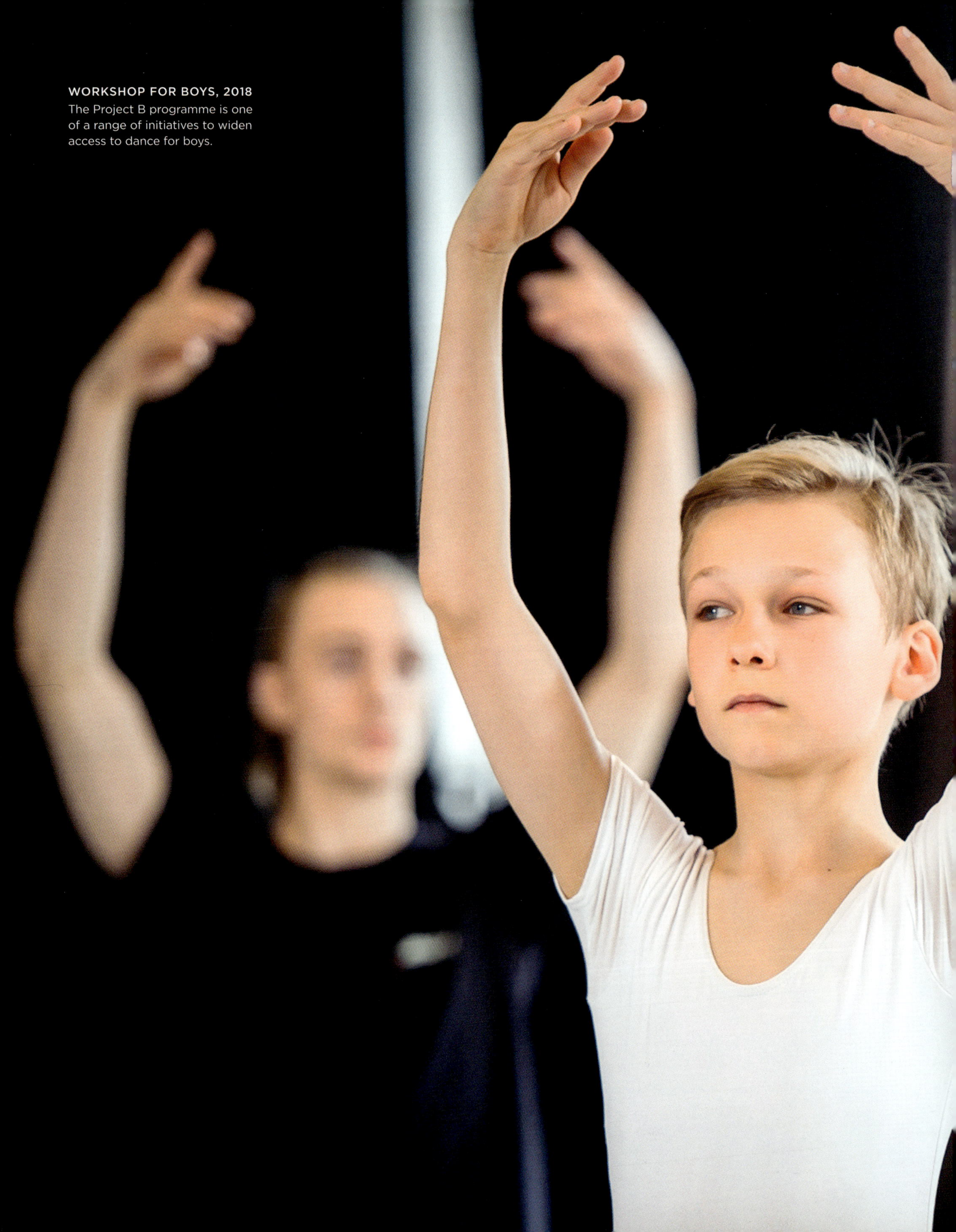

WORKSHOP FOR BOYS, 2018
The Project B programme is one
of a range of initiatives to widen
access to dance for boys.

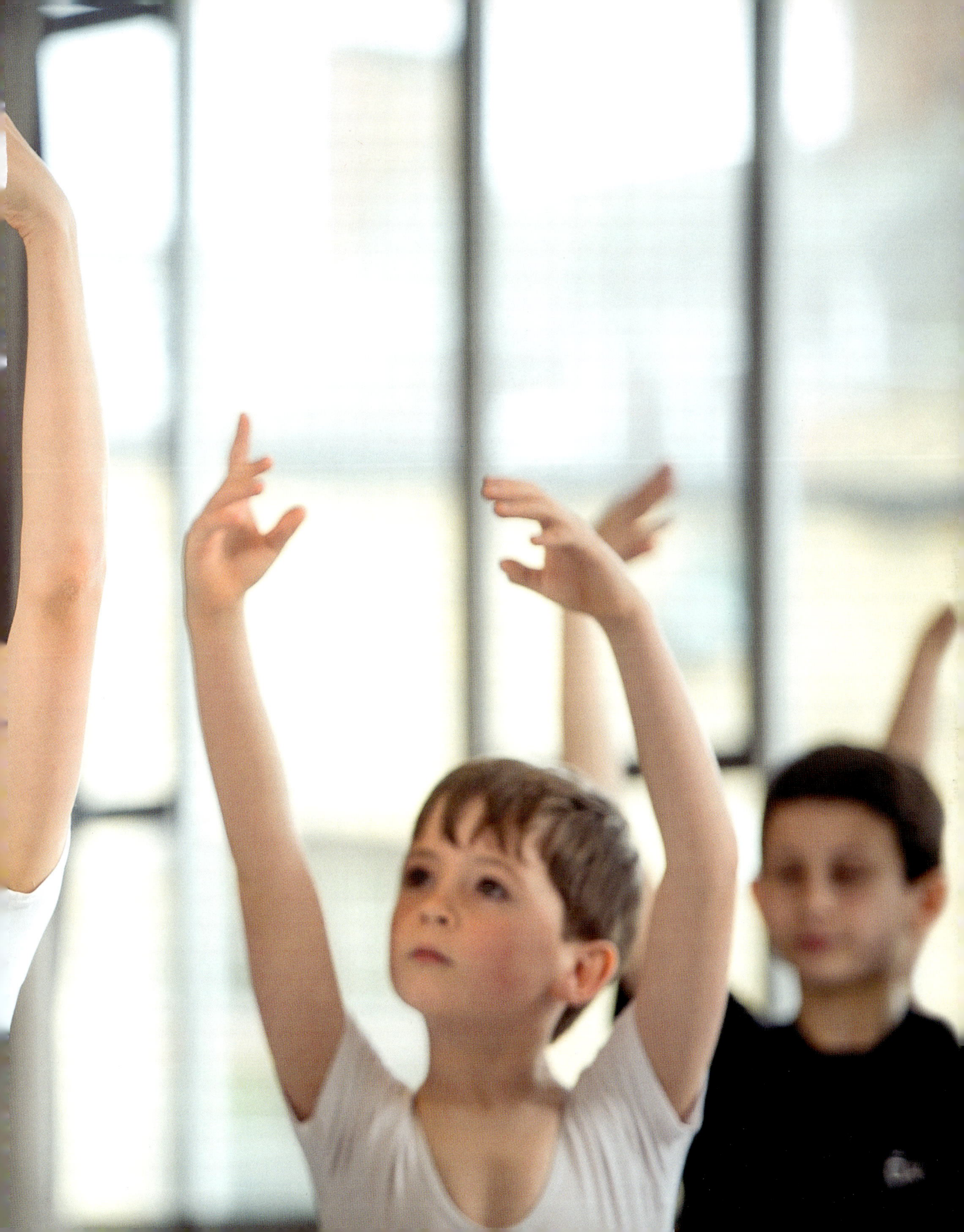

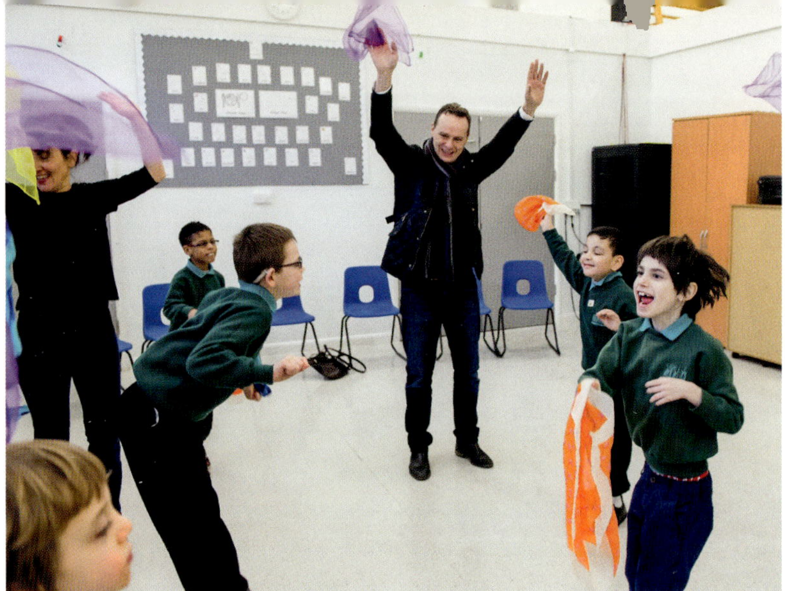

RADiate

The benefits of dance for children with special needs have been well established through the Academy's RADiate project, which began with funding from the Ward Blenkinsop Trust in the 1990s. It provides subsidised dance classes to children with a variety of learning, behavioural and emotional difficulties. The weekly sessions take place at primary schools in South West London as well as at the RAD headquarters and are led by a team of teachers experienced in making the group activities fun for children who often find it difficult to engage. Working in close collaboration with the staff at the school, the teachers help the children use dance to express themselves and their individuality in an alternative, non-verbal way, using their own imagination and creativity. RADiate Lead Tutor, Sue Burton, noted impressive developments in the dance skills of students who attended sessions for two years, 'including the ability to remember and anticipate long sequences of movement and to focus and co-operate with a partner and in a group, as well as significant developments in their social, language and communication skills'.

Michael Nunn, RAD's RADiate Ambassador, believes the classes 'celebrate ability rather than disability and promote a real sense of joy'. The RADiate sessions give the students a break from the pressures of the classroom, where they often feel out of their depth and unable to cope with the demanding curriculum. Dancing develops their personal strengths, boosts their self-esteem and allows them to relax and have fun. This in turn gives them more confidence to engage not only with their own bodies but with the bodies of others, and to move more freely in space.

The changes in those who find communication challenging are not instantaneous, but parents remark on the pure enjoyment their children take in the RADiate classes and how, in the longer term, their social skills improve noticeably. The children themselves are able to express what the classes mean to them. 'I feel free', one said, while another commented, 'when I'm dancing I feel happy'.

The RAD has long been an outward-looking organisation that has always interacted with the rest of the dance world, whether that be through glamorous galas, the Queen Elizabeth II Coronation Award or events with visiting dancers such as the recent Question and Answer session with the US ballerina Misty Copeland. However, its centenary in 2020 is being marked with a determination to engage even more with the wider community and to think about new ways to relate some of the skills of dance – discipline, focus, presentation and performance – to everyday life in work and other settings. Most importantly, however, the centenary of the RAD is an opportunity to encourage the idea that dance offers something for everyone, regardless of gender, age, ability or background.

'The classes celebrate ability rather than disability and
promote a real sense of joy.'

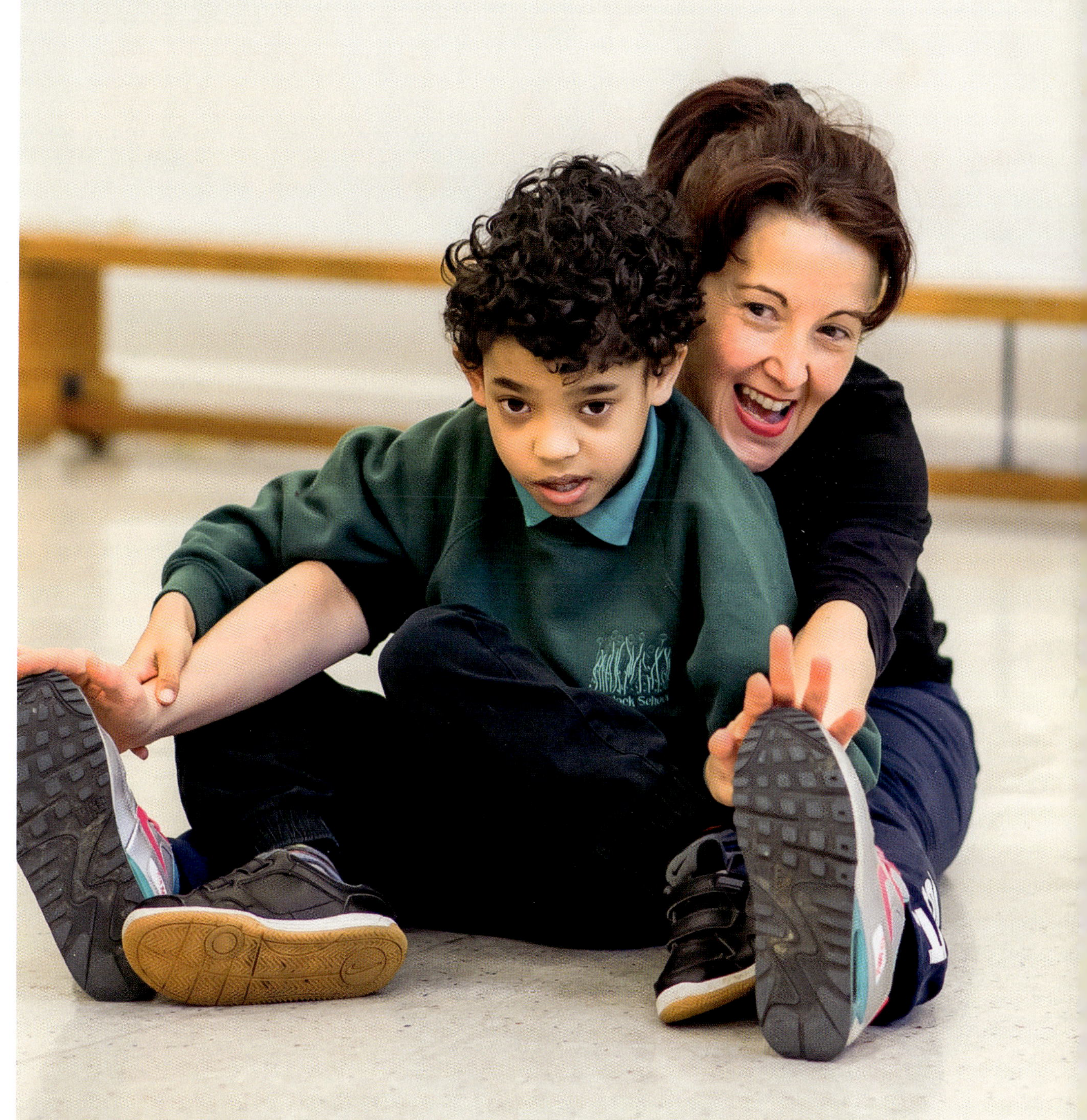

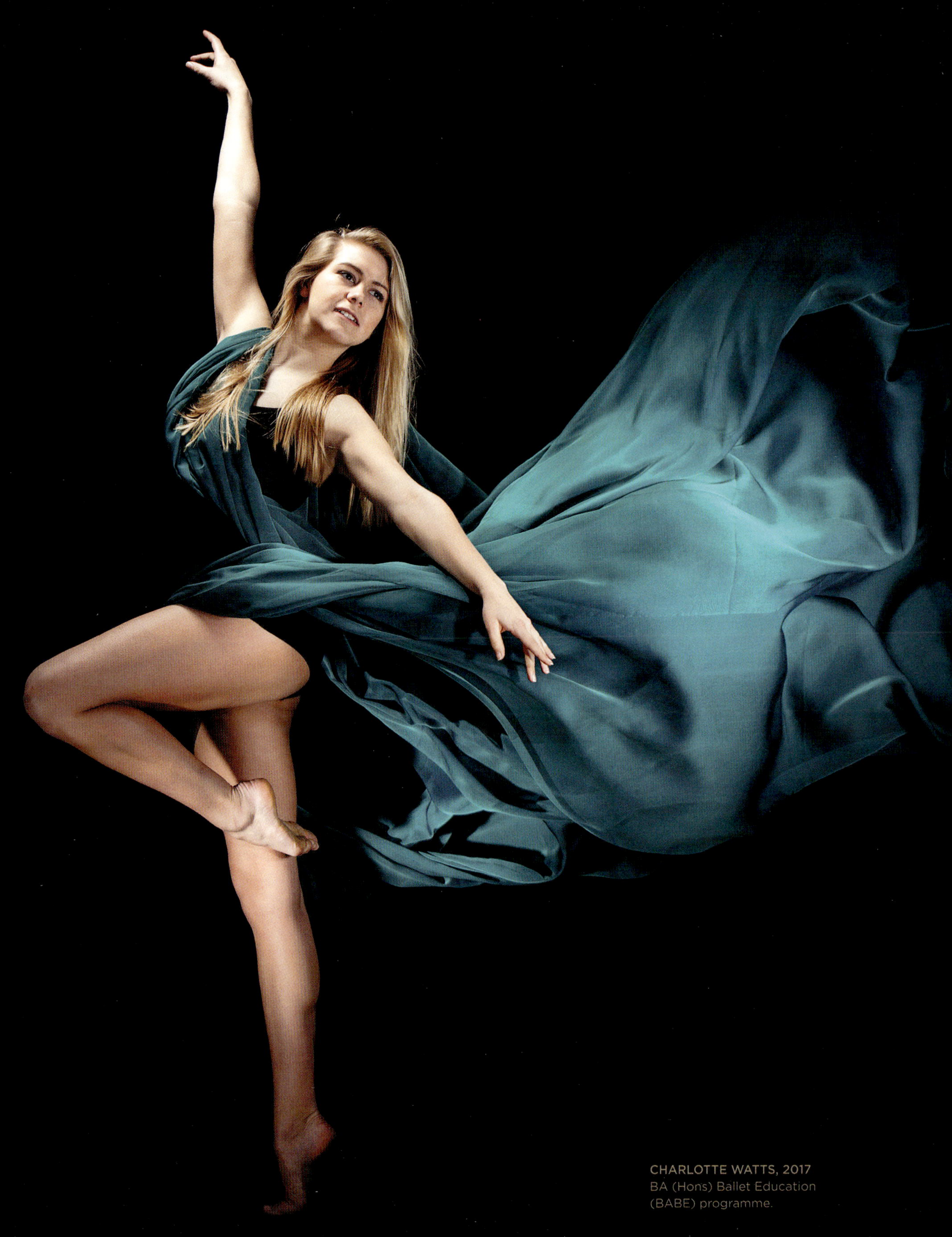

CHARLOTTE WATTS, 2017
BA (Hons) Ballet Education
(BABE) programme.

LOOKING TO THE FUTURE

A UNIVERSAL human activity, dance is a force for joy everywhere. It liberates. It empowers. It improves health and well-being. It offers moments of exquisite beauty and passion. From studio to stage, through community and creativity, the Royal Academy of Dance has been teaching the world to dance for 100 years.

As the RAD reaches its centenary, it is a good moment to look back on how much has been achieved since its foundation in 1920. From modest beginnings, with a committee of six, the Academy has grown to become one of the largest dance examining bodies in the world. The century has brought extraordinary changes to the organisation, but there is much, too, about the RAD that its founders and first members would recognise: a dedication to standards and quality; the value of membership; a structured approach to teaching and to assessment; and an innate sense of the importance of the art of dance. These are beliefs that were as core to the early members of the Academy as they are to a worldwide membership today.

In a world that is increasingly complex and increasingly interconnected, dance and the arts are proving more significant than ever as they bring people together in celebration of their shared humanity. A centenary is certainly a moment to look back, to take stock and celebrate achievements, but it is a time, too, to look forward. For the RAD it means continuing to build on the foundations of the past to ensure the future not only of the Academy but of dance as a whole.

The RAD supports dance in a wide variety of ways: training dance teachers; awarding degrees in dance; examining dance students; supporting community dance projects. It runs a dance school, dance workshops, dance summer schools, dance competitions. It awards dance bursaries and sells dance products. The sheer range of its activities

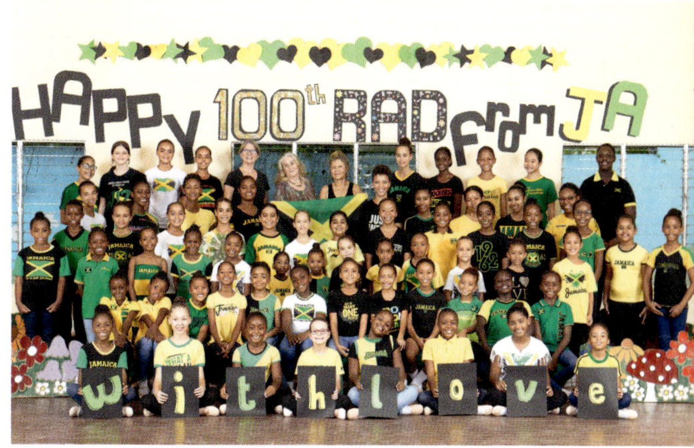

100 YEARS
Celebrating the RAD's centenary in Jamaica.

makes the Academy unique. Everyone has their own view and experience of the RAD but it can sometimes be a challenge to convey a sense of passion and vibrancy of the organisation as a whole.

The opening chapter of the next phase of its history therefore sees the RAD putting down tangible foundations as it moves into a new global headquarters in London. On the surface, the new premises offer an opportunity to double the RAD's physical footprint, providing the space and the facilities both to cater to students of all kinds and to administer to its worldwide business. The move enables the Academy to expand provision for its growing membership. But the new headquarters represent more than a move from one building to another. The building represents a physical expression of the RAD's vision of a future in which it continues to forge strong links with the local community as well as at national and international level, and in which it looks forward to the next 100 years as a home for dance for everyone.

WHERE ARE THEY NOW?

Alexander Campbell

Alexander Campbell studied the RAD syllabus
at Academy Ballet in Sydney, Australia, up to
Advanced 2 level. He competed in the Genée
International Ballet Competition in Sydney
(2002) and Birmingham (2003). He then
graduated from the Royal Ballet School in 2005
and subsequently pursued his dance career with
Birmingham Royal Ballet (2005–11) and with
The Royal Ballet (2011 to the present). Campbell
became a principal dancer with The Royal Ballet
in 2016. Recently he became an ambassador for
Dance Down the Wicket (see p. 151).

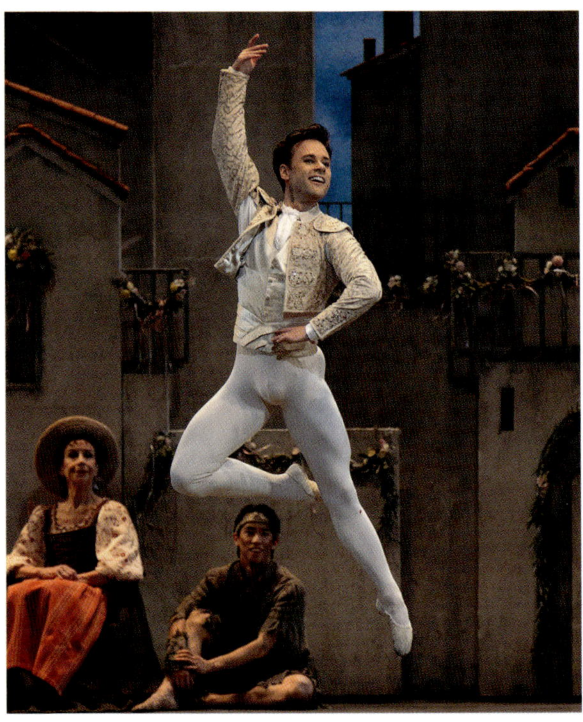

Flora Zeta Cheong-Leen

Flora Zeta Cheong-Leen was the first Chinese dancer
to be accepted into the Royal Ballet School. She won
the silver medal at the Genée International Ballet
Competition in 1975 and was also the winner of the
Ninette de Valois Choreographic Award from the
Royal Ballet School, among other honours. She joined
The Royal Ballet and later worked as guest principal
dancer and choreographer for the Hong Kong Ballet.
Cheong-Leen is now a member of the Board of
Governors of the Hong Kong Ballet. She went on to
a successful career as a fashion designer, earning awards
such as the China International Grand Master Fashion
Design Award (2003), and started the Tian Art
Foundation charity, giving dance scholarships to orphans
and underprivileged children. After moving to China in
2009 she started the Conservatory of International
Style and Cultural Arts, which now consists of 13 dance
schools in Beijing and Shanghai. In 2013 she founded
the professional dance company Ballet Octahedron.
Cheong-Leen is also an RAD Professional Dancers'
Teaching Diploma (PDTD) graduate.

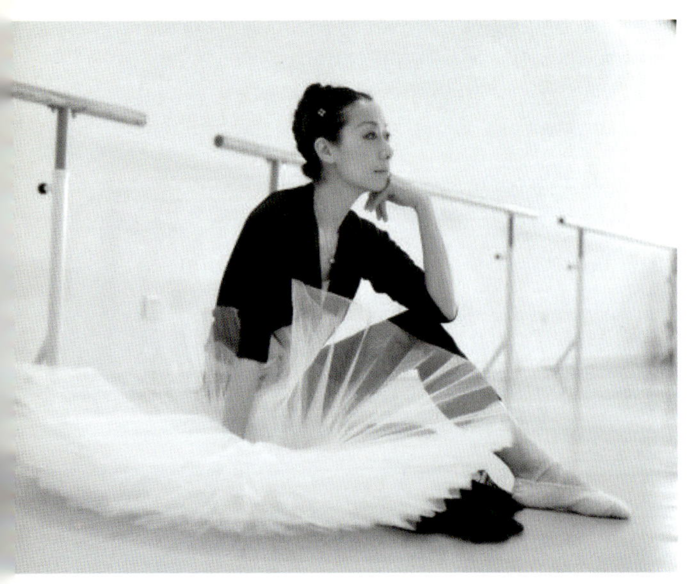

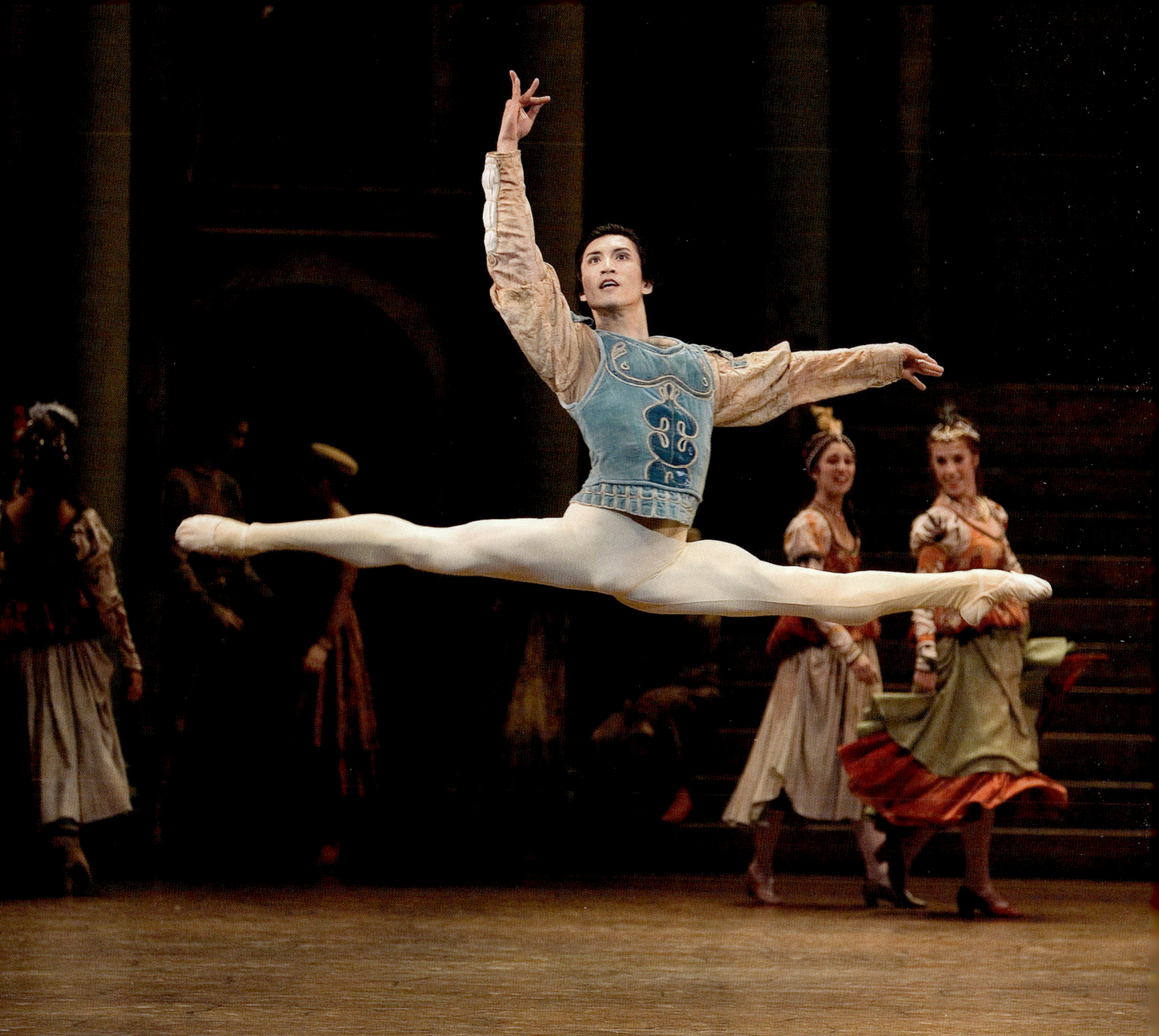

Chi Cao

Born in China, Chi Cao trained at Beijing Dance Academy and at the Royal Ballet School after winning the Prix de Lausanne in 1994. In 1995 he joined Birmingham Royal Ballet and won the gold medal at the Varna International Ballet Competition in 1998 (becoming the first Chinese-born male dancer to do so). He was named principal dancer at Birmingham Royal Ballet in 2002. Cao has guested with companies and festivals all over the world, including the National Ballet of China, Houston Ballet, The Royal Ballet and Bayerisches Staatsballett (Munich), among others. In 2010 Cao appeared as Li Cunxin in the film *Mao's Last Dancer* (directed by Bruce Beresford). He has been a member of the jury for the Genée International Ballet Competition and is an RAD Professional Dancers' Teaching Diploma (PDTD) graduate (2018).

Lisa-Maree Cullum

Born in New Zealand, Lisa-Maree Cullum started ballet at the age of three with her mother. In 1988, while studying in Sydney, Australia, she won the gold medal in the Genée International Ballet Competition at the age of 15, followed by a Prix de Lausanne scholarship. She went on to study at the Académie de Danse Princesse Grace in Monaco, and joined the English National Ballet before becoming principal dancer with the Deutsche Oper Berlin and subsequently with the Bayerisches Staatsballett in Munich. In 2008 Cullum was awarded the honorary title of 'Kammertänzerin' by the Bavarian Ministry of Culture, as an acknowledgement of her outstanding career as a dancer in Germany. She is now the Associate Artistic Director and permanent teacher at the Bottaini Merlo International Centre of Arts (BMICA) in Munich.

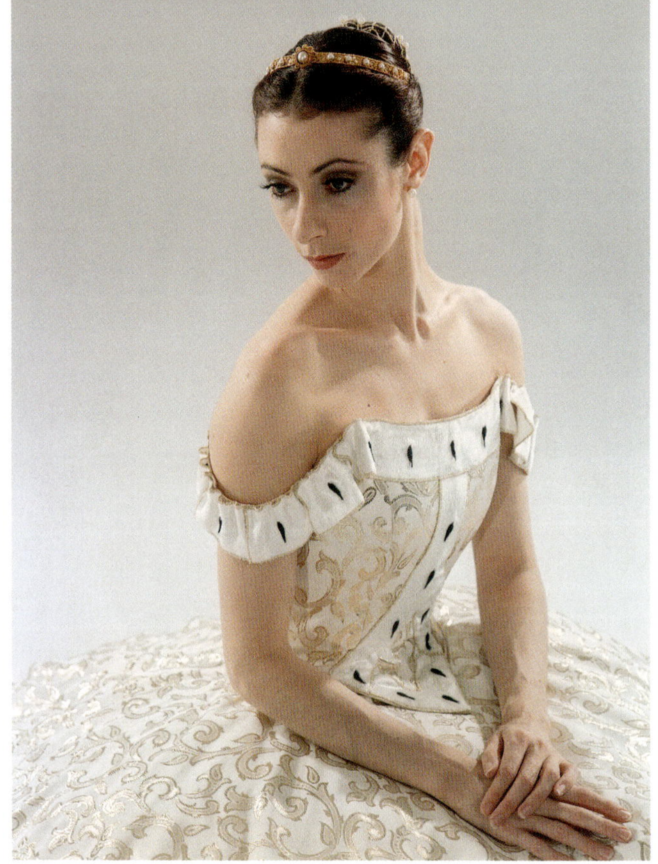

Shevelle Dynott

Shevelle Dynott started dancing at the age of seven and studied the RAD syllabus up to Advanced 2 level. He trained at the Royal Ballet School and won the bronze medal at the Genée International Ballet Competition in 2004, subsequently joining the English National Ballet in 2005. His career highlights with the ENB have included his performance in Akram Khan's groundbreaking version of *Giselle* and as the Moor in *Petrushka*. In 2017 Dynott's portrait was added to the National Portrait Gallery's permanent collection as part of a portfolio showcasing Black British individuals who have achieved success in a variety of fields, with a public exhibition in 2018. He is an Ambassador for the RAD's Project B, and in 2018 he also hosted the RAD's first live broadcast for World Ballet Day, seen by over 300,000 people worldwide.

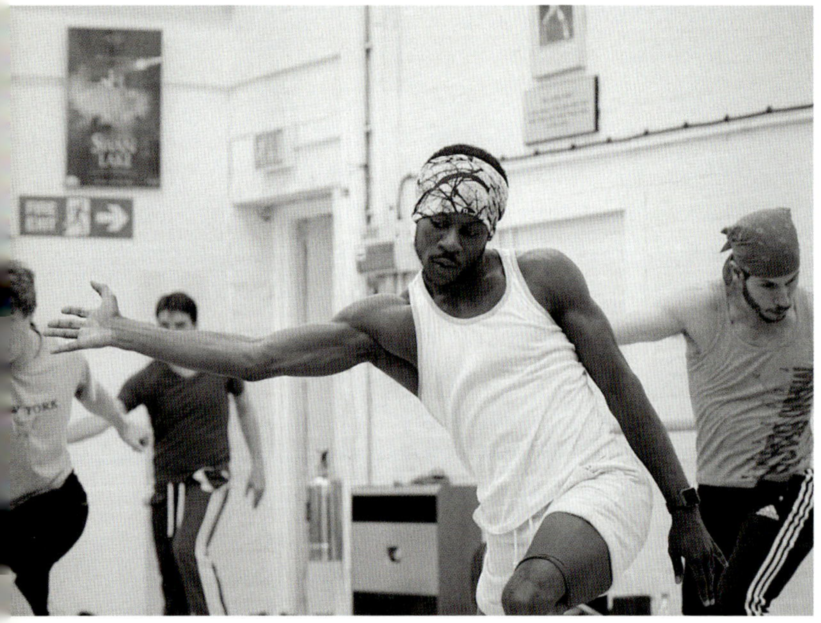

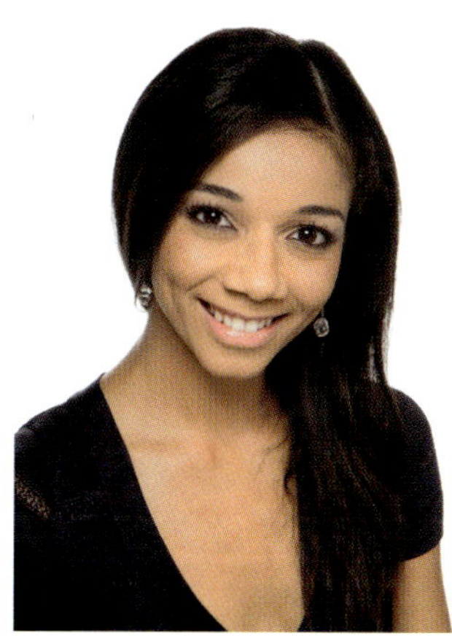

Céline Gittens was born in Trinidad and trained at the Goh Ballet Academy in Vancouver, Canada. She was awarded the RAD's Solo Seal in 2004 and won the gold medal and the Audience Choice Award at the Genée International Ballet Competition in 2005. She went on to a career with Birmingham Royal Ballet in 2006, becoming a principal dancer in 2016. In 2012 Gittens was the first black ballerina in the UK to dance the lead role of Odette/Odile in *Swan Lake*. She has been acclaimed for her performances in lead roles such as Lise in Frederick Ashton's *La fille mal gardée* and Juliet in Kenneth Macmillan's *Romeo and Juliet*, among many others. She also holds a Master's degree in Philosophy from the University of Birmingham (2012).

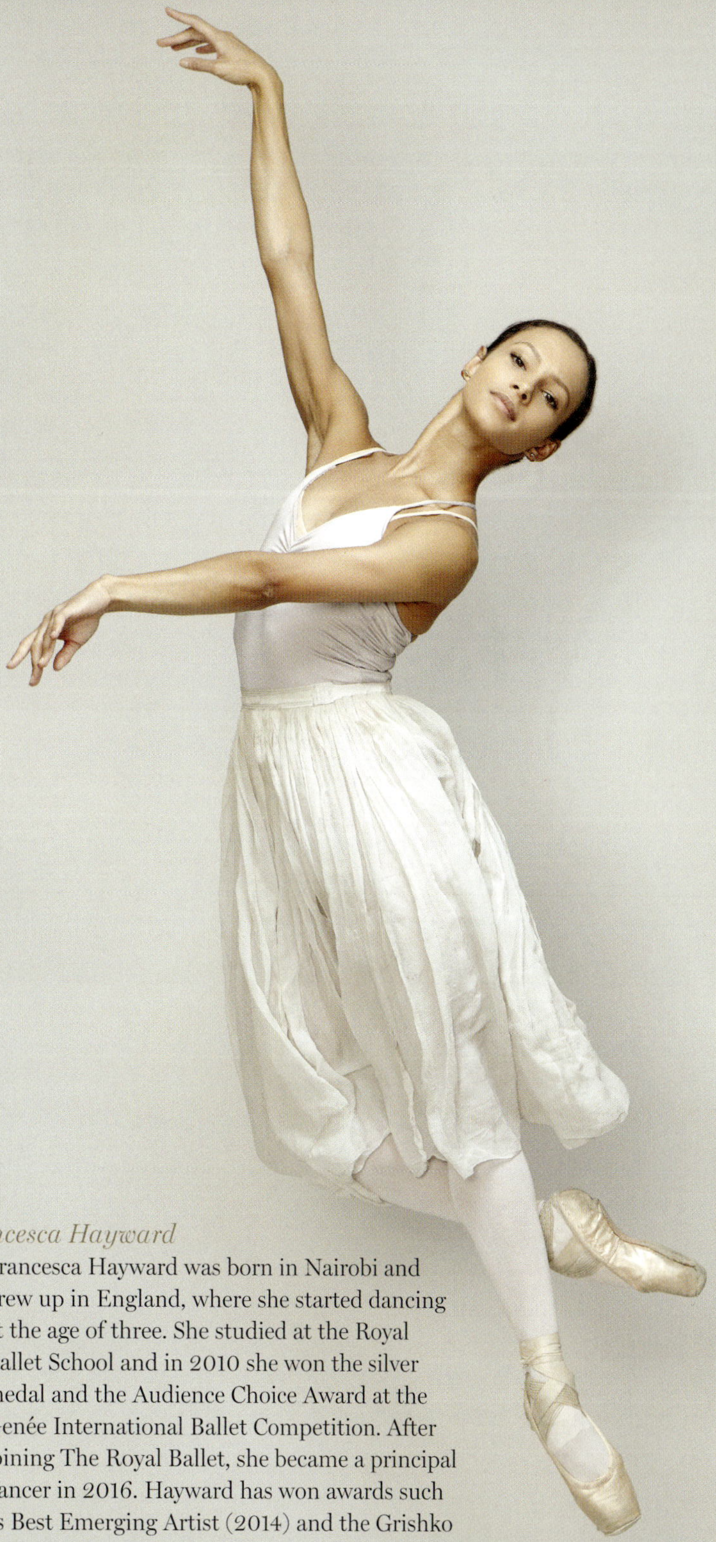

Francesca Hayward was born in Nairobi and grew up in England, where she started dancing at the age of three. She studied at the Royal Ballet School and in 2010 she won the silver medal and the Audience Choice Award at the Genée International Ballet Competition. After joining The Royal Ballet, she became a principal dancer in 2016. Hayward has won awards such as Best Emerging Artist (2014) and the Grishko Award for Best Female Dancer (2016) at the Critics' Circle National Dance Awards. Her many acclaimed performances have included Aurora in *The Sleeping Beauty* and the lead role in *Giselle*, and she will portray Victoria in the forthcoming film of *Cats*.

Born in Sydney, Australia, Steven McRae won the gold medal at the Genée International Ballet Competition in 2002, followed by the Prix de Lausanne in 2003. He studied at the Royal Ballet School and joined The Royal Ballet in 2004, becoming a principal dancer in 2009. McRae has created many roles such as the Magician/Mad Hatter in *Alice's Adventures in Wonderland* and Florizel in *The Winter's Tale* (both choreographed by Christopher Wheeldon). He has appeared with companies worldwide, such as the National Ballet of Canada and Australian Ballet, and in international galas. He also holds a BA (Hons) in Business Management and Leadership from the Open University. McRae will play the role of Skimbleshanks in the forthcoming film of *Cats*.

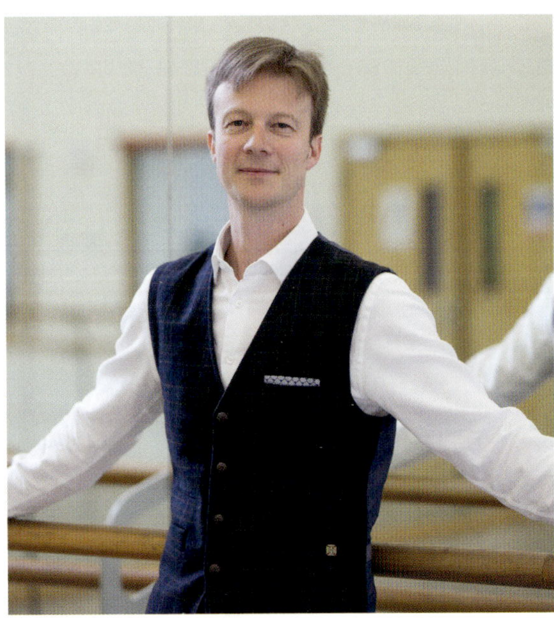

Robert Parker

Robert Parker trained at the Royal Ballet School and joined the Birmingham Royal Ballet in 1994. He became a principal dancer in 1999 and collaborated with the Artistic Director and choreographer David Bintley to create many leading roles for the company. He made guest appearances with The Royal Ballet and around the world, and received honours, including a Critics' Circle Award for Outstanding Male Artist in 2003. Parker later completed a Master's degree in Philosophy in Education. After retiring from Birmingham Royal Ballet he passed his RAD Professional Dancers' Teaching Diploma (PDTD) with distinction in 2012 and became the Artistic Director of Elmhurst Ballet School in Birmingham.

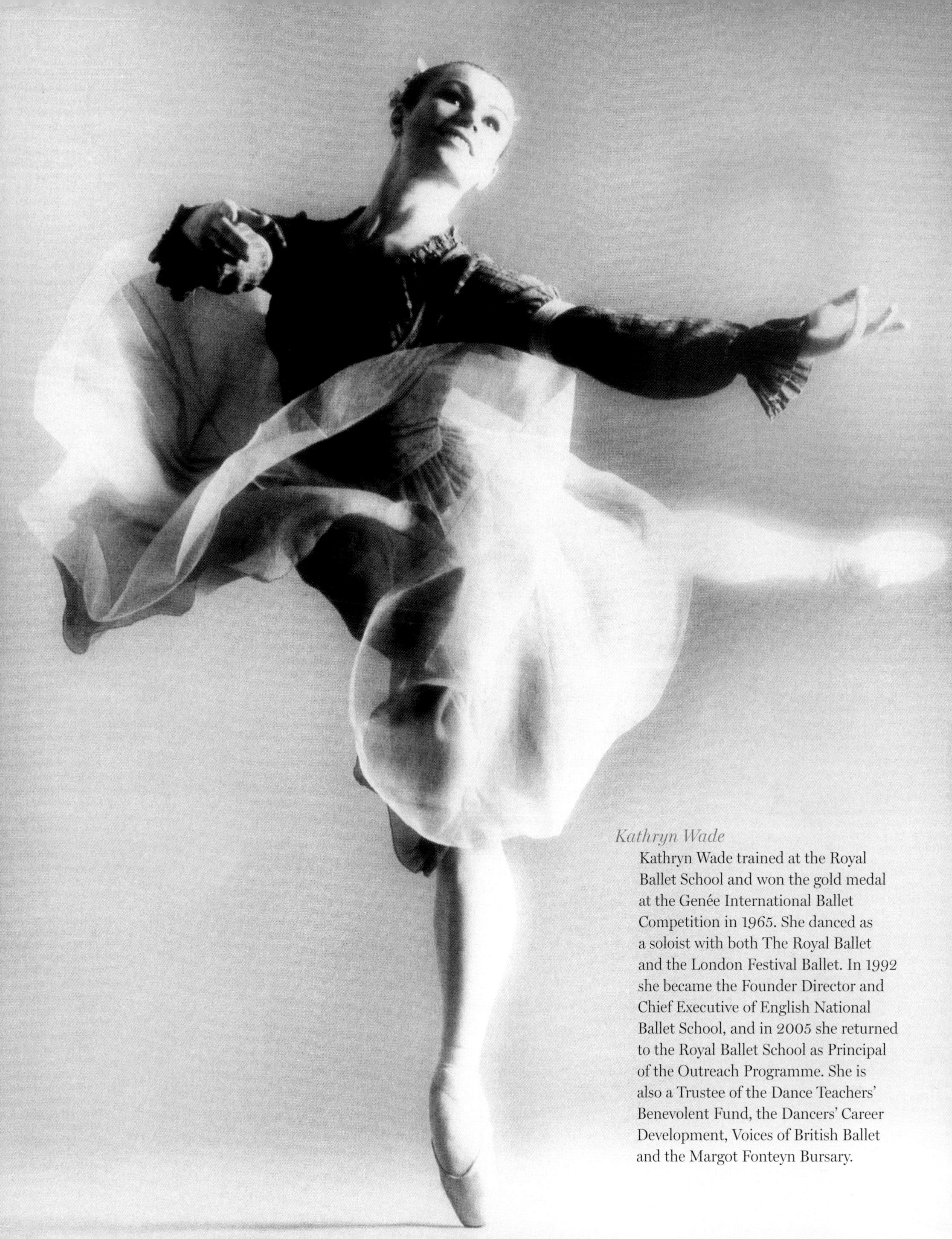

Kathryn Wade
Kathryn Wade trained at the Royal
Ballet School and won the gold medal
at the Genée International Ballet
Competition in 1965. She danced as
a soloist with both The Royal Ballet
and the London Festival Ballet. In 1992
she became the Founder Director and
Chief Executive of English National
Ballet School, and in 2005 she returned
to the Royal Ballet School as Principal
of the Outreach Programme. She is
also a Trustee of the Dance Teachers'
Benevolent Fund, the Dancers' Career
Development, Voices of British Ballet
and the Margot Fonteyn Bursary.

PRESIDENTS OF THE ROYAL ACADEMY OF DANCE

DAME ADELINE GENÉE (1878–1970)
RAD PRESIDENT 1920 to 1954

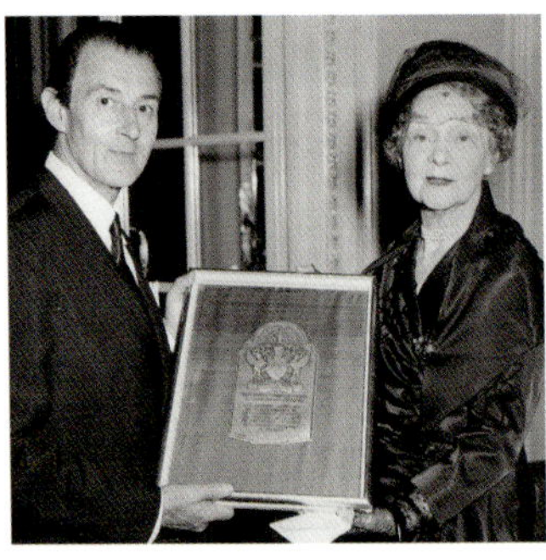

Born Anina Margarete Kirstina Petra Jensen in Hinnerup, Denmark, the young Genée studied dancing with her uncle, Alexander, from the age of three. Like many theatre performers of the time, Genée changed her name and, after early appearances in Denmark and Germany, pursued a long and illustrious career in London's Music Hall Ballet. Genée was prima ballerina of the famous Empire Theatre in Leicester Square for over ten years (1897–1909) and did much to raise the status and respectability of ballet during her time. Critically acclaimed for both her technical and expressive qualities, Genée also created much of her own choreography and enjoyed successful tours of America, Australia and New Zealand. In 1920 she became a founding member of the Association of Teachers of Operatic Dancing and was elected its first President.

Genée worked tirelessly to promote ballet and raise standards in its teaching, ensuring that the Danish ballet tradition was incorporated (alongside the French, Italian, English and Russian) in RAD syllabi. Under her oversight the Association became known as the Royal Academy of Dancing and she instigated a successful application for a Royal Charter in 1935, as well as introducing the Adeline Genée Gold Medal Awards (in 1931) and the Queen Elizabeth II Coronation Award (in 1954). The RAD today owes a great debt to its founding President, who served for nearly 35 years.

In 1923 Genée was awarded the Ingenio et arti medal by the King of Denmark; in 1950 she became a Dame Commander of the Order of the British Empire (DBE). The Genée Studio at the RAD Battersea headquarters is named in her honour and a number of items relating to her life and career are held in the RAD Archive.

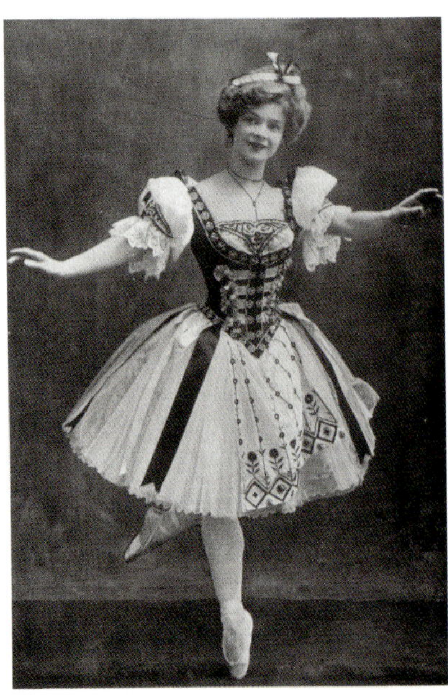

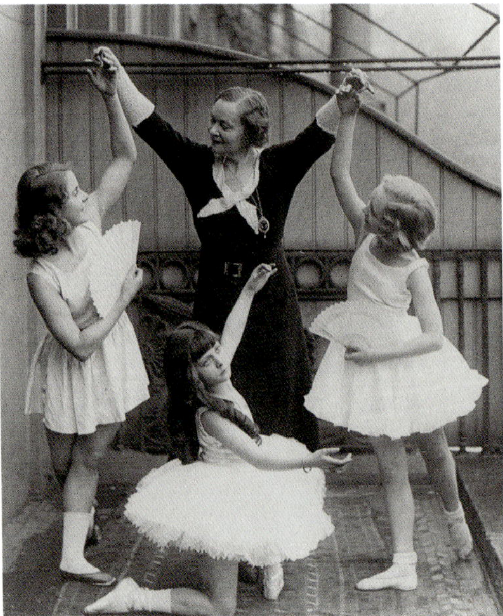

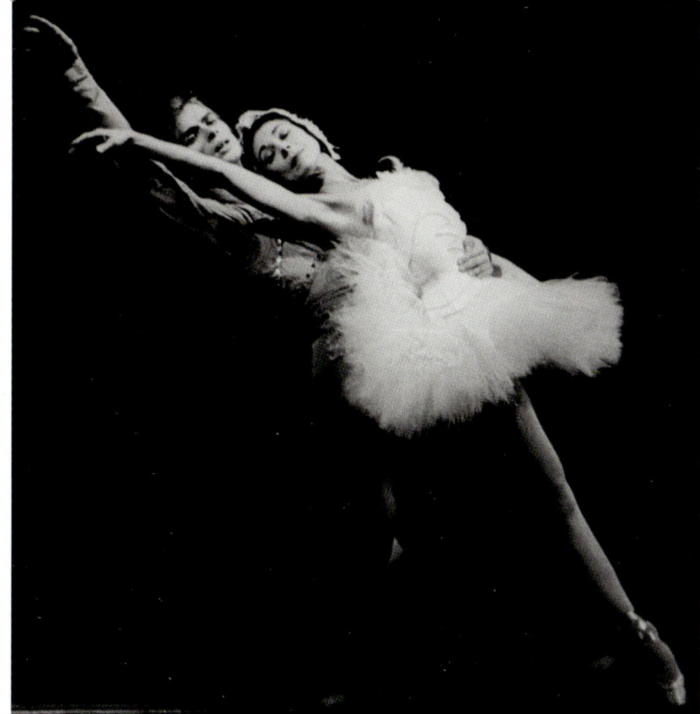

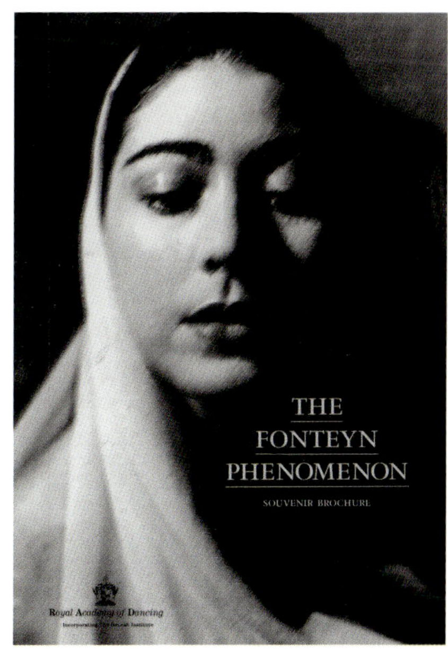

DAME MARGOT FONTEYN (1919–1991)
RAD PRESIDENT 1954 to 1991

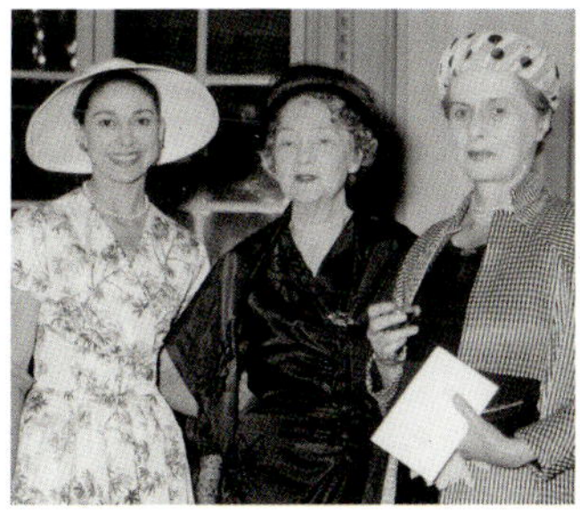

Margaret Hookham was born in Reigate, Surrey, and as Margot Fonteyn was to become a legendary ballerina and the subject of numerous books, films and television programmes. After studying with Nicholas Legat and Serafina Astafieva in London, Fonteyn was accepted at Ninette de Valois's Sadler's Wells School in 1934. A year later she joined the Vic-Wells Ballet, where she created many roles in ballets by Frederick Ashton. During the Second World War Fonteyn toured widely with the Vic-Wells Ballet company and gained critical acclaim for the purity of her line, her musicality and her expressive quality. Her popularity continued to grow throughout the 1950s and reached new heights when she found the perfect partner in Rudolf Nureyev. Their partnership was to last for nearly 15 years and remains one of the most celebrated collaborations in ballet history.

Fonteyn succeeded Adeline Genée as President of the RAD, a role that she maintained until her death in 1991. Combining an international performance career with her commitment to the Academy's work, Fonteyn organised a series of glittering charity galas to raise money for the RAD Building Fund as well as overseeing developments in syllabi, examinations and teacher training. She found time to attend meetings in London, often flying in from another continent, as well as visiting international summer schools and events. In 1990 the RAD named its new building The Fonteyn Centre in her memory and in 2000 it hosted a conference entitled 'The Fonteyn Phenomenon'. One hundred years after her birth Fonteyn continues to inspire ballet students around the world.

In 1956 Margot Fonteyn was awarded a DBE; she held several honorary doctorates and served as Chancellor of the University of Durham from 1981 to 1991. Her autobiography was published in 1975, and in 1979 she presented the popular TV series *The Magic of Dance*. A statue of Fonteyn as *Ondine* still stands in her hometown in Reigate, Surrey.

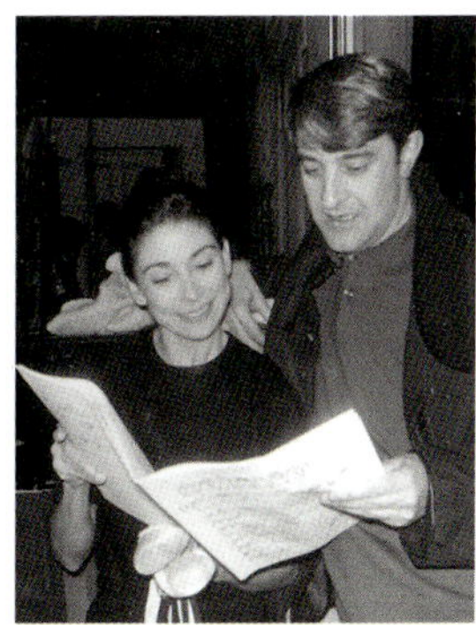

Margot Fonteyn with Rudolf Nureyev in Swan Lake, Vienna, 1964; *The Fonteyn Phenomenon* souvenir brochure, 1999; with Adeline Genée and Ninette de Valois at an RAD luncheon to celebrate the 21st anniversary of the Royal Charter in 1957; with Kenneth MacMillan at rehearsals for the RAD Gala Matinée performance in 1963.

DAME ANTOINETTE SIBLEY (b.1939)
RAD PRESIDENT 1991 to 2012

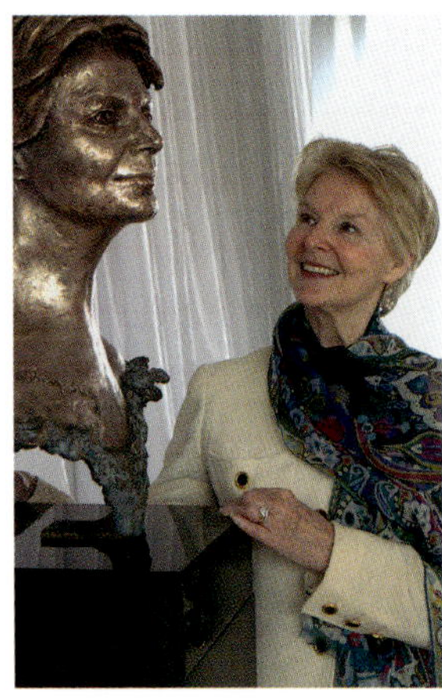

Born in Bromley, Surrey, Sibley joined the Sadler's Wells Ballet in 1956 (just before it became The Royal Ballet) and was quickly promoted to Soloist (in 1959) and then Principal (in 1960). She danced her first Odette/Odile at the tender age of 20 and went on to form a celebrated partnership with Anthony Dowell. Her purity of line and innate musicality were much admired but she also developed dramatic qualities demonstrated in Ashton's *The Dream* and *Enigma Variations*, and MacMillan's *Manon* and *Anastasia*. Sibley retired in 1979 but returned to The Royal Ballet as a guest artist from 1981 to 1989. She was elected a Vice President of the RAD in 1989 and became its third President (succeeding Fonteyn) in 1991.

Sibley's presidency marked a period of expansion and modernisation as the Academy entered the twenty-first century. The inauguration of the President's Award, the incorporation of the Benesh Institute (now Benesh International) and the creation of the Faculty of Education all took place during her years at the helm. A natural teacher, Sibley's skills as a coach were a highlight of the Academy's 'Revealing MacMillan' conference (in 2002) and she graced many awards and presentation ceremonies. On retirement, her contribution to the RAD was marked with a bronze bust by Frances Segelman, which is currently displayed in the reception area of the Battersea headquarters. In 1996 Antoinette Sibley was awarded a DBE.

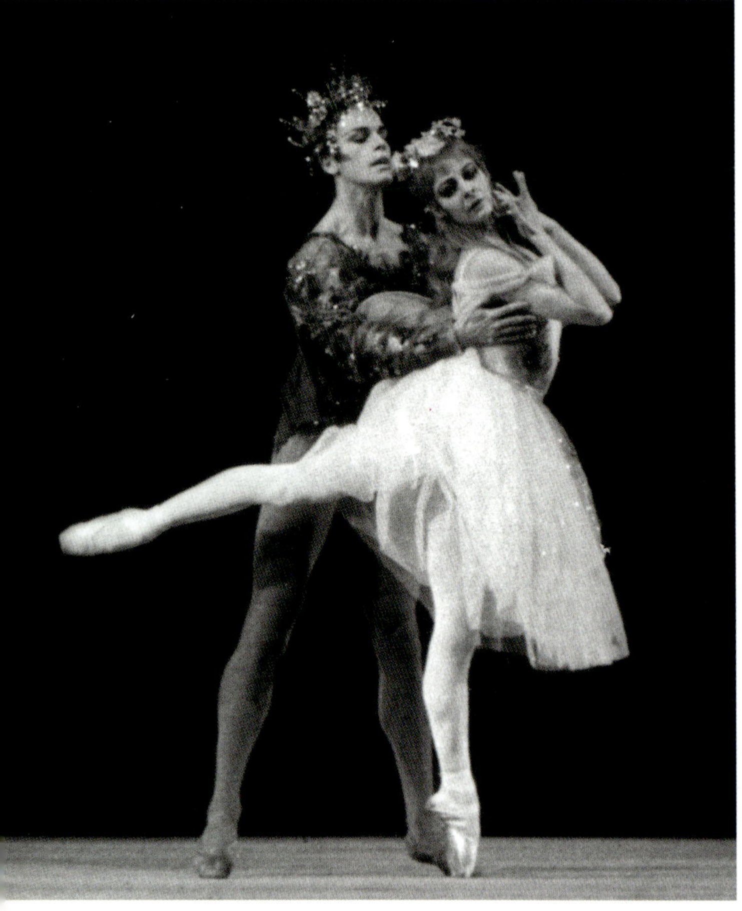

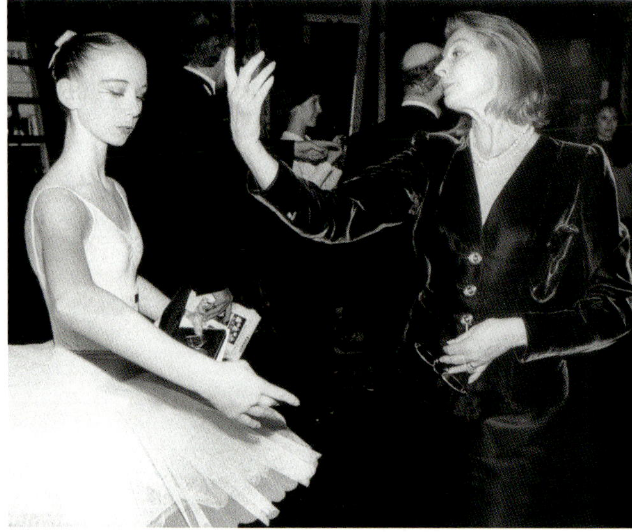

Antoinette Sibley with the bronze bust by sculptor Frances Segelman, 2012; with Anthony Dowell in Frederick Ashton's *The Dream*, 1970; coaching Elisha Willis, silver medallist at the Genée, 1996.

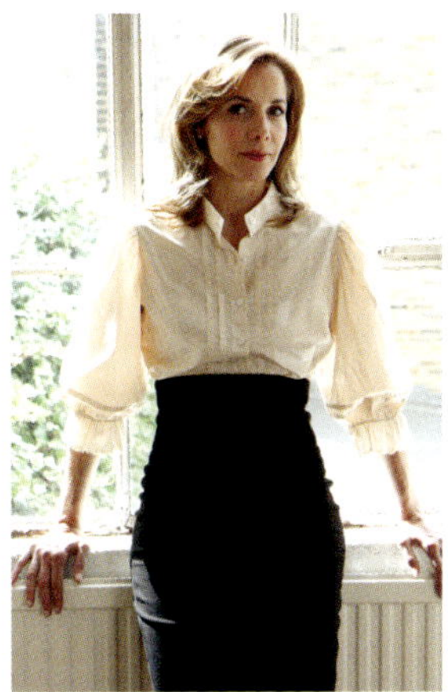

Darcey Bussell was born in London and attended the Royal Ballet School from 1982 until 1987, winning the prestigious Prix de Lausanne in 1986. She joined the Sadler's Wells Royal Ballet (now Birmingham Royal Ballet) in 1987, where she was picked by Kenneth MacMillan to create the leading role in his new production of *The Prince of the Pagodas*. Following the première in December 1989 she became principal dancer of The Royal Ballet at Covent Garden, where she was to remain for twenty years. Tall and long-limbed, Bussell challenged traditional notions of the English ballerina and was noted for her athleticism and range of movement as well as her classical line. She excelled as Aurora in *Sleeping Beauty* and Odette/Odile in *Swan Lake* but was also acclaimed in Balanchine repertoire and created roles for a wide range of choreographers, including Twyla Tharp, Christopher Wheeldon, Mark Baldwin and John Neumeier. Bussell performed as guest artist with New York City Ballet, Kirov Ballet, Hamburg Ballet and the Australian Ballet. Retiring in 2007, her last performance was broadcast live on British television (BBC2).

As President of the RAD, Bussell has inspired a new era of growth and development. Her energy, glamour and self-effacing manner continue to win the hearts of audiences, from the Genée International Ballet Competition and annual Awards Ceremony to the building site of the Academy's new home. The Dame Darcey Bussell Genée Bursary Scheme was set up in her honour in 2015.

Bussell has forged a highly successful career in books, modelling, health and fitness, and television. She initiated a series of children's books, *Magic Ballerina* (published by HarperCollins), has appeared on the cover of numerous magazines and created her own dance fitness programme (DDMIX). Her television career has brought her widespread recognition, with documentaries such as *Darcey Dances Hollywood*, *Darcey Bussell: Looking for Margot* and *Darcey Bussell: Looking for Fred*, all made for the BBC. She is also well known as a panel judge on the internationally popular BBC1 show *Strictly Come Dancing*.

Bussell was awarded a DBE in 2018 and holds numerous honorary awards, including an Honorary Doctorate from the University of Oxford. A full-length portrait by Allen Jones RA was commissioned by the National Portrait Gallery and unveiled in 1994.

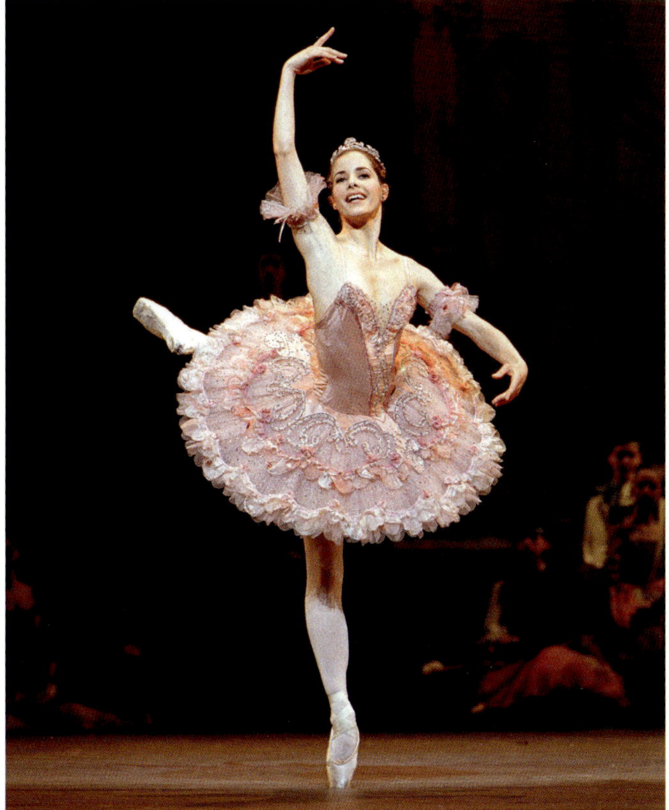

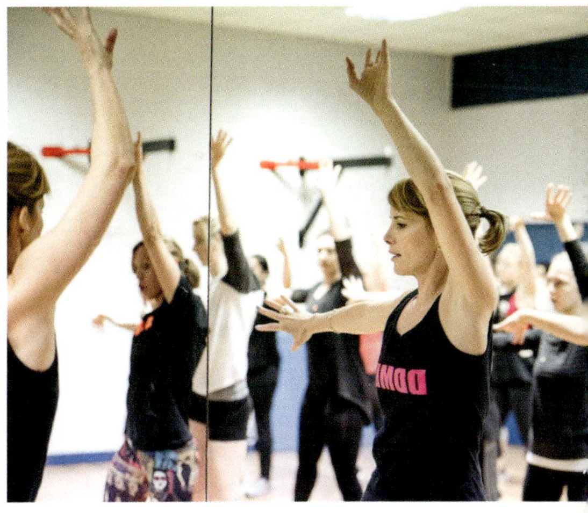

FROM TOP:
Darcey Bussell in 2012; as Princess Aurora in *The Sleeping Beauty*, 2003 (left) and creating her own dance fitness programme DDMIX (right), 2015.

LEADERSHIP PAST AND PRESENT

PRESIDENT

Adeline Genée (1920–1954)
Margot Fonteyn (1954–1991)
Antoinette Sibley (1991–2012)
Darcey Bussell (2012–present)

CHAIRMAN OF THE EXECUTIVE COMMITTEE/BOARD OF TRUSTEES

Adeline Genée (1934–1954)
Margot Fonteyn (1954–1958)
Sir Frederic Hooper (1959–1963)
Sir Ashley Clarke (1964–1969)
Ivor Guest (1970–1993)
Roger Harrison (1993–2006)
Kerry Rubie (2006–2015)
Guy Perricone (2015–present)

GENERAL SECRETARY

Philip Richardson (1920–1937)
Kathleen Gordon (1937–1947)*
Muriel Lehmann (1947–1968)
Marjorie Kimberley (1968–1970)
Barrie G. Dumont (1970–1972)
Philip E. Starr (1972–1976)
John Field (1976–1979)
John Saunders (1979–1982)
Alan Hooper (1982–1983)
Donald Scrimgeour (1983–1986)
David Wall (1986–1990)**

CHIEF EXECUTIVE OFFICER

David Watchman (1991–1999)
Luke Rittner (1999–present)

ARTISTIC DIRECTOR

John Field (1975–1976)
Alan Hooper (1980–1982)
Julia Farron (1983–1989)
John Byrne (1991–1993)
Lynn Wallis (1994–2016)
Paula Hunt (2017–2018)
Gerard Charles (2018–present)

PATRON

HM Queen Elizabeth II

PRESIDENT

Dame Darcey Bussell, DBE

VICE PRESIDENTS

David Bintley, CBE
Li Cunxin
Dame Beryl Grey, CH DBE DMus DLitt DEd FRSA
David McAllister, OAM
Wayne Sleep, OBE
Sir Peter Wright, CBE DMus DLitt FBSM

ADVISORY COUNCIL

Joy W. Brown
Barbara Fewster OBE, FISTD
Dr Stanley Ho, OBE GrOIH Chev Leg d'Hon
  DSoc Sc CStJ
Lady Porter
Sir Roy Strong, CH DLitt PhD FRSA FRSL

TRUSTEES

Justine Berry, PDTD PGCE MA ARAD RTS
Joanna Binder
Julia Bond, OBE
Thérèse Cantine, ARAD Dip PDTC RTS
Hilary Clark, ARAD Dip PDTC RTS
Deborah Coultish, Adv Tch Dip RTS
Sarah Dickinson, ARAD Adv Tch Dip RTS
Peter Flew
Imogen FF Knight, BA (Hons) Dip RAD Dip TD
  (NBS) ARAD AISTD RAD STC
Ida Levine, BA Juris Doctor JD
Andrew McIntee
David Nixon, OBE
Kevin O'Hare, CBE
Darren Parish, PDTD DPBMN RAD RTS
Penny Parks RAD RTS
Guy Perricone
Aliceson Robinson
Catherine Weate, BA DipEd LSDA FRSA Hon FLAM

---

* Kathleen Gordon also held the role of Director from 1947 to 1968. She was succeeded as Director by Peter Brinson,
  who held the role from 1968 to 1969, but after this time the duties of this position reverted to the General Secretary.
** David Wall also held the role of Associate Director from 1984 to 1986.

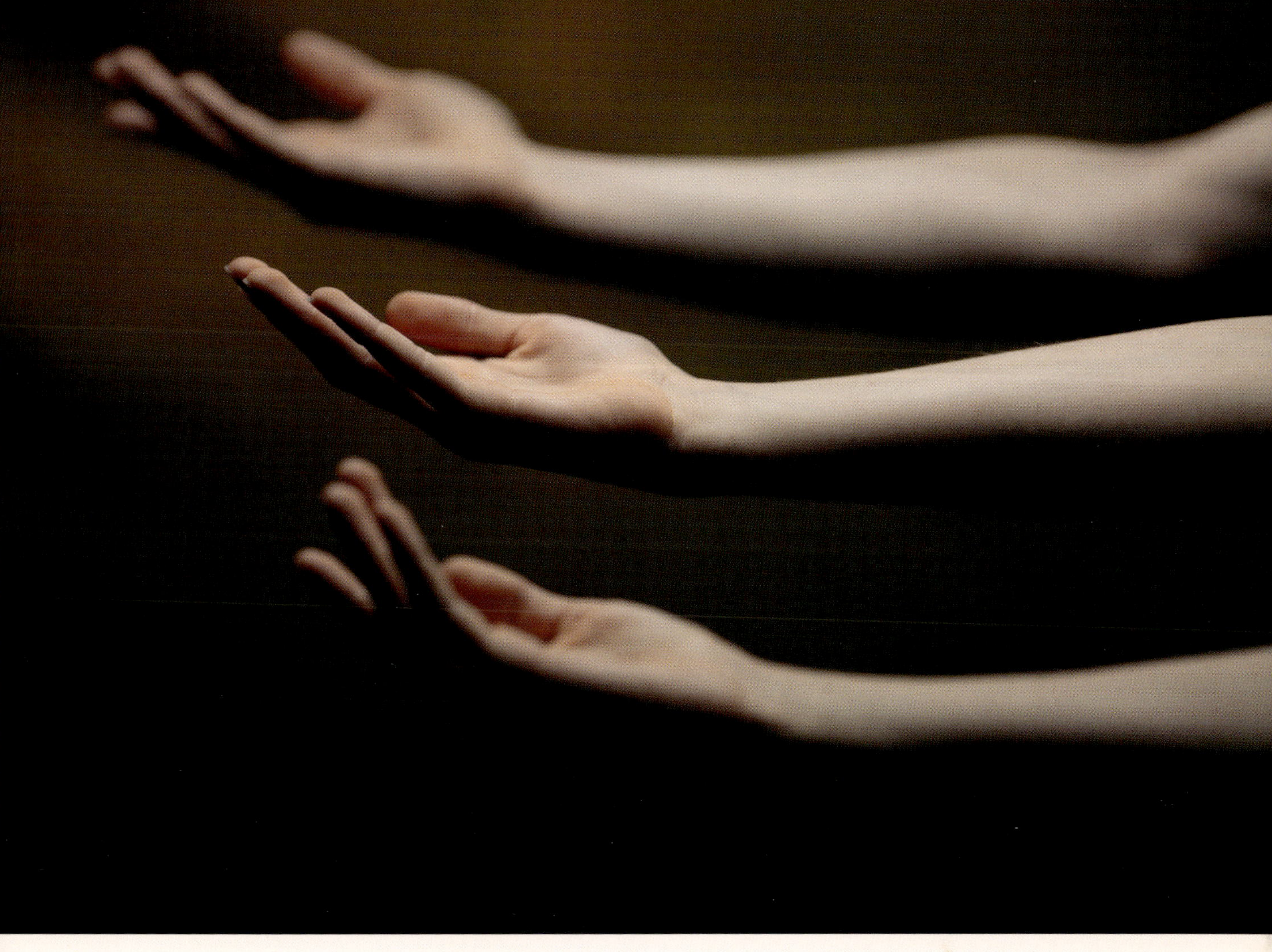

Over the years, many people have contributed to the development of the Academy's unique syllabi, including the following:

Margaret Barnes
Karen Berry
Morwenna Bowen
John Byrne
June Christian
Martin Cleave
Susan Cooper

Diana Curry
Kit Dickinson
Vanessa Donkin
Julia Farron, OBE
Jacqueline Ferguson
Valerie Hitchen
Paula Hunt, MNZM

Hilary Kaplan
Grant Kennedy
Pamela May, OBE
Sara Neil
Carolyn Parker
Antoinette Sibley, DBE
Jonathan Still

Valerie Sunderland
Alfreda Thorogood
Iris Truscott
Lynn Wallis, OBE
Eileen Ward

FURTHER READING

Anderson, Zoë. 2009. 'Full Circle: Dame Antoinette Sibley celebrates her 70th birthday'. *Dance Gazette*, 2, pp. 22–4

Baronova, Irina. 2005. *Irina: Ballet, Life and Love*. Gainesville, FL: University of Florida Press

Beaumont, Cyril. 1948. *Margot Fonteyn*. London: C.W. Beaumont

Bedells, Phyllis. 1954. *My Dancing Days*. London: Phoenix House

Bedells, Phyllis. 1971. 'The First Fifty Years'. *Dance Gazette*, 1 (autumn), pp. 5–27

Bussell, Darcey. 2016. *Darcey Bussell: A Life in Pictures*. London: Hardie Grant

Bussell, Darcey. 2018. *Darcey Bussell: Evolved*. London: Hardie Grant

Carter, Alexandra. 2005. *Dance and Dancers in the Victorian and Edwardian Music Hall Ballet*. Farnham: Ashgate

Clarke, Mary. 1991. 'Thanksgiving for Margot'. *Dancing Times*, 81, 971 (August), pp. 1022–3

Daneman, Meredith. 2004. *Margot Fonteyn*. London: Viking

De Valois, Ninette. 1937. *Invitation to the Ballet*. London: Bodley Head

De Valois, Ninette. 1992. *Come Dance With Me: A Memoir*. London: Dance Books

Dolin, Anton. 1960. *Autobiography*. London: Oldbourne

Dolin, Anton. 1985. *Last Words: A Final Autobiography*. London: Century

Espinosa, Edouard. 1913. 'Technical Dictionary of Dancing'. London: *The Dancing Times*

Espinosa, Edouard. 1916. 'What Every Teacher of Operatic Dancing Ought to Know and Be Able to Teach'. *The Dancing Times*, 6, 72 (September), p. 327

Espinosa, Edouard. 1946. *And Then He Danced: The Life of Espinosa by Himself*. London: Sampson Low, Marston & Co.

Espinosa, Edouard. 1948. *Technical Vade Mecum*. London: Eve Kelland

Fonteyn, Margot. 1975. *Autobiography*. London: Hamish Hamilton

Fonteyn, Margot. 1979. *The Magic of Dance*. New York: Alfred A. Knopf

French, Ruth and Felix Demery. 1934. *First Steps*. London: Ruth French and Felix Demery

Genèe, Adeline, Tamara Karsavina and Phyllis Bedells. 1920. 'The Future of Ballet'. *The Dancing Times*, 11, 123 (December), pp. 177–80

Genée, Adeline. 1937. 'Foreword'. *Dance Gazette*, 29 (November), p. 1

Genée, Adeline. 1954. 'Foreword'. *Dance Gazette*, 96 (August), p. 1

Genné, Beth. 1995. 'Openly English: Phyllis Bedells and the Birth of British Ballet'. *Dance Chronicle*, 18, 3, pp. 437–51

Guest, Ivor. 1958. *Adeline Genée: A Lifetime of Ballet under Six Reigns*. London: A. & C. Black

Haskell, Arnold. 1934. *Balletomania*. London: Victor Gollancz

Hogan, Anne (ed). 2014. *The Song of the Body: Dance for Lifelong Wellbeing*. London: Royal Academy of Dance Enterprises Ltd

Karsavina, Tamara. 1930. *Theatre Street: The Reminiscences of Tamara Karsavina*. London: Heinemann

Markova, Alicia. 1986. *Markova Remembers*. London: Hamish Hamilton

Money, Keith. 1974. *Fonteyn: The Making of a Legend*. New York: Reynal and Company

Parker, Derek. 1995. *Royal Academy of Dancing: The First Seventy Five Years*. London: Royal Academy of Dancing

Rambert, Marie. 1962. *Dancers of Mercury*. London: A. & C. Black

Rambert, Marie. 1972. *Quicksilver: An Autobiography*. London: Macmillan

Richardson, Philip. 1916. 'The Sitter Out'. *The Dancing Times*, 72 (September), pp. 326–9

Richardson, Philip. 1923. 'Non-competitive Dancing Examinations for Children'. *The Dancing Times*, 152 (June), pp. 900, 902

Rittner, Luke. 2000. 'Wanted: A Blueprint for the Future'. *Dance Gazette*, 1, pp. 26–7

Royal Academy of Dancing. 1991. 'A New Chief Executive for the Academy'. *Dance Gazette*, 206 (February), p. 38

Spatt, Leslie and Nicholas Dromgoole. 1976. *Sibley and Dowell*. London: Collins

Sutton, Tina. 2013. *The Making of Markova: Diaghilev's Baby Ballerina to Groundbreaking Icon*. New York: Pegasus

Walker, Katherine Sorley. 1995. 'The Karsavina Syllabus'. *Dance Now*, 4, 2, pp. 48–54

Walker, Katherine Sorley. 2007. 'The Espinosas: A Dancing Dynasty, 1825–1992'. *Dance Chronicle*, 30, 2, pp. 155–235

Watchman, David. 1992. 'Looking Ahead'. *Dance Gazette*, 209 (February), p. 14

ACKNOWLEDGEMENTS

The reach and complexity of the RAD's accomplishments over the past century, and the number of people who have offered their time and dedication to its work, make the task of recognising every individual contribution almost impossible. While we have done our very best to ensure credit has been given wherever it is due, we regret any and all inadvertent omissions.

RAD offices, representatives and members around the world kindly offered their photographs and memories, and while it was not possible to include all of them, these contributions were all greatly appreciated.

The Academy would particularly like to thank Clarissa Aykroyd, Joy Brown, Darcey Bussell, Li Cunxin, Gerald Dowler, Eleanor Fitzpatrick, Pamela Hartshorne, Carol Martin, Caroline O'Brien, Jane Pritchard, Johanna Stephenson, Jonathan Still, Valerie Sunderland, Richard Thom, Jennie Walton, Ray Watkins and RAD Enterprises Ltd for their assistance in the development of this book, as well as all RAD staff members who helped in various ways.

PICTURE CREDITS

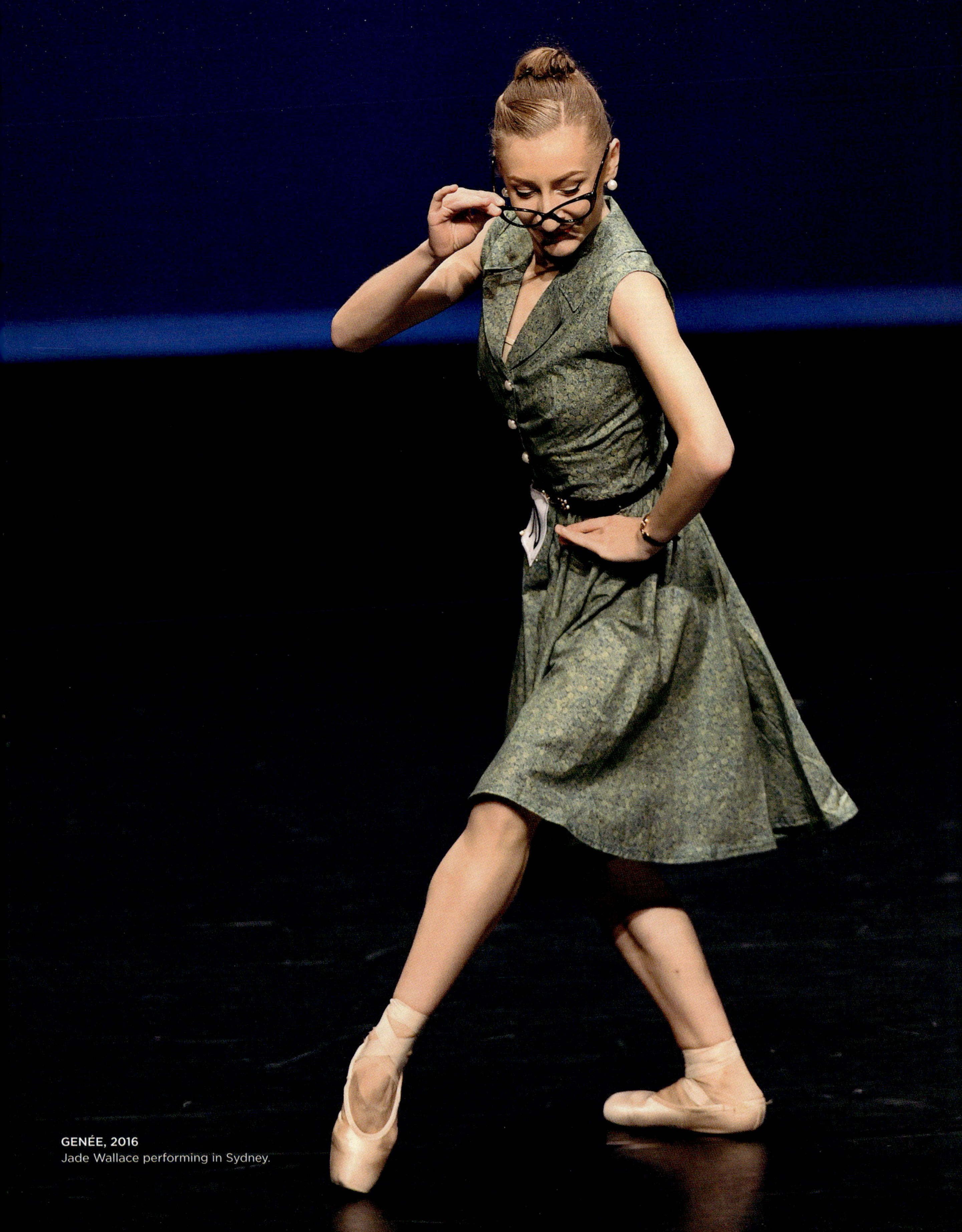

GENÉE, 2016
Jade Wallace performing in Sydney.

First published in 2019 by
Scala Arts & Heritage Publishers Ltd
10 Lion Yard
Tremadoc Road
London SW4 7NQ, UK
www.scalapublishers.com

In association with
Royal Academy of Dance
www.royalacademyofdance.org

ISBN 978-1-78551-217-9

Edited by Johanna Stephenson
Designed by Raymonde Watkins
Printed in Italy

10 9 8 7 6 5 4 3 2 1

Front cover: Jessica Templeton, 2018.
Back cover: Meriel Evans rehearses RAD Scholars in
Make Believe, ahead of their performance at the RAD
Gala Matinée in 1961.
Page 1: Early RAD Scholars Kathleen Pearce,
Anna Vaughan and Margaret Turner, 1926.
Pages 2–3: Anya Mercer, 2018.
Page 4: Behind the scenes at the Genée, London, 2005.

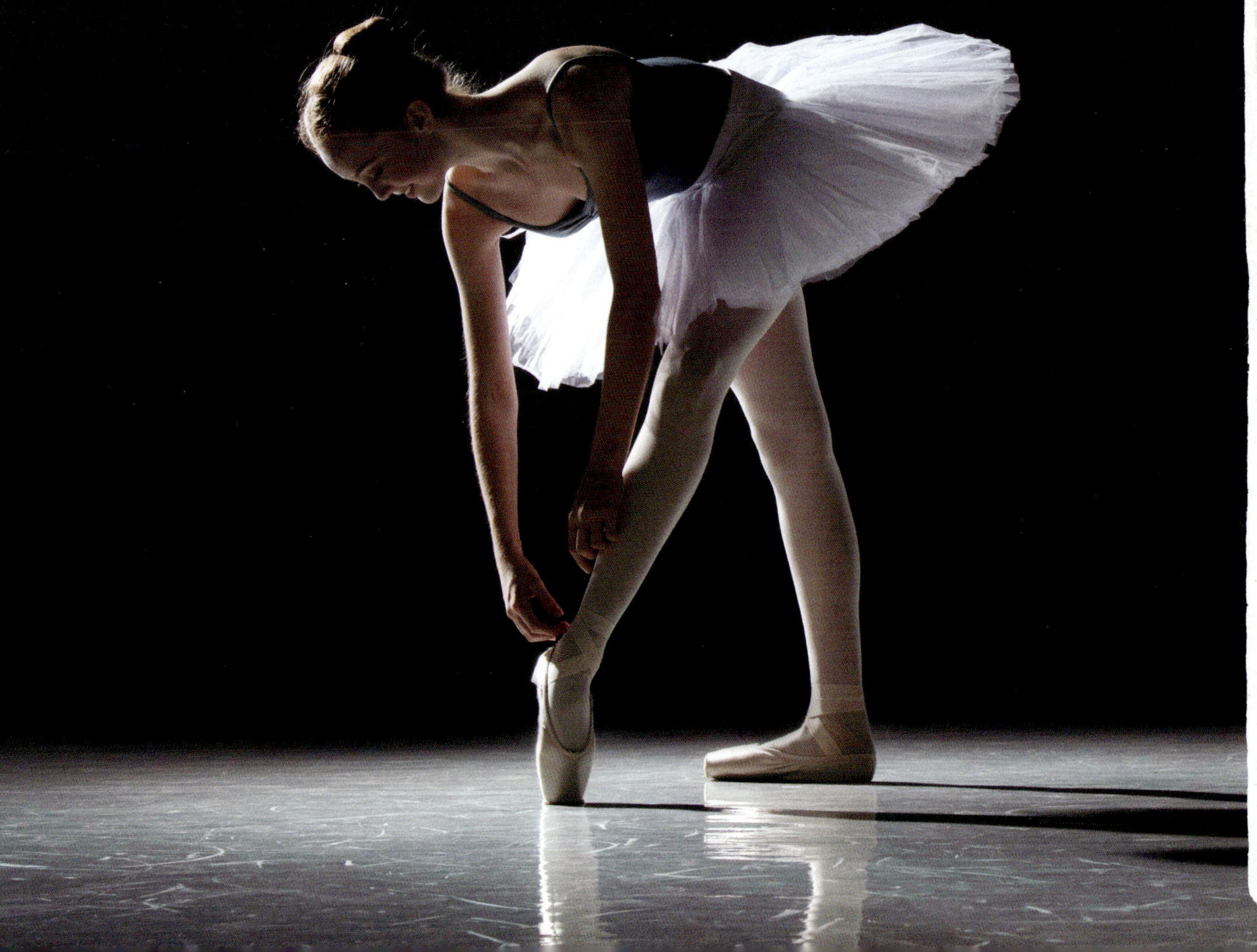